D1554818

Sai Baba Gita

The Way to Self-Realization and Liberation in this Age

Compiled and Edited

by

Al Drucker

Atma Press
Crestone, Colorado

ISBN 0-9638449-0-3

51250>

9 780963 844903

Due to recent increases in paper, postage and production costs, we regretfully have had to raise the price of this book. For orders within the U.S.A, copies can be obtained by sending a check for $12.50 plus $2.50 for shipping and handling per book to Atma Press, P.O. Box 337, Crestone, CO 81131. For orders of 5 or more, for Sai Centers, or for orders abroad, kindly inquire at this address, or by calling (719) 256-4357, or by faxing 256-4355 for current pricing.

Many individuals helped in the preparation of this book. In particular, the following were instrumental in getting this edition into print: Janny DeHoog, Jack Scher and Judy Warner Scher. The following individuals' efforts helped make possible the previous edition printed in India: Laura Marshall, Rilla Reynolds, Raju Reddy, Joan Brown and John Behmer. Prof. N. Kasturi, Prof. Nanjudaiah and Prof. Rama Raju reviewed the manuscript of the earlier Indian edition to ensure that the text remained true to the essence of Baba's original Gita discourses given in Telugu. The editor expresses his deepest appreciation to Sai Baba for making these profound teachings available to the world. The editor is solely responsible for any errors of commission or omission in rendering them into print. Neither the editor nor Atma Press are connected with the Sathya Sai Baba Organization, the Sathya Sai Book Center of America or the Sathya Sai Book Trust of India.

Published by Atma Press

Crestone, Colorado 81131

Printed in the U.S.A.

Messages

Suppose you are asked: "Who created all this multiplicity in the world; who is responsible for all this variety?" What will you answer?.... The correct response is, "There is no multiplicity at all!".... The one divine self remains the one self forever. You mistake it as many. The fault is in you. Correct your vision. Remove your delusion. The divinity did not change into the world just as the rope did not change into a snake. In the dark you mistook the rope to be a snake but it remains a rope. So also, the divine self remains the divine self though your ignorance of this fact makes you see it as world.... The world of diversity stands on one leg called delusion. Cut down that leg and the world falls.... I often tell you not to identify even me with this particular body. You do not understand. You call me by only one name and believe I have only one form, but there is no name I do not bear and there is no form which is not mine.

After long searches here and there in temples and in churches, at last you come back completing the circle from where you started, and find that he for whom you have been seeking all over the world, for whom you have been weeping and praying in churches and temples, on whom you were looking as the mystery of all mysteries, is the nearest of the near.... your very self.... the reality of your life, body and soul. Assert it! Manifest it!

You as body, mind or soul are a dream. But what you really are is pure existence, knowledge, bliss. You are the God of this universe. You are creating this whole universe and drawing it in. To gain the Infinite, the miserable little prison individuality must go.... Follow the heart. A pure heart seeks beyond the intellect. It gets inspired. Within you is the real happiness. Within you is the mighty ocean of nectar divine. Seek it within you. Feel it. Feel it. It is here, the self. It is not the body, the mind, the intellect. All these are simply manifestations. Above all these you are. You appear as the smiling flower, as the twinkling stars. What is there in the world which can make you desire anything?

— From sayings and writings of Sai Baba —

Sai Baba

For the countless millions of devotees who have come into his fold, Sai Baba is the *avatar* of this age. He is revered as the incarnation of the full power of divinity. Such an auspicious advent has not occurred since ancient days when the divinity came into human form 5000 years ago, in another major age of mankind. Then he came as Krishna, to enact the role of *avatar* of that particular age. Now, the divinity has come again in the role of world teacher, to guide and uplift mankind at this present critical time in human history.

Just as sweetness cannot be understood through words alone, but must be experienced directly through the taste, so also the Sai phenomenon cannot be understood by merely reading about him or studying his words or even experiencing him first-hand. His truth can be known only by fully living his teachings and practicing them in every thought, word and action of daily life. By transforming our lives in this way, we discover our own truth. This is the rarest of all jewels that this *avatar* has come to bestow on us. It is the deeper message of the mission for which he has incarnated, namely, that the divinity appears among us in order to remind us of **our** divinity. "I know who I am," he says. "I have come to help you to realize who you are." In essence, we are no less than he. We are God incarnate. That is the principal teaching of his *Gita*. He has come as the guide to help us realize our truth and return mankind to its divine source.

The Three Incarnations of Sai

Like Allah of the Muslims, or Jahweh of the Jews, or Divine Father of the Christians, or the Buddha Nature of the Buddhists, or Ahura Mazda of the Parses, or the Supreme Self of the Vedantins, or the Great Spirit of the native Americans, Sai Baba is a name for the omnipresent, supreme reality, which in most religions is known as God. The one divinity takes on countless names and manifests itself in countless forms. It has chosen a 250 year period beginning in the early 19th century to manifest successively in three human forms as *avatar* for this *kali* age, to restore righteousness to floundering humanity. All three of these incarnations are called Sai Baba, which means divine mother-father.

The present Sai Baba, born in 1926, is the second in a succession of three incarnations of the Sai *avatar*. He is known as Sathya Sai Baba. The first incarnation was Shirdi Sai Baba, who left his mortal body eight years earlier in 1918. Shirdi Sai Baba lived his life exemplifying the unity of God and the brotherhood of man, by ministering to both the Hindu and Muslim communities of central India, each of which claimed him as their own. For many years, he would spend alternate days living in a Hindu temple and in a Muslim mosque.

The Sai *avatar* will remain in the present Sathya Sai form until his mid 90's, well into the 21st century. Then, shortly after leaving his physical body, he will be born again in the south of India, appearing as the third and final incarnation. At that time he will be known as Prema Sai Baba and will complete the mission of the Sai *avatar* to end this *kali* age and usher in the golden age for mankind.

Sai Baba's *Ashram* – Prashanti Nilayam

Sathya Sai Baba took birth in the little out-of-the-way hamlet of Puttaparthi in the south of India, near Bangalore. Now, a modern township has sprung up there, called Prashanti Nilayam, the abode of ultimate peace, which is his main *ashram*. It provides accommodations for thousands of pilgrims from all over India and from all parts of the globe, who come to experience Sai Baba's daily public contacts with the devotees and private interviews for those who are fortunate to be chosen.

The *ashram* houses a comprehensive educational complex where students come from all parts of India and abroad to live and study together. Small children can come into the residential program starting at the age of five in the primary school, then go on to the high school, college and university levels, and finally on to the postgraduate and doctoral levels, to complete their education twenty years later. The Sai educational system, with campuses in various states of India, is wholly non-denominational and completely cost-free. All the educational costs for thousands of students are borne directly by the Sathya Sai Baba Trust.

Also at Prashanti Nilayam is the central headquarters for the worldwide network of Sai service organizations, engaged in a wide range of community service projects and in bringing education in human values into government and private school systems throughout the world. Recently, the largest specialty hospital in Asia was inaugurated at the *ashram*. Here patients, no matter how poor, can come from all over the globe for open heart surgery. They stay at the hospital with no charge for doctors, medicine, hospital services, food or room.

Sai Baba, The Human Being And The God-Man

The hub of all this activity is Sai Baba, who from his earliest days has attracted large numbers of people to him through his unique personal presence. He can only be described as the personification of pure, selfless love, the embodiment of perfect peace and bliss, the essence of all goodness. He manifests every noble human quality that mankind admires and he incorporates every divine quality that is characteristic of the *avatar*. He has the full power of nature in his hand. He has all knowledge at his command. He knows the past, present and future of everyone who comes to him. He manifests himself in many parts of the world for the sake of his devotees. These characteristics, namely omnipotence, omniscience and omnipresence, are the mark of a full incarnation of the divinity.

In his teachings he befriends all faiths and emphasizes the unity of all religions in the oneness of divinity. In his personal manner, Sai Baba displays a majestic grace, and at the same time, an exquisite joyfulness. In the midst of a splendorous temple and *ashram*, he lives in a small, simple room, and maintains an austere life style, completely committing his time from early morning to late at night to ministering to the needs of those who come to him.

Not being limited to the physical plane, Sai Baba works in all dimensions, gross and subtle, appearing through visions and dreams and inner experiences, as well as in his physical form. As the divine teacher guiding the spiritual unfoldment of his devotees, he inspires from within and directs from without. He illuminates the heart and transforms the mind and reveals the greatest of all treasures, the immortal *atma*, the universal self abiding in every heart.

The Sai Advent

These two and a half centuries encompassing the Sai advent are a unique time of great spiritual significance in the history of the world. During this period, many saints and sages are also appearing on the earth in order to advance the divine mission of revitalizing spiritual values and reversing the present downward trend of moral degeneration which is engulfing the world. In the millenia to come, generations will look back with great awe at those of us who lived during this sacred time, much as we might look back at those fortunate ones in other ages, who were the contemporaries of Rama or Krishna, or of Moses, Jesus, Buddha, Mohammed or Zoroaster, and who had the unique chance to experience their sacred presence directly.

Very rarely in the long span of human existence, has the divinity taken a human form on earth and allowed itself to be widely recognized by many. And even more rarely has the divinity come in all its fullness and glory as *avatar* of the age, as is true today in the form of Sai Baba. Now, the full power of God can be directly approached and experienced by all, and his teachings, which have the authority of the source of all wisdom, can be understood by everyone, for he speaks to us in the language and the idiom of our present time.

Introduction to the Gita

Gita means song. But the *Gita* is no ordinary song. It is the divine song of emancipation. It is given by God to free us of the illusions that have kept us bound. The *Gita* celebrates our highest truth, the *atma*.

Atma means self. But *atma* also means God. *Atma* is our god-self, our true self. And since God is always one, *atma* is the one true self of everyone and everything. Illusion makes it appear as the many. Our destiny is to dispel the clouds of illusion so that our truth is revealed and the *atma* is realized. That is self-knowledge.

When self-knowledge comes, the illusion of separate beings and separate objects goes, and is replaced by unity consciousness. Self-knowledge is the only knowledge that has truly eternal and lasting value, for it enables us to transcend all limitations of time and space, and be immersed in the bliss of the *atma*.

In every major age, God comes as *avatar* and teaches the *Gita* to initiate us into self-knowledge and dispel the veils which hide our divine nature. 5000 years ago, God came as Krishna, to render this song of truth at a time of great moral decline. At that time, he gave the *Gita* in order to rescue Arjuna, and through him all of mankind, from the fog of illusion and attachment. In this age, he has come again as Sai Baba, to give this sacred teaching at another time of great turmoil and deteriorating values. The malady he is treating is the same, and the remedy he prescribes is also the same, stemming from the same ancient wisdom. But, being the very source of eternal wisdom, he knows how to transmit it in a way which makes it come alive today and be meaningful in this present age.

In his *Gita* teachings, Baba shows us how to transcend the false perception of our senses and mind, which constantly support the illusion of separate existence. Step by step, he directs us onto the inner path to discover who we truly are. When all illusion is stripped away, we realize that we are not these bodies and personalities, we are not separate beings individualized into name and form. The truth is, and he emphasizes it over and over again, that we are not different from God. Our unchanging reality, which was the same before we took on the limitations of these bodies, and which is the same after we let go of these bodies, is the one divine self, the *atma*. Inexplicably, *atma* has become cloaked with the changing names and forms which make up the covering veil of *maya*, or illusion. But, under the layers of obscuration, hidden from view, *atma* shines in everyone as the unvarying radiance of divine light.

To realize this requires a purification of consciousness, until only pure awareness, unbefogged by illusory mind-stuff, remains. Baba tells us that when we give up our outer vision and our fascination for the world and, instead, turn our mind inwards to gain the integral vision, we become steeped in unity consciousness. When we give up body-consciousness we gain God-consciousness. When we expand beyond our limited human awareness into the fullness of our potential, we become who we truly are. We transcend the illusion of separation of God, man and world and merge into the one divine principle. That is the essential teaching of the *Gita*.

The *Gita* is the very heart of the ancient wisdom making up the perennial philosophy of the East. It is the basis of all spirituality. We are told that it had a profound influence on Jesus, as well as on the Buddha, not to speak of the countless spiritual lights who have graced this planet in the millenia since the *Gita* was given by Krishna on the battlefield.

The *Gita* has something for everyone at every level of the spiritual path. Baba talks to each of us at the level at which we are ready, pointing us from wherever we are, to our final destination. If we incorporate this *Gita* into our daily lives, we will never need to read another book nor study another teaching. By following the directions given here, we will be led home to our own unchanging truth. First, however, there are a number of stages we must go through. They are best spoken of in terms of the *yogas*. The Sanskrit word *yoga* speaks of union, referring to union with God.

There are three principal *yogas* which Baba takes up here. They are *karma yoga*, the path of selfless service; *bhakti yoga*, the path of devotion wherein we see the divinity in everything we see; and *jnana yoga*, the path of wisdom, the culmination of the spiritual journey, wherein we dwell constantly on our highest truth. These *yogas* are the soap which purifies us and strips away the layers of unreality that have covered the *atma*. For too long, illusion and unreality have posed, bizarrely, but totally convincingly, as the only true reality and kept the bona fide reality, the *atma*, hidden. These *yogas* help return us to unity consciousness.

A question may arise as to why, when the verses of Krishna's *Bhagavad Gita* are freely available, Baba has elaborated this new version of the *Gita*. Baba explains that this present age is different from Krishna's time and different from Rama's time, as well. In the age of Rama, the forces of darkness were embodied as demonic hordes, external enemies that disturbed the inner peace and tranquillity of the people. Rama, God incarnated as *avatar*, personally took up arms and went into the forest to destroy this evil. Tens of thousands of years later, in the age of Krishna, the forces of evil were not outside in the forest, but right at home in the same family. Now the *avatar* did not take up arms directly. Instead, he drove the chariot and galvanized Arjuna to fight the battle and win the victory.

In truth, the divinity had already decided the outcome. To make it clear to Arjuna that he was merely an actor in this drama, Krishna gave Arjuna a vision of the cosmic form of God. Suddenly, Arjuna could see all of time, past, present and future. He saw all the combatants on both sides, engulfed in their inescapable destiny, following the play orchestrated by the Lord. Though he was engaged in fighting all the battles, Arjuna saw that he was merely the instrument carrying out the will of the Lord, and that the ultimate conclusion of the war, the triumph of righteousness over evil, had been decided even before the first battle commenced.

In those days people lived much longer than they do now. Baba mentioned that at the time of the *Mahabharata* war, Krishna and Arjuna were both in their eighties. Krishna and Arjuna had known each other for over 70 years. They were the closest of friends, spent most of their time together, and were related as brothers-in-law. In all this time spent together, the *Gita* never came up. For years, Arjuna, along with the other Pandava brothers, had nobly borne every insult and indignity perpetrated by their wicked cousins. But, the forces of evil were unrelenting. The conflict was destined to culminate in war. Preparations for the battle commenced. Now, on the eve of the war, when Arjuna saw his beloved grandfather and his revered teacher ready to fight on the opposing side, and all his other close relations arrayed for battle, he threw down his bow in despondency.

In speaking of this, Baba said that Arjuna had faced many worldly dilemmas in his life and knew how to deal with them. But, at that point, Arjuna was facing a spiritual dilemma. He was overwhelmed with a feeling of helplessness that stemmed from the onslaught of his inner enemies, attachment, infatuation, deluded vision, and the rest, which had made him forget his own truth and his commitment to preserve righteousness at all cost. Now, in desperation, he turned to Krishna, knowing that Krishna alone could rescue him from this quagmire. He declared, "Lord, command me. I will do as you say." At that moment, their relationship changed from chums and co-equals to master and disciple. And it was at this point, Baba tells us, that Krishna chose to teach Arjuna the *Gita.* Surrender of the individual will to the divine will was the key to proper preparation in receiving this age-old wisdom.

Baba said that the sage Vyasa tuned in on their dialogue with his *yogic* powers of subtle hearing. Vyasa elaborated Krishna's teachings into 700 verses in the Sanskrit poetic form, which have been preserved through time as the *Bhagavad Gita*. But, Baba said that in the 20 minutes or so, when Krishna spoke to Arjuna on the battlefield, he did not actually expound all these verses or render them in poetic meter. Krishna's goal was very specific.

Krishna who was the divinity incarnate was always unremittingly happy. Arjuna, like the rest of humanity, experienced periods of joy and sorrow. Here, on the eve of the battle, Arjuna was deeply depressed, but earlier that day, Arjuna had been highly elated, eager to fight. Krishna knew that all of these changes of mood were caused by illusion. Arjuna was out of touch with his true nature, the *atma*, which is synonymous with eternal delight. Krishna resolved to dispel Arjuna's confusion and bolster his courage by teaching him the knowledge of the *atma*, so that Arjuna would discover his own divine truth and be forever immersed in unchanging inner joy.

In these chapters, Baba gives us an insight into the main points of Lord Krishna's *Gita*. Since this present book is the *Gita* for this present age, Baba gives many additional directions for our spiritual advancement, which are particularly applicable to these troubled times and our needs. His goal is the same as Krishna's, namely to establish us in *ananda*, the eternal delight which is our true nature.

This age is different in many ways from Krishna's age. In this age, the forces of good and evil are not only battling in the same family, but they are battling inside of every being. Baba tells us that if the Lord were to come today, sword in hand, to stamp out all traces of evil, no one alive would escape or survive. He comes, instead, as the inner director. Following his guidance, we must fight our own inner battles, conquer our own inner enemies, and gain the ultimate victory of salvation and awakening.

This *kali* age, in which we are now living, wherein gross materialism and lawlessness have run rampant and spiritual values have declined, is, in many ways the worst of all ages. But, from the spiritual point of view, this age is the best of all ages for the transformation of the individual. In this age we can most readily throw off the bonds of illusion and realize the *atma*. But, it requires swimming up-stream against the powerful current and rapids of worldly life, which try to sweep us into the abyss and keep us locked onto the endless cycle of birth and death. Now, the *avatar* of this age, through his teachings, shows us how to navigate these rapids. He works internally as the indweller in every being, directing us how to confront our own inner enemies and win this war of good and evil inside.

In ages past, Baba points out, the spiritual path was primarily devoted to rituals and religious practices, such as meditation, penances, chanting of *mantras*, prayers and other worshipful activities. These practices are still important, but they are not enough. Baba often says, "Hands that work in the service of society are much holier than lips that pray." He wants us to do *karma yoga* and engage in selfless service to mankind. All our work must be pure and done to the full extent of our capacity for excellence. At the same time, we must have no attachment to the fruits of our labors, but instead, offer up all our actions and their results to God.

When we see the divinity everywhere, installed as the indweller in every being, and we serve that omni-present divinity in all we do, then *karma yoga* automatically becomes *bhakti yoga*. Our work becomes worship. But in this there is still some separation between ourselves and God; there is still some duality. Baba is not satisfied with our spiritual progress until we become totally immersed in non-duality and reach our highest truth, the realization of the immortal self. That is the final stage.

Baba tells a little story of an old woman who was sewing in her home at night. She was working on her tapestry when she lost her needle. The light being very dim in her house, she went out to the street lamp where the light was bright, to look for her needle. Baba ends the story there. Whenever he tells this story he always seems a little amused by the silliness of it.

We are like that old woman. We have also lost our needle while working on the tapestry of our many lives. Our lost needle is the knowledge of our truth, without which we cannot finish our work. After groping through countless lives caught up in illusion, we now know that there is something vital to our existence that we have lost. We go to great teachers and to *ashrams* where the spiritual light is intense, hoping to find there what we have lost.

We get great solace being in the light and we gain deeper understanding of what we are looking for, but the final discovery of what we have lost can only happen when we look inside our own heart of hearts. There within, deeper than the body and the mind, deeper than our sense of *I-ness* which stands at the core of our individual self, beyond all sheaths, subtle and causal, which cover our truth, we find the brightest light of all, the light of *atma*. When the *atma*, our true self is realized, the tapestry of our long journey in the world which we have been working on for so many eons and so many lives, is finally complete.

Baba assures us that, just as was true in the vision given to Arjuna showing the final outcome of the war, the outcome of our long trek and our inner war has also already been determined by the divine will. We are destined to return home. Nevertheless, we must still tread the path and fight the battles and win final victory over our inner enemies. We initiate this process by making friends with the divinity in our hearts, keeping it as our steady companion and allowing it to guide our inner journey.

As we proceed on our path the clouds of illusion thin out and we become aware of a great mystery. We realize that the spiritual journey we thought we were on is itself an illusion. We are not individuals on the spiritual path following the direction of the divine inner *guru*. In truth, we are the totality. We are the divinity itself. We are and always have been the *atma*. *Atma* is neither born nor reborn; nor does it ever die. As *atma* we have not come from somewhere nor are we going somewhere. We have never changed. Only the illusion of individuality and separateness has changed. Ultimately that illusion disappears and we discover the glorious truth that we have always been one with God. Baba tells us, "God if you think, God you are. Dust if you think, dust you are. Think God. Be God. You are God. Realize it."

Some years ago in a public discourse, Baba directed us to repeat several times daily, "I am God, I am God, I am no different from God. I am the infinite supreme. I am the one reality." If we allow this declaration of truth to suffuse our lives and fill us with the consummate love that is God, these powerful words will gradually become our direct inner experience. More and more we will identify ourselves with the divinity, our real self, and less and less with these ephemeral personalities which are but shadow selves. Thus we realize who we are, the immortal self, the one divinity, which is love itself.

That is the inspiring message of this *Gita*.

The Essence of the Gita

For Western readers who may not be familiar with it, here follows a summary of the traditional *Bhagavad Gita*, as set down by the sage Vyasa. That *Gita* was given by Krishna to Arjuna, just before a great war involving huge armies with millions of combatants, coming from kingdoms scattered all over the Indian subcontinent. In massive encounters that raged daily for 18 days, the forces of good were pitted against the forces of evil. This war proved to be one of the bloodiest of all time. When it was over, only a handful of men survived.

In this war, Krishna, who was God incarnate, took the humble role of a charioteer, to guide Arjuna and the Pandava brothers to victory. But, on the eve of the great war, it looked like the battle was lost before it even started. Arjuna, the foremost warrior on the side of good, had become overwhelmed with doubts; he decided to throw down his bow and not fight. This situation came about after Krishna had driven Arjuna's chariot onto the battlefield between the two armies. There Arjuna saw his beloved grandfather, his teacher and his kinsmen on the opposite side, getting ready to fight and die for their cause. They had allied themselves with the forces of unrighteouseousness.

Filled with a deep despondency, Arjuna said, "O Krishna! I cannot fight! I feel overcome by a sense of helplessness! What good is winning this war when it will lead to the destruction of all these kinsmen, teachers and heroes. I do not know where my duty lies! I beg you to tell me what is right for me! I surrender myself fully to you! I am your disciple! Please teach me!" Then the blessed Lord gave him the great wisdom teachings of the *Gita*.

Krishna started the *Gita* teachings with an admonishment, "Arjuna! Shake off this faint-heartedness. It is not worthy of you. Do not yield to weakness. You have been preparing so long for this battle to preserve righteousness.

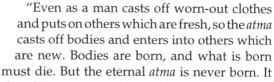 "Even as a man casts off worn-out clothes and puts on others which are fresh, so the *atma* casts off bodies and enters into others which are new. Bodies are born, and what is born must die. But the eternal *atma* is never born. It never dies. Weapons cannot cut it, fire cannot burn it, water cannot wet it and wind cannot dry it.

"This *atma* is not your perishable body. It is your immortal self, the imperishable self of everyone. Once that is known, then what is there to grieve for? The wise never grieve... neither for the dead nor for the living.

"I am that *atma*, Arjuna. I am the supreme Lord of all, residing in the heart of every being. I am the father of this world and also its mother and sustainer. I am the beginning, the middle and the end. Everything is produced out of me. Everything is pervaded by me. No creature can exist without me. Whatever path men travel, it is my path. Whichever way they go they reach me.

"Though I am eternally birthless and unchanging, yet, I incarnate myself from age to age. Whenever righteousness declines and unrighteousness prevails, I take on a form, to protect the good and to destroy evil.

"Veiled as I am by my inscrutable power of illusion, my *maya*, the world does not recognize me. Although they do not know me, Arjuna, I know them all. I know their past, present and future. In truth, I am ever unmanifest and imperishable; but not understanding this transcendental nature of mine, the ignorant regard me as a mere mortal.

"Knowing nothing of my reality, they ignore me and become occupied in the world with vain hopes, vain works and vain knowledge. Lost in the maze of *maya*, they are spun around like puppet-dolls on a merry-go-round.

"This divine illusion of mine is most difficult to overcome. Among thousands of human beings, only a few struggle to know my truth; even amongst these that struggle, only one, perchance, comes to know me in reality. Such a one is a *yogi*, one steeped in the highest wisdom. Therefore, Arjuna, you should be a *yogi*! With all your being take refuge in me alone, and by my grace you will attain supreme peace.

"From this moment on, fix your mind steadily on me dwelling in your heart. Be devoted to me, bow down to me, worship me. Know that I am always within you and soon you will become one with me. Yes, truly do I promise this to you, Arjuna, for you are very dear to me.

He who knows my divine birth and work, will not be born again after death. He will not lose sight of me, nor I of him.

"Arjuna, whoever works for me and has me as his supreme goal, whoever is devoted to me and is unattached, bearing no malice towards any creature, will quickly come to me. Such a one sees me everywhere, residing in all beings, as the imperishable amidst the perishable.

"For these, who have me ever present in their mind's eye and serve me steadfastly with affection, I will carry their burdens and I will give them what they need. Talking about me to each other, they are forever satisfied and delighted. Out of my compassion for them, I strengthen their power of discrimination and destroy the darkness of ignorance that beclouds their vision. Bringing their senses under control they transcend the world of death and decay, and attain immortality.

"Arjuna, whoever offers me with love, either a leaf, a flower, a fruit, or even some water... such devout offerings coming from a pure heart, I will surely accept. Whatever you do, whatever you eat or sacrifice or give away, whatever austerity you perform, offer that first to me. Then you will be free of the consequences of your actions, and soon your mind will become calm and wise, steeped in renunciation. Endowed with evenness of mind and having abandoned the fruits of your actions, you will be freed forever from the fetters of birth.

"Arjuna, resign every action to me. Fix your mind firmly on me. I will perform all your actions through you and liberate you from all sins. Fear not. By my grace you will overcome all obstacles.

"But if from self-conceit you do not listen to me, you will surely perish. You may think, 'I will not fight!' But impelled by your sense of duty, your own nature will compel you to fight. What out of delusion you do not wish to do, you shall do in spite of yourself. Arise, Arjuna! With the sword of wisdom that I have given to you, cut to pieces this ignorance which doubts the truth that the divinity is everpresent in your heart. Arjuna, stand up and achieve glory! You are pledged to uphold righteousness! The forces of unrighteousness have become rampant. You must encounter them and destroy them!

"Take refuge in me, Arjuna. Think of me at all times and fight! It is not you who will kill these heroes, but I. I am the world's creator and sustainer, but I am also the mighty world-destroying time that devours all. Truly, these warriors in hostile armies have already been slain by me. You are merely the instrument through which I act.

"Here, I give you a vision of my universal form in which you can see the oneness of all existence! Behold my divine power! Behold the whole universe, moving and unmoving, all unified in me!"

Overwhelmed with wonder and amazement, Arjuna bowed his head in adoration and spoke with palms joined, "O supreme Lord! Hail to you! Hail, again and again! If the effulgence of a thousand suns were to blaze forth together in the skies, their glory could compare only a little with your infinite splendor! You are the imperishable Lord, the undying guardian of the eternal *dharma*. You are everything that can ever be known. Seeing your awesome form, all the worlds are trembling with fear. And so am I. Just as the many rivers flow towards the sea, so do all these heroes in the world of men enter your flaming mouths."

Then the blessed Lord again assumed his usual gentle form as Krishna, and said, "Graciously have I shown to you this infinite, primeval form of mine. It is very rare, indeed, to see what you have just seen. Neither by study of the scriptures, nor by austerities, nor by charity, nor by rituals, but only by single-minded devotion can I be seen thus. This experience of my cosmic form and this sacred knowledge that I have taught you are the most precious of all treasures.

"Arjuna, have you listened to me with full concentration? Has the delusion caused by your ignorance been dispelled? Think over everything that I have said to you, reflect on it fully, and then do what pleases you."

Arjuna answered, "O Lord of the universe! Your powerful and wonderful words contain the highest wisdom, and you have spoken them with so much compassion. Through your grace, my delusion is now destroyed. I stand free of all doubts. Please direct me! I will do as you command!"

Foreword to the American Edition

I would like to give you, dear reader, some background on how this book came about. In August and September of 1984, there were extensive riots in South India. There were shootings not far from Sai Baba's *ashram* and the *ashram* gates were locked. Armed soldiers were patrolling outside and escorting the college students into the *ashram* for the evening meetings. For 34 days during the height of the tension, Sai Baba spoke in daily discourses to the students on the *Gita*. He spoke in Telugu, his native language. These talks form the chapters of this book.

I was living in Baba's *ashram* at the time and teaching in his university. With Baba's permission, I used these powerful *Gita* teachings over the years as the basis for my scheduled talks to visitors who came to the *ashram* from all over the world. It has been my good fortune to work with this material now for almost 9 years. Every moment spent on it has brought new light and depth of understanding, and, as has happened to many others, these teachings have unalterably transformed my life.

Five years ago, I had the chance to publish this *Gita* in India, from the edited translations of Baba's talks. 12,000 copies in English were printed and distributed, and translations were published in a number of European and Asian languages. The original manuscript was presented to Sai Baba on the stage of the auditorium during the Christmas function in 1987, and he graciously blessed it and signed the title page. That work contained extensive Sanskrit phrases and references to traditional Indian themes, which were familiar to Indian devotees.

In the intervening years, the Indian English edition has gone out of print. With the intention of making these teachings widely available without need for the reader to have an extensive background in Sanskrit or Indian philosophy or prior knowledge of the characters and stories that fill Baba's talks, this book was prepared in the present edition. Here, the majority of Sanskrit terms have been deleted and incorporated in their English equivalents into the body of the text. Also, the chapters have been freely edited to clarify any difficult passages or obscure references and to convert the spoken words into easily readable text. Every chapter has been arranged to stand on its own, with the effect that you can turn to any chapter whose subject matter particularly interests you, without first having to study all the previous chapters in the book.

In editing the text my primary focus was on clarity in conveying Baba's teachings to the Western reader, rather than on literal translation. I acknowledge the grave responsibility of editing the *avatar's* words and urge scholars to study the tapes of Baba's *Gita* discourses in Telugu.

Al Drucker,
Crestone, Colorado, October 1993

Contents

Sai Baba   i

An Introduction To The Gita   v

The Essence Of The Gita   xi

Foreword To The American Edition   xv

Table of Contents   xvii

Part One – Path Of Devotion

1st Chapter   **Love And Duty – The Path Of Perfection**   1

Self-Knowledge Is God-Knowledge   1
Faith In Yourself And Faith In God   3
The Formless Takes A Form   4
Divine Consciousness   4
Work, Worship And Wisdom   5
Extinction Of Delusion   6

2nd Chapter   **Surrender – Transformation Of Man Into God**   8

The Universe   8
The Path Of Devotion   9
Your Highest Self Is God   10
The Unlimited Power Of God   11
The Devotee Is Even Greater Than God   12
You Can Bind God With The Power Of Love   13
From Duality To Non-Duality   14
Near And Dear   15
Show No Hatred Towards Any Being   16

3rd Chapter   **Earning God's Love**   17

The Love Of God   17
True Joy   18
Courage And Steadiness   18
Worship Of God With And Without A Form   19
Only The Formless Is The Permanent Aspect Of The Lord   20
Steady Your Mind By Worshipping The Divinity With Form   21
Worshipping The Formless God In Your Heart   22
Inner Peace And Contentment   23
Love All   23

4th Chapter   **Inner Inquiry – The Path Of Wisdom**   25

The Three Stages On The Wisdom Path   25
God Is The Master Of Time   27
The Veil Of Illusion   28
The World As A River Of Truth And Untruth   29
Hold On To God Alone   29
Conquer Your Senses   30
Give Your Burdens To God   31
Surrender Fully To God   33

5th Chapter   **Find God In Your Own Heart**   34

The Indwelling God   34
Within The Body Is Pure Consciousness   35
See God In Everything   36
The Diseases Of Mankind   37
Seek The Lord Inside Your Own Body   38

Harmonize All Your Thoughts, Words And Deeds   39
Forbearance, The Primary Spiritual Quality   40
You Can Experience God Through Love Alone   40

6th Chapter   **The Three Stages On The Spiritual Path**   42

First Know That God Is Here Then Experience God Directly   42
The Cowherd Boy   43
Anguished Yearning For The Lord's Presence   43
The Vision Of The Lord   44
Beyond Dualism   45
Becoming One With The Lord   46
The Three Stages In Secular Life   46
Knowing, Seeing And Becoming One   47
Reaching The Abiding Peace Of The Immortal Self   48
The Sacred Names Of Arjuna   49

7th Chapter   **Restraining The Tongue In Food And Speech**   51

The Dual Power Of The Tongue   51
Control Of The Tongue   52
Develop A Discriminating Mind   53
Purity Of The Food, The Cooking Vessels And The Cook   54
The Blessing Offering Food To God   54
The Role Of The Tongue In Speech   55
The Story Of The Officer And The Preceptor   55
The Power Of Words   57
Sacrifice And Forbearance   57
Talk Wastes Spiritual Energy   58
Self-Confidence   59
Efface Selfishness, Pride And Jealousy   60

8th Chapter   **You Can Reach God Through Love Alone**   61

Devotion   61
Meditation And Devotion Are One And The Same   62
The Householder And The Monk   63
I Am God   63
From The Form To The Formless   64
Surrender To The Divinity Within You   65
Transforming Desires Into Wisdom   65
Renouncing The Fruits Of Your Labor   66
Love Is The Root Of All Spiritual Practices   67
Fill Your Heart With Love And Faith   68
Love Is The Most Important Of All Human Qualities   69

9th Chapter   **Desire And Anger – The Twin Evils**   70

Use Sacred Thoughts To Destroy Dark Thoughts   70
Good Character, Good Behavior And Knowledge Of The Self   71
Divine Power And Physical Power   72
The Three Worlds And The Lord Beyond   72
Wherever You Look You See Your One Self   73
You Are Not A Sinner — You Are God   74
The Sweetness Of The Servant Path   75
Controlling Desires And Anger   75
Attraction And Repulsion   76
Character Not Belief Is What Is Important   77

10th Chapter   **Love & Sacrifice – The Cure For Desire And Anger**   79

The Fire Of Desire   79
Make Love The Dominant Force In Your Life   80
The Nature Of Anger   81
Sacrifice Conquers Desire   81
The Pest Of Desire And Hatred   82

Let All The Noble Human Qualities Shine Within You 83
Replacing Bad Habits With Good Habits 84
Steady Practice Is The Key To All Accomplishments In Life 85
Keeping The Senses Within Their Normal Limits 86

11th Chapter **Renunciation – Focus On God, Not The World** 87

Control Of The Mind 87
Detachment 88
Make The Best Use Of Every Object 88
Harischandra And Buddha 90
Worldly Attachments Are Like Poison 91
King Janaka's Dream 92
The Anguish Of Separation From God 93
True Renunciation Is Turning Your Mind Towards God 94

12th Chapter **Detachment – Unify Thoughts, Words & Deeds** 96

Detachment Leads To Self-Realization 96
Detach Yourself From Objects Which You Think Belong To You 97
Give Up The Fruits Of Your Actions 98
Everything Undergoes Change 99
Constant Practice 100
The Three Austerities, Physical, Vocal And Mental 100
Better Be Quiet Than Tell An Untruth 101
Every Day Observe A Period Of Silence 102
Free Yourself From All Bondage 103

13th Chapter **Time Wasted Is Life Wasted** 105

Start Your Spiritual Practice When You Are Young 105
Do Not Waste Your Youth 106
Use Your Body For The Sake Of God 107
You Cannot Start Spiritual Life When Death Is At The Door 108
True Human Life Involves Discrimination & Renunciation 109
Keep Your Concentration Unwaveringly On God 110
Be Steady In Your Practice 111
Tell The Truth But Use Discretion In Your Words 113
The Four Types Of Anger 113

14th Chapter **Remember God – Forget The World** 115

Find Out Who You Truly Are 115
Youth Is The Most Precious Period Of Life 116
Develop Self-Confidence And A Firm Resolve 117
Birth Is Sorrowful, Life Is Sorrowful And Death Is Sorrowful 118
The Field And The Knower Of The Field 119
The Whole World Is Illusion 120
The Four Types Of Devotees 121
The Story Of The Wealthy Man And His Four Wives 123
God Answers Everyone's Requests 124
You Are Not Mortal, You Are Immortal 125

Part Two – Path Of Wisdom 127

15th Chapter **Give Up Self-Delusion – Know Your Real Self** 131

Infatuation And Attachment Lead To Sorrow 131
Infatuation Will Destroy Your Courage And Will 132
Ignorance Is The Cause Of All Sorrow 133
The Cure For Ignorance 134
The War Between Selfishness And Selflessness 135
Foresight & Compassion – Qualities Found In A Pure Heart 136
The Transformation From Kinsman Or Friend To Disciple 138

Be Courageous, Be Fearless, Be Discriminating 139

16th Chapter **Banish Ignorance And Sorrow Will Leave You** 141

Your True Nature Is Eternal Joy 141
The Body Is The Outer Garment You As Pure Spirit Wear 142
This Body Is Only One Of Many You Have Worn 143
Ignorance Is Being Unaware Of Your True Nature 144
The Danger Of Being Attached To The Body 145
You Must Live The Teachings 146
Ignorance Must Be Completely Dispelled 147

17th Chapter **Master Your Senses & The World Will Be Yours** 149

The Transitory Nature Of All Things 149
The 24 Impermanent Principles 150
The Immortal Self Beyond The Ephemeral Individual 150
The Noble And The Ignoble 151
The Nature Of The Sense Organs 152
Those Bound By The Senses Are Destroyed By The Senses 153
The King Who Was Ruled By His Five Wives 154
The Mind With Its Five Wives, The Senses 155
Being Ever Vigilant In Controlling The Senses 156
Victory Over The Senses Through Self-Inquiry 157
Control Of The Tongue, The First Step In Sense-Control 158
The Pure Brother Of The Impure Demon King 159

18th Chapter **You Are The Indweller – Not The Body Or Mind** 160

You Are The Atma, You Are God 160
Keep The Atma In View And Nothing Can Harm You 161
Sense-Control Is Easy When You Understand The Senses 163
Realize The Transitoriness Of All Sense Objects 164
Focus On The Divinity, Your True Self, And Do Your Duty 165
Intellect Surpasses All Your Senses 165
A Wise Man Never Forgets The Atma 166
God Does Not Wish To Be Praised By Anyone 168

19th Chapter **Sense Control – The Key To The Highest Wisdom** 170

Sense-Control, The Foundation For Self-Knowledge 170
Sense Enjoyment Is An Illusory Joy 171
All Joy Comes Only From The Self 172
Sense Objects Can Only Give Temporary Joy 173
Self-Knowledge Gives The Greatest Joy 175
Beauty And Joy 175
The Light Of Atma Illuminates Everything 176
The Joy Of The Self Is The Only True Joy 178
Do Not Drive With Your Foot On The Brake 179
Detachment, Devotion And Sense-Control 180

20th Chapter **Knowledge Is Useless Without Self-Knowledge** 181

The Light Of Wisdom Dispels The Darkness Of Ignorance 181
Atma Remains Unchanged, The Individual Changes 182
The Two States Of The Mind, Pure And Impure 183
Give The Mind Some Peace – Turn It Towards God 184
How To Cross The Turbulent River Of Worldly Life 185
External Freedom And Inner Freedom 186
You Need The Lord's Grace To Achieve Anything Worthwhile 187
God's Grace Is Earned Through Purity Of The Heart 189
There Are Many Beings But Only One Underlying Divinity 190
Only Wisdom Can Conquer Ignorance 191
Develop Wisdom Through Inner Inquiry 192

21st Chapter **To Know The Divinity Is To Become The Divinity** 194

The Atmic Light Gets Hidden By The Impure Senses 194
See Unity In All Diversity 196
You Are A Human Being, Not An Animal 196
Desire Makes You Break Your Resolutions 197
The Body Is Given To You To Realize The Indweller 198
Everything Comes From The One Indwelling Divinity 199
Association With The Divinity Makes You Divine 201

22nd Chapter **The Three Worlds – The Gross, Subtle & Causal** 203

The Five Elements, Gross And Subtle 203
Life Is A Series Of Waves 204
But For The Divine Principle, The World Is Totally Inert 205
The Artist Who Tried To Capture The Image Of The Lord 206
To Reach The Permanent, Go Beyond The Impermanent 207
You Are Not One But Three 209
Behind The Gross The Subtle, Behind The Subtle The Causal 210
Samadhi Is Equal-Mindedness 211
You Alone Are True 212
The Qualities Of The Truly Wise 213

23rd Chapter **Limit Desires, Be Content & Become Dear To God** 215

Be Satisfied, Do Not Chase After Desires 215
You Must Win God's Love 216
Contentment Is The Real Wealth 217
Atma Is Never Born, Atma Never Dies 219
Reduce Your Desires And Remember The Atma 221

24th Chapter **Patience And Forbearance** 222

Realize The Atma Through Your Direct Experience 222
You Gain Forbearance Through Difficult Circumstances 223
The Tree, The River And The Cow 224
There Are Times When You Should Withhold Forbearance 225
When To Use Forbearance And When It Is Inappropriate 226
Undue Haste And Delay Are Two Extremes To Be Avoided 227
To Adhere To Truth Is The Same As Practicing Forbearance 228
At Times You Have To Alter Your Voice In Telling The Truth 229
Negative Qualities Must Be Uprooted And Destroyed 230

25th Chapter **Jealousy And Hatred** 231

Discover The Indweller Through Your Own Inner Practice 231
The Five Characteristics That Make Up Everything 232
Jealousy And Hatred 233
Being Jealous Of The Divinity 234
The Divinity Never Has Selfish Motives 235
Conquer Jealousy And You Can Conquer Anything 236
Forbearance Will Overcome Hatred 237
Behind Jealousy And Hatred Is Egoism 238
Destroy Egoism, Jealousy & Hatred With Love & Forbearance 240
Only Through Love Can You Experience God 241
Jealousy And Hatred Destroy Those Who Possess Them 242

26th Chapter **Truth And Good Character – The Breath Of Life** 244

Truth And Dharma 244
Truth Needs To Be Established From The Earliest Age 245
Even A Little Fib Can Lead To Unhappiness Later 246
When One Bad Quality Goes The Rest Cannot Long Remain 247
Dharma Is Changeless But Its Practice Changes In Each Age 250
Not Harming Others Is Dharma 252
Social Duty, Obligatory Duty And Family Duty 252

Sense-Control Is The Key To Doing Your Duty Properly   253

27th Chapter **Kindness & Compassion**   255

The Unity Of The Self, The One Atma Existing Everywhere   255
Harmonization Of Thought, Word And Deed   256
Kindness Is The Hallmark Of A True Human Being   257
A Child Suffused With The Nectar Of Human Kindness   257
God Showers His Grace On Those Who Have Kindness   259
Inner And Outer Purity   260
Conquer Your Inner Enemies   261
The Two Banks Of The River Of Life   262
The Three Principles That Take You To Your Divine Goal   262

28th Chapter **Fearlessness – Seeing The One Self In Everyone**   263

Divinity Is The Basis For Everything   263
Fearlessness Is Beyond Body-Consciousness   264
Fear Of Death – The Most Powerful Of All Fears   265
Fearlessness Is The Very Nature Of A Human Being   266
The Grand Meeting Of All The Animals   267
In What Way Are Human Beings Better Than Animals?   269
Through Effort Humans Can Transform Their Lower Nature   270
The Vital Difference Between Human Beings And Animals   272
Most Human Beings Behave Even Worse Than Animals   273
When You Have A Firm Faith In God You Will Be Fearless   273
Develop Good Qualities And Gain The Grace Of The Lord   274

29th Chapter **Turn Towards God & God Will Turn Towards You** 276

Sacred Vision   276
Chariot Festivals   277
The Chariot Of The Human Body   278
The Field Of The Heart   280
True Fearlessness   281
The Story Of Gajendra, The Elephant   282
Turn Your Vision Towards God And See Your Self   283
The Elephant Of Arrogance And The Crocodile Of Attachment   284

30th Chapter **To Become Free Surrender Your Mind To God**   285

Root Out The Weeds Of Tamas And Rajas   285
Clean Your Heart Thoroughly To Welcome God There   286
Devotion, Wisdom And Detachment Will Keep You Pure   287
The Characteristics Of Rajas   288
Remove All Three Qualities And Gain Liberation   288
King Janaka's Challenge To Gain Self-Knowledge   289
Janaka Achieves Self-Realization   291
For Self-Knowledge Total Surrender To The Guru Is Required   292
Offer Up Your Mind To The Lord   294
Steady Your Mind And Your Body   295

Part Three – Path Of Action   297

31st Chapter **Do Your Duty–Without Concern For The Results** 301

The Shield Of Devotion And The Armor Of Wisdom   301
Use Wisdom To Conquer Your Inner Enemies   302
Every Worldly Experience Can Be Traced To Karma   303
Egoism Develops When You Forget The Indweller   303
The Body Is An Inert Thing Made Of The Five Elements   305
From Sacred Actions To Devotional Feelings To Bliss   306
Food Gives Rise To Thoughts, Feelings And Actions   306
Focus On The Action, Not On The Fruit   307

Time, Action, Purpose And Result Apply Only To The Body 308
Turn Desire Towards Wisdom To Gain The Divine Light 309
The Three Types Of Actions 310
Aspire For The Supreme And Never Come Back 311

32nd Chapter **The Yoga Of Action – Relinquishing The Fruit** 313

Transform All Your Actions Into Sacred Actions And Be Free 313
Turn Actions Into Yoga Not Roga 314
The Joy Of Doing Is Greater Than The Joy Of The Rewards 315
The Gita Brings The Highest Wisdom Into Daily Life 316
Janaka And Suka 318
The Venom Must Come Out Before Teachings Can Go In 319
The Fire That Brought Out The Attachments Of The Disciples 320
Through Arjuna Krishna Taught The Whole World 321
Ordinary Actions, Detached Actions And Sacred Actions 322
The Gita Will Give You Whatever You Are Ready To Receive 323

33rd Chapter **Developing The Inner Vision** 325

You Cannot Run From Your Inner Enemies 325
Transform All Self-Serving Actions Into Selfless Actions 326
Purify Your Actions Before Offering Them To God 327
The Characteristics Of An Enlightened Being 327
By Their Actions People Will Reveal Their Inner Natures 329
The Spell Of Illsuion And Its Two Powerful Forces 330
The Power Of Maya To Delude Can Be Permanently Dispelled 331
A Pure Heart Is Free Of Attachment And Illusion 332
Actions Without Attachment To The Fruits 333
From Ordinary Actions To Buddhi Yoga To Karma Yoga 334
Astravakra At The Assembly Of Scholars 335
Without Inner Vision They Were Shoemakers Not Scholars 337
Let All The Poisons Emerge Without Interference 338
The Six Spiritual Treasures 339

34th Chapter **Remove Body-Consciousness And Realize God** 341

You Perform Actions In Order To Sanctify Your Life 342
Make All Your Actions A Sacrifice Not A Battle 343
You Are The Atma, You Are Not This Body 343
God In Human Form Is Not Limited To The Avatars 344
Expand Your View Of Yourself To Understand The Divinity 344
Go From The Individual To The Society To The Divinity 346
The Nature Of Dharma 347
Peace Can Only Be Found Within Yourself 347
For A Marriage There Must Be A Husband 348
Use The Hardships You Encounter As Opportunities & Tests 349
No Need To Carry Your Luggage On Your Head 350
Identify Yourself With The Divinity Not With Your Body 351

Part One

PATH
of
DEVOTION

LOVE AND DUTY -
THE PATH OF PERFECTION

If you want peace and if you want happiness
You must live in love.
Only through love will you find inner peace.
Only through love will you find true happiness.
Love flourishes through giving and forgiving.
Develop your love.
Immerse yourself in love.
These words of Sai are a stream of love
Flowing out to you.

Embodiments of Love,

There are many fields of knowledge but there is only one supreme knowledge. This supreme knowledge is self-knowledge, the knowledge of the immortal self. It is the knowledge of your unchanging reality, your true self – that which was never born and which will never die. There are many other types of knowledge. There are the different fields of art, science, commerce and education. But, these will only help you to gain some transitory worldly objectives and worldly pleasures. To realize the eternal bliss that is your own true nature you must have self-knowledge. It is the only knowledge that enables you to know the inner peace and the unending joy which is your own truth, your real identity. When you shine with self-knowledge, you become love itself. You become pure and completely selfless. Then you will always be in perfect harmony with all existence.

Self-Knowledge is God-Knowledge

Self-knowledge is not different from God-knowledge. The sacred knowledge of God and the sacred knowledge of the immortal self are one and the same. They are the one divine wisdom. When you realize the one self everywhere, you become established in unity consciousness. Then you see only the oneness in all the diversity that is around you. From that moment on, you transcend worldly existence and gain the immortality you have been seeking.

What is the basis for this supreme knowledge? Its basis is purity of the mind. To purify your mind you must suffuse your whole life with spirituality. Engage yourself in noble activities. Associate with spiritually-minded people. Observe exemplary conduct in your daily life. Strive to do your duty to perfection. Live your life so that it is one of selfless service and virtuous deeds. And study the wisdom teachings of the ages; put them into daily practice; let these teachings serve as your guideposts. Then your mind will become purified. And with a pure mind you will be able to discriminate between the permanent and the temporary, between that which is beneficial and that which is detrimental to your spiritual progress. Then all your ordinary daily activities will become sacred and God's grace will be showered upon you.

Now, you may be highly learned in secular knowledge, you may be a great scholar or you may be a world-renown expert in a number of fields. But all your titles and achievements cannot confer on you real wisdom. To be truly wise and remove the grief from your heart, you must know who you really are. You must realize your immortal self. You cannot transcend grief by any other path. Only the knowledge of your true self will allow you to overcome all suffering and misery. This is the only knowledge that can bestow on you all happiness. When you master a worldly field of knowledge you earn the respect of your peers. You may become famous and fulfill your worldly aspirations, but it is only when you acquire self-knowledge that you deserve and earn the grace of God. When you have that, you become ever blissful. You enjoy the ultimate happiness.

Who are those who deserve to learn this sacred knowledge? Is it, as some would contend, exclusively reserved for old people, or does a child deserve to learn it? Is it to be given only to religious initiates or should it be made available also to those who have no previous religious background? Should it be kept for men alone or are women equally eligible? Truly, to gain this wisdom, race, color, age, gender, nationality or social status are of no consequence. The sage Valmiki in his earlier life had been a highway robber, the sage Narada was born of a lowly maidservant; yet, they both became great spiritual lights. Everyone is equally entitled to acquire this supreme wisdom.

The Lord comes to those who have devotion for him; he looks at the heart and not at the outer status. Develop your devotion. Devotion is very important to human life. The Lord said in the *Gita*, "You become very dear to me when you serve me with a loving heart."

Faith in Yourself and Faith in God

When the Lord counsels you to develop your devotion it does not mean that you should neglect your worldly duties. Prepare yourself thoroughly for all your worldly tasks. Take great care to properly learn the secular knowledge which you need to discharge your duties. Most importantly, always have faith in yourself, faith that you will be able to fulfill the role for which you have taken human life. Faith in yourself and faith in God is the real secret of greatness. In truth, they are the same, for faith in yourself means having faith in your innate divinity.

Worldly knowledge can only give you food and shelter, whereas self-knowledge gives you the greatest treasure of all, the realization of your own reality. Still, without some worldly knowledge, you will not be able to obtain the knowledge of the eternal. You should not be careless in the sphere of worldly knowledge. Spiritual knowledge needs to be balanced with worldly knowledge. The sages Valmiki and Vyasa were honored by everyone. They wrote many holy scriptures, including those timeless epics, the *Ramayana* and the *Mahabharata*. They were great spiritual lights, but they were also very well versed in worldly knowledge. Otherwise, how could they ever have written such great classics?

Everything in the world is derived from God. When everything comes from him, what can you possibly offer him? The only thing you can offer him is your love. That is all he expects from you. That is why a great poet sang,

> **Beloved Lord.** *You are the all-pervading reality.*
> *When the entire universe is filled with you,*
> *How can I build a temple to you?*
> *When you are effulgent like millions upon millions of suns,*
> *How can I offer you my small candle light?*
> *When you are the indwelling reality of all beings,*
> *How can I call you by a particular name?*
> *When the entire universe is in your stomach,*
> *How can I offer you a little food in worship?*
> *All I can offer you is my love,*
> *And all I can hope to do is to empty myself in you,*
> *Who are the ocean of divine love.*

The Formless takes a Form

For the sake of human satisfaction you give name and form to the Lord. But in reality he does not have any form at all. Yet, he will take on a form so that you can express your devotion to him and worship him, and thereby satisfy some of your spiritual yearnings. Whatever form of the Lord you choose to follow, worship him with a loving heart.

Ramakrishna was not a learned man in secular matters; he was barely literate. But his mind was always engaged in worshipping the divine mother. With his heart brimming with love, he dedicated his entire life to the worship of the divine mother. He was living on only five rupees per month; that was enough for all his needs. Through his intense, one-pointed devotion, he became luminous. Today he is well-known throughout the world; you can find Ramakrishna Missions everywhere. He is universally honored.

Similarly, a robber like Ratnakara became the great sage Valmiki because of his love for God. Prahlada was the son of a demon, nevertheless he became luminous and pure with the divine love he had for God. Hanuman, a monkey, by repeating the name of Rama, became a glorious being who is honored throughout India. Jatayu was a bird, who because of his great love for Rama merged in the divine principle when he gave up his life. For devotion towards God, race, creed, gender or any other distinctions make no difference at all. Everyone is equally eligible.

The chapter on devotion is the most important chapter in the *Gita*. That is why we have started with it today. Devotion is not merely repeating the name of God. It is an undying and pure love for God. It is completely selfless in its nature, bereft of any worldly desires. It is pure, permanent and eternal. This divine love should be practiced constantly in your daily life.

Divine Consciousness

To begin with, you must know who you really are. Are you the body? If you are the body then why do you say, "This is my body"? Since you call it, "my body", you must be something different from the body. When you say, "my heart", then that means that you are something different from your heart. Your heart is an object possessed by you, its owner. You declare, "This is my brother, this is my sister, this is my mind, my body, my intellect". The unchanging element in all of these declarations is *my*. There is a true *I*, which stands behind this little *my* and gives rise to it. It is really the deepest consciousness in everyone and in everything. It is the universal *I*, the divine consciousness. This divine consciousness is all-pervading. It is within you, around you, below you, above you, and beside you. Truly, it is you.

This divine consciousness can be found everywhere, in everything in the world. But to realize it, the mind must be turned inwards. You must become inner-directed and search out your own truth. You must realize that you are not this, you are not that... you are not the mind, you are not the body, you are not the intellect. Then who are you? The answer comes, "I am I". This is the right path to follow for self-realization. This can only develop when you follow the path of love, the path of devotion. To search for God there is no other way.

Everywhere you look, the formless has taken on forms. God is present everywhere. But in order that you may comprehend him, he has taken on a particular name and form. He is everywhere as the formless divinity, but before you can get that realization, you have to develop your love and devotion for the Lord with form. Therefore, in the beginning, you enter the devotional path at the lowest rung, and worship the Lord with a name and form. Then steadily, inch by inch, you rise to a higher state. You withdraw your mind from the external world and worship the formless, until finally you realize your own reality as the formless divine principle. That is self-realization.

Work, Worship and Wisdom

Without flowers you cannot have fruits. The maturation of the flowers into the unripe fruits and then into the ripe fruits, is the path of self-realization. The flowering stage is the path of service. When it progresses to the unripe fruits it is the path of devotion. When the fruits become ripe and full of the sweet nectar of wisdom, then it becomes the path of self-knowledge. At that point, the flowers of good works and service have transformed themselves through love and devotion into the sweet fruits of wisdom. Therefore, good works lead naturally to worship and detachment, and on to wisdom. On the spiritual path, it is not enough to just worship; you must also engage in good works. But your works become worship when you steep every deed with love for the Lord and offer all your works to him.

As long as you are in this world, you must be engaged in work. Work is very important for human beings. It is through your work and activities that you learn to harmonize thoughts, words and deeds. For great souls, thoughts, words and deeds are always one. At first you will yearn for the fruits of your work. In the beginning, when there is still a great deal of desire, you will not be able to perform your work without a desire to enjoy the fruits. Later, however, you will become totally selfless and unconcerned with the fruits of your work. In that way, gradually, your work becomes converted into worship and, in time, you will be doing everything only for the love of God.

Truth is one, but the sages call it by many names. The divinity is one, but many names are used to speak of this one absolute reality. From the one come the many. When a child is born it is called a baby. As it grows up it becomes a youth. After twenty years it becomes an adult and later a parent. Later still in life, it becomes a grandparent. But these are all one and the same entity. Similarly, the ultimate reality is always one and the same. When you realize this unity and remain firmly established in the one divinity underlying all the changing names and forms, you will have achieved something that is truly worthwhile.

Extinction of Delusion

Have a clear understanding of the *Gita* in your heart. What is the essence of the *Gita* teachings? Some say that it is the path of service and action, and others say that it is the path of love and devotion. Still others say that it is the path of knowledge and wisdom. But these are all partial truths. The *Gita* starts with a verse whose first word is *dharma*, which means duty or right action. The concluding verse of the *Gita* ends with the word 'my'. When these words are taken together they become 'my duty' or 'my work'. That summarizes the whole teaching of the *Gita*. It means you should perform your prescribed duty to the very limits of the human capacity for excellence and perfection, doing the work that is appropriate to your stage of life.

When you are a student study your lessons well. When you are a householder perform your work and family responsibilities properly. When you are retired perform the duties appropriate to that stage, and if you have renounced the world to engage yourself in contemplation of the reality, then stick to that path. When you follow your prescribed duty in the very best way possible, discharging your duty sincerely and conscientiously, then there will be no confusion or misery.

Arjuna had to perform his duty on the battlefield. His calling was to be a warrior and to combat evil and protect the good. But, when he saw his friends and relations arrayed on both sides of the battlefield, he forgot his strong resolve to fight for right, the fight for which he had been preparing for so long. He became full of attachments and delusion, and threw down his bow. He abandoned his duty and became miserable. Krishna taught Arjuna how to free himself from despair by adhering to his prescribed duty. Krishna taught Arjuna the truth of the immortal self, and showed him that his duty was to follow the inner promptings of the Lord, who was enshrined in his heart. When Krishna finished his teachings, he asked Arjuna, "Have your attachments and delusions disappeared?" Arjuna picked up his bow and answered, "My despair has completely vanished. All my delusion is now gone. I will do as you command!"

As long as you have delusion you will be in a state of bondage. When you suffer from delusion and infatuation, liberation is impossible. Liberation has nothing to do with worldly pleasures. It is not an air-conditioned car or a comfortable life. It is the complete destruction of delusion. It is the extinction of all worldly attachments, the incineration of all selfish desires.

From now on, do your duty to perfection and become ideals for mankind. Apply the teachings of the *Gita* in your daily life and be blessed with grace. Many of you are just wasting your time. Start today to reform yourself. Don't waste time. Time is God. Every day spend some time on these holy teachings and contemplate their inner meaning. Once they are understood, put them into practice. Only in this way will you be able to attain a sacred life, a life of purity and perfection, which is the mark of a true human being.

Second Chapter

SURRENDER -
TRANSFORMATION OF MAN INTO GOD

*K*rishna declared in the Gita, "If you surrender yourself fully
to me and take shelter in me, you will be protected by me. I
will drive away your sins and guide you towards self-realization." You must treasure this statement in your heart.
Steadfastly follow the path of surrender to the Lord and he
will look after you and take you to him.

Embodiments of Love,

God's power is immeasurable and unlimited. The huge diversity
you see when you look out at the universe is all the result of the illusory power of God. The physical universe visible to your human
eyes is just a very small part of the infinite power of the Lord. All
the worlds can be covered by a fraction of the foot of the Lord. It is
impossible to understand the greatness of the Lord. He pervades
the entire universe, gross and subtle. No place exists where he is
not.

The Universe

The universe is the body of God. He has embodied himself in the
creation. To understand the divine principle on which the universe
rests, you can begin by considering the vast size of the universe. The
moon is hundreds of thousands of miles away from the earth. The
sun is many tens of millions of miles away. Even the nearest of stars
is millions upon millions of miles away; and beyond that, in the
furthest reaches of the visible universe, there are stars that are
still billions of times further away. But, all of this, which constitutes the physical universe, and which to our limited view is so infinitely vast, is only the minutest part of the subtle universe.
Compared to this subtle universe, the whole grand physical universe is no more than the size of an atom.

The subtle universe, which is so indescribably huge when compared to the physical universe, is itself only a microscopic part of a

much, much vaster aspect of the universe, which can be described as the causal universe. It is known as the causal universe because it is out of this finest aspect that the gross and subtle worlds arise. All of these three worlds, the physical, the subtle (or mental), and the causal, are so enormously big, the scriptures have declared that they cannot possibly be understood by the human mind or depicted in words. They are beyond the imagination, beyond the ability of the mind to grasp. And yet beyond all these, transcending the gross, the subtle and the causal, is the divine principle, the ultimate cause of all.

The Path of Devotion

God is beyond the gross, the subtle and the causal. But, as Lord, he rules over all of them. He is the master of time, past, present and future. Human beings have been given limited capacities and may find it very difficult to understand this divine principle. In that case, the easiest path to follow is the path of devotion. This is what Krishna taught Arjuna. Krishna described the path of devotion in three steps.

First and foremost is:

Work for God! – You may not be aware of it, but every bit of work you do is already being done for God. He is the supreme master of this world and everything in this world belongs to him. Knowing this, consciously make every action you undertake an offering to God. Devote all your labors to him, while being ever mindful that God is not outside of you.

The second step is:

For the sake of God alone! – Up to this point you have been thinking only about yourself. But who are you? Who is this *I* that you use to refer to yourself? Krishna said, "It is I who am shining in you." This word *I* does not belong to the body, neither to your own body nor to Krishna's. This *I* emanates from the highest self, the immortal self, the *atma*. This *I* should not be equated with the body or the mind or the intuitive faculty or any other aspect of the individual. It transcends the limited personal self of the individual. This *I* relates only to the unlimited, impersonal self, the divine self, which is the real self of everyone.

The limited personal self by calling itself "I", has associated itself with the universal. But the personal self is not the real self. It is merely a reflection of the one immortal, divine self. Whatever you have been doing has been for the satisfaction of the divine self alone. Not realizing this sacred truth, you have been caught up and swept away by delusion. Krishna told Arjuna, "Whatever you do, do it for my satisfaction, for my sake. Do everything you do for me. Perform all your actions on my behalf. Act as my agent." This *me or my* or *I* which Krishna is speaking of, is not God outside of yourself. It refers to the *atma*, your divine self. Do everything you do for the sake of God alone, who is none other than your highest self.

The third step is:

Be devoted only to God! – Understand the inner secret of this directive. Devotion is the expression of love, and the emotion which is called love emanates from God, your highest self. Love comes from God and is directed towards God.

Love has nothing at all to do with worldly feelings and secular things. Love, which is just another word for devotion, is the very name of your highest self. This principle of love emanating from the core of your heart must saturate every action, word and thought. This will happen when you think that everything you do, say or think is for the satisfaction of God alone.

Your Highest Self is God

In the waking state, you may think that you are doing everything for the sake of your body and mind. But in deep sleep you are not conscious of your body or your mind. Then for whose sake are you enjoying the rest and peace of sleep? It is for the sake of yourself. Sleeping, taking food, all the various activities of your daily life, are performed only out of love for yourself. You believe that you are doing all these for your personal self which you experience to be separate from God, but the I that you call yourself really emerges from your highest self which is no different from God. Whatever you do out of love for yourself reaches your highest self and, therefore, reaches God. So you must do everything with the awareness that whatever action you undertake, good or bad, will certainly reach God. Devotion means making all your actions sacred and dedicating them to God alone.

In the ancient scripture we find a conversation between a sage and his wife in which the sage explained these inner meaning to his wife. He said to her, "For whose sake are you loving me? If you examine your deepest intentions you will discover that it is for your self. The wife does not love the husband for the husband's sake. It is for herself that she loves the husband and that self is the true self, her highest self. You may think that the mother loves the child for the sake of the child, but it is not so. It is for herself that she loves the child. Again, it is for her highest self. You may feel that the teacher loves the student for the student's sake, but it is really for the teacher's sake that he loves the student. Similarly, the devotee does not love God for God's sake; it is really for himself that he loves God."

When the devotee feels the deep joy of love for God, he believes it is his personal self that is feeling this joy. And so his love for God is tinged with selfishness. But, God's love for the devotee is totally different. God's love for the devotee is not selfish. It is only for the devotee's sake. Herein lies an important hidden truth which can be found behind every spiritual practice. God has no sense of individuality or separation. He does not feel that some things are his and others are not his. When there exists a feeling of difference and individuality, then selfishness and the sense of *I-ness* and *my-ness* arise. But God does not limit himself to any particular form. He has no separate feeling of *mine* and *thine*. He has no selfishness. These three injunctions, "Work for God!... For the sake of God alone!... Be devoted only to God!..." are given for your sake. They are not given for the benefit of God but for your benefit. They are intended to help you realize your true self by removing all traces of selfishness and separation which becloud your truth and keep you from being one with God.

The Unlimited Power of God

If you want a little breeze you may take a hand-fan and wave it so that you get a little air. On the other hand, when there is a powerful whirlwind you find very big waves crashing against the shore of the ocean and even huge trees being uprooted. The breeze you can get from a hand-fan will be very limited, but the power of God is tremendous; it is unlimited. Consider some other examples. When you try to draw water from a well, you can draw only a very small quantity. But when there is a heavy downpour, streams will become rushing rivers which join together in one great flood. One comes from the limited power of man, the other comes from the unlimited power of God.

Take the example of wanting some light in your house. You may light a candle or switch on an electric lamp. But at dawn when the sun rises, the whole city and forest will soon be flooded with the sun's light. The little light of your lamp is very weak compared to the splendor of the sun, shining magnificently everywhere. Again, this is the unlimited power of God, compared to the limited power of man. How can you reach this unlimited power of God? How can the limited capacity of a human being be transformed into the unlimited capacity of God? The means is surrender.

The Lord has declared in the *Gita*, "I will destroy all your sins and raise you to the supreme position which is my own." How can that happen? The physical world that you see with your human eyes is the gross aspect of the universe. When this gross aspect takes a subtle form in the mind you have the subtle universe. And when the mental takes a still finer and more subtle form in the heart, then you have the causal universe. The infinite Lord is beyond all these. He is the biggest of the big, but he takes the form of the smallest of the small, and installs himself in the very heart of the devotee, deep in the causal aspect. The wonderful truth is that such a vast, unlimited and powerful Lord allows himself to be imprisoned in the heart of the devotee. Here is a story to illustrate this.

The Devotee is Even Greater Than God

Once upon a time, sage Narada came into the presence of the Lord. The Lord asked him, "Narada, in all your travels through the world have you been able to discover the principal secret of the universe? Have you been able to understand the mystery behind this world? Everywhere you look you see the five great elements, earth, water, fire, air and ether. Which do you think occupies the first place? Of everything that is to be found in the universe what is the most important of all?"

Narada thought for awhile and then answered, "Lord, of the five elements the densest, biggest and most important is surely the earth element." The Lord answered, "How can the earth element be biggest when three-fourths of the earth is covered by water and only one-fourth is land? Such a big earth is being swallowed by the water. What is bigger, the thing that is being swallowed or that which is swallowing it?" Narada acknowledged that water must be bigger because it had swallowed the Earth.

The Lord continued his questioning. He said, "But Narada, we have the ancient tale that when the demons hid in the waters, then in order to find them, a great sage came and swallowed up the whole ocean in one gulp. Do you think the sage is greater or the ocean is greater?" Narada had to agree that without doubt the sage was certainly greater than the water he had swallowed. "But," continued the Lord, "it is said that when he left his earthly body, this same sage became a star in the heavens. Such a great sage is now appearing only as a small star in the vast expanse of the sky. Then what do you think is bigger; is it the sage or is it the sky that is bigger?" Narada answered, "Swami, the sky is surely bigger than the sage." Then the Lord asked, "Yet we know that one time when the Lord came as *avatar* and incarnated in a dwarf-body, he expanded himself so hugely that he was able to cover both the earth and the sky with his one foot. Do you think God's foot is bigger or the sky?" "O, God's foot is certainly bigger," Narada replied. But, the Lord asked, "If God's foot is so big, then what about his infinite form?"

Now, Narada felt that he had come to the final conclusion. "Yes," he said exultantly, "the Lord is the biggest of all. He is infinite beyond measure. In all the worlds there is nothing greater than he." But the Lord had still one more question. "What about the devotee who has been able to imprison this infinite Lord within his own heart? Now tell me, Narada, who is greater, the devotee who has the Lord locked up or the Lord who is locked up by the devotee?" Narada had to admit that the devotee was even greater than the Lord, and that, therefore, the devotee must rank first in importance over everything, surpassing even the Lord.

You Can Bind God With the Power Of Love

Such an enormous power which can bind even God, is within the scope of every devotee. Whatever be the immensity and capacity of any power, however magnificent it may be, if it is bound by something else, then that which binds it must be considered more powerful. The awesome power of God has been bound by the power of love; therefore, in this path of devotion, you can tie up the Lord himself and keep him locked in your heart.

If you take a drop of water from the ocean and keep it in the palm of your hand, compared with the ocean the drop appears very, very small. But put that same drop of water back into the ocean and it becomes a part of the infinite ocean. If your smallness as a human being is joined together with the vast power of the Lord, you become infinite and all-powerful; you become one with God. In the scriptures it is said, "The knower of God verily becomes God." In other words, the very process of knowing God merges you into oneness with God. This process which joins God and you together is called the path of devotion.

Unfortunately, many people today choose not to even recognize God; instead they prefer to rely only on their own limited strength and to be impressed only by human achievement. They are prepared to bend low before a village officer or a petty government official, but they refuse to show humility and obedience to the all-powerful cosmic personality, who is the master of the universe. God, who is the origin and cause of everything seen and unseen, is being ignored. The reason for this sad state is that very few have been able to understand the underlying truth behind this vast manifested universe. If they were to see that everything is but a reflection of the one divinity, they would never follow the wrong path.

If you have a wish-fulfilling tree in your courtyard why search for wild fruits in the forest? If you have the all-giving celestial cow in your house why wander around the market place looking for milk to buy? If you recognize the unlimited benefits you derive from having the celestial cow, you would never look elsewhere and get caught up in trivial pursuits. For little minds even small things look very big. You get what you deserve; think little and you become little. Little thoughts breed little natures. You are attracted by small things because you think that your power is limited. But truly speaking, your power is unlimited.

From Duality to Non-Duality

You remain small by identifying yourself with the body. You think, 'I am the body'. This thought keeps you in a state of littleness. But expand your view from 'I am the body' to 'I am the soul, the spark of the divine.' In this way rise up from the stage of dualism to the intermediary stage of qualified non-dualism. Then, you must expand further from 'I am the soul, a part of the divine' to 'I am the divinity itself, I am no different from God. God and I are always one.' That is the highest spiritual stage, the stage of complete non-dualism. The feeling you start with, that you are the body, is steeped in dualism; it is the very birthplace of sorrow. As long as you are immersed in duality everything is sorrow and grief. If you identify yourself with the supreme self everything will be happiness and joy.

You must elevate your thinking and always identify yourself with your highest self, thus giving up the false identification with the body. This is the proper attitude for worship. Worship in Sanskrit is called *upasana*, which means sitting near to God. But it is not enough to just sit close by and be near. The frog sits on the lotus but does it benefit from the sweet nectar that is in the lotus? Just being near the Lord is of no use; you must also be dear to him. You must be able to taste the honey.

Your neighbors may be very near to you, but you do not get too deeply affected by whatever problems and difficulties they may be experiencing. Compared with this, if your husband or son is half a world away and you don't get a letter for even one week, you begin to worry. In this case the body is far away, but your mutual love makes you near and dear. Your relationship with your neighbors is not charged with the same love, although they are very near. Consider another example. In a house there may be some mice and ants running around. Do you call them your friends? Along with physical nearness there must also be dearness. A deep feeling of love must develop and permeate the relationship. You must be near and dear to the Lord.

Near and Dear

What benefit will you derive by being near and dear? If you sit close to a lamp you get light, and with the help of its illumination you are able to do some useful activities at night. If you sit under a fan you get a cool breeze and the heat that was causing you discomfort will be dispelled. During the cold season of the year, if you sit near a fire you will be protected from the cold which may be bothering you then. In each case, one quality is removed and another takes its place.

Similarly, if you are close to the Lord, if you become dear to him, then you will get his love, and soon all the bad qualities in you will vanish away and be replaced by the good qualities that God embodies. Develop your love so that you may get ever nearer and nearer and dearer and dearer to God. The easiest way to get closer to God is to remember him in whatever you see, whatever you say and whatever you do. Think only of God and how to get nearer and dearer to him.

On the path of devotion it is not enough for you to love God but you must also engage in activities which are pleasing to the Lord, so that you can evoke God's love and feel his love for you. There are a number of characteristics that a devotee should possess which will endear him to the Lord. Treat censure or praise, heat or cold, profit or loss, joy or sorrow, honor or dishonor, or any of the other pairs of opposites, with an equal mind. Do not get dejected when you are criticized or elated when you are praised. Do not be overjoyed by profit or come to grief when there is loss. Treat heat and cold with an equal attitude, they can both be a source of joy to you.

During the winter warm clothing will be desirable and being near a source of heat will give you comfort from the cold. But, during the summer you will want thin clothes and you will welcome the cold. Heat gives joy sometimes, cold gives joy at other times; the way you use them determines whether you experience this joy or not. Heat and cold, profit and loss, and, in fact, all the various pairs of opposites and everything else in the world have their usefulness. Everything has been created for a purpose; but you need to use them in a way which is appropriate to your life and your stage of development.

Show No Hatred Towards Any Being

It would be utter foolishness to give a golden cup to a child or to give a sword to a madman. A golden cup, which is highly valuable, should be given only to a person who would appreciate its value. . Such a person will derive great joy from it and know how to use it. In the same way, the one who knows the value of devotion will use it to fill himself and others with pure joy. Genuine love will never give trouble to anyone, it will never lead one to hate another. In the 12th chapter of the *Gita* the desirable qualities of a devotee are enumerated; they start with 'Let there be no enmity directed towards any creature in the world.' Repeating parrot-like, "Lord, I love you", "Lord, I love you", while at the same time giving trouble to others cannot be considered devotion.

You become a devotee, filled with love and devotion, when you surrender yourself completely and are ready to carry out every command of the Lord. Arjuna, out of pride and egoism was feeling dejected; but after listening to the Lord, Arjuna fell at the divine feet and said, "Lord, I am your disciple. Teach me what is good for me. I surrender myself fully to you." Up until that time they were treating each other as brothers-in-law. Arjuna was married to Krishna's sister. But once Arjuna said, "I will do as you say. I will carry out your commands!", he became a devotee. The transformation took place in his mind, as he changed the relationship from a brother-in-law to that of a disciple, with the Lord as his teacher. Such a mental transformation is absolutely essential for a devotee. Without this, whatever level of closeness you feel you may have developed with the Lord, your devotion will remain fruitless and useless.

Being aware of these high principles, do your duty in life. Maintain an even mind and make sure that the work you do is good, and that it is always appropriate to the occasion. These verses from the *Gita* should not merely be memorized but they must be put into practice. When you fully understand their meaning and practice them in your daily life, your worries will soon leave you and all your sorrows will disappear.

Third Chapter

EARNING GOD'S LOVE

The Lord said in the Gita, "Develop steady and unwavering devotion for me and you will become very dear to me."

Embodiments of Love,

In the world, you can earn money, you can gain wealth and property, you can attain honor and prestige, you can gain position and power. All these are rewards you can attain from your worldly endeavors. But the Lord declared in the *Gita* that these are but temporary fruits. They are transient and have no lasting value. The only thing you can attain through your life here on earth that is of real value, that remains with you permanently and eternally, is the love of God. This divine love is extraordinary. No price can ever be set upon it. It is a treasure that is valuable beyond all measure. You must make every effort to discover the means for acquiring this precious love of God.

The Love of God

God's love is unconditional. It is the same for all. But what must you do to experience this extraordinary love of God? What path should you follow ? If you sow some seeds without first weeding and properly preparing the field, you cannot expect to get a good crop. In the same way, in the field of the heart, unless all the bad traits of selfishness are first removed, you will not get a good crop. In the *Gita* it is taught that the principal weed that has to be removed from the field of the heart is the attachment to and identification with the body. Even now, you may imagine that you love God; but merely having this thought will not produce any worthwhile result for you. It is like sowing good seeds on barren, unprepared soil. The most important thing for you to find out is if you are dear to God. Even if you love God, if you haven't transformed your life to become very dear to him and feel his boundless, unvarying love, then your devotion will not have taken you very far.

What, then, is the way to become dear to God? You will find the answer to this question in the *Gita*, in the chapter on the path of devotion. The chapter on devotion gives a number of human qualities that are very pleasing to God. It speaks of being resolute and making a firm commitment to practice only the spiritual teachings in your daily life. It puts great emphasis on developing steadiness of mind under all circumstances. And it enjoins you to be fully contented and joyful at all times, under all conditions. What is the inner meaning of this last directive?

True Joy

Consider the feelings you get from singing devotional songs at a spiritual function. If a song is being sung that is not very familiar to you or whose melody is not especially pleasing to your ear or if you are not drawn to the particular aspect of the divinity to which it is being sung, you might find that you have very little real feeling towards the song. You merely follow the song perfunctorily with your lips. What a great difference between that and a song which you love, which comes from the very core of your heart, emerging freely, spontaneously, with a great deal of joy, filling you with rapture and devotion for God.

In the same way, there is a vast difference between the temporary joys you derive from this apparent world and its transitory objects and phenomena, and the true joy that emerges from the depths of your heart. The latter joy is totally different from the temporary satisfaction you get from worldly things. This deep joy coming from the heart is associated with truth. It is permanent. It is detached from all transient worldly concerns. It represents the unity of the spirit. For this joy there is no possibility of change. There is nothing that can be added to true joy. It is full and complete in itself.

True joy comes from equanimity. Do not be carried away by or attach any importance to worldly things. Use your time and effort to control the vagaries of the mind and develop mental steadiness. Equal-mindedness means that you remain unaffected by victory or defeat, by profit or loss, by joy or sorrow. Accept whatever happens, whatever comes your way, as the gift of God, to be enjoyed with great satisfaction, regarding it as a gift of love given to you for your own good. When your heart is not swayed by worldly things, when you treat all people and all things with equal-mindedness, then you will experience true joy. Then your heart will be filled with feelings of love and satisfaction, and you will know the true joy of devotion.

Courage and Steadiness

Another important quality that every devotee must possess is to be resolute and courageous. It is completely natural for you to have courage and a firm resolve. You can manifest these qualities in a number of ways in life. You may use these attributes to climb mountains. The same sense of adventure and courage may be used for crossing the ocean or traversing through wild jungles. You may also behave in a courageous and resolute manner in earning wealth, acquiring properties and making a profit. Or, you may be brave and courageous, but manifest these qualities in a merciless manner. You may choose to abandon all the noble qualities of humanity and divinity and, instead, acquire the qualities of a demon. This firmness and resolve may be used either for good or for bad. How you use these God-given qualities depends upon you.

Earlier in his life, the great sage Valmiki was Ratnakara, the despicable robber. At that time he was using all his courage, prowess and firmness in an evil way. Thanks to his association with the seven sages, and listening to their teachings advising him to constantly repeat the name of God, he was able to transform his life, and use his strong determination and powers for the good of mankind. Soon he had the name of Rama constantly on his tongue. That is how he became the author of the *Ramayana*, the great epic recounting the life of Rama. Therefore, you should not use your steadiness and firmness in doing bad things or even for ordinary worldly things. Instead, use your courage and resolve to acquire the grace of God.

Worship of God With and Without a Form

In the chapter on devotion, Krishna expounds on the worship of God both with and without a form. The *Gita* compares these two modes of worship and points out which is better, which is easier and safer for devotees at each stage of their spiritual progress. The *Gita* declares that it is impossible to realize the formless and attributeless divine principle except by going through the stage of worshipping God with form and attributes.

As long as you have attachment to your body and remain steeped in body consciousness, you will not be able to understand and reach the formless aspect of the Supreme. You attain the necessary qualifications to worship the formless only after you have overcome your attachment to the body, your attachment to the world, and all your other attachments. Therefore, as long as you identify yourself with the body, and think that you have a particular form, then you must also visualize God with a form. So, you start your spiritual journey by worshipping God in a particular incarnation, having certain recognizable divine qualities. Gradually, after following this path for some time, you can change your practice to worshipping the formless aspect of the Supreme.

In truth, the whole world is the form of God. Everything you see everywhere is the form of God. But to begin with, you focus on a particular form of God, one of the *avatars* or incarnations of God. These divine incarnations are associated with the physical universe. Corresponding to these physical forms there are the subtle forms of the Lord which are in the mental or the subtle aspect of the universe. The physical and mental domains have to do with the senses and the mind. Transcending both the senses and the mind is the causal universe. This causal universe is made up of the subtlest manifestation of matter, containing in potential form the seeds of all names and forms. This causal aspect is experienced every night in deep sleep. Here the formless aspect of the Lord can be experienced.

During the waking state the effect of the mind and the senses will be very strong because they are associated with the phenomenal world. During the dream state, associated with the subtle world, the senses will not hold sway over you, but the mind will be very active. In the deep sleep state, associated with the causal world, the mind gets dissolved and does not comprehend the sense impressions. It is only in such a state, when the mind and senses are totally inactive, that it is possible to experience the formless aspect óf the divinity. But, this can be experienced even in the waking state, when the mind becomes perfectly steady and equanimous and the senses are maintained tranquil and inactive. Then, you enter the causal state while awake and experience the formless aspect of divinity.

Many devotees base their spiritual experiences only on God manifest in name and form. The form and the formless are both essential for a devotee. It is like having two legs for walking or having two wings to fly. To reach the final spiritual goal you must have the two legs of form and formless, putting one in front of the other, with the one leg representing form, taking its support from the other, which is the formless. It is important to realize that the manifestation of the Lord with form is only transient, whereas the formless aspect of the divinity is permanent. It is everpresent and unchanging. Here is a small example to illustrate this principle.

Only the Formless is the Permanent Aspect of the Lord

When you come to hear Baba give a spiritual discourse, you will be with about a thousand others seated in the temple. This will be happening in the physical domain, and may last for one to two hours. Associated with this experience is a given time and activity. But this very same experience can be re-experienced even after you go home. Whenever you want to think of it, it will be there in your mind... one thousand people seated in the temple and Sai Baba giving the discourse. In the external vision and in your experience in the waking state, you can see that all of you are sitting in the temple. What happens when you are back in your home? You find this temple will be in your heart and can be recalled to your mind at any time.

You were there for one hour, but this can become a permanent experience for you forever, even after you leave the *ashram*. Having initially had the physical experience in the phenomenal world, it becomes a permanent record in the subtle universe of the mind, which can then be recalled at some later time. As you repeatedly recollect this experience and ruminate on Baba's teachings, its message becomes permanently embedded in your heart.

Without first having had the actual experience in the hall, there would have been no permanent impression in your heart which you could later re-experience in your mind. Once the impression has been made in the mind, there is no need for actually being physically present in the temple or seeing Baba's physical form. In the same way, once you have experienced God in form, you will certainly be able to get the experience of the formless God later on. The form is momentary whereas the formless is eternal; but the formless will live on as a permanent entity for you only after first having experienced the divine form and imprinted it on your heart through worship and devotion.

Consider another example. Suppose you want to teach the word 'chair' to a small child. If you merely utter the word 'chair' it does not become clear to him what its form is. However, you can show him a chair like this and ask him to look it over carefully. While he is doing this you repeat the word 'chair'. Then later on, whenever he sees a chair he will remember the word associated with the form you have shown him and he will repeat to himself 'chair'. The form of the particular chair you used to teach him the meaning of the word may be impermanent. That chair will change, but the word 'chair' and the type of objects it represents will remain. Unless he sees the impermanent form he will not learn the permanent word 'chair'. The permanent element is understood through the impermanent one. Therefore, though divinity is formless, you first have to associate it with a particular form to understand it.

Steady Your Mind By Worshipping the Divinity With Form

To start with, many people do not even have a firm faith in the existence of God. Most of the time their mind will be wavering, and they will ask themselves, "Does God really exist? Is it really true that there is a God?" An iron resolve is most essential to cultivate constant faith in God. You can travel from an unsteady mind to a steady mind with firm faith only through the process of worshipping the divinity with form. Consider one more small example.

Here is a pillow stuffed with loose cotton. What covers this pillow? A piece of cloth. What is the content of this cloth? Cotton. So externally you have a piece of cloth and internally there is the cotton. But, in fact, the internal and the external are both cotton. The formless cotton has taken the form of thread, and this thread has become cloth, and this cloth is covering the formless cotton. Cloth is form and raw cotton is formless. From the formless to the form and then from the form to the formless, these are the transformations that make up divinity. To have a pillow you cannot use the formless cotton alone. So, you must first convert the cotton into cloth and this cloth having form can then cover the formless cotton inside.

In the same way, the divinity in form and in its formless aspect are exactly the same. Both are essential. Through the impermanent form you become aware of the permanent formless. While you still identify yourself in terms of body-consciousness and feel that who you are is related to your body, it will be impossible for you to give up the aspect of form. As your mind becomes steady, rooted in faith, and you move beyond body-consciousness, you will be able to experience the permanent formless aspect of the divinity.

Worshipping the Formless God in Your Heart

Traditionally, in the worship of the God with form, you may become engaged in many types of ritual worship. You may offer flowers to the Lord, you may bathe his statue with holy water, you may burn incense or use other forms of worship. These will give you some satisfaction. Worshipping the Lord's form externally with various sacred articles yields satisfaction. But, once you establish God inside your heart, then you will worship him through the flowers of your heart. After body consciousness and the delusion associated with it is destroyed, then the divinity that you previously worshipped externally in form, with flowers and various articles of external worship, will now become established in its formless aspect in the depths of your heart, and you will want to worship it with the sweet flowers of your feelings. This will bring true unchanging joy.

As long as you are worshipping the Lord with form, you will use physical flowers such as roses, marigolds and jasmine. These are all impermanent and the body which performs this worship is also impermanent. But if you want to worship the formless God in your heart, then the flowers are different. Those flowers will be permanent. Those flowers are the noble qualities that you develop in your heart and offer to the Lord. They are the flowers of nonviolence, of sense restraint, of truth, of patience and forbearance, of perseverance, of love and compassion, of charity and sacrifice. All these flowers are meant for inner worship. To elevate yourself to the worship of the formless principle, you will have to develop these flowers of the heart and use them in your worship. Then you will experience the ineffable and unchanging joy of the spirit, and enter the path that takes you home to your divine source.

Inner Peace and Contentment

In the 12th chapter of the *Gita*, Krishna taught the essential characteristics that a true devotee should possess. These are the qualities which you have to develop if you want to be loved by God. To begin with, if you want to be a devotee of God you have to develop inner peace and a firm resolve. You should always be contented. You should never give room to worry and allow any pain to enter and disturb your heart.

The great devotional scripture called the *Bhagavatam*, gives the example of Prahlada as the ideal devotee who possessed all these qualities. When the demons were troubling Prahlada, who himself was the son of the lord of the demons, Prahlada never allowed any pain to trouble his heart, no matter what trials and difficulties he was passing through. He just kept on repeating the name of the Lord, taking shelter in him as his protector and savior. He never shed one tear in the midst of all these troubles. Therefore, Prahlada has been described as the one who was fully established in union with the Lord. Even though he was living in the phenomenal world and had a form, he did not allow any desires or attachments to enter his heart.

Love All

For a true devotee there should be no evil traits such as hatred, jealousy, anger or greed. These are the main obstacles to devotion which enter your being. You must develop a sense of unity with everyone. If you develop hatred towards anyone, you will be hating the very Lord whom you worship. It is because of your inflated ego that you take action against another, in the course of which, hatred, jealousy and anger arise. Therefore, the primary warning given in the *Gita* says, "Show no hatred towards any being".

Without uprooting the weeds from the field and preparing it for cultivation, the seeds will not yield a good crop. In the same way, without removing the weed of ego from within your heart, all attempts at spiritual practice will be useless. The most important thing to be learned from the path of devotion is that you should not only love God but you should also love all beings, treating everyone as God. Worshipping God while harming others cannot be called devotion. It only reveals the depths of one's ignorance. Such people will never progress on the spiritual path.

In the days to come you will learn the ways that you can develop your faith, and through your good actions sanctify your life. It is by developing these desirable qualities and practicing them in your daily life that you will call forth the love and grace of the Lord.

Fourth Chapter

INNER INQUIRY – THE PATH OF WISDOM

Meditation is the steady, uninterrupted practice of contemplating God. This is the principal spiritual activity taught in the Gita. Thinking of God now and then cannot be called meditation. Meditation is thinking of God at all times, under all circumstances. It is a continuous, unceasing process.

Embodiments of Love,

The constant remembrance of God is the method in which you continuously keep turning the mind inwards to become united with the indwelling Lord. This can correctly be called meditation. Any practice that you engage in periodically is a concentration practice. Such a practice will usually focus on a chosen object and be associated with a particular place and time. True meditation, on the other hand, goes on continuously. It is completely free of all objects and phenomena and completely transcends the element of place and time. Therefore, in the *Gita*, the ongoing practice of meditation has been described as superior to any type of periodic practice.

But, there is a practice even superior to meditation. The ultimate spiritual practice is the development of wisdom. Wisdom emerges from inner inquiry. It is the spiritual practice of looking deep into the essential nature of everything. If you faithfully pursue this inquiry, you will gradually reach the supreme state of peace and bliss. This is the unique goal of human life, a goal which all mankind will one day achieve.

The Three Stages on the Wisdom Path

To reach the state of abiding inner peace, you begin by inquiring into the very heart of everything. This is the process of inner inquiry, the first stage on the wisdom path. Then you must make use of the deep insights you have gained by applying the spiritual teachings to every detail of your daily life. This is the second stage. If you continue with this practice unfailingly, then, in time, you will reach the goal of God-realization and enjoy unending bliss. This is the third and final stage on the wisdom path.

You can compare the first stage to the period of life when you are a student. As a student and spiritual seeker you are most active in acquiring knowledge. While you are in this stage you inquire into the principle which underlies everything in the universe. You try to understand the deeper meaning of the great wisdom sayings, such as *that thou art*. Here, *that* refers to the eternal divine principle we call God, and *thou* refers to the immortal self, which is the one true reality of everyone. In this first stage you try to understand this saying, which states that the highest self and God are one and the same, and you look for this oneness in the core of everything.

So, you start off by seeking the unity underlying everything in existence. Then, having become aware of it, you live your life by applying this great truth to all your daily activities. This second stage can be compared to the period of life when you are employed and busy in your profession. If you have not pursued your education and earned good qualifications, you will not be able to find an appropriate position. Therefore, in the first stage you acquire a good education and develop your knowledge so that in the next stage you can put that education into practice and use it to do your life's work. The third stage can be likened to the later period of life when you are retired and become a pensioner.

You receive a pension only after you have completed your working career. You start your career and gain employment, in the first place, only after you have successfully completed your education and acquired qualifications. These then are the three stages in your path through life; namely, first is the stage when you are a student, then there is the stage when you are a professional, and lastly, there is the stage when you are a pensioner.

Similarly, on the path of wisdom, you start out as a seeker, then you become a practitioner, and finally, you become a wise illumined one. In this final stage you enjoy complete peace of mind and realize the unity of all of creation.

To permanently acquire peace of mind and the state of unending inner joy, you first have to enter into the stage of inquiry and give up all attachments to the world. These days, so-called spiritual seekers are first entering into the stage of attachment, and later they try to enter the stage of inner inquiry. They call each other brother and sister and aspire to practice unity, while at the same time taking on new worldly attachments. At best, they can only be described as part-time devotees. The *Gita* does not condone such part-time devotion. The *Gita* teaches complete surrender by offering oneself and everything one has to God.

God is the Master of Time

In order to experience the principle of complete surrender you need to become aware of time, and how it exercises total power over all that is changing, and yet, how it is utterly powerless over the unchanging divinity, which is its master. God is not subject to time. He not only is not under the spell of time, but he keeps time under his control. The one who is bound by time is man; the one who transcends time is God. The one who is mortal is man; the one who is immortal is God. Only when you take shelter in divinity will you be able to transcend this element of time. Time consumes man, whereas God consumes time itself. It is time which is responsible for man's progress or man's decline, for the promotion of his good or his fall into evil, for his earning merit or storing demerit. Therefore, in the ancient scriptures we find this prayer:

> *O God, you are the very embodiment of time. Please, help me*
> *to sanctify my life and spend all my time in remembrance*
> *of you, so that I may safely reach your lotus feet.*

The entire world is inextricably enmeshed in the grip of time. It is not possible to fight against this element of time. Time does not wait for anyone. You are bound by time, time is not bound by you. Time can be compared to a great flowing river. All living beings are washed away by this flow of time. If you are washed away by a flood you cannot take protection and shelter in someone or something which is also being washed away. You, as well as the people and objects in which you try to find security, are all being washed away by the flood of time. If you seek to gain protection from something that is itself being washed away, it is like a blind person following another blind person. In the end, they both get lost. But if you were to be helped by someone who is standing securely on the bank, you would surely be saved.

The one on the bank who is not caught up in the flood of time is God. If you take refuge in God you will be able to free yourself from all the troubles and problems associated with time. God has proclaimed the principle of surrender and emphasized its importance by telling man, "O man, you are being washed away by the flood of time. The only one who can shelter you is myself. Take refuge in me, and I will save you." When you obey this divine command and offer yourself, your wealth, your property, your entire family at the Lord's feet and surrender yourself completely, then you will surely be saved.

The Veil of Illusion

At first it is difficult to experience this principle of surrender because there is a very big veil between you and God. Due to this veil, you are easily subject to doubt and confusion, and then you feel yourself unable to surrender completely. This veil is illusion. What is the meaning of illusion? Illusion refers to that which does not exist. When you are under the spell of illusion you imagine that which does not really exist to exist. And you imagine that which really exists to not exist. What never changes really exists and is true. What changes does not really exist and is not true. The one thing which always exists, which is true and unchanging is God, the one without a second. The world, when thought to be devoid of God, will be seen as constantly changing. Since it is changing, it cannot be true and, therefore, cannot really exist. But, in this, you are not seeing the world correctly.

When you are under the spell of illusion, you see the world as separate from God. You do not see the divinity as the principle underlying everything in the world, and as a result, you become afraid and find it impossible to surrender yourself completely. It is like seeing a rope and thinking that it is a snake. But there is no snake there at all. You are subjected to fear and tension by imagining that there is a snake where there really is no snake, at all. What is the reason for this fear? Imagining things which really do not exist, as existing, is the cause of fear. This feeling is responsible for all your troubles. If you were to see all this in total awareness, you would find that there is only a rope; there is no snake. Then you would have no fear whatsoever. You would not be afraid to reach out to it, to hold it and to play with it, because you would realize that all there is, is only a rope.

You are subject to many sorrows because you forget the fact that the entire world is the embodiment of God. It is not just the world as you think it is. You see the world only from the phenomenal point of view; you are not looking at it through the eyes of inquiry. If you were to look at the world correctly, you would realize that it is a stream of continuous change. This ongoing, uninterrupted flow of change is the basic characteristic of the phenomenal world. But within and governing that flow of change, is the one divine principle which is forever unchanging.

It can be likened to a river. The water in the river will flow continuously and give rise to the apparent effect of a steady stream, flowing without end. But at any given period of time, and at any particular place along the river, the particles of water rushing by will all be different; some will be muddy, some will contain rocks, some will be foamy, some will be pure water. Although the flow is continuous, the exact makeup of the water is constantly changing. We see that the river is a combination of both changing and unchanging elements.

In a similar way beings, which are the expressions of life, are born and die. Although they come and they go, there is a continuity of life in the world. Life which goes on continuously can be considered to be truth, whereas living beings which are born and die and are constantly changing, represent untruth. Therefore, the changing expressions of life are untrue, but life itself, which is a steady stream whose essence is the divinity, is true.

The World as a River of Truth and Untruth

That is why the world has been likened to a river, where reality has become associated with unreality, or change. You can consider it a stream of changing truth, a truth which is qualified and not fully true. The world is a combination of pure truth, which remains the same and never changes, and untruth, which deals with things that are constantly changing. The wisdom teachings have described this state as truth-untruth, namely, a mixture or combination wherein both truth and untruth coexist. Spiritual practice is the process whereby you separate the truth from the untruth, and retain the truth. You see the illusion that the world exists separately from yourself and God for what it is, namely untruth. Once recognized as untruth you are no longer deluded by it, and the truth, which is the unity of God, man and world, stands revealed.

Ignorance, nature, world, illusion, mind, *maya* are all synonymous. They are all the illusory power of God. Thinking that things exist which do not really exist, and coming under their spell, is illusion. A saint summarized this as, "God is true but the world is false". You must understand this statement correctly. What it means is that our mistaken perception and experience of the world is untrue. The world itself, in essence, is true. God is the one, unchanging basis of this world of change. When you examine this in some depth you discover that the world is truly not world, but the divinity itself.

Hold on to God Alone

In the *Gita*, Krishna told Arjuna, "Arjuna, you are subjecting yourself to this element of time. You are getting yourself caught up in its flow, and you are going far, far away from me. Surrender yourself to me and all your sorrows will soon be removed." When you are associated with God, when you are near him, illusion cannot harm you. Here is a small example for this.

In the expensive homes of the wealthy there will often be a watchdog guarding the gate to keep people out. This dog is not like a street dog; it has been brought up by its owners with great affection and has been carefully trained. This dog does not go on barking whenever it sees people walking or moving about. It starts barking only when someone comes near the gate and tries to get in. When they see the dog and hear the barking, most visitors will quickly leave the gate and go away. Others, however, who have taken a firm resolve to meet the owner of the house, will continue to stand there and loudly call out to the owner of the house. Eventually, the owner, hearing all the commotion at the gate, will look out from his upstairs window to see who is standing at the gate. Once the owner recognizes the person waiting there to be his friend, he will come down, go to the gate, let his friend in, and take him upstairs into the house.

When this apparent stranger, who had been waiting at the gate turns out to be a friend of the master of the house and goes with him, the dog will no longer bark at him or try to harm him. The dog now knows that this person is being allowed in by the owner himself. Illusion can be compared to this dog. It guards the gate of liberation and bliss. If a person comes who is not a friend of the master of the house, if he has nothing to do there, but insists on coming in through the gate, the dog will catch hold of him. Fearing the consequences of being accosted by the dog, most people will run away. In a similar fashion, most people, as soon as they experience some difficulties on the spiritual path, will choose to turn away, instead of persisting on their quest, undaunted by difficulties. And so, they do not reach their goal and thus continue to be buffeted by the spell of illusion.

But a real devotee, who in this example is the person with a strong determination to reach the owner of the house, does not mind the dog at all. He remains at the gate and attracts the attention of the master, and stays there until the master comes out. To such a persistent one waiting at the gate, even the barking of the dog, even the pain caused by illusion is helpful, because the pain draws the attention and compassion of the master inside. The master turns his gaze on the devotee, recognizes him, and takes him into the house. Therefore, only the one with courage and a strong resolute nature, who has decided to remain there no matter how ferociously the dog is barking, will get to see the master and be able to enter this palace of ultimate peace.

Conquer Your Senses

The five senses and the sense objects we perceive with them represent this dog of illusion which will distract you and keep you from reaching God. It is for this reason that Krishna told Arjuna, "Arjuna, you are attached to so many sense objects; therefore you are ruffled by events. You have not been able to control your senses and you have not been able to develop concentration. Therefore, you have not been able to establish the divinity in your heart. Continue to cultivate your practice of constantly turning your mind back to God dwelling in your heart. Then you will gain concentration of mind. Only when you have concentration of mind will you be able to fully surrender to God. At all times and in all places always think of God. Whatever work you are doing, think of God. Remember God with love. Remember God with faith.

"Even when you are waging a war, think first of God, then fight. This is not an ordinary war; this fight you are now becoming involved in is not like a quarrel between you and some other individuals. What you are fighting most of all is your own weakness, your bad habits, all your limitations and frailties. With warm thoughts of love for the divinity dwelling in your heart, wage this inner war and win. Remember you are not just fighting a war against others. You are fighting your own inner sense organs. So, do not quit until you have achieved victory, until you have conquered your senses and fully mastered them."

In an earlier age, Prahlada also spoke of this inner fight to his father, the powerful demon king. He said, "Father, you have won many wars and have gained lordship over numerous worlds, but you have not been able to win a victory over your own senses. By winning all the worlds outside you have become a powerful king, but only when you can control your own senses will you be king of the whole universe. If you keep being defeated by your inner senses, how can you ever win a lasting victory against your enemies outside? When you win over your inner enemies, you can easily win over the external ones, also."

When is this possible? Only when you surrender yourself completely to the divinity. You say, 'my objects', 'myself', 'my people'. As long as you have such feelings it will not be possible for you to surrender. These are all attachments associated with the physical realm. You will have to gain mastery over not only the physical, but over the mental realm as well. Finally you will have to gain entry into the spiritual realm. Once you have fully surrendered yourself and entered the spiritual realm everything will be taken care of automatically, and you will no longer be bothered by any burdens and cares.

Give Your Burdens to God

When you take a train journey, upon reaching the railway station you have to transport your luggage via a porter, or by one means or another. If there is no one to help you, you have to carry the luggage yourself. But once you enter the train you can put the luggage down anywhere you like. Then you can relax and there is no further bother with the luggage. The train will carry you and your luggage. Nevertheless, there are some fools who will sit in the train and carry their luggage on their heads. Those are the ones who have been blessed with God's grace but still doubt and continue to follow their own independent will. They have not surrendered fully.

Once you surrender yourself fully to the Lord and offer up everything that is to be done, as well as when it is to be done and how it is to be done, at the Lord's feet, he will take care of everything. To achieve this level of surrender there can be no trace of ego left; there should be no sense of yourself remaining. This has been shown in a particularly clear manner in the *Ramayana* by Lakshmana, the brother of Rama.

Let us pick up the story when Rama, Sita and Lakshmana during their exile in the forest, were moving through a mountainous area. As is the Lord's nature, he always loves to carry on some playful sport; he is the perfect actor. He never has any sorrow or pain whatsoever, but sometimes he will act as though he has these feelings. Whenever God comes down in human form he acts this way in order to conduct himself in a natural way as man. The human form is taken on by him so that he can be easily accessible to people. On that particular day, Rama, the incarnation of God, acted as though he was very tired. He was removing the sweat from his brow and telling Lakshmana, "Lakshmana, I am so tired. I don't think I will be able to go any further. Please put up a hut somewhere nearby, so that we can take a little rest."

Lakshmana asked Rama, "Brother, where shall we have this cottage?" Rama said, "You can decide for yourself which place will be most appropriate, and then put it up." Lakshmana responded, "Rama! Rama! What have I done? What is my error? What sins have I committed to hear these words? Please let me know why you have spoken to me like this!" Now, Rama knew the mind of Lakshmana and so he knew why Lakshmana was saying this, but in order to help Sita understand the level of Lakshmana's surrender, Rama said, "Lakshmana, please tell me what is troubling you. What have I said that has made you feel so much pain?"

Lakshmana replied, "I have given up everything. I have given up wife, mother, father, kingdom, everything. I have come along with you feeling that you are the father, that Sita is the mother, and that wherever you are is our beautiful capital city of Ayodhya. I have come only to implement your will. I have given up my own individual will, and now you ask me to construct a hut and choose the place in which to build it. Your command is my only thought. I have no other thoughts than that. Whatever is your will, I will do. My only duty is to obey you. My only goal, truly my everything, is you. You alone must tell me where the hut is to be put up." Sita realized the depth of Lakshmana's devotion and surrender. She turned to Rama and asked him to relieve Lakshmana's distress by designating the site for the hut himself.

Surrender Fully to God

The basic lesson of this story is that man should not have any desires separate from the one desire to fully surrender to God. Everything belongs to God, and only to God. Surrender means implicitly following the commands given to you by the Lord, whose directions will be clearly heard when he is enshrined in your heart. Surrender is the basis of the declaration, "Come and sit in my train and I will look after you. Let go of your ego-sense and desire. Don't carry your baggage on your head and suffer."

In this context, Krishna taught surrender as the highest and most important stage of devotion. Once you have surrendered yourself fully to the Lord, you will gain his grace. "Wherever you are, be it in a town, in a village, in a forest or in the sky, I will be your refuge. Come and surrender to me!" That is the command of the Lord, and that is also his promise. Once you are his, he will shelter you and protect you from all harm.

But, surrender does not mean giving up your discriminating faculty. You must discern what are desires and what is truly divine, and surrender all your worldly desires, offering them to the divine. Make every effort to discover the right way to surrender yourself, and thereby sanctify your life and reach the goal.

FIND GOD IN YOUR OWN HEART

The Lord stated in the Gita, "Only when you renounce all selfishness and attachment, only when you treat joy and sorrow with an equal mind and practice forbearance in all circumstances, will you become my devotee and very dear to me."

Embodiments of Love,

To have an equal mind, to be free of attachments and concern for yourself and your family, is difficult for ordinary spiritual seekers. Particularly for householders, such equanimity of mind and detachment is almost impossible. They are able to worship God through the various types of spiritual practices which have been prescribed in the scriptures. But for them to destroy their ego and remove all sense of *I-ness* and *my-ness* would be very difficult. Why is that so? It is difficult to eliminate the ego as long as you differentiate your own will from the command and will of the Lord. You have doubts and are unable to surrender because you see others and the world as separate from God. It is only when you recognize that God is dwelling in all people everywhere, in the form of an ever-luminous light shining in the temple of their hearts, that you will be able to eliminate your egoism and surrender fully to God. Once you recognize the all-pervasive unity of the Lord you will have no difficulty following him. Know that the self-effulgent flame of God's presence which resides in all people also resides in you. The one who protects all people is an integral part of your own form.

The Indwelling God

From time immemorial, the inquiry has been going on whether or not God exists. Once you have convinced yourself that he exists, the next step is to find the way to reach him. Just as was true in ancient times, this problem of how and where to find God has become a perplexing question for mankind today. To solve this problem, numerous sages made a determined effort to use all their skills and their penance to find the solution. These sages revealed where they searched and how they came to know about the existence of the effulgent Lord. They declared to the world at large:

> *"O citizens, we have been able to perceive the transcendental principle which exists beyond this visible and created world. It will not be found in the external world or in outer space, but only within your own inner self. It is there in your inner vision within your soul, in the sacred heart inside your deepest self. It is there that the blissful Lord resides."*

This was their great discovery, that God dwells within the body itself. God is the imperishable one who lives within the perishable body. The body is inert; it does not know itself. In the *Gita*, God has been called the knower of the body and the one who gives consciousness to the body. To penetrate through the veils of ignorance that hide your truth, you must make a determined effort to discover the immortal Lord residing resplendently in your mortal body. Not only must you find the Lord installed in your own body and the bodies of other creatures, but you must also find him installed in every object, in every thing. He is the indweller of all the five elements, space, air, fire, water and earth. He is the very basis of the creation.

To find a diamond you must dig deep within the earth. You will not find it hanging outside on a tree. In the same way, you will not find this most valuable diamond which is the Lord, lying around somewhere outside, easily visible to all. With the help of the teachings of great souls you will have to make the effort to find God within. The body is not an ordinary thing. It is the temple of God, it is a chariot which carries the Lord. In the world, which can be thought of as a grand village, the Lord is being taken in procession everywhere in this chariot called the body.

Within the Body is Pure Consciousness

Since the body is the temple of the Lord, it is not proper to be indifferent towards it or to neglect it, or to use it in an inappropriate or unrighteous manner. The body must be used only to perform activities which are sacred and selfless. You must take good care of the body and sanctify it by using it to do holy tasks. The body is inert no doubt, but within it lives the principle which is pure consciousness. This body may be compared to a boat which will help you cross the ocean of worldly existence. This body was not so easily obtained by you. Because of innumerable merits and numerous births in other forms, you have been able to obtain this human body. To use it improperly is to waste all the merits you have earned in all those countless lives.

It is your extraordinary good fortune to have been able to get this birth as a human being. Therefore, this sacred boat which can take you to your destination, has to be used very carefully so that you can cross the ocean of worldly existence safely. In this ocean there are terrible crocodiles and all kinds of terrifying creatures which are very harmful to you. These menacing crocodiles are the six inner enemies of man, in the form of lust, anger, greed, attachment, pride and jealousy. They inhabit this unfathomable ocean of worldly existence at every level.

The water of this ocean of world existence which supports all these horrendous creatures, is made up of a mixture of opposites like joy and grief, attraction and repulsion. When you are in this ocean of life it is very difficult to say when you will obtain happiness and when you will suffer pain. When you are beset with so many crocodiles, the very best means for completing this journey safely is to see the unity in everything. You have to firmly believe that the divine principle, the godhead in the form of the self-effulgent flame, resides in everybody and in every thing. Once you recognize the presence of God dwelling in everyone, once the unity is recognized in all this apparent diversity, then you will no longer be able to hate anyone. That is why in the *Gita* the injunction, *show no hatred towards any being* is given first place.

The various acts of ritual worship, such as singing devotional songs and repeating the holy name, which at one time may have seemed so important to you, will seem very small in comparison, once you recognize this principle of God dwelling in every heart. It is only when you are ignorant of this great truth, that you consider the various devotional practices as paramount in your spiritual life. However, until you have mastered the art of swimming there is a need to use various flotation-aids for support. Once you have learned to swim, these aids will no longer be necessary. In the same way, all the various ritual practices are necessary until you truly understand the meaning of the *Gita*. Once you have comprehended the sweet essence of the *Gita*, all these rituals will appear quite trivial.

See God in Everything

In the chapter on devotion in the *Gita* , the noble characteristics that endear a devotee to God are described. It is emphasized there that once the six inner enemies of man are brought under control, these characteristics will naturally blossom forth in the individual. Can this ever be done easily? Yes. These six enemies can be readily conquered once you recognize the truth that the one God resides in all of the five elements everywhere, and that it is he who activates all beings. Before you recognize this and experience it, you will not realize true satisfaction in anything you undertake.

If you keep some salt in your mouth then even if you try to swallow some sweet juice, you will still get the taste of salt. First you have to get rid of the salt and wash your mouth well, then you will be able to taste the sweetness. When the salt is gone you can enjoy the full unpolluted sweetness of the juice you have taken in. Similarly, it is only when you are able to conquer the ego by removing all the bad traits which have become an integral part of you, that you will be able to enjoy the sweetness of compassion, the sweetness of sacrifice, the sweetness of charity, the sweetness of sympathy and the sweetness of divine love.

To begin with, try to understand what true devotion really means. Devotion means an all-absorbing love for God. When you develop devotion and turn all your love towards God, everything that is necessary will be added unto you. You will develop the capacity to sacrifice yourself. You will expand in love. Love is the very life breath of a human being. Without love you cannot live. Love is a very sacred quality. As was referred to earlier, a great sage in ancient times told his wife, "All the love that you have is really for the sake of your higher self. Love is not for the sake of others but only for the higher self." But all too frequently, through delusion, this sacred love for the *atma*, the one self, is diverted towards the body. Everywhere in the world we find this disease of identification with the body.

The Diseases of Mankind

Many of the enjoyments you experience in life are really just the relief you feel when you temporarily soothe the pains of a disease you are suffering. For example, you think that taking food is an enjoyment, but it is really only a medicine. Food is the medicine for the disease of hunger. When you give the medicine the disease is temporarily forgotten. You cook many varieties of delicious food and consider the taste of these prepared dishes to be most enjoyable, but that is not the real purpose for which you take food. As you know, medicines are sometimes given in the form of a mixture which contains some sweetener to make it more palatable. In the same way, to treat the disease of hunger there will be a meal containing a mixture of ingredients, some of which are particularly flavorful and pleasant to the taste. But in the final analysis, the meal can only be thought of as a form of medicine to treat the disease of hunger that afflicts you. After you have eaten, the symptoms of the disease disappear. Similarly, when you take some cool water, the symptoms of the disease of thirst disappear.

We have previously discussed the six inner enemies of man: lust, anger, greed, attachment, pride and jealousy. They can also be described as desire, hatred, possessiveness, infatuation, arrogance, and envy. These are the most deep-seated diseases of mankind. It is only when you engage in practices which serve as medicines to counteract these diseases, that they will diminish and disappear. During your whole life you have been deluded into thinking that you are enjoying different types of pleasures, but in fact you are afflicted with these diseases. Until you recognize that the resident of the body is God, you will continue to be burdened by these diseases and the sufferings they bring.

Seek the Lord inside Your Own Body

All spiritual practices can only be done with the help of the body. All the education that you have acquired has been obtained by means of the body. The magnificence and extraordinary characteristics of God have been learned through the facility of the body. Taking the body as the basis, you have to make an all-out effort to see the Lord inside it. Do not keep thinking that God resides somewhere, in another world. He actually is present in the body itself. Sin does not exist in some distant world far away; it depends upon the actions that you perform with your body. Both your merit and demerit are the result of the actions you performed with the help of your body. You have to make an incessant search, a serious attempt, to find God inside your own body.

Only when you knock at the door will the master inside open it. Even your own mother will serve you food only when you ask her for it. Therefore, you will have to ask and go on asking, knock on the door and go on knocking, search and go on searching, seek and go on seeking. If you search for God within you, with all earnestness, you will surely be able to find him. If you go to a room where a great number of articles are stored, it is only if you search carefully that you will be able to find the particular article for which you are looking. Without searching you will never find the article you want. Therefore, it is said, 'Seek, seek, and it shall be found; knock, knock, and the door shall be opened.'

Perhaps you feel that you have already been knocking at the door for a long time and it has not opened for you. But find out if you have been knocking at the right door. Are you knocking at the door of liberation, or are you knocking at the door of attachment? Are you knocking at the door where God is residing or are you knocking at the door where the devil is dwelling? Whom are you approaching? In whom are you taking shelter? Are you asking the most merciful one, the one who comes in human form and holds out his own life as an example? Are you asking the mother of the universe? Are you asking for food from her, or are you asking for food from the devil?

You may even be looking at the Lord, but you are not asking for the divinity itself. No doubt, you are praying to God, but you are asking for petty material things and worldly things. You are at the wish-fulfilling tree and you are asking for trivial coffee powder. You have to pray for the wish-fulfilling tree to grant you the transcendental principle which will fill you forever with eternal bliss.

Your devotion must go on increasing and progressing, keeping in mind the firm belief that God is residing inside your own body. If you want to seek and search for the Lord who is residing inside you, you have to turn your vision inwards. How should you aspire for the Lord? You have to cry the way a calf cries for its mother who has left it and gone off with the herd. You have to cry like a chaste woman who has lost her husband and wails in pain at the separation. You have to cry in the way that a childless couple implores and pleads with God for a child. This is how you should pray to the Lord, full of devotion, longing to realize his presence within you.

Harmonize All Your Thoughts, Words and Deeds

But today, most of your prayers are filled with pompous words, devoid of feeling. Inside the mind there is one thing, on your lips there is something else. It is only when you synchronize the thoughts in your mind with the words in your mouth, that your words can turn into prayer and become effective. Then you must put your prayers into practice. When your activities in daily life are coordinated with your thoughts and words then your prayers can become worship; and when you achieve full unity in thought, word and action then you become a great soul.

You have to examine yourself to see whether you are following this path of harmony in thought, word and deed. When you examine yourself honestly you may find that most of the time these three, thought, word and deed, will be going off in three different directions, without any unity between them. When thoughts are different, words are different and actions are different, you have the characteristics of a demon, not of a saint. Such disharmony will not benefit you nor endear you to the Lord.

Forbearance, the Primary Spiritual Quality

Whatever thoughts you have, they will bring you the corresponding results. Whatever you are feeling will be reflected in your way of talking and acting. In the very first place, you must endeavor to purify your feelings. You have to make your love pure. To do so you have to develop forbearance, which is a serene patience and self-restraint under all circumstances, giving good to all, even to those who may want to harm you. There is nothing greater than having this quality of forbearance. Forbearance is equivalent to truth itself, forbearance is the heart of righteousness, forbearance is the very essence of the ancient wisdom, forbearance is nonviolence in practice, forbearance is contentment, it is compassion. Truly, forbearance is everything in all the worlds. Only when you have developed patience and forbearance will you be able to obtain the Lord.

Now, over minor insignificant things you lose your temper and become ridden with tension. Anger and temper are dangerous. They can ruin your life. If you suffer from anger you will not be able to achieve anything worthwhile. You will be looked upon with disgust and derision. You will lose your wealth. All the honors you have enjoyed will turn to ashes. Your anger will even separate you from those who are closest to you. Because of anger people lose everything, and their life becomes a waste. Therefore, in the *Gita*, Krishna taught the principle of love and the need to cultivate love to counter hatred, jealousy, anger and all the other bad traits that cause so much harm to you.

> *Love knows no hatred.*
> *Love is free from all selfishness.*
> *Love is far removed from anger.*
> *Love never takes; it knows only giving.*
> *Love is God.*

You Can Experience God Through Love Alone

If you want God, you will have to develop this sacred quality of love. Only through love will you be able to experience him, who is love itself.

If you want to see the moon there is no need to use a candle or a torch light. The light of the moon is enough to see the moon. If you want to see God you need only to immerse yourself in love. Fill yourself with love and you will surely succeed in acquiring God. But as long as this love has not yet become clearly established, there is a need for spiritual practices such as devotional singing, repetition of the name of God, and other forms of worship. Once pure love has developed these spiritual practices are no longer necessary.

Yet, even when the moon shines brightly, you will not be able to see it if your eyes are closed. In the same way, if your eyes are still closed to the loving presence of God within you, then good actions, including the various spiritual exercises, will help open your eyes and clarify your vision, so that you can see and enjoy the Lord. That is the import of Krishna's teaching in the *Gita*.

Only when you listen to such great words, and only when you understand them clearly, and only when you practice them, will you be able to reach your divine goal. Set aside at least one hour per day to study these teachings and incorporate them in all your daily activities. In so doing you will be using your time wisely and you will be sanctifying your life.

Sixth Chapter

THE THREE STAGES ON THE SPIRITUAL PATH

Fill your heart with one-pointed devotion and God will reveal himself within you. Then you will see him as he truly is. In time, you will merge with him and become one with him.

Embodiments of Love,

There are three principal stages that you must follow on the spiritual path in order to reach your spiritual goal. They have been described in a number of different ways in the Gita. At the end of the 11th chapter, wherein Lord Krishna gives Arjuna the vision of his cosmic form, you will find the three stages presented as follows:

First, you must know that God is here.
Then you must have a direct vision of him.
Finally, you must merge with him.

These three steps will lead you to liberation.

Know That God Is Here Then Experience God Directly

In the first step, you learn through the words of the scriptures or a teacher, that God really exists. But merely knowing this truth does not give you unlimited joy. You discover that God is here, but you also realize that you and God are separate. This feeling of separation can serve as the basis for subsequent steps on the path, but in itself it does not provide much lasting satisfaction.

Gradually, the anguish of separation from God moves you on to the next step. The desire develops in you to gain the direct personal experience and vision of God. You feel, "I want to see you, dear Lord. How can I experience you directly?" But, you find that it does not happen so easily just by wishing for it. You must deeply pine and yearn for this vision; you must constantly aspire to see him. Whatever form or aspect of God you have come to love in your devotion, you must now yearn for it with all your heart and wish to see it directly. If your yearning is sincere, then after some time he will make himself known to you in a most personal way, and give you this sought-for vision of himself. Here is a small story to illustrate this.

The Cowherd Boy

There was a poor cowherd boy, who had a great deal of faith and an intense yearning to see God. One day, in the village where this boy lived, a preacher came to deliver some spiritual discourses. The preacher would gather together an audience and sing the glories and exploits of the Lord. It was not possible for this cowherd boy to give up his work and come to all the meetings, because all day long he had to attend to his cows. But in the evenings he would bring the animals into a sheltered place and then go to hear the preacher give his talk. The cowherd boy would listen with great earnestness and care to all that was being said.

The preacher was a follower of Lord Vishnu, and so he related the characteristic features of God in the form of Vishnu, or Narayana, as he is also called. In the course of the discourse the preacher repeatedly described the traditional image of the Lord as one who was dark-complexioned, who wore a white mark on his forehead and rode on a white eagle. The preacher also explained that Lord Vishnu was always prepared to go to the rescue of those who sought shelter in him, and that he would accept as an offering anything that was given to him with full faith and love.

As the preacher repeatedly described these characteristics of the Lord, they made an indelible impression on the heart of that boy. The preacher also said that God is a great lover of music, and that he could be won by directing one's prayers to him in song, sung most reverently from the heart.

Well, this cowherd boy used to carry some food with him for his noontime lunch. Daily he would offer this food to God with all sincerity and devotion, praying to the Lord to partake of it. He began his prayers by singing this song, "O loving Lord, You ride on a white eagle, so I have been told. Come. Please come to me and accept this food." The boy went on praying like this to the Lord for one whole week continuously. He never touched his food because it was not shared by the Lord. By the end of the week he became extremely weak.

Anguished Yearning for the Lord's Presence

Besides his weakened physical condition, he was also suffering from extreme anguish because he felt that he wasn't singing properly and therefore the Lord did not respond. He was sure that it was because of his own shortcomings in his songs that the Lord did not come to partake of his food. And so with great determination and devotion he continued to practice his singing, thinking that in the end he would surely win the grace of the Lord.

In his weakened condition he reached the forest. He was feeling extremely exhausted but he was determined not to eat unless his offering was accepted by the Lord. Now his prayerful song poured out of him in a most melodious and sacred way. The boy just kept on singing and singing all the time, imploring the Lord to come down and accept the food and drink that he was offering with so much yearning. When there was perfect harmony in the feeling, in the tune and in the content of the song, the Lord descended. How did he appear before that cowherd boy? He came as a boy of the same age, wearing the simple ochre cloth of a saddhu, a mendicant holy man.

The young cowherd asked the boy he saw standing before him, "Please, dear friend, may I know who you are? Are you a traveler passing through this forest?" The holy boy answered, "I am the Lord. I am Narayana. You prayed to see me and so I have come to give you a vision of myself." Remembering that the Lord liked the sweet sound of music, the cowherd boy continued his questioning in the form of a most melodious song, "But you don't conform to the description given of the Lord, who is dark-complexioned, who wears a white mark on his forehead and who rides a white eagle. The preacher said that is how we can know the Lord. But it doesn't seem to be true. O, dear one, if you are really the blessed Lord, please resolve my doubt and let me see you in your true form."

The Vision of the Lord

The boy had heard a description of the Lord; now he wanted to see and experience him directly, exactly as he had heard him described and come to believe in him. But God doesn't have any specific name or form; he has a thousand eyes, a thousand ears, a thousand hands and a thousand feet. Yet in order to please and satisfy his devotees who are aspiring to see him, he takes on the particular form which has been earnestly prayed for. To satisfy this cowherd boy the Lord revealed himself by taking on the lustrous form of Vishnu, and accepted the food and drink so lovingly offered by the boy. This is the second stage when one yearns for the vision of the Lord. Even when that vision comes, it will still not be the true form of God but the one chosen through the prayers of the devotee. God loves sincere, heartfelt feelings, and therefore, in keeping with the feeling of his devotee, he will give his vision in the form which pleases the devotee most.

After the Lord left the boy thought to himself, "First I heard a description of him, and then I prayed for a vision of him. Now he has come down and I have seen him directly. But, how can I reach him and be ever with him?" By merely knowing that God exists, a devotee will not be satisfied. Nor does he get full satisfaction by just having a vision of the Lord. Having had the vision, he yearns to be fully merged with him. It is only then that the devotee will be in unending bliss. In the case of this boy, the Lord had given a vision of himself, and then disappeared. But from that moment on the boy kept the picture of the Lord as he had just seen him, in the form of Vishnu, continuously imprinted in his heart. With that lovely form in his mind's eye, he now began inquiring and thinking only of how he could reach him and merge with him. This is the third stage.

Beyond Dualism

In the same way, by either listening to learned people or by reading and studying the scriptures you can get some idea of what God is like. But ultimately you will not be satisfied and happy with just this. It is still only a stage of dualism, for in this stage you and God remain separate. Therefore, you will make an attempt to go beyond the stage of dualism to the next step, which is qualified non-dualism. This refers to the deep aspiration to see and experience God directly. How can you get a vision of him? By picturing in your own heart the form of God you heard described, and then continuously thinking and contemplating on that form. Whatever you do, whatever you say, whatever you see and whatever you listen to, you have to become one with that sacred form.

The specific form of God you have pictured becomes a thought form in your mind. The thought form should then become saturated with the feeling of devotion so that it becomes a feeling form in your heart. Gradually, gradually, these feelings will deepen and strengthen until one day you will have a real vision of the Lord. So, first the Lord is heard of and thought of, then he is sought through intense feelings of devotion and yearning, and finally he reveals himself in form and can be directly experienced. In other words, the thought form turns into a feeling form, which then becomes transformed into real experience. That describes the second stage on the path. Not only do you get the personal vision of the Lord, whom you have aspired to see, but you also get the chance to converse with him face-to-face.

After seeing the Lord thus and talking to him directly, you gain a little more satisfaction. But if you are a true devotee, even this golden opportunity will not give you the full joy you long for. Now you want to reach God and merge with him. You think, "I have heard... I have seen... now I must reach him and be one with him." In the first stage, when through reading and hearing you come to know that God exists, you feel that God is separate and you are separate. This is the state of dualism. But in the second stage you see the Lord and get the feeling that you are part of him. This is the state of qualified non-dualism. Finally you move on to the feeling, 'The Lord and I are one and the same'. This is the stage of complete non-dualism. Here you think, 'Either I must get merged with him or he must become one with me.' Then there is complete unity.

Becoming One With the Lord

So long as there remains a separate river distant from the ocean, which is its source and its goal, then the river will retain a separate name and have an individual identity. But once the river merges into the ocean it gets the taste of the ocean, it gets the form of the ocean, and it takes on the name of the ocean. If you want to become one with the Lord, you have to acquire the feelings of the Lord, you have to acquire the form of the Lord and you have to acquire all the sacred characteristics of the Lord. Only then will you be one with him.

You have to feel that all the attributes of the Lord must manifest themselves in you. Affirm to yourself: "The broadmindedness of the Lord is within me. All the selfless feelings of the Lord are within me. The unbounded love of the Lord is within me." When you faithfully live this conviction then you eventually attain the realization that you and he are one. Then there is perfect unity.

You must continuously strive for this feeling of unity. You must make every effort to gain it. Then you will reach that fulfillment one day. This is the ultimate goal of human life. It is only when you reach that place, the place from which you have originally come, that true fulfillment will be yours.

The Three Stages in Secular Life

Even in your secular life you can recognize these progressive stages necessary for reaching a goal. Consider the following example. Suppose some mangoes have arrived in the market place and that mangoes are fruits which you love immensely. There may be one particular type of mango which you especially favor and relish. Now a friend comes to you and informs you that they are selling these particular mangoes that you enjoy so much. The moment you hear this you get a certain amount of satisfaction; you are happy just thinking about these mangoes, even though you have not acquired them and tasted them.

The moment you get the news you rush to the bazaar to find out where those mangoes are and whether there are any still available. Yes, they are there. Now you get a good look at them. This gives you still more satisfaction. But even then you are not yet fully happy. So you put some choice mangoes in your bag and pay for them. Then, until you reach home you go on thinking about those fruits, reflecting on your good fortune to find such nice ones, and looking forward to eating them. Why do you spend so much time thinking about them? Because you have an extraordinary liking for these fruits, and your actions in going after them and getting them are proof of this strong love you have for them.

You can get a lot of joy when a feeling that you have been experiencing strongly inside you, takes on a form which you can see externally. In truth, whatever you see outside of you is always only a reflection of your inner thoughts. When you have a strong enough desire, you will manifest externally what you wish for so strongly internally. Your desire for the mangoes brought you to the market. Now you have bought them and brought them home. You wash them nicely and peel them. Then you start eating them with great relish and anticipation. As you consume them, you blissfully enjoy the nectarine juice of these lovely fruits. Soon, the juice is no longer something outside of you, but it will have become part of you. With that you get immense joy; you feel complete bliss.

Knowing, Seeing and Becoming One With the Divinity

What is the reason for such great joy? Let us recapitulate the process. First you came to know that the particular fruit you love had become available in the bazaar. That is knowing. After hearing about it, you didn't get discouraged but developed the intense desire to get them and enjoy them. You went to the bazaar with great intensity of desire, yearning to see the fruits there. Finally, you found them and got a good look at those fruits. That is the stage of seeing. After seeing the fruit, you acquired them and ate them. This is the stage of entering into and becoming one with the object of your desire.

Do you have such intense feelings for God? That is the one desire you really should develop. After listening to a number of discourses, after reading many scriptures, after knowing that God exists and after having spent much time in worshipping him, you will have to develop a strong yearning to see him; otherwise, all your efforts will be in vain. You have to fervently strive, making an all-out effort to get a direct vision of the Lord.

A student, after having entered a particular grade and spent the year studying the subjects at that level, will not get any satisfaction in remaining in that grade for the next year. He will aspire to progress to a higher grade. If a student is in the same class for two years he develops a sense of despair and despondency. Not only does he get discouraged but he is also put through a lot of ridicule by his fellow-students. In the same way, you will be poorer in the eyes of other devotees if you continuously remain in the first stages of dualistic worship, without moving on in your spiritual development. Other devotees will say, "Look at this person. He has been attending so many discourses over a long period of time and he's read all the great scriptures, but what is the use of all that? There doesn't seem to be any progress in him."

This unfortunate process of remaining stuck in the first stage, is the characteristic feature of the slothful quality of inertia and laziness. You have to remove this quality and go on from the dualistic state to the next state of internalizing the Lord. In this state, through the continuous contemplation of the Divinity inside, you try to gain a direct vision of God in the particular form you choose. With intense desire you will get that coveted chance to see the Lord, converse with him and serve him.

Reaching the Abiding Peace of the Immortal Self

But even then you should not be satisfied. You should strive to reach the final and highest state. There should be no rest, no peace of mind or contentment until you reach the state of complete mergence with God and the realization of his oneness. These days you are only aspiring to obtain rest for your body and trying to get a little peace of mind. But this is not good. You have to reach the abiding peace of the *atma*. This is your true self, the immortal self, the one universal self. When you become reunited with it, you become peace itself. Your individual self has to merge with the universal self. Then the long journey is complete and permanent bliss is realized.

A river is born from the ocean and ends in the ocean. But how did the river originate? Initially some of the water of the ocean turned into clouds. Once the ocean water becomes a cloud there is separation and duality. Clouds are separate; ocean is separate. The water of the ocean is saltish. After it turns into a cloud it becomes sweet. But now the water which has become a cloud comes in the form of rain. You can say it is a rain of love, because this rain water becomes a river and with great enthusiasm rushes to rejoin the ocean. This may be compared to the state wherein a great anguish and aspiration develops to get nearer and nearer to the final goal.

When you are in that state you yearn with all your heart to reach the native land from which you have become separated. In the case of the water in the form of a river, it is impelled to merge back into the ocean from whence it came. Only then will it have reached its goal. Such is the pure non-dualistic state of total mergence with the source.

You are born as a human being and you have lived part of your life as an ordinary human being. But you have chosen to take up the path of spiritual life. You find yourself seeking out the company of spiritually-minded people. You find yourself listening to the great scriptural stories describing the sacred characteristics of the Lord. But now, you find that this is not enough. You yearn to have a direct vision of the Lord. Even then, you are not satisfied with just that. Merely having had the opportunity to see and talk with the Lord you still do not find that your happiness lasts. But when you finally get fully merged and united with him, then you gain the complete fulfillment you have been seeking. Then you are one with the unending peace and bliss that is the Lord. This was the teaching that Krishna imparted to Arjuna on the battlefield.

The Sacred Names of Arjuna

In the *Gita*, Krishna used a number of names to address Arjuna. Even in worldly life, a number of titles and names may be conferred on people. In the *Gita*, it was the embodiment of divinity, Lord Krishna, who conferred the different names on Arjuna. Krishna told Arjuna, "O Arjuna. You are not a child of mortality. You are the divinity itself. You are the son of immortality." In his life Arjuna found himself in a number of trying circumstances in which he acquitted himself heroically. As a result, he was given various titles. To obtain his bow, which was a sacred weapon, he performed severe penance and faced a number of difficult problems. But throughout he persisted with a great deal of faith, courage and conviction.

His determination in the face of all obstacles was ultimately rewarded by gaining the grace of Lord Shiva and winning the bow directly from him. In the process of getting this celestial weapon even the elements of nature went against him, but nothing could deter him from his firm resoluteness and purpose. Because he was able to win that bow, the Lord conferred on him the title, the victor of the bow.

From a worldly point of view, Arjuna could also be thought of as the one who was victorious in gaining wealth. There is a story for this. The oldest of the Pandava brothers, Dharmaraja, who was the king, decided to undertake a great ceremonial sacrifice, performed only by reigning kings. At that time the Pandavas were opposed by the wicked Kauravas. The treasury of the Pandavas was completely empty. They had no money available at all. In the face of such obstacles it would have been nearly impossible to proceed with such a grand ceremony. Still, Dharmaraja insisted on going ahead with the ceremonial sacrifice. He said to Arjuna, "Brother, this occasion will require a very heavy expenditure of funds. We will need a great deal of wealth. How might we raise this money?" Arjuna replied, "Dharmaraja, why worry about money when we have with us the wish-fulfilling tree in the form of Krishna? Why should we be afraid? Once Krishna blesses us we will be able to get any amount of money."

Arjuna went around to the different kings ruling over the surrounding areas to inform them of Dharmaraja's wish to hold the great sacrifice. As soon as these kings heard that Dharmaraja was planning to perform the ceremony, they offered to support Dharmaraja with their own treasuries, and so Arjuna brought back wealth in such huge quantities that it took dozens of elephants to carry it. There were great heaps of gold, silver and jewels. Krishna who had prompted all this, came and acted as if he didn't know anything. He asked Dharmaraja, "Wherever did you get so much wealth? Where did it all come from?" Dharmaraja, out of ignorance and fraternal pride, replied, "It is because of my brother Arjuna that I got all this."

From that day on, Krishna addressed Arjuna as the conqueror of wealth, in this way concealing his own role and announcing to the world that it was Arjuna who was able to gather so much wealth. There were many other names given to Arjuna, such as son of the earth. These names were not intended for Arjuna alone. As you hear these various names you can start applying them to yourself; each contains a deeper meaning and shows how the Lord showers his grace on his devotees. Make them part of you; fully live them by striving to understand their deeper meaning and by putting them into practice in your daily life.

Seventh Chapter

RESTRAINING THE TONGUE
IN BOTH FOOD AND SPEECH

One of the most important disciplines necessary for coming into union with God is control of the tongue. This must be exercised both in the area of food and in the area of speech. Without control of the tongue it is impossible to follow the path of devotion and become one with God.

Embodiments of Love,

Together with most animals and birds, human beings have five sense organs. These sense organs must be used extremely carefully, always being aware of their capabilities and limitations. You must exercise the same control over them as you do in controlling some of the powerful energies and tools that are used in daily life. For example, fire when used with care and intelligence can serve you in many useful ways. But when it is out of control it can be very harmful. Or take a knife or electricity; if you know the proper way to use them, they will be beneficial. Otherwise they can be quite dangerous. It all depends on the care you take and how well you use your intelligence. The spiritual teachings have laid great emphasis on knowing the proper use of the sense organs and applying that understanding to your day-to-day life.

The Dual Power of the Tongue

Each sense organ given to human beings has one particular use, but the tongue is endowed with dual power. It has both the power of speech and the power of taste. In the *Gita*, the Lord cautions you to be very careful in using your tongue. He praises the devotee who has attained complete control over the tongue, for such a one will soon develop a pure and steady heart and feel the constant presence of the Lord. To gain such control, devotees have been practicing a number of special disciplines, such as observing silence, controlling their diet, or maintaining a complete fast.

Fasting promotes health for the physical body. In the mental realm it gives joy and bliss. Unlimited and unregulated food is very harmful for devotees. Indulging indiscriminately in unwholesome foods is likely to lead the devotee into the torpidity of inertia. To think that you can go on wantonly indulging yourself in food, while at the same time trying to please God and enjoy the nearness of God, is extremely foolish. These two, indulging in food and gaining the nearness of God, are not compatible. Therefore, right from the beginning you must make a determined effort to keep the tongue under control. Once you gain mastery over the tongue, the other sense organs will automatically come under control.

Control of the Tongue

Today's devotees have imposed on themselves all sorts of rules and regulations in order to live a disciplined spiritual life. Unfortunately, these have not been effective in gaining control over the tongue. Truly speaking, it is not necessary to make such strenuous efforts to control the various sense organs. If the tongue is properly controlled all the other sense organs will come in line by themselves. Because people have not been able to gain control over the tongue, they are afflicted with numerous doubts, emotional turmoil, contradictions and confusion. Control of the tongue refers not only to food but also to speech. You must recognize that there is nothing more powerful than the power of words. For this reason, you must keep your talk strictly under control.

In life, you can observe that even for little things a number of sacrifices have to be made. You cannot get anything without paying for it. You are prepared to sacrifice even your own life to obtain some small, petty, useless things. But, you are not seeking that which is exceedingly important, that which includes all other things and is the very basis of everything worthwhile. That greatest of all treasures is the immortal self. Only when you give up one thing can you get another in its place. Should you not then give up everything else for the sake of gaining this most important and most valuable of all possessions? Should you not sacrifice everything for the sake of reaching your highest self?

In the market place, if you want some vegetables you will have to give some money in exchange. Without offering to pay, and thereby sacrificing some of your money, you will not be able to get those vegetables. By giving up one thing you can then acquire another. In the same way, if you want to acquire virtues, you will have to give up your bad qualities. Only by sacrificing your likes and dislikes can you obtain equal-mindedness. Only by sacrificing your bad qualities can you attain the noble qualities. Only by giving up your bad thoughts, bad habits and bad behavior can you possibly achieve good thoughts, good habits and good behavior.

Many sages have described how the tongue always longs to enjoy good things, and how everything will be easy once you can gain control over it. The principal way of exercising this control is by observing silence. Silence does not merely refer to restraint of the tongue. Not only should you exercise silence in speech but you should also be silent in thoughts. Your mind should remain free of all thoughts. That is true silence.

Develop a Discriminating Mind

If you want to gain control over the food that you take in, you should not go on feeding the tongue whatever it desires. You have to develop discrimination. In every activity of life you have to apply your discriminating faculties to determine if what you are doing will benefit you spiritually. In the area of food, you have to explore and find out whether the food you take in is pure, or if it inflames the senses and passions, or if it is of a dull, unhealthy quality that produces a sleepy slothful reaction.

According to the *Gita*, maintaining control over the tongue by taking in pure food in limited quantities is absolutely essential for the devotee. Use your powers of discrimination with every item of food and ask the question, "Is this food pure, or will it disturb or lower my consciousness?" If you were to examine every item of food you use in this way, and take food in judiciously, you would always remain equal-minded. You would not be affected by censure or praise.

But, if you were to indulge in food without discrimination, without trying to find out whether it was desirable or not, paying attention only to satisfying your hunger and catering to your taste buds, you would not be able to control your attachments and feelings. You would sink down into weakness. If someone were to make adverse comments about you, you would soon conclude that the whole world was against you and you would feel depressed. The moment you were criticized or blamed by anyone your happiness would go, you would become grief stricken and regard all of life as meaningless.

On the other hand, if anyone were to praise you and appreciate you, you would start bloating up with ego and pride. It would be practically impossible to hold you down. What is the reason for such instability? The single most important reason for these weaknesses is the type of food you take in. All these adverse feelings come about because of your lack of control and discrimination in the area of food. The *Gita* has emphasized the need for exercising extreme care in selecting the food you eat. You must constantly keep in mind the importance of pure food for helping you to maintain equanimity in all situations, so that you become neither elated when praise is showered, nor depressed when criticism is heaped upon you.

Purity of the Food, the Cooking Vessels and the Cook

The *Gita* has also declared that there should be purity of the vessels and utensils used in cooking, and purity of the cooking process itself. The vessels used must be absolutely clean. Purity refers not only to physical cleanliness but also to the way in which the implements and the articles of food have been acquired. You have to see whether these things have been acquired by proper means and honest work or whether they have come through dishonest means. Articles which are acquired by improper means and used for cooking food, will not only generate bad thoughts but will lead you down the wrong path.

The next step is to inquire into the purity of the cooking process itself by ascertaining the thoughts and feelings of the person who is cooking the food. There are three things that have been mentioned that must be carefully looked into and controlled. Normally, you pay attention only to the purity of the vessels and not the other two, namely, the purity of the person cooking and the purity of the food itself. You do not know the feelings in the mind of the cook and you do not know if the shopkeeper has acquired the articles you buy in the market by proper or improper means.

Therefore, just before taking your food, you should pray and offer the entire meal to God in order to cleanse and purify it. This prayer which is offered before food is not for the benefit of God but for your own benefit. It will purify your food by evoking God's blessing. Before eating, you can say your own sincere prayer from your heart asking God to purify and bless the food. Or, you can use formal prayers such as the verses from the *Gita* that are traditionally used before food. These are the 24th verse from the 4th chapter and the 14th verse from the 15th chapter, which are particularly efficacious.

The Blessing Offering Food to God

In Sanskrit the *Gita* verses used before food are:

Brahmaarpanam, brahma havir,
Brahmaagnau brahmanaa hutam,

Brahmaiva tena gantavyam,
Brahma karma samaadhinaha.

Aham vaishvaanaro bhutvaa,
Praaninaam dehamaashritaha,
Praanaapaana samaa yuktaha,
Pachaamy annam chatur vidham.

which mean:

The offering is God, the act of offering is God,
Offered by God in the sacred fire which is God.
He alone attains God
Who in all his actions is fully absorbed in God.

I am the all-pervading cosmic energy,
Lodged in the bodies of living beings.
United with their ingoing and outgoing life-breaths,
I consume all the various foods.

This prayer before eating removes all the defects and flaws in the vessels and in the articles of food, as well as removing any negative influence acquired during the cooking process. Before offering the prayer the food is merely food; but once you offer it to the Lord it becomes consecrated food.

The Role of the Tongue in Speech

The second aspect of the tongue is speech. As has already been mentioned, speech has its own powerful impact on the mind and the entire mental process. It has a tremendous power. It can perplex your mind. It can break your heart. It can even kill you. It can also give life and encouragement and help you to reach your divine goal. These are two opposite and contradictory results, both effected by the spoken word.

By the use of appropriate words, it is possible to transform the entire mind of an individual. Unfortunately, many people do not believe this. They raise objections like, "How is it possible to transform the mind through mere words? What experiments have been conducted to prove that there is this power in the faculty of speech? Words are only gross sounds heard through the ear." Or else they think, "The mind is a very subtle thing. How can mere sounds transform something that is so subtle and fine? It is not possible." In this way they will argue that it is impossible to bring about a mental transformation through words. There is a small story to illustrate this attitude.

The Story of the Officer and the Preceptor

There was once a government officer who did not believe in the great power of words to transform minds, particularly when it came to spiritual teachings. He happened to be the education secretary for a district, and included among the schools he had under his auspices were some religious institutions. One day he visited one of these schools where a preceptor was teaching the holy scriptures to a number of young students. This spiritual teacher was expounding on some very profound concepts. Sitting there listening to this, the officer developed a headache. Finally, he told the teacher, "My dear fellow. These are small children. There is no need to burden them unnecessarily with such lectures. This will be completely useless to them. Such scriptural truths and deep philosophical concepts cannot possibly be grasped and understood by such small children."

The teacher replied that only when children are at such a tender and impressionable age can they be led onto the proper path. Being taught these noble truths from the very beginning, he felt, would clear their hearts of doubts and put them on the right track in life. The officer said, "I do not believe in all these words. How can mere words transform the mind? I do not think this will ever be possible." The teacher tried to convince him through various explanations and arguments, but the officer would not listen and allow any of the teacher's wisdom to penetrate into him. It was a case of a closed mind. Too much authority often results in cynicism and an exaggerated sense of self-importance. Cleverness follows and in a short time all the virtues disappear and the reason becomes impaired.

When the teacher realized that no matter how hard he tried it was impossible to explain his point of view to this officer, he decided to prove his point by a practical lesson that the officer was sure to understand. He asked the youngest of the students to get up and told this small boy, "Child, you go and physically throw this officer out of the room. Do it immediately!" The moment he heard these words, the officer got very angry. He started shouting at the teacher, "Who do you think you are? I am a government officer, I am the education secretary of this district, and you are asking a small child to send me out! How dare you do this?"

The teacher then told the officer, "Well sir, I did not beat you or hit you or even touch you. I did not do anything to you. Just by merely hearing some words you seem to be getting very upset. What could be the reason for your becoming so angry? It is because of these few words I used, isn't it?" This is how the teacher demonstrated to him that words can be very powerful. They have an enormous capability for doing great harm or great good, according to the way they are used. After this personal lesson the officer left, but now much wiser and humbled by his experience.

The Power of Words

In the scriptures you will also find statements that point out how words are extremely powerful and can destroy the world itself. There it is said that if you were to cut a tree, it could still sprout; or if a piece of iron were broken in two, a blacksmith could make the two pieces come together again by heating and pounding them until they were one. But if you were to break a heart by venomous words, it would not be possible to ever make it whole again. Words can cause endless troubles and they can also give boundless joy. Therefore, you should be most careful that the words you use do not hurt or give pain to others.

If you were to physically slip and fall there might be some small injury that could cause you some inconvenience for a while. But there would not be any grave consequences resulting from this in the long term. There might only have been a small wound, which you can get easily dressed, and which would soon heal. But if your tongue were to slip and you were to hurt the mind or the heart of another person with harsh words, it would create a wound in that person which could not be cured by any doctor in the world. Therefore, you should never use words which are likely to hurt another's feelings. One day the words which you have used will come back to you. So, always use sweet and good words.

It has been said that the tongue relishes sweet things. You can talk to it and say, "O tongue, you like sweet things so much, why don't you linger on the sweet name of the Lord? O tongue, you know what true sacrifice means; you are the very embodiment of sacrifice. Use yourself only for singing the name of the Lord. Sing of God and become sacred and holy thereby."

Sacrifice and Forbearance

Now, why do we say that the tongue knows the true meaning of sacrifice and is absolutely selfless? Well, this is really what you experience every day. For example, when you give some sweet things to the tongue it tastes them, and as soon as it finds out that they are delightfully sweet, it says to itself, "O let me pass these lovely sweet things on to the stomach so that it can also enjoy this delight." But if what is tasted is not pleasant, if for example it is something that is bitter, then the tongue will not pass this on to the stomach but will immediately spit the offensive substance out of the mouth to save the stomach from grief. Good or bad, sweet or bitter, the tongue does not try to keep anything just for itself and only for its own enjoyment. It lives selflessly and with honor, knowing its own limits very well. For any number of years it is content to remain shut up inside the mouth. Does it come outside even once? No. Whatever work it does, it does uncomplainingly inside the mouth.

There is still another important feature of the tongue; it has extraordinary forbearance. Whatever are its difficulties and problems, and whatever troubles others give it, it remains focused within itself, never exceeding its own limits, and always observing forbearance. It lives in the midst of exceedingly harmful companions, namely, very sharp and powerful teeth. With a great deal of skill it manages not to be bitten or hurt by these aggressive fellow-residents that share its tight quarters. With unusual skill and forbearance it has been existing very well with such dreadful neighbors, without even once coming to any harm.

In this way, the tongue can teach a number of very important lessons which can be quite useful to you. For instance, it teaches you that you can live in the midst of people who are very difficult to live with. With a lot of care, forbearance and skill, you should be able to enjoy a happy life despite such trying circumstances. But in today's world there will be very few who follow such good examples. For most individuals, once they come in touch with bad people, they also tend to become bad. All the good feelings, the good qualities, the good thoughts and the good behavior disappear in a moment, and they lose all their merit and virtues. In order that you do not suffer such bad consequences, it is necessary that you gain complete control over your tongue.

Talk Wastes Spiritual Energy

Baba quite often tells the students, "Dear students, you should not talk too much. The divine energy which is in you will get wasted in the process. By engaging in too much talk, your memory power will be reduced and weakness will develop in your body. Premature old age will be the final result. Besides that, you will also get a bad name."

Now, consider that you have a radio. You may switch it on to hear a news broadcast, but then you leave the room and forget to switch it off. The radio just continues to play without purpose and uses up costly energy. Your body can be compared to that radio and the intellect may be thought of as the switch that has turned it on but failed to turn it off again. In this comparison, your mind will be the useless sound coming forth in the form of words and talk, ceaselessly babbling all day. The sacred divine energy in you will get wasted by this kind of endless talk.

Right from dawn when you get up until dusk when you go to bed you go on talking, if not loudly then within yourself. The volume might be turned down but nevertheless the talk will be going on all the time. The radio inside just keeps on playing non-stop and the valuable spiritual energy that is within you gets wasted, just as electricity is consumed in the case of the radio, whether it is playing loudly or softly. The energy just drains away.

The most common cause of premature old age and senility is this talk, and more talk, and still more talk. All this talk is not good. You have to observe silence. From birth you have not developed the habit of inner silence. You have to develop it now. Actually, the two functions of the tongue are closely related. Too much talk leads to unnatural hunger. When the talker feels more hungry he will, of course, take more food. Because of this excess food, feelings will arise which will express themselves in still more talk. In this process, controlling the senses becomes an almost impossible task.

If you were to give a horse very concentrated food and then confine it or tie it up, it would become very nervous and upset, and would not be able to keep quiet. After you feed a horse it is necessary to exercise it also. In the same way, if you take in rich food without working hard and taking some exercise, you will become nervous and restless, and you will also develop egoistic feelings of selfishness and pride. Proper exercise will strengthen your health and proper food taken in moderation will control the negative tendencies.

One of the main purposes of spiritual practice is to see to it that the food you take in will be used in the service of society. You must be firmly resolved to always do good. In the face of some adversity, you should not flicker like a flame in the wind. You must have strong self-confidence.

Self-Confidence

Consider a tiny bird which has come and landed on a branch where it continues to sit for some time afterwards. Now, suppose a wind comes up and the branch starts to move, swaying back and forth. The little bird will not get frightened by this movement of the branch. Why? Because it does not depend entirely on the branch for its support. It depends on its wings and so it has strong self-confidence that no amount of movement of the branch would disturb it. Even if the branch were to break, this would not threaten it or cause it to fall. But today's man gets easily frightened by the smallest difficulties in day-to-day life. He does not have the self-confidence which even a little bird has. What is the reason for this? The reason is too much food. He takes in food which is full of dross and which, in turn, generates feelings that are saturated with the quality of *rajas*, excessive nervous energy and activity, which promotes apprehension and anger. As a result, he has no chance to experience his true nature which is even-minded and pure.

The youth of today have many doubts. They see animals and birds relating to one another in all kinds of ways, enjoying a great deal of freedom. The youth wonder why they should not have the same freedom and independence that the animals enjoy. The proper answer to this question is, "Yes, you are also entitled to freedom, but it is the freedom appropriate to a human being, not that of an animal." Animals enjoy the freedom which is natural to animals. You should enjoy human freedom, the freedom that is natural to human beings.

Live as a true human being; develop the qualities appropriate to a human being. Calling yourself human but trying to enjoy the freedom of an animal will not get you far. The human characteristics are sacrifice, love, compassion, generosity, sympathy, nonviolence and other such noble qualities. Do not develop the qualities associated with an animal. And even worse than that, do not succumb to qualities much lower than an animal, namely, the qualities of a demon such as selfishness, anger, hatred, lust, jealousy and the like. These demonic qualities have no place in a human being.

Efface Selfishness, Pride and Jealousy

In particular, you should never allow selfishness, pride and jealousy to take up residence within you. These three are the worst of the bad traits that infest man. If you wish to acquire only good qualities, the human qualities instead of animal or demonic qualities, then you will have to acquire control of the tongue, in both the areas of speech and food. This is the royal road for human beings. The path of devotion, requires that you use the tongue properly, which means that you use food properly and use words properly.

Especially in this dark age of materialism and unrighteousness, the tongue can get easily sanctified by repeating the holy name. Instead of wasting your precious divine energy and your precious time in idle talk, let the tongue constantly sing the praises of God and repeat his name. Sing the name of the Lord! That is the proper way to spend your life. Use every moment of the day to saturate yourself with the glory and the holiness of his presence.

Eighth Chapter

YOU CAN REACH GOD THROUGH LOVE ALONE

The Lord declared in the Gita, "When you constantly think of me with love, I will bless you with the gift of spiritual discrimination. This will lead you to permanent union with me. I promise this to you."

Embodiments of Love,

The *buddhi* is the discriminating faculty through which you can separate that which is real from that which is unreal, that which is permanent from that which is changing. This power of spiritual discernment becomes available only to people who have developed sacred devotion and are filled with love for God. Devotion is the royal road to attaining the highest wisdom. In truth, it is the only path leading to self-knowledge. Devotion evokes the grace of God. The Lord proclaimed in the twelfth chapter of the *Gita*, "The one who is devoted to me is very dear to me."

Devotion

What is devotion? It is the steady flow of love towards God. When your love flows towards individuals or towards transient, worldly things it cannot be called devotion; it is really only a form of attachment. But when your love flows unceasingly towards God, the one unchanging principle behind this world of change, then your love becomes devotion.

Initially, you develop your devotion by turning towards God and approaching him. Then, you strengthen your love for God by cultivating the attitude that you are his devotee or his servant and you surrender yourself to his will. As your love for God deepens, you progress to the stage where you feel an intimate closeness to God and experience his presence continuously. Finally, you reach the consummation of your spiritual journey when you fully realize the truth, "I am God. God and I are one."

In practice, devotion takes two forms. First, there is the type of devotion which involves various devotional practices and rituals engaged in by devotees, such as the traditional practice of worshipping the Lord with ritual offerings, making pilgrimages to spiritual centers and attending spiritual functions, singing devotional songs and studying devotional literature, and so on. These are the ordinary types of devotion. In the *Gita* the Lord taught that these various practices can be considered to be of a lower type. But, when your worship expands into a total absorption in God, when your love for God enters into every activity of your daily life and you develop a flawless, sacred character, then you are expressing the higher devotion which very much pleases the Lord.

There is a clear distinction, therefore, between this devotion which is particularly dear to the Lord and the more ordinary type of devotion. The latter uses the things of the phenomenal world to worship the Lord, such as flowers, for example. Where have these articles come from? Have you been able to manufacture them? Have you created these flowers? No. They have all been created by the Lord. Where, then, is the sacrifice in offering to the Lord things which he himself has created? Such offerings will not get you very far on your spiritual path. But to offer to the Lord the sacred flowers of your heart, which are not related to the world, and to offer these in loving worship to the one who is seated in your heart, that is the highest form of devotion. That is the devotion you should aspire for.

Meditation And Devotion Are One And The Same

Another way of thinking of this highest form of devotion is as the uninterrupted meditation on God alone. In the popular understanding of the word, meditation refers to concentrating on an object, and through that object reaching a higher state of consciousness. But this is not the correct approach to meditation. True meditation is meditation on God, and only on God. Therefore, meditation and devotion are really the same; both are the process of concentrating on God to the exclusion of everything else, thinking only of him. Without such meditation or devotion it is impossible to realize the constant presence of God everywhere, in everything, and thereby, gain true spiritual knowledge.

You long to enjoy the fruit, but you will not be able to get it without first having the flower. First comes the blossom, then comes the fruit. Devotion is like the flower. Without first developing the flower of unshakable love for God and allowing it to blossom forth, it will be impossible for you to acquire the fruit of spiritual wisdom. This flower of love may express itself in different ways as the following example shows.

The Householder and the Monk

There were two devotees who both had an all-consuming love for God. One was a householder leading a family life and the other was a renunciate monk. The family man felt himself to be the servant of the Lord and always practiced the principle of total surrender to God. The great virtue of the servant stage is that through the practice of humility and surrender, the ego quickly disappears. As long as you have egoism, you will not be able to gain the sacred knowledge of the supreme self.

Egoism can be found everywhere. Even Arjuna, whom Krishna befriended for so long, and to whom Krishna gave so much encouragement, was riddled with egoistic feelings throughout his life. It was only after Arjuna threw down his bow and surrendered himself completely to the Lord, saying, "Command me, O Lord, I will do whatever you say," that Krishna taught him the highest wisdom of the *Gita*.

So, the householder started from the very humble beginning which is associated with "I am your servant, O Lord, I am your instrument", and he expressed his unshakable love for God that way. On the other hand, the monk, expressed his love for God by seeking God everywhere he went, in everyone and in everything he encountered. He would constantly repeat, "Everywhere I look I find only God. Everything I see is created by God and imbued with God. Everyone I meet is but God. I too am truly God."

Because of the different circumstances of their lives, these two individuals adopted different paths to overcome the power of illusion. The householder, by following the path of a servant became smaller and smaller, until he became so small that he slipped through the clutches of that fierce tiger *maya*, the terrible power of illusion, which had held him in its claws. By losing his ego he became free. For the monk, the shackles of illusion which had been binding him were broken to pieces when he transcended his ego limitations by absorbing himself in the conviction "Everywhere there is only God. All is God. I too am God. I am God." Through their deep love of God, each in his own way was able to transcend the power of illusion.

I Am God

If you develop within yourself the sacred and lofty idea, "I am God", you will not be bothered by anything; nothing can come in your way. Of course, it is of no use to merely utter these words. You must first overcome your body consciousness and maintain a firm control over your senses. At the same time, you must develop an intense love for God and live it by continuously identifying yourself with the divine. This will lead you to the supreme wisdom. Or, you can express your love for God by following the path of the servant. This will quickly remove the egoism from your heart and fill you with bliss.

There are three successive stages on the way to God-realization. In the very beginning you will declare, "I am a devotee of God." Here there are two entities, one is God and the other is you, the devotee. God is believed to be away somewhere, and your approach will be to try to find God, to get closer to him, and become very near to him. Gradually you progress along this path and, in time, you will come face to face with God. Then you say to him, "Dear Lord, I belong to you." In this second stage, you stand erect before God and declare yourself as his own, very close to him. Then in the third stage you know yourself to be one with God and you state, "You and I are one."

The first stage, which is characterized by the declaration, "I am the servant of God," and where God is cognized as a faraway form, is dualism. The second stage, where you say directly to God, "O Lord, I am your devotee", and feel him inside your heart, is the stage of qualified non-dualism. The third stage, in which the ultimate truth dawns within you and you say to God, "I am you and you are me", is non-dualism. At that point there is no distinction between you and God.

From the Form to the Formless

You commence your journey from the stage of dualism and finally end up in the stage of non-dualism. You start your spiritual practice with the very ordinary type of devotion, worshipping God with form and attributes and using rituals and external forms of worship. But then you quickly progress onto the formless, the absolute aspect of the Divinity. In this way, you initially develop yourself spiritually by being a servant of God, but eventually you become fully identified with God.

Consider, for a moment, a very big circle, and consider that just by its side and separate from it there is another circle, one which is very much smaller. The big circle may be thought of as God, the small one as the individual soul. Here the individual is different and distinct from God; this is dualism. When you bring the smaller circle in so that it lies within the bigger circle, you have qualified non-dualism; now the individual is part of the Divinity, he exists in God. What then is the meaning of the individual becoming totally merged in God? The small circle has to broaden itself and grow bigger and bigger until it has fully expanded to the size of the big circle. At that point the two circles are indistinguishable and man has merged himself into God. This is complete non-dualism.

Surrender to the Divinity Within You

On the path of devotion it is absolute surrender which makes the individual soul expand and become merged with God. It is when you relinquish your limited individuality by surrendering yourself to the divinity inherent within you that all your weaknesses will leave you and you will develop the broadness of mind that finally culminates in your mergence with God. How can you gain this understanding of your divine nature? How can you recognize the divinity within you so that you can follow its directions? It is only through steady practice that you will acquire this realization.

To acquire even the smallest skills in the world, you have to constantly practice, be it reading, writing, walking or talking. All of these are developed through practice alone. If you start your practice at the first step then eventually you will be able to reach the last step. In this case, the last step means acquiring the supreme knowledge that makes you free.

There are two types of knowledge. One refers to spiritual knowledge, the other to knowledge of the physical world. Inquiring into the various properties of an object is the ordinary knowledge associated with the world. But understanding the inner principle, the underlying basis and purpose of every object that has ever existed in the world, is spiritual knowledge; that is what can be called wisdom. This is a very important quality to cultivate. Even for understanding the world in its deeper aspects, you first have to acquire spiritual wisdom.

To gain spiritual wisdom you must use your body wisely and have your mind and your senses under control. Without the body it is not possible to perform any activity. For all types of work and activities, the body is needed; it is the basis for all practices. Use your body for the purpose of reaching your goal and in performing activities which will be useful to others. Here is a small example.

Transforming Desires Into Wisdom

Consider for a moment that you have gone on a picnic to a forest, and that you have taken along all the articles necessary for cooking and preparing your food. Just before you start your meal preparations, you gather up three stones and arrange them as a base for the cooking vessels. Next you put some water in the vessel and then you add the rice. Underneath the vessel, in between the stones, you make a fire.

What is the purpose of the fire beneath the vessel? It is through the heat of the fire that you can cook the rice which is in the vessel. Without the vessel, if the rice were to be put straight into the fire, you would not be able to get the food that you want. The heat of the fire gets transmitted to the vessel, and on from the vessel to the water, and finally from the water to the rice. In this way the rice gets cooked and you enjoy your meal.

In this forest of life, you are searching for bliss, which can be compared to the food that you prepare. The three stones are the three basic qualities of inertia, activity and purity, underlying all natural phenomena and human activities. Your body may be considered the vessel. Your feelings and desires are the water, and your spiritual yearnings and aspirations are the rice. The fire which you have put between these three stones is the purifying practice which is used to acquire wisdom. This purifying fire which must continue for some time, has to be applied to the body, and through the body to the feelings and desires; these in turn will be cooked and transmuted into the highest spiritual yearnings. Finally, this process results in the cooked product, the spiritual food, the knowledge of the true self, which you have been aspiring for. This knowledge grants eternal bliss.

It would not be possible for you to realize such spiritual wisdom directly in your heart, straight off, without first going through the cooking process. Through the body and your good actions you have to burn up your desires, transform them into spiritual yearnings; this will then lead to the realization of the highest knowledge.

Renouncing the Fruits of Your Labor

The correct application of the practice of meditation is the gradual, slow and steady control of all desires through the constant practice of love for God. By controlling the sense organs and controlling your desires it will become possible to carry on all your activities in a totally natural and spontaneous way, without expecting to reap any fruits from your labors. Actually, it is impossible to have work without fruits. Whenever you engage in an activity there will necessarily follow some consequence or result; this is the fruit of that action. So, it is not that there are no fruits, but the *Gita* teaches that you should give up interest in the fruits. The fruits will always be there, but do not work for the purpose of obtaining these fruits. Work only because it is your duty to work, because it is God's will.

While discharging your duty there will incidentally be some desires and there will also be some results, in other words, some fruits. There is no harm in that. Just continue doing your duty. *Gita* has not taught that actions will be without fruits. People who have not correctly understood the meaning of sacrificing the fruits of action are giving up the action itself. But actions must be engaged in. What the *Gita* stresses is renunciation in action and not renunciation of action. Until the food is cooked there is need for the fire. Until you understand the inner secret of work, and that of sacrificing the fruits of work, you will have to continue to engage in activities and discharge your duties.

Love Is the Root of All Spiritual Practices

A noble character and good behavior announces the inner truth of a person; this truth is based on love. Whether you are engaged in sacrificing the fruits of your actions, or contemplating on the omnipresent Lord, or practicing inner inquiry and aspiring to gain wisdom, the root of all these spiritual exercises is love. There are five major human values that distinguish a noble human being. These are truth, righteousness, peace, love and nonviolence. But they do not exist separately. They are all essentially dependent on one of these five, which is the primary value. That is love.

When love enters the thoughts it becomes truth. When love manifest itself in the form of action it becomes righteousness. When your feelings become saturated with love you become peace itself. The very meaning of the word peace is love. When you fill your understanding with love it is nonviolence. For all these noble human qualities it is love which flows as the undercurrent.

Another way of saying this is when you saturate every thought of yours with love then you are immersed in truth. When you practice love in your daily life it is *dharma* or righteous living. When you feel love all the time you are established in abiding peace. And when you have a deep understanding of the divine principle of love you become steeped in nonviolence. In the *Gita*, in the chapter on devotion, it says, "Fill yourself with love and use this love to reach me. In that way, you will develop both nearness and dearness to me."

Dear devotee. Your hands are very small but with these
little hands you are trying to serve me. Your eyes are

very small but with these two little eyes you are trying to see my infinite vastness. Your ears are very small but with these two little ears you are trying to follow my sacred words. With your two little feet you are attempting to come towards me.

But merely serving me with your two little hands will not achieve very much. Merely looking at my infinite form with your two little eyes will also not be of much use. Merely listening to my divine words through your two little ears will not get you very far. And merely coming into my presence with your two little feet will not serve you so strongly. But there is one thing you can do which will have a great impact, which will produce a truly significant effect. That is: Install me permanently in your heart! Once you bring me into your heart then all these other activities will no longer appear very important.

Whatever worship you have been engaged in, using your eyes and your ears and your hands and your feet, has only served to control your mind. But when you invite the Lord to enter your heart, then control of the mind and the senses becomes very easy. The mind and senses will become still on their own. There will be no need for any special effort to be made for sacrificing the fruits of your actions. Krishna said, "Once you start thinking only of me, and keeping your thoughts constantly fixed on me, then I will automatically take care of all the rest." To achieve this state of total one-pointed focus on the Lord, you must develop a firm resolve and an unshakable faith that the Lord is ever-present in your own heart. Your heart is his residence.

Fill Your heart With Love and Faith

God is always full and complete; to reach such infinite fullness you must have full faith. When God is full and complete and you are not full and complete, there cannot develop the necessary binding force that will hold you and God together. To reach the full and complete love that is God, you must also have a full heart, full of love and faith. If, instead, you are filled with doubts, you will undermine this pure principle of love which is your true nature; your doubts will blemish your heart and distance you from the omniscient, omnipotent and omnipresent Lord, who is aware of your every thought.

Whatever thoughts you have, fill them with him. Think of him with a full heart saturated with love and faith; then you will certainly reach him. In the *Gita,* He said that you will become dear to him when you worship him fully with all your heart. That means seeing him everywhere, in everything. The *Gita* proclaimed, in all of the creation do not hate anyone or anything, for he is in every name and form. When you have the feeling of love permeating your whole being, you become very dear to him.

All the noble human qualities are already there in their fullness in every human being, but very few people are making any effort to become aware of them. They are wasting their time in pursuing only outer activities in the world. But you must also engage in inner activities which will help you to reach your goal. For example, you perform your worship using external rituals, but you must perform your worship internally, as well, offering God the flowers of your heart. Then there will be unity and harmony in your life. Once you achieve such unity in all your activities, both inner and outer, your life becomes sanctified and you will experience fulfillment in whatever you do.

Love Is the Most Important of All Human Qualities

In the path of devotion, it has been taught that love is the basis of everything. It is the single most important quality that has to be developed. All your thoughts must become immersed in this quality of love... then truth will naturally establish itself in your heart. All your acts must be saturated with love... then righteousness will naturally manifest itself in all your undertakings. All your feelings must be soaked in love... then you will be able to enjoy immense peace. And all your understanding must be filled with love... then you cannot hate or hurt anything. Therefore, love is the very basis of peace of mind. Love is the very birthplace of truth. Love is the very foundation of righteousness and nonviolence. That is why Baba has so often said, "Love is God. God is love."

The essence of the teaching of the path of devotion is to develop and practice this selfless love. Then you will become broadminded and, in that way, fully develop all the greatness that is inherent within you.

Ninth Chapter

DESIRE AND ANGER - THE TWIN EVILS

O nly when you can still your thoughts will you be able to overcome desires, and only after you have controlled your desires will you be able to conquer anger. Therefore, the first step in conquering desires and anger is to become free of the thought process.

Embodiments of Love,

Stilling the mind is an essential practice for both devotees and ordinary people, but, as has been taught in the *Gita* chapter on devotion, the calming of all thoughts is especially important for devotees. Thoughts are charged with energy and life. They can even be stronger than the strongest matter. You begin thinking right from the moment of birth. The material making up your thoughts is extremely subtle; it arises from the food you eat. Therefore, if you consume food that has been sanctified you will get only sacred thoughts.

Use Sacred Thoughts to Destroy Dark Thoughts

When a person is filled with sacred thoughts all his actions will be sacred. His words will also be sacred. Such sacred thoughts are like a sword or a sharp knife. You can use sacred thoughts to search out dark thoughts, dark feelings and dark actions, and cut them to pieces. On the other hand, if you take in food that is not sanctified, dark feelings, dark actions and dark thoughts will flourish. Not only this, but because of unwholesome food you will weaken the body and lose the power of digestion, and suffer all sorts of bodily discomforts.

In the *Gita* the Lord has emphasized that for worldly prosperity as well as for developing the spiritual potential that is inherent in man, a strong and pure body is essential. For this it is important that only wholesome food be consumed and that it be sanctified by being offered to the Lord before it is eaten.

Thoughts and the thought process constitute the very form of the mind. If thoughts are turned towards the phenomenal world and the things related to it, then these thought processes become concerned with wealth and property, for these are the very basis of life in the phenomenal world. The word wealth usually refers to your worldly possessions and attachments, such as money, houses and land. Another form of wealth is your fame, your position and station in life. But the *Gita* does not consider either possessions or status as your real wealth. It declares that character is your wealth, good behavior is your wealth, and above all, knowledge of the supreme self is your true wealth.

Good Character, Good Behavior and Knowledge of the Self

Worldly name and fame, property and family are all ephemeral. They may disappear even while you are still alive. Calamity and misfortune may bring about the loss of name and fame, property and family. What is more, none of these will have any connection with you after your death. But good character, good behavior and all the noble qualities which they give rise to, will help you not only during your lifetime but also when this life is over. They will remain your steadfast companions forever. They will be by your side to help you gain the knowledge of your true self, and thereby reach the Lord and merge with him.

Your true fame does not depend on your physical beauty or your charm. It does not depend on your riches. It does not depend on your physical strength. It depends only on your good character. In the scriptures, you will find the story of Vishvamitra who, at that time, was a powerful and ruthless king obsessed with ego and pride in his physical prowess. One time, he decided to take revenge on the sage Vashishta. Of course, Vashishta based his strength only on divinity. He was a very great soul who was ever established in God-consciousness. He wore an invisible protective shield, the protection that comes from being immersed in the divine principle.

When attacked by the deadly arrows and missiles of Vishvamitra, the sage remained completely unruffled. The arrows that Vishvamitra launched towards Vashishta became utterly powerless, as if they were aimed at a mountain of stone. All the missiles Vishvamitra used broke into pieces the moment they touched Vashishta's body and fell harmlessly to the ground.

In fact, physical strength is really a kind of weakness. Only power which is based on divinity and has the strength of righteousness is true strength. When Vishvamitra realized this, he undertook severe penance so as to reach the same lofty spiritual state that Vashishta was always in. After engaging in prolonged austerities, Vishvamitra was finally able to acquire the knowledge of the divine and have Vashishta himself proclaim him a God-conscious sage.

Divine Power and Physical Power

The Kauravas, the evil cousins that Arjuna and the Pandavas had to encounter in the great war, together were one hundred brothers. The Kauravas had also based their strength on military might. In the end, all these brothers died in the war which they had fomented and not even a single son was left to perform the funeral rites for the parents, when the parents died. What a terrible fate that was. Instead of seeking divine help, the Kaurava brothers took refuge only in physical power, in money and in the strength of individuals. On the other hand, the Pandava brothers surrendered everything to Krishna, and sought only his grace.

When Arjuna fell at the feet of Krishna and surrendered to him, Krishna was very pleased and lifted him up, saying, "Get up, Arjuna. Real power lies in faith. In the end, justice will always triumph and selfishness will always perish; this is the one unchanging righteous truth that applies in every age." He assured Arjuna on the day of the battle that whoever takes refuge in the Lord will win the Grace of the Lord, and will be successful in whatever he undertakes. Whereas one who refuses the protection of the Lord will not be able to win his grace, and in the end, will surely fail and be destroyed.

If you aspire to earn the grace of the Lord, you have to control your worldly desires. All your activities in the phenomenal world have to do with the waking state. The results that arise from these activities are no more real than the results you get in dreams. The mansions and big bungalows you see in dreams vanish in a flash once you open your eyes and wake up. They are not real and were never real. The experiences of your dream state disappear in your waking state and the experiences of your waking state disappear in your dream state. And in your deep-sleep state they both vanish.

The Three Worlds and The Lord Beyond

Krishna taught in the *Gita* that there are three worlds, the physical, the mental and the causal. The mental world is a subtle form of the physical world, and the causal world is an even subtler form of the mental world. Of these three inter-penetrating worlds of your waking, dream and deep-sleep consciousness, the causal is the subtlest. It is all-pervasive. But beyond all these is the infinite Lord, the supreme principle of divinity. This divine principle is the subtlest of the subtle, the smallest of the small, but also the biggest of the big. Among the mighty ones, the divinity is the mightiest of all. There can be nothing greater. Seek him. Install him in your heart and be saved. Know that that mightiest of the mighty is your very self. This is the truth of divinity. This is your truth.

To reach the principle of Godhead, which is the goal supreme, you have to start your journey with the first stage of the path, wherein you consider yourself to be the servant or the messenger of God. This is the stage of dualism. Gradually you enter the stage of qualified non-dualism, the second major step on the spiritual path. Here you experience the divinity within yourself, in your own heart. At this stage you identify yourself very closely with the Lord. You will have the feeling, "God is within me. He is the one I truly am. I am he. I am he." Then, as you continue still further on the spiritual path, all duality will disappear completely and you will be left with only the *I*, the pure self, without any modifications or limitations.

This whole journey is a little like the healing process that takes place with a wound. Initially, a protective layer of hard skin forms over the wound. Eventually this covering falls off by itself as the wound heals. When both the feeling that you are the servant of the Lord and the feeling that you are one with the Lord, both of which cover the pure *I*, fall off, then you will be in the final stage of non-dualism. Then you are immersed in the one truth, *I am I.*

Wherever You Look You See Your One Self

When you declare, "I am he. I am God", there is still some duality, because there are still two entities, I and God. So, this is still not complete non-dualism. At the very beginning, when you say, "O Lord, I am your servant," the Lord is separate and the servant is separate, and their status is clearly different. On the other hand, when you say, "I am God," although there is still a trace of duality, the distinction is not one of separate subject and object but more like seeing the reflection or image of yourself in a mirror.

Whenever people are different, when there are many separate entities, then there will also be many different images or reflections. But in the stage of qualified non-dualism, you see only your own image everywhere, because you are all there is. You are the one self being reflected as many images, just like the one sun is seen as separate images in a number of different water-filled pots. So, in the stage of qualified non-dualism, you are alone; there is none other. The only thing that still comes between you and the divinity is the mirror. You constantly perceive your own reflection, and so you see yourself as very near and very dear to the Lord — face to face with him.

But when you perceive only the one God who is all-pervasive, then where is the need for any image at all? Can there be a place where he is not? When the entire world is the mansion of the omnipresent Lord, then where should you look to find the door to enter his mansion? If there were a separate street and a separate house then there would have to be a door which opens onto the street; but in truth, there is no street at all. When the all-pervasive Lord is everywhere, how can there be any special place where you must seek him to find him? No, there is no special place where he resides.

Once you realize that he is everywhere at all times, then the true perception of the divinity is not that of an object whose reflection is seen in various places but the realization that there is only you, the one immortal self, abiding everywhere, present in everything in all its fullness. This all-pervasive perception of the divinity as the one without a second, is called non-dualism.

You Are Not a Sinner — You Are God

As part of their religious observances, people will sometimes say in their prayers, "O Lord, I am a sinner, my soul is full of sin, I have been performing so many sinful acts." But who is this person who is sinning? Can there ever be anyone who is separate from the Lord? Can such a one exist? These declarations about sinning and being a sinner are not good practices for devotees to engage in. Rather you should think, "In truth, I am God. I am not different from God. I am peace itself. I am love eternal. I am pure bliss without end." Keeping such lofty ideas and thoughts in your mind is the best way to reach the goal.

In the *Gita*, in the list of noble qualities that a devotee should possess, the Lord started with, "Be without hatred towards any living being." If you treat happiness and misery with an equal mind then the question of hatred does not arise at all. If you recognize that the same transcendental principle is embodied in all human beings as well as in all creatures, then there cannot be any room for hatred. If you realize that the one divinity resides equally in all, then how could you ever hate another? Where is the other? In this context, you might ask for whom the phrase, "Be without hatred towards any living being" is intended. Is it meant for those who have realized the one transcendental principle which exists equally in themselves and in everyone else? No, it is obviously not intended for them. This injunction is given for the sake of those who have not yet realized this great truth of the unity of all beings.

The Sweetness of the Servant Path

There is an extraordinary joy which you obtain when you immerse yourself in the attitude of being the servant of the Lord. You soon become filled with delight from having imbibed the Lord's sweetness, and you never want to leave that happy state. You come to the conclusion that if ever you were to move on from this feeling of being the servant to the state of "I am he", you would not be able to continue to enjoy the consummate sweetness of the Lord. Sugar does not know its own sweetness. You may be concerned that if you were to become one with the sugar you would no longer be able to enjoy its sweetness. Since you partake of the Lord's sweetness in the servant stage, you may prefer to remain in this stage so that you will always be able to taste the nectarine sweetness of the Lord, rather than being one with him.

For example, Hanuman, the great devotee of God, had the experience of extreme bliss arising from his unwavering attitude of "I am the servant of Lord Rama". But how long can such a feeling last? It can last only as long as you have the grace of the Lord and are near to him. If you were to ever become separated from him, then in all likelihood you would experience extreme anguish.

In the stage of qualified non-dualism, the question of suffering does not arise at all, because in that exalted state you are unceasingly with the Lord, and there is no possibility of experiencing any separation or suffering. In the servant stage there is the possibility of separation between the Lord and the servant, but in the second stage of qualified non-dualism there cannot be any discontinuity in the bliss since no possibility of separation can arise.

Controlling Desires and Anger

If you want to reach the ultimate truth of your being and be immersed in the bliss of your own divine principle, you need to develop complete control over your desires. The moment any thought arises, you should inquire into the nature of this thought. Ask yourself, "Is this thought desirable or is it harmful for my spiritual progress?" Devotees should be extremely careful right from the very beginning, to see to it that dark thoughts do not remain in their minds. For most people, it is impossible to remain without any thoughts at all. But, at least, when dark thoughts arise you can do something about it. Do not harbor them. Give them no shelter.

Immediately transform any dark thoughts into sacred ones. In the same way, see to it that you undertake only good actions, and take every opportunity to transform these actions into worship by consecrating them to the Lord. By transforming all thoughts into noble thoughts and all work into worship, you will naturally progress on the sacred path. By controlling your thoughts in this way, you will also be able to control any anger that might arise.

Quite a few people worry about anger, wondering what is the best way to control it when it comes on and tries to overwhelm them. The easiest way to control anger is this. The moment you become aware that anger is rising within you, just laugh very loudly. Or go to the bathroom and have a cool bath. You can also take a glass of cool water and relax in a cool place. The moment anger comes it is most helpful to leave the place where you are and go somewhere else. If with all these measures you still have not been able to control your anger, then stand in front of a mirror and examine your face. After seeing your appearance you will surely feel so much disgust that at once you will be able to control your anger.

One other thing you can do whenever anger comes is to inquire into the cause of this anger. Is it justified? Remember that if someone is going to be harmed in the process of your anger, you will be committing a sin, and that cannot possibly be good for you. To undertake all these methods will be quite difficult, but it is enough to remember not to let your tongue go into action immediately after you get angry and spill out a torrent of angry words. Take some time to think things over. In a number of ways anger weakens a person who is trying to undertake a spiritual practice. If you make some effort to control anger when it arises, these efforts will act to strengthen your body and purify your mind.

Attraction and Repulsion

The *Gita* declared that a weak person can never gain self-realization. Therefore, in order to acquire the knowledge of your true self, it is most important that you gain full control over your attachments and hatreds, over your desires and anger. These pairs of opposites arise from the primary qualities of attraction and repulsion which are inherent in the human psyche as well as within all phenomenal things and beings. Attraction and repulsion are responsible for everything that makes up the world. They keep you bound to the world, and as long as you are preoccupied with the world, the light of truth will not shine for you. Therefore, this attraction and repulsion for things of the world must be banished from your heart. Then the knowledge of the true self can take root there.

When you have the sacred knowledge of the *atma* in your heart, you will be able to enjoy peace. That fragrance of peace will spread all around you and affect everyone you see and touch. On the other hand, if you are filled with dark feelings, dark thoughts and dark actions, these will pollute your heart and infect others with your poison. Whether good or bad, the thoughts that suffuse your heart and take shelter there, will spread to others around you, and these others will soon emanate the same feelings.

Sometimes there may be some difficulty in distinguishing good from bad. The real distinction is not in outer appearances and labels but in the inner purity and intentions. If you hold a rose in your right hand, which in the East is considered your sacred hand, the fragrance of the flower will not only reach you but also the people in the surrounding area. But even when you take the same rose and hold it in your left hand, which in the East is considered the unsacred hand, the rose will spread its sweet fragrance to all. You might make a difference between right and left, but for the fragrance there is no distinction whatsoever. It spreads to all who are near just as profusely from the unsacred hand as from the sacred one.

Likewise, whether you are a theist or an atheist, this relates only to your own feelings and beliefs. As far as God is concerned, if you have sacred thoughts and engage in good works and good words, then even if you are an atheist you will be dear to him. The Lord of the *Gita* declared, "Whoever he is, if he has control over his desires and anger, if he has subdued either his attraction or his abhorrence to people and things of the world, then he is very dear to me."

Character Not Belief Is What Is Important

Indian philosophy has been classified according to those who believe in God and those who do not believe in God. But to the divinity, what counts are the qualities of men's character rather than their beliefs. Prahlada, who was the son of a demon king, was one of the greatest devotees of the Lord. He was put to great trouble by his father and his teachers who tried to impress on him their demonic traits. Although he was born a demon, Prahlada always displayed a noble and sterling character. And despite all the difficulties he was put to, Prahlada was able to continuously enjoy the bliss of his own immortal self, and know the presence of the Lord in his heart. Prahlada means the one who is continuously happy. So, if you go on thinking of the Lord continuously, these feelings of joy will shine forth with an effulgent splendor, and you will become one with God.

Right at the outset of your spiritual journey you have to make determined efforts to control your desires and anger, your attachments and hatred. This will permit the divine principle to shine forth from within you. Controlling desire and anger is a most important spiritual practice. It is the primary task of every devotee. If you succeed in controlling desire and anger, attachments and hatred, you will be able to justify your life and reach your goal. But if you allow them to remain within you, then whatever spiritual exercises you undertake will be wasted and your life too will become an utter waste.

LOVE AND SACRIFICE –
THE CURE FOR DESIRE AND ANGER

Anger is born of desire and desire arises from thoughts. Therefore, thoughts alone are responsible for both desire and anger. Just as you cannot get cloth without thread and thread without cotton, you cannot get anger without desire and desire without thoughts.

Embodiments of Love,

In the *Gita*, the divine teacher has termed desire and anger as fire. There is danger of being harmed by fire even when it is some distance from you. When this is true for a fire that is burning outside then how much more careful you must be when the fire is burning fiercely in your own heart. This fire of desire and anger has an extraordinary capacity to destroy all your human qualities and to suppress the divine nature within you, leaving only the demonic qualities raging inside.

The Fire of Desire

Most things in the world have prescribed limits but the fire of desire and anger is limitless in its hunger. Whatever fuel you give to fire, whether it be wood, oil, or anything else, it will never have enough. But even the most destructive fire eventually burns itself out and becomes extinguished when it uses up its fuel, whereas this fire of desire and anger knows no such limitation. It has a voracious appetite that is endless. It will not exhaust itself. It cannot be appeased. It will never be satisfied. This fire of desire and anger has no contentment at all.

That being its nature, is there any way to control it? The Lord declared in the *Gita*, "You can conquer anger through love and you can conquer desire through renunciation and sacrifice." Where there is love there can be no anger. If you develop your love, then there will be no room left in your heart for hatred and anger to take root. The heart is like a chair, there is room for only one occupant at a time. Therefore, only one quality can establish itself there. It leaves no place for another to enter and occupy it at the same time. You must make every effort to establish love and only love in your heart. You must never allow your heart to become like a 'musical chair', giving room for love at one time and for anger and hatred at other times.

If you want to conquer anger through your love then you must develop your love in a most magnificent way. Love is always prepared to shower itself freely and to overlook the defects and weaknesses in others. Love has this extraordinary quality, it lives by giving and forgiving, whereas the little ego-self lives by getting and forgetting. Where there is love there can be no room for selfishness, and where there is selfishness there will be no love.

Make Love the Dominant Force in Your Life

There is absolutely nothing in the world which you cannot achieve when you shine with this principle of love. With love you can conquer all obstacles. Therefore, to achieve total victory over anger you have to fill your heart with love and make love the dominant force in your life. Once you recognize that the indweller of your heart is the indweller of every heart, that the beloved Lord whom you worship seated on the throne of your heart is also dwelling in every other heart, then there can be no possibility of hating or being angry with any person in the world. When the same Lord is in every heart how can you look down with contempt at another? Therefore, immerse yourself fully in this principle of love and establish it indelibly in your heart.

As has been mentioned before by Baba, when love is associated with thoughts, it becomes truth; when love is introduced into your activities, your actions become righteous; when your feelings are saturated with love, your heart is filled with supreme peace; and when you allow love to guide your understanding and reasoning, then your intelligence becomes saturated with a deep respect and caring for all life, and you manifest the quality of nonviolence. Therefore, love is truth, love is right action, love is peace, love is nonviolence. For all these noble human qualities love is the undercurrent. If your thoughts are not filled with love, there will be no truth. If there is no love in your actions, righteousness will not be present. If you do not feel love in your heart, there will be no peace. And if you do not base your understanding on love, nonviolence will not establish itself in your intellect.

So, just as sugar is the basis of all different kinds of sweets, so also love is the basic ingredient for truth, righteousness, peace and nonviolence. Love is the divinity itself. Love is God and God is love.

Love is the divine power that activates everything. Through love you can easily conquer hatred and anger. Therefore, always live in love.

The Nature of Anger

Anger can be the source of numerous difficulties and expose you to countless problems. It destroys your dignity and undermines the principle of humanness that exists within you. Anger first enters in a very subtle form and gradually becomes all-pervasive. Initially, when it comes in, it will only ask for a small bit of space. "Just give me a little room to sit down in," it says. Once it has established itself, it declares, "Now, I'll make myself enough space to lie down and stay." But you must not permit even the least room in your heart for such bad traits. Once you let anger in, it will be impossible to get rid of it. Even if you make friends with it and give it all your wealth it will not leave you. It is a most dangerous poison which should not be given even the least space to get a foothold within you.

In a car the red tail-light goes on as a warning before the car comes to a stop. In the same way, before you explode into anger, your eyes become red, your lips begin to quiver and the whole body becomes hot. The moment you start having any of these symptoms, you had best leave the place you are in immediately and go to a solitary spot and sit there until peace returns. As was mentioned yesterday, you can also take a cold-water bath.

Once anger expresses itself in words it may lead to endless complications and problems later on. Even if your anger is justifiable and you are protecting the truth, you will still have to learn how to express that truth in a sweet way, in a dear way, in an acceptable way that would be received by the other person without hurting him in any way. Therefore, every devotee must learn to control his anger by developing and saturating his heart with love.

Sacrifice Conquers Desire

Next, let us consider how to deal with desire. To conquer desire you have to develop a sacrificing nature; you must be steeped in renunciation. Renunciation does not mean that you give up your family and go to the forest; nor does it require you to give up all your property. Once you realize the defects in any object, once you recognize its transitoriness and worthlessness in helping you to reach your goal, you will automatically stop desiring it.

Even when living the life of a householder immersed in the world, you can recognize the defects and weaknesses of the things of the world. For example, there may be a certain kind of food that you enjoy very much, like a curry, for example, and you ask your cook to prepare a variety of dishes made with this curry. You sit down to eat, the meal is brought in and you are about to eat it with great relish. But then the cook comes running in and says, "Stop! Please sir, don't eat this food! I just discovered a poisonous lizard has fallen into the pot and is dead inside!" The moment you hear this and recognize the harmful nature of the food you were about to eat, you would under no circumstances consider eating it anymore, no matter how much you previously cherished that dish and looked forward to having it.

In the same way, you have to recognize the nature of the things of the world. They are ever changing and some day they must cease to exist. Once you know this, how can you remain enthusiastic about acquiring them and trying to get lasting enjoyment from them? Food is only medicine for the disease called hunger. How can it ever be an item of luxurious indulgence? When you are sick and medicines are given, do you refuse them if they are not tasty? Therefore, recognize the fact that the things you use in the world are only medicines for the diseases that you have.

As the disease declines, the need for medicine diminishes. When you are well you do not need to take any medicines at all; but when you are sick you must take the right medicine which will cure you of your illness. You cannot refuse to take the medicine just because it is not very tasty, while at the same time hoping to get cured. Now you are running after all sorts of attractive and tasty things which instead of curing your ills worsen them. You rejoice that you have discovered so many delights in the world and that you are living a very happy life, enjoying many things which seem to give you a lot of comfort and joy. But these are not real enjoyments, for, in the future, you will surely have to face the consequences of all these indulgences you are engaging in now.

The Pest of Desire and Hatred

Consider a giant tree which has a number of branches heaped with flowers and fruits. It is a very grand and attractive tree. One day, this tree begins to dry up and its flowers fall off. Is it because there is a shortage of water or manure? Has there been some neglect in feeding it? No, there is some kind of pest that has attacked its roots and is destroying this beautiful tree. Through the roots the pest enters and starts to eat up this giant tree. In the same way, once you allow these pests of desire and hatred to enter your heart, then one day you will quite suddenly come to ruin. This is absolutely certain.

In the material world you think that a rich man is a very important individual, but in the world of the spirit, material wealth is of no consequence. Charity is a quality that is much greater than all the possessions associated with wealth. If there is no charity, wealth has no intrinsic value at all. You have four heirs, each of whom will enter a claim to your wealth. The first is charity. The second is the government. The third is the thief. And the fourth is fire. Each of them expects to inherit your wealth, but if you were to hand over all your wealth to your first heir, charity, then the others will get no share of it. When you give freely to charity, you will find that the other claimants will show great respect for your decision and will not press their own claims.

For example, we know that the government gives you an income-tax exemption when you donate to charity. Even fire will be a little frightened of you, and thieves will leave you alone. So, when you give to charity, which may be considered your oldest son and your natural heir, then the others who would otherwise try to claim your wealth will respect your action and not interfere. But if you possess wealth and do not give it in charity, then the thief will have his eye on you and the government will also try to catch hold of you and claim your riches as its own. If these two for some reason choose to ignore you, then fire will come one day and destroy your possessions.

Let All the Noble Human Qualities Shine Within You

The *Gita* has declared that it is charity, not wealth, which is really important. In a similar way, in human beings, it is not the ability to speak well but the truth which is uttered, that is important. If there is no truth in your speech, then whatever you say will have no value at all. The *Gita* has also declared that it is not life itself but a good character that is important. A life devoid of good character is useless. You have to develop your character and earn a good name so that all the noble human qualities will shine forth in you.

Your most important duty is to harbor good thoughts, to have good behavior, to speak good words and to lead a good life. You must be very careful with your words and actions so that you will never earn a bad name. Instead of living the life of a crow for a hundred years scavenging off others, it is far better to live a few moments as a swan, with an untainted name and an unblemished character. The *Gita* extols such a sterling soul whose life is replete with goodness.

Good actions are far more important than physical strength. A body that is not being used to serve others is nothing but a dead body. Use your body in the service of mankind, not just for the purpose of catering to your own selfish needs. Today, whatever man does, thinks or utters is primarily prompted by selfishness. In order to overcome this tendency, you have to constantly seek opportunities to help others and develop the principle of service. In this process, by your good actions, all of humanity will get sanctified. It is very difficult to obtain birth as a human being. You must spend some time thinking over how to properly utilize this rare life that has been given to you and develop good habits which will overcome these weaknesses of desire and anger that waste your golden chance.

Replacing Bad Habits With Good Habits

How do you best overcome the deeply ingrained bad habits and replace them with good habits? Consider a small example.

One day a beautiful dog happens to come to your house; you do not know to whom it belongs. It is such an attractive thing, in order to keep it there for some time and enjoy its presence, you give it a little food. Next day it comes about the same time, and again you feed it and enjoy having it visit you. In this way it comes back every day to get fed, and gradually over a period of time, attachment increases and this dog now regularly visits your house, spending more and more time there. One day you find that it will no longer leave; it just continues to live at your house from that time on.

But the happiness that you enjoy in looking at physical beauty does not last very long. Once the beauty is no longer accompanied by joy, it becomes obnoxious to you. In the case of this dog, you soon get tired of having it around all the time, and so you look for a way to get rid of it.

To begin with you must ask yourself why that dog has attached itself to you and is now living in the house. The reason is that right from the very beginning you have been feeding it regularly every day; you have also been stroking it, playing with it, and paying so much attention to it. It is this repeated daily practice which has created the attachment between yourself and the dog. Now you must develop a new regular practice, which will break this attachment and help you to get rid of the dog. For this the best method is to reverse the original process that created the attachment and made the object so dear to you.

Steady Practice Is the Key To All Accomplishments in Life

In the case of the dog, if no food is given for some days and everyone is indifferent to it, paying no attention to it whatsoever, then soon, of its own accord, the dog will go away. Therefore, it is the practice that is important. It is through practice that you have developed certain attachments and undesirable qualities, and it is through practice that you can change them. The *Gita* has said that for everything practice is the starting point. In the 12th verse of the chapter on devotion, it says, "Through practice you will be able to get knowledge, through knowledge you will be able to develop meditation, through meditation you will develop sacrifice, and only when you have sacrifice will you obtain peace of mind." Therefore, it all starts with steady practice.

For many births, you have been enamored with beauty and you have engaged yourself in desire and anger until these passions have struck deep roots in your heart. Now you have become a slave of your desires. Mere words will not be enough to get rid of them. After having practiced attachment for so long, these negative qualities have developed such strong roots, that even if you were to cut them off at the surface, they would sprout up again and again. When desires have become an integral part of you, it is only by reversing the process and practicing detachment and renunciation that you will be able to get rid of these deeply ingrained pests.

In the beginning, desires are extremely attractive and sweet. After some time you develop a disgust for them; but then it is already quite difficult, in fact, almost impossible to get rid of them. Therefore, it is best if right from the very beginning you develop renunciation and detachment as part of your nature and give no place or importance to desires. Unless you have such an attitude of sacrifice and a capacity to resist desires, you will not be ready to receive the grace of God.

A bullock or a horse which cannot be controlled, a car without brakes, or a life which is not based on control of the senses, are all dangerous. Control of the senses is very important. You need to tightly control the tendencies of the mind to go off in all directions, running after desires. Mind and senses must be kept in check within limited bounds. Even happiness which exceeds certain limits can be harmful. For everything there is a limit, there is a range of healthy functioning.

Keeping the Senses Within Their Normal Limits

The normal body temperature is 98.6 degrees Fahrenheit; if it goes up even one degree there will be a disease in progress. Only when it is within the appropriate level does it indicate a healthy body. In the same way, your blood pressure is normal when it is 120 over 80. If the blood pressure goes up to 150 over 90 it indicates an abnormal condition in the body, which may be indicative of an illness. Similarly, the heart beat should be around 75; if it increases an ailment will be in progress.

The same is also true for your senses. There is a range of light that is appropriate to healthy functioning of the eyes. If the light is too bright the eyes cannot see and will be harmed. This is true, as well, in the case of the ears; there is a proper range of sound. If the level of sound exceeds that range, such as may happen close to an airplane, a train or a loudspeaker, the hearing will become impaired. Like this, all the senses are limited to a normal range of operation.

We see that life functions a lot like a limited company in the business world. If you want to carry on unlimited business with this limited company then you will be subject to a great deal of distress. Therefore, you have to impose restrictions on your behavior, and spend your life acting always within certain prescribed limits. This can also be called discipline. Discipline is particularly necessary for the spiritual progress of an individual. Without discipline a person is likely to become nothing but an animal. But discipline, too, has to be exercised within limits. There is even a need to regulate your discipline if you are to enjoy life. You see that for everything there is a limit and a boundary. If you stay within these limits you will not be troubled by life.

The *Gita* has taught that desire and anger are the primary obstacles to liberation, so it is vitally important that they be curbed. You need to take proper notice of these two dreadful enemies of man and develop complete control over them. These enemies are not external to you; they are your inner enemies. If you are defeated by your inner enemies, how can you ever hope to conquer your external ones? Once you keep desire and anger under firm check you will be able to defeat your outer enemies quite easily. The *Gita* has shown that the way to conquer desire and anger is by saturating your life with renunciation, sacrifice and love.

Eleventh Chapter

TRUE RENUNCIATION -
FOCUS ON GOD, NOT THE WORLD

If you want to reach the Lord and have a vision of him, the most important quality that you need to develop is detachment. Detachment endows you with the capacity to internalize your vision. Detachment allows you to introvert your mind and dwell on your inner beauty.

Embodiments of Love,

Once you recognize the defects and weaknesses in the objects of the world you soon lose your desire to possess them. The mind is very strong and fickle. It is also very obstinate. It is forever determined to get its way. Arjuna prayed to Krishna for help in controlling his mind. He lamented, "O Lord, the mind is very powerful and wayward." Krishna replied, "Arjuna, if you practice detachment you will certainly be able to control your mind."

Control of the Mind

The mind can be compared to a poplar tree. The poplar leaves are always shaking whether there is a wind or not. Similarly, the mind is always unsteady and wavering. In addition to its wavering quality the mind is also strong and stubborn. Take for example an elephant. It is very strong and it can be quite cruel, too. However with the help of a goad you can bring it under control. Likewise, the horse is rarely still. It is always moving its limbs, its ears, its head or its tail. Being unsteady, it will first go one way and then another. But with a bit, it can be controlled and made to go in the direction that the rider wants.

Another example is the monkey, which roams here and there, the very picture of unsteadiness and fickleness. But with training, it too can be brought under control. Therefore, just as with a goad you can control an elephant which may be very cruel and strong, just as with a bit you can control a horse which is nervous and unstable, just as with training even a monkey can be controlled, in the same way the mind, which is also strong and fickle, can be controlled by detachment and constant practice.

Detachment

True detachment means realizing the temporary nature of objects and not allowing your mind to get attached to these transient things. It does not necessarily mean that you feel disgust or hatred for them. It means that you feel no mental attachment towards them. Totally giving up all the objects of the phenomenal world is not possible. However, you can give up your *my-ness*, your sense of possessiveness. Once you give that up, then you can go ahead and enjoy the various objects of the world. They will cause you no harm.

In the phenomenal world, every thing, every person and every object undergoes change. The world consists of six types of change: birth, growth, maturity, decline, degeneration and death. These are the changes to which all objects are subjected. To delude yourself into thinking that this transient impermanent world is permanent and become attached to the objects in it is very foolish indeed.

In the temple of Vishnu you will see statues and pictures of Garuda, the eagle. Similarly, in the temple of Shiva you will find statues and pictures of Nandi, the bull. And, in the temple of Rama, you will see a portrayal of Hanuman, the monkey. In all these depictions the concentration of each of these beings, Nandi, Garuda and Hanuman, is on the feet of the Lord; they see only the Lord, not the world. All of these demonstrate the right kind of attachment. Their attachment is to the Lord who is permanent. And their detachment is from the world which is transient. The significance of all these symbolic representations is that you should not care much for what is transient, but always concentrate and dwell on the permanent entity, which is the Lord himself.

Once you recognize the defects of objects, their transitoriness and impermanence, then you will gradually lose your desire to have them. There are a number of stories which show how emperors who had a lot of wealth at their disposal and possessed all the luxuries and properties one could dream of, did not derive much joy or peace of mind from them. In order to get peace of mind they would go to the forest and perform penance. From this they ultimately derived the satisfaction and inner solace for which they had been yearning.

Make the Best Use of Every Object

Detachment involves more than just recognizing the defects and weaknesses in objects which results from their transitory nature.

Detachment also involves the positive quality of getting the most out of the objects of the world. You should always strive to make the best use of an object and appreciate it for what it is. There is no point in just dwelling on the limitation and sorrow that objects of the world produce, but you should know to properly use objects to perform your duty in the world. Then you will acquire some satisfaction. In the larger sense, it is really giving up worldly sorrow and gaining the bliss of the supreme self that is true detachment. Giving up family, wife, children and properties and then going to the forest cannot be called detachment. Detachment is recognizing the weak aspects in the nature of the objects, as well as accepting their positive and strong points.

Whenever you get into difficulty, whether physical, mental, financial or any other type of problem, you may develop a sense of detachment towards the objects causing this state. This is quite natural. For example, suppose a person dies and his body is taken to the burning ground where it is cremated. When you look at such a situation you develop a particular type of detachment, philosophizing that the body has to come to an end some time or another. But this detachment is only a temporary phenomenon, a temporary feeling; it cannot be considered true detachment.

Another example is when a mother is delivering her first baby. Not being able to suffer the pain, she shouts that she would rather die. This also is not true detachment. As soon as the baby is born, suppose she has a girl, she immediately wants to get a boy the next time. A similar situation develops when someone does not get his wishes fulfilled. Here also he develops a certain type of detachment. All these attitudes are temporary. Permanent detachment is something quite different.

Permanent detachment is an intense detachment, as opposed to dull or weak detachment. For example, a person may have resolved to go on a pilgrimage to one of the holy places in India, but then there may be a strong tendency to postpone it to the next month. If it is a matter of doing something good such as going on a pilgrimage, one will tend to postpone it. On the other hand, if it is a matter of doing something bad, one prefers to do it right on the spot, without wasting any time. People usually will not make very great efforts to perform good deeds. This may be seen as a type of weak detachment which tends to postpone implementing good resolutions and performing good actions. But such behavior will not help you to reach your spiritual goal. It is intense detachment which is essential for progress on the spiritual path.

Harischandra and Buddha

If you decide that a particular activity is good and sacred, you should not postpone it. You should immediately implement it and see to it that this good action is successfully carried out. This was the royal path laid down for all by the Buddha. Once Gautama Buddha realized that the body was impermanent, that none of the worldly things were going to last, he resolved to seek out and discover the unchanging truth. He gave up his family and his kingdom and went into the forest to realize the ultimate reality.

There was another great ruler who had an intense sense of sacrifice and detachment. His name was Harischandra. Although he was an emperor, through a series of unfortunate circumstances he lost everything he had in the world, his kingdom, his wife and family, and spent his days as caretaker of a cremation ground.

One day, when Harischandra first started performing his duties in the cremation ground, the corpse of a rich man was brought there by a large number of friends. They brought the body, set it on fire and immediately went back to their homes. Usually when a body is set on fire, a little weight is put on it. Otherwise, as soon as the heat comes, the body bends as if it was getting up, and then lies down again. Only Harischandra remained in the burning ground that day. No friends or relatives of the dead man stayed behind to keep a watch on the body. Harischandra went to get a little more fuel to put on the fire. Suddenly he saw the body lift itself up. He was surprised and went near it to have a closer look.

As Harischandra approached the pyre, he noticed that the body had by itself returned to a prone position. For an instant he thought that it was still alive as if sitting up to look for its relatives and friends, but then he realized that the whole episode was just a momentary illusion of a corpse appearing alive, caused by the heat of the fire. Harischandra thought to himself, "In the same way that I mistook this corpse to be alive, I thought this world to be real. But it is unreal, it gives only an illusion of reality."

Harischandra lamented that such a wealthy man whose corpse was brought there had no relatives or friends to stay with his body until the end. He thought, whatever may be the position and the riches of a person, not even his wife or children retain any attachment to him after his death. As a result of this experience, Harischandra developed an intense detachment towards the objects and forms of the world.

Worldly Attachments Are Like Poison

Every day, at every time, there will be changes occurring in all the objects of creation. These changes are not artificial, they are not imaginary, they are natural and inherent in the very nature of the objects. Once you recognize that the world is basically a stage for the continuous natural occurrence of changes, and that change is inherent in the very nature of the objects of the world, then you will become free from suffering. Anyone who realizes that there is a lethal toxin contained in the fangs of a poisonous snake will not casually go near it. If you see an approaching scorpion with its poisonous tail held up, ready to strike, would you not run away from it? Only a small, innocent child or a totally ignorant person would go near it, get stung and die.

You make every effort to avoid a poisonous creature because you know its harmful nature. In the same way, you would make every effort to avoid worldly attachments if you knew their harmful nature. The Lord taught in the *Gita*, that instead of undergoing all the sufferings that go with developing attachments and then getting disillusioned when the inevitable changes begin to happen, it would be far better from the very beginning to remain unattached towards the things and objects of the world. But now you go on planning many things and attaching yourself to many things in order to gain some short-term joys. You exhaust yourself thinking and planning, "I should do this, I should do that" or "I should do this instead of that" and get yourself involved in countless projects and activities. But you will have to bear the consequences of all these actions in the future.

The seeds you have sown by your actions will mature and you will reap the harvest of those seeds. If the seed belongs to one variety, you cannot expect to get back a different kind of result. Whatever acts you have indulged in, the appropriate fruits thereof will be given to you in the form of an invisible garland which is hung around your neck. When you are born from the womb of your mother, no garland can be seen. Neither a garland of pearls nor one of precious gemstones nor a necklace of gold will be visible around your neck. Nevertheless, there surely is a garland there. That garland is composed of the consequences of your past deeds which you have performed during your previous births. That garland given to you by the Creator will adorn your neck, although it will not be seen by the physical eyes.

The person who recognizes the truth, that for every action there will be a resulting consequence, will take up only good activities and will spend his life indulging only in actions that will earn him good results. This has been taught by the *Gita* as a spiritual exercise of particular importance to devotees. It leads eventually to developing indifference and detachment to the things of the world, and it results in the acquisition of true wisdom. Here is an example which illustrates this illusory nature of the world and the detachment you should have to it.

King Janaka's Dream

King Janaka had acquired extraordinary proficiency in the knowledge of God. He was called "the king devoid of body". In other words, he had been able to transcend body-consciousness. One particular night after dinner, he was discussing certain administrative problems with his ministers. He got back to his bedroom a little late. A meal had been set out for him but he did not touch it. He relaxed on a sofa while the queen massaged his feet. Soon the king fell asleep. The queen asked the various attendants present to leave the room and made sure that the king, who was extremely tired, would not be disturbed in his sleep. She covered him with a blanket and banked the light low, quietly remaining by his side.

Shortly afterwards, King Janaka quite suddenly opened his eyes, sat up, looked around incredulously at his surroundings, and in a most peculiar way began to ask, "Is this real or is that real? Is this the truth or is that the truth?"

The queen became a little frightened by his bewildered look and strange question. She tried to find out what exactly he was asking, but he would not explain or answer any of her queries. He just went on saying, "Is this the truth or is that the truth?" She called for the ministers, counselors and other important officials. They all assembled and began questioning the king. "Maharaja, what is your doubt? What exactly are you asking?" But the Maharaja would not respond to them. Finally the ministers brought the great Sage Vashishta to the court. Vashishta asked the king, "What are you asking? What is troubling you?" The king was replying to all the questions with the same query, "Is that the truth or is this the truth? Is this reality or is that reality?"

Sage Vashishta being omniscient closed his eyes and meditated for a while to find out the cause of the king's strange behavior. Vashishta realized that the king had suddenly awakened from a vivid dream in which he had forfeited his kingdom and found himself wandering lost, alone and despondent in a forest. He was feeling very hungry and also very tired and forsaken. As he wandered through that forest he kept shouting, "I am hungry, I am hungry." It happened that there were some robbers in that forest. Those robbers were just sitting down in a glade nearby to have their meal, eating from plates made of leaves. Taking pity on him, the robbers made themselves known and invited Janaka to join them, offering him a portion of their meal.

Just at that moment, a tiger came upon them and they all ran for their lives. The tiger helped himself to all the food. Again Janaka found himself staggering through the forest crying out, "O, I am so hungry. I am so very hungry." When he woke up he discovered he was in a palace, on a royal sofa by the side of the queen, with a silver tray filled with luxurious food and dainties sitting on the table nearby, and he began asking whether he was the starving, forsaken wretch begging food from robbers in a fearful forest or whether he was a king living in a sumptuous palace surrounded by all possible luxuries. "Is this true or is that true? Is this real or is that real?"

Maharishi Vashishta immediately recognized the king's confusion and said, "King Janaka, neither beggar nor emperor is real. You alone are real. You, yourself, are the truth. The *you* who was present as pure consciousness in the dream state playing the role of the beggar and who is present in the waking state playing the role of the king, this *you* who witnessed both these states, is your true reality. Life during the daytime is a day-dream, during the night it is a night-dream. They are both illusions. They are filled with defects and flaws because they constantly change from one thing to another; so they cannot be real. Only you who remain unchanged in all these states are real, free of all change and illusion."

This was also emphasized in the *Gita*, where Krishna pointed out the important truth that the world is constantly changing and that the *atma* alone is real and ever unchanging.

The Anguish of Separation from God

Detachment does not mean leaving behind everything to go to the forest and adopt the life of a renunciate. Penance does not refer to certain postures or bodily deprivations. Penance refers to the intense anguish you experience when you feel yourself separated from God. Whenever that anguish of separation is with you, wherever you may be, then you are engaged in penance. All worldly experiences are governed by combinations of the three attributes, inertia or chaos, action or reaction, and rhythm or calm. The anguish of penance with its intense aspiration for reaching God, takes you into a state of being which transcends these three worldly qualities. At that time, you will experience a deep inner serenity and unity of thought, word and deed.

Thought, word and deed are the causes of *karma*. They are called the instruments of action, It is the union of these three instruments of action which may be described as penance. When that union is complete there follows an ineffable joy, which is the very bliss of the *atma*. So true penance is the point at which the three instruments of action merge together into one and you experience the eternal delight of your immortal self.

Consider the following example. Every day you enjoy the benefits of electricity. In your room you may have an electric fan. There are three blades attached to the motor of the fan. If they were to rotate in three different directions you would not get much of a breeze. But when they rotate in unison, as if there were a single blade going around, then you can enjoy a very good flow of air from the fan. So, enjoyment of the cool breeze comes only when all the three blades are working together and rotate as one. In the very same way, when the three instruments of action, thought, word and deed, merge together and work as one, you can enjoy real bliss.

In this illustration your heart may be compared to the room containing the fan. The three instruments of action may be compared to the three blades of the fan. Your intellect may be thought of as the electric switch. Your spiritual power, the energy emanating from the supreme self, may be thought of as the electricity that energizes the fan. Your spiritual practice is the process of clarifying your intellect, and thereby turning on the switch. When the three instruments of action work together in harmony, just as the three blades of the fan go around together, then all your anguish becomes transformed into bliss. In this way, you can convert your life-force and your entire spiritual power into bliss.

True Renunciation Is Turning Your Mind Towards God

Mankind has forgotten the ability to perform penance. When you let your vision roam in the temporary and transient world, your spiritual path spirals downward into inertia and stasis. When you concentrate your vision and your awareness on the permanent God, then you are practicing penance and your spiritual progress leaps ahead. If a door is locked and you want to open it, you must put the key inside the lock and turn it towards the right. Then it will open. But if you turn the key to the left, the lock remains closed. It is the same lock and the same key. The difference is in the way you turn the key. Your heart is that lock and your mind the key. If you turn your mind towards God, you get liberation. If you turn it towards the objective world, you remain in bondage. It is the same mind that is responsible for both liberation and bondage.

True renunciation is turning your mind towards God. It means constantly bringing your mind back from other thoughts to dwell on the permanent entity. Such mental detachment and sacrifice must be developed into a very intense feeling. You should not keep on postponing the practice to the next day, and then the day following that, and so on.

Suppose you expect to go to a marriage; you would keep certain clothes ready several days before the occasion. Or suppose you had a chance to go to the movies; then you will get ready very fast. Even for just going for a walk you make yourself ready in a trice. Well, if you cannot go to the cinema today you can easily postpone it to another day. If you do not go for a walk now you can always go another time. But the Lord's journey cannot be postponed or canceled. You must always be ready to accept whatever comes your way. Time waits for no one. Time does not follow man. Man has to follow time. Time flows on continuously and takes everything with it.

The *Gita* teaches you that you may enjoy the various objects of the world, but while enjoying them you should not get yourself attached to them, thinking that you possess them. This feeling of renunciation or detachment is one of the most essential aspects of the spiritual philosophy propounded in the *Gita*.

Twelfth Chapter

DETACHMENT –
UNIFYING THOUGHTS, WORDS & DEEDS

For the wheel of existence, the mind is the focal point, the central hub from which all worldly activities emerge. To be able to penetrate this focal point and obtain a vision of the immortal self that is beyond, you must cultivate the practice of non-attachment. Make every effort to develop this most important discipline.

Embodiments of Love,

Renunciation or detachment can also be thought of as non-attachment. Non-attachment is when the mind and the senses become unaffected by the objects of the world and remain indifferent to their attraction and repulsion. The mind covers the true self; therefore, the mind can be described as a veil. It is a veil of ignorance, for it hides your true self and keeps you unaware of its magnificent presence within you. But, the mind, itself, is tied down by the sense organs, and the sense organs are attracted to the objects of the phenomenal world, and get bound by them. Therefore, the first step in realizing your true self is to gain control over your sense organs. For this, the practice of non-attachment is essential.

Detachment Leads to Self-Realization

Once you are free of attachment to the sense objects, then the sense organs will no longer be able to bind your mind. A mind unencumbered by the senses becomes pure and transparent. It no longer imposes its covering influence over the *atma*. When the veil of the mind dissolves, your true self becomes aware of itself. Then you are immersed in the unity of all existence and enjoy the bliss which is your true nature. The *Gita* has taught that non-attachment is crucial for realizing your true self. That true self is the one supreme self.

Detachment or non-attachment has also been emphasized in the *yoga* classic of Patanjali, a great seer of ancient India. He taught that detachment is the natural property of a mind which remains that detachment is the natural property of a mind which remains unswayed by the sense organs and the objects which attract them. Such a mind, being free from the slavery of the sense organs and sense objects, is pure and unaffected by delusion. You gain a pure mind when you see all the objects of this world as transient and changing. The ancient wisdom teachings have declared that from the lowest creature in the phenomenal world to the highest, right up to the heavenly beings, everything is ephemeral and undergoing change. Knowing this, you should relinquish all attachments to sense objects. Any attachment will gradually but steadily lead to bondage.

Just as removing the firewood from the fire automatically extinguished the flame, removing the sense objects from the senses automatically renders them impotent. The wisdom teachings have stressed in a most forceful way that only that person who does not care for anything less than full realization of the supreme self, is a person of true renunciation. Neither objects of the world nor even the heavenly abode of the Lord could sway him from his one-pointed focus.

There is a story related in one of the ancient wisdom teachings about a very wise young boy, who, because of an oath made by his father, found himself in the realm of death. The god of death tried to win over the boy. He said to him, "I will give you complete mastery and lordship over all the wealth and all the power of the world, and I will give you all the pleasures of the heavenly world." But the boy replied, "This world and all the worlds beyond are but transient; they will not last. I do not want anything to do with that which comes and goes. I only want to have the vision of the supreme self. I want to realize the ultimate truth, that which never changes. The world with its bondage and all the sorrow that goes with it is for the person who is swayed by the objects of the senses. They do not interest me in the least."

Attachment to Objects Which You Think Belong to You

Let us suppose that you have been living in a particular house for a long time. One day you have to shift to another dwelling. You pack all your belongings and put them in a conveyance and bring them to the new house. Now, it is a common experience that you even go to the extent of wrapping the worn out slippers and the old broomsticks in newspapers to carry them with you because you think that they belong to you. What is the reason for this attitude? The reason is that you have become bound by your attachments to the sense objects. You have so much interest in packing up all those old things and taking them with you because you are attached to them. You feel they are yours.

But then, consider another example, that of a college principal or the headmaster of a school. In every educational institution there will be a number of valuable articles. For instance, in the lab there will be some highly valuable equipment, many tables, chairs, other items of furniture, a wall clock and so on. When the headmaster of that school retires or is transferred, he feels no attachment to these things. And so he leaves with the same free mind that he had when he came. He does not worry and bother himself about leaving behind all those valuable articles when he goes. The reason is that he knows perfectly well that none of those things belong to him. They belong to the management or to the school trust or to the government. Therefore, with a sense of detachment and indifference to those objects he leaves the school.

Where there is a sense of *my-ness* and possessiveness, there will be suffering. If you do not have that feeling of possessiveness you will not be bound by anything and will not suffer. Therefore, for all bondage, suffering and sorrow, it is just the *I-ness* or *my-ness* that is responsible. Like the school principal, you may make use of all the objects that you find in the world. Do not give up the objects themselves, and do not give up your actions and activities. Just give up the attachment that you have towards the objects and give up the attachment that you have towards the world and your activities in it.

Give Up the Fruits of Your Actions

Another way of saying this is, give up the fruits of your actions. Perform your duty with a sense of complete detachment, realizing the defects in the objects. Once you understand the underlying laws that govern the world and recognize the defects that are inherent in both the objects of the world and the relationships you have in the world, you will quickly be able to overcome the attachments you have towards them.

Before you were born, who was the parent and who was the child? Before marriage, who was the husband and who was the wife? Only after birth was there a parent and a child. Before birth there was no such relationship and after death there will be no such relationship. It is only during the short transitional period in-between that the feeling of possessiveness and attachment arises. This is all due to defects in your vision and defects in your approach. It comes from a narrow-minded, short-sighted attitude. For all your sorrows, it is your feelings and attitudes alone that are responsible. Once you recognize the defects in objects and relationships you will have no desire to possess them.

Try to understand the principle of detachment. You must reach a state in which you do not have any kind of attachment and bondage even during the dream and deep sleep states. If you encourage a sense of attachment during the waking state, it will also be there in a subtle form during the dream state and the deep-sleep state. The dream state may be compared to a reflection in the mirror. Whatever you experience in the waking state will impress itself into the dream state, and will be seen as a reflection there. Therefore, the waking and dream states are something like the object and its image. If in the waking state you take the right path, recognizing truth and conducting yourself in the light of this truth, then you will be treading the right path even in the dream state. To succeed you have to recognize the defects of the sense objects and overcome them by giving up your attachment to them.

Everything Undergoes Change

Because of the passage of time everything undergoes change. Food which is freshly cooked today is tasty and delicious. While it is fresh, its potentiality for giving strength and health are very good. But the very same articles of food become toxic after a lapse of two days. Whatever food you consider to be good, to be useful, to be healthy and beneficial, will after a period of time change into something bad, something useless, something unhealthy and harmful. These changes are unavoidable.

In the context of change, you can also see the four types of devotees: the one who is afflicted and seeks relief from pain and suffering, the one who seeks material boons and prosperity, the one who seeks spiritual knowledge, and the wise one. Over a period of time the very same person is likely to progress through all these stages.

We can also consider the changes that occur in the course of a lifetime. Immediately after birth the new-born is called a baby; after a few years it is described as a child; twenty years later the same person is considered an adult; and after another 30 years it will have become a grandparent. These are not four different people. It is the same person all the time, but because of the passage of time different names are given, in accordance with the different stages of life that the individual is passing through.

A human being's life, which is most difficult to obtain, undergoes many changes as time goes by. When this is true for human beings, then how much more must it be true for all the other beings and objects of the world? If you ask what is the greatest defect in a human being, you will find that it is the changes which occur in one's physical being. Whether good or bad, these changes cannot be avoided. As changes are inherent in everything in the phenomenal world, you should not develop any attachment or any sense of *myness* for anything or anyone.

Who is the father? Who is the mother? Who are the children? Who are the family members? Who are the friends? These are all changing forms. You cannot answer these questions for all time. As you become aware of all these changes that are constantly occurring in all these relationships, then how can you develop any attachment to them? The *Gita* has taught that one has to recognize all the changes that come about with time as fundamental defects and flaws. Therefore, develop complete detachment from the defective forms which are experiencing these changes. They have no permanence.

Constant Practice

Detachment or non-attachment is the first important discipline that should be undertaken. The second is constant practice. What kind of practice can be called constant? One kind is austerity or penance. The moment people hear this word austerity they get a little frightened. They inevitably associate austerity with going into the forest, eating whatever fruits and roots are available there and exposing themselves to all kinds of risks and sufferings. Truly speaking, that is not austerity; that is just putting the body through some suffering and punishment.

It is not the body that must undergo the suffering, but the mind. The mind tends towards either sloth and chaos or endless activity, and is filled with the sense of doership and possessiveness. Austerity is putting such a mind with all these negative tendencies that cling to it, through real torture, until all these tendencies let go their hold. Austerity also means removing the defects that are inherent in the sense organs. This is the real austerity. There are three types of austerity. One is the physical austerity of the body, the second one is the vocal austerity of the tongue and the third is mental austerity of the mind.

The Three Austerities, Physical, Vocal and Mental

Physical austerity refers to using the body to perform good actions, which includes worshipping the Lord and expressing your sense of gratitude by serving great souls. If you earn their grace, the selfish aspects of *I-ness* and *my-ness* will slowly get reduced. Once these negative qualities decline, then automatically positive qualities and actions will develop. At that point, you will naturally be attracted to the company of like-minded spiritual beings and be inspired to study the *Gita* and other sacred texts.

In addition to this, you will undertake charity for education, for medicine and hospitals, for poor feedings and other good causes. And just as, traditionally, the different types of charities such as giving away gold and cows and land were the means for using the body in sacred activities, so also you will now be using your body in a sacred way. Since you will not be doing any harmful or prohibited activities, you will not put yourself under the spell of the sense of doership and possessiveness. You will free yourself from bondage to these two qualities. All of this can be described as bodily penance.

Vocal penance is the use of good and noble words. Even when you speak the truth you should not be severe or sharp-tongued. You must be careful not to hurt anyone. In this context, the *Gita* has said that truth must be sweet and nonviolent. Use the sacred tongue which has been given to you for giving joy and delight to others and for helping them. Do not give any suffering to another's mind. Use your thoughts to help you concentrate and think of the Lord. Use your tongue to describe all the glorious attributes of the Lord. Use words which are highly helpful to others. Use your talk to show the right path to others. Explain to others all the great and good spiritual experiences that you have had. Correct people if they are going on the wrong path by using good words and a sweet tongue. Make sure that no amount of falsehood enters your heart, or enters your talk. This is the way to become an adept of truth and nonviolence.

Better Be Quiet Than Tell An Untruth

If you are following the path of truth there may be quite a few problems that you will encounter. A particular sage performing penance had taken an oath to take the path of truth and nonviolence, come what may. A cruel hunter who heard of this tried to induce the sage to break his vow. The hunter pursued a deer and drove it in such a way that it had to pass in front of the sage, immersed in his austerities. The sage saw the deer hiding in the bush. The hunter came running and asked the sage, "Have you seen a deer passing this way?" The sage was in great conflict. If he told the truth he would cause harm to the deer, but if he did not tell the truth he would be breaking his vow. On the one hand, he would commit the sin of causing harm to another being, and on the other hand, he would commit the sin of lying.

The sage found a very good way of dealing with this dilemma. He answered the hunter's query in a somewhat enigmatic way. He said, "The eyes which see cannot speak and the mouth which speaks cannot see. I cannot make that which has seen speak, and that which can speak see. That is the truth." Even in such difficult situations one should not tell an untruth, but one may not be able to tell the truth either. When you are engaged in the vocal type of austerity, difficult situations of this kind may arise. You should make every effort to see to it that you escape without uttering any falsehood. Whatever be the circumstances, do not tell a lie. If you cannot tell the truth then it is best for you to keep quiet and observe silence, rather than uttering an untruth.

Consider the third austerity, the mental austerity. In this type of austerity you will have to develop good qualities and virtues. Whatever thoughts may be flashing through your mind, your face will show the reflection of them. That is why it is said that the face is the index of the mind. All thoughts will be reflected on your face. If you are grief-stricken mentally, your face will reflect that state. If there are sacred thoughts in your mind your face will be very cheerful. The effect of the mind and its thoughts can easily be seen in this way.

Only when you have sacred thoughts, sacred feelings and sacred ideas in your mind, will you be able to live a happy and cheerful life. If there are bad thoughts torturing you, then whenever somebody comes and talks to you, even if you try to smile, your smile will be artificial and it will betray the disturbed inner state in your heart. You should not allow yourself to be driven to such a state. Always keep yourself happy. When will you be happy and joyous? Only when your thoughts are good and sacred. In order to have such good and sacred thoughts in your mind you should exercise control over your thoughts.

Every Day Observe A Period Of Silence

At least for a few hours a day you should observe silence. Then the mind will get some rest from words and thought waves. Repetition of the holy name and concentration on the Lord can also be practiced to give some rest to the mind. Repetition of the name and thinking of the Lord brings about both inner and outer purity. Just as you bathe your body every day and transform it into a clean outer vehicle, the mind, too, has to be given a regular purification bath to renew its freshness and sacredness. Now you are concerned mostly with physical cleanliness, but you must also engage in mental cleanliness, which is equally essential to life. Good thoughts, good feelings and good actions go a long way to bring about inner cleanliness.

Austerity truly means bringing about a physical, vocal and mental unity by letting actions words and thoughts become one. This is the real austerity. A great soul is one who has been able to enjoy the unity of all these three attributes. If the thoughts, the words, and the actions are different, then a person cannot be considered a great person.

Worldly experiences are governed by combinations of the three attributes. Of these, inertia and chaos give rise to a slothful nature, action and reaction give rise to an active, passionate nature, and rhythm or calm gives rise to a pure, harmonious nature. Austerity refers to transforming the first of these two, the slothful and passionate natures, into the pure, calm, harmonious nature. This can be brought about by controlling sloth with the help of the passionate nature and then by controlling passion with the help of the pure calm nature. In this way you can enjoy the harmony of all three natures, being joined together as one. Ultimately, when all your actions, words and deeds have become totally unified, you will have overcome all worldly attributes and you will be free even from the limitations of the pure calm nature.

For example, suppose you have stepped on a thorn. If you want to remove the thorn from your foot there is no need to look for a special instrument. Another thorn is sufficient to remove the first one. Then you can throw both thorns away. In the same way, the two lower natures which have been giving you so much trouble, can be removed with the help of the thorn of the calm pure nature. Until you have removed these two lower qualities, you need the calm quality. The calm quality may be described as a golden chain, the passionate quality as a copper chain and the slothful quality as an iron one. All three chains bind you in the same way. The value of the metal of the chain may be different, but they all bind nevertheless.

Free Yourself From All Bondage

If an individual is bound by a golden chain, will he be happy in that situation? No! Bondage remains bondage, be it from a chain made of gold or one made of copper or iron. So, even a pure, calm nature causes bondage, and in the end you have to get rid of this also. You must free yourself from all bondage. But until you reach divinity you need the pure, calm, harmonious quality. Once you merge in the Lord, there are no more distinguishing qualities of any kind. In that state the question of the three qualities does not arise at all.

When you have offered up everything and become one with the Lord you rise above these attributes and become totally free of all chains.

The *Gita* has taught that in order to control the mind, constant practice and renunciation, are essential. Practice does not refer to just the observance of daily religious rituals. Practice means using the body, using the tongue and using the mind in such a way that you do not develop attachment. Practice means orienting your whole life towards the one goal of reaching the divinity. Every word you utter, every thought you think and every deed you perform should be pure and associated with truth. This is the essence of all austerities. Truth and purity are the real instruments for success on the spiritual path. My wish is that you develop these noble qualities and thereby sanctify your life.

Thirteenth Chapter

TIME WASTED IS LIFE WASTED

The Lord declared in the Gita, "Whoever remembers me is very dear to me." Therefore, remember the Lord always. Offer him your mind and your will. Surrender everything to him and you will quickly reach him."

Embodiments of Love,

In the *Gita* the Lord taught that joy and sorrow, cold and heat, profit and loss, criticism and praise, must all be faced with an equal mind. This equanimity of mind is one of the most important attributes of a true devotee. There are many other attributes of a true devotee, but these are all contained in two principal qualities: discipline and renunciation. Discipline refers to the three types of penance: bodily penance, mental penance and vocal penance. Renunciation refers to understanding the defects in objects, and living a life which does not get attached to these things; in other words, living as a witness. If you can incorporate these two important qualities, discipline and renunciation in your daily life, then there will be no need for any other spiritual practice.

Start Your Spiritual Practice When You Are Young

If you want to develop these two qualities you have to start in your childhood and use this early period of your life in a sacred and ennobling way. In the world today many people undertake spiritual practice only when they reach old age. After they have thoroughly enjoyed the objects of luxury and have become disgusted and exhausted by worldly pleasures, they consider embarking on the spiritual path. Having spent their lives concentrating on sense objects, on family life, on children, on wealth, on properties, on name and fame, they become disillusioned in old age. They realize that there is nothing true in these things and that peace of mind and lasting joy cannot come from the phenomenal world and from worldly pursuits. After they come into the evening of their lives and are haunted by the emptiness of their experiences, they begin to do spiritual exercises.

But in old age, when you are suffering from all sorts of physical and mental weaknesses, it will be very difficult to practice and live a rigorous spiritual life. Even then you should not be discouraged, thinking that there is no possibility for spiritual advancement in old people. Opportunities for spiritual experiences are certainly available to them. Instead of not thinking of the Lord at all, it is far better to think of him, at least in old age. When it comes to thinking of the Lord, there are no restrictions whatsoever with respect to time, place or age. That is why the divine teacher has declared in the *Gita*, "At all times, in all places, think of me." But he has also declared that the best opportunity for practicing these spiritual exercises in a determined way is in your youth. When your physical strength, the strength of your sense organs, and your mental strength are there in abundance, that is the best time to undertake spiritual exercises.

The process is something like reserving a plane ticket before embarking on a journey. When you arrive at the airport, after first having reserved your place, you are likely to proceed smoothly with your journey. On the other hand, if you go to the airport only at the last minute, without having a reservation, you may not get on the plane. It all depends on chance. You may end up having to go by a slower way or you may have to delay your journey. It is the same way with people who start thinking about spiritual matters in their old age. They may or may not be able to advance spiritually in a significant way at that point in their lives. But if the same individuals had in earnest undertaken spiritual exercises from an early age, they would be sure to achieve spiritual success in their old age.

Do Not Waste Your Youth

If you waste your time enjoying the pleasures of life during your youth, wasting the power of your body and your sense organs, then if you want to reach your goal of merging with the Lord in your old age, you may not get that chance. There is no meaning whatsoever in serving delicious food to the demons, and then, when they have consumed everything worthwhile, offering the leftovers to God. Do you think that will please God? No! After all your powers and capacities have been dissipated by the demons of anger, greed, lust and pride, you try to offer God what little is left. But that offering will not be accepted by him. In this context, the *Gita* has emphasized that your youth is a very precious period which has to be used with great care to advance yourself spiritually.

When you have had something for a long time and taken it for granted, you may not appreciate its real value. It is only after losing it that you truly appreciate it. As long as you have your eyes, you do not know the value and the preciousness of your eyes. You only realize the importance of vision when you lose your eyesight. In the same way, when you have good health and all your faculties are in their full glory, you do not understand their true value. After having lost your health, and when your faculties have become impaired, then you repent and lament that all your capacities and powers are gone. But lamenting at that point is useless. During youth you have allowed the bad habits and bad traits to become your great friends and get deeply rooted within you. You squandered and misused the capacities that have been given to you, blindly following your sensual desires. Later, these bad habits and bad traits become your principal enemies in old age.

Most young people do not use their powers of discrimination properly. They do not try to sort out who is their true friend and who is their foe. If you follow only your senses and lower instincts, and have not developed your intelligence to understand the meaning of life, then is there any reason for calling you a human being? Should you not be called a mere animal? Once you understand the significance of human life and fill yourself with the noble qualities of a human being, your senses will no longer be able to confuse you.

Use Your Body for the Sake of God

These days you are using God for the sake of the body. You are not using your body to worship God. You pray to God for good health whenever you are sick, but you are not using all your physical strength and faculties, when you have them, to worship God. You imagine that there will be plenty of time later on to engage in worship, and so you go on wasting your time. You think that after retirement you can begin to take up the contemplation of God and do spiritual exercises. Perhaps you feel that it is better in the meantime to enjoy life and to enjoy the objects of the world while you are still young. But how can you start thinking of God when you become old, after having lost all your capacities.

If you are not using all your physical powers and capacities for the worship of the Lord now, then later it will be too late. When children make fun of you and call you 'old monkey!', will you then have the strength to start an intensive spiritual life? When your hair is gray, when you are hardly able to move, when you are barely able to see, when all the sense organs have become weak, will you then be able to use them for the worship of the Lord? No, it will not be possible. The scriptures have very forcefully described the futility of starting your spiritual practices only during your last days. It is stated that when the god of death finds you and shouts, "Come! Come!", when your own relations are anxious to get the corpse out of the house, when they are all shouting, "Take it away! Take it away!", and when your wife and children are there sobbing, can you think of the Lord at that time? Can you tell your relatives to stop crying, can you tell death to wait a little bit because you want to think of the Lord for a few moments?

You should accumulate in youth all the things which are necessary to lay a strong foundation for a happy future. Do you really think that it is possible to think of the Lord only after you retire? No, it is not possible. You should be fully engaged in regular spiritual practice before retirement. But instead, you immerse yourself in business, and continue with that even after retirement, or waste your time going to clubs, and in many other ways dissipate your precious life.

You Cannot Start Spiritual Life When Death Is At The Door

A housewife once asked her husband, "At least now in your old age shouldn't you be thinking of God? You never took the time to do it before, during your busy period. Please, do it now!" The business man replied, "I have no time even to die, no less to think of God." But do you think that death will not come to someone who says that he has no time to die? Will death come only according to his wishes? No, time waits for no one. Therefore, while you still have time you have to make use of it in a proper way.

The enemy called death, along with his soldiers called disease, will be waiting to wage war against your body. Men die most pitifully and helplessly during such periods of time when they are attacked by disease and death. But no army can attack those who have won the grace of the Lord. Therefore, during youth itself you have to earn the grace of God and equip yourself to meet all the challenges of your enemies when they come to lay siege on you. Above all, you must be firmly convinced in your own heart that this journey of life is going to be a long one. Any other journey, whether it be by bus, train or plane lasts for only a short time; you need not make too many preparations for these. But for this journey of life you must equip yourself for all the contingencies of a long journey; otherwise you will be suffering greatly later on when you are faced with real problems and real troubles.

In the compartment of freight trains used to transport chemically-active substances, a stamp is placed at the time of manufacture giving a particular date in the future. It is the day when that container has used up its normal service life and must be returned to the depot for recycling. It is the same for the container that is your body. Here also a return date has been written on it by God himself.

You do not remember that you have to go back. People totally forget this all-important truth. If you really want to enjoy all the pleasures of life at a later stage, then during youth you have to earn the grace of God. In the course of human life the early periods of childhood and youth are very important. Not realizing the great value of this period of your life, you waste your time during youth. You use a golden cup, adorned with precious gems and jewels, for a low, mean, contemptible purpose. To feed the fire of your senses you are using costly sandalwood as fuel. The vessel is very precious, the fuel is also precious, but the food you are choosing to cook with their help, is insipid and worthless. Such a precious body and such sacred fuel is being squandered away for the sake of enjoying useless trivial things in life. Things without value are put in this precious vessel and used for sordid enjoyment. You are using a golden plough to plough the field of your heart, but you produce nothing but useless weeds.

True Human Life Involves Discrimination & Renunciation

The field of your heart is most precious and sacred. The divine teacher has declared that even that field belongs to him. The Lord has declared that he is both the field and its knower. He is the true owner of your heart and of your body. He has identified himself with them. What are you doing with this sacred heart and body? You are using a golden plough to raise useless crops of sensual pleasures. Any person who is aware of the preciousness of the heart and the preciousness of the feelings that are there will not misuse these things. Life must be used for good, for the welfare of others, for reaching the sacred goal and for treading the sacred path, and for bringing about a shining effulgence in the heart and mind. You have to use this life for merging yourself in the divinity. Only then will you have the authority to say that your life has become sanctified and genuine.

It is said that it is very difficult and almost impossible to get a human life. What is so special about human life? Why is it so difficult to get? All the pleasures which animals and birds enjoy, you can also enjoy. In that case, what is the meaning in declaring that human life is so very precious, so very special? It is because you have the ability to discriminate between right and wrong. It is because you have the ability to give up attachments and hatred. Therefore, you have to use the intelligence given to you to make a distinction between the animal way of life and the human way of life. By not discriminating between the true self and the lower self, by not developing your higher intelligence, you become the victim of agitation and sorrow. You cannot find inner peace because you do not follow the right path.

With a firm determination, young people need to undertake the three types of penance, physical, mental and vocal, and thereby set an example for the world. You have to use the active principle within you to subdue the slothful principle, and then, you have to use the serene principle to subdue the active principle. It is impossible to be serene as long as your heart is filled with the slothful and active natures. When the head is empty you can hope to fill it with some good ideas, but if your head is already full of all sorts of useless thoughts, how is it be possible to fill it up with any thing sacred and great? You have filled your head with all sorts of unnecessary worldly stuff. You will have to first empty all that out. Only then will you be able to fill your head with sacred feelings and sacred thoughts.

Keep Your Concentration Unwaveringly on God

Many of you are following a meaningless path and living a meaningless life. You cry when you are born and you cry when you die. In between, through your whole span of life, you go on crying for useless things. Do you cry when you see the decline of righteousness? That is what you should cry for, that is what you should use your strength and abilities for, to correct the decline of righteousness and to help heal the wounds that follow its decline. What is right living? It is the constant remembrance and uninterrupted contemplation of the Lord. It is discharging your daily duties thinking of the Lord. The *Gita* has not taught that you should give up your family, that you should give up your wealth and property, and then go to the forest. No! Take care of your family. Do your duty. But keep your concentration constantly on the Lord. Whatever you do, do not forget your goal. If you give it up, you will get lost and stray onto the wrong path. Your divine goal must be solidly set in your mind. Keeping your goal in view, perform your daily duties.

Do not allow any flaw or defect to taint your words. Always adhere to truth. Some people think that in times of difficulty they can modify the truth. They may even feel that it is necessary to tell untruth sometimes. But in difficult situations you can develop sufficient presence of mind to keep silent, instead of telling either the truth or an untruth. If you tell the truth, tell it dearly and sweetly. Do not tell the truth in an unpleasant way, or tell an untruth in a pleasant way. Whenever there comes a difficult testing time, you should learn how to avoid compromising situations without ever telling an untruth. In certain circumstances you will have to conduct yourself in an extremely careful way. You should know how to use words without hurting people. It has been said that, "He is the fortunate one who knows how to talk without ever hurting anyone." You should neither hurt others nor be hurt by others. Here is a small story.

Be Steady In Your Practice

A housewife attended a series of meetings at which a spiritual teacher was expounding the scriptures. She was concentrating and listening with great attention to everything that was being said. One day, the speaker recounted the story of Rama and Sita, and in that connection declared that for a wife, the husband was the only goal in life. He said, "It is the responsibility of the wife to satisfy her husband and make him happy. Always treat the husband as God." The housewife after hearing all this went back home. She was so impressed by this discourse that she resolved to put into practice immediately all that she had learned. As soon as the husband returned home for his midday meal, she took a container of water and poured it over his feet, thinking that she was worshipfully serving her husband thereby. The husband was confused and flabbergasted. He entered the house and sat down to dry his feet, but before he could do so she insisted on doing it for him.

After seeing all this, the husband went into his office and rang up the doctor. Her husband did not know that his wife had been attending the discourses. The doctor came and decided to give her some sleeping pills. He said that it looked like an attack of hysteria, but after a rest of one or two days she probably would be all right. The husband ate his meal and told his wife to go and have some rest; then he went to his office. His wife went right back again to the meeting to hear the next lecture. That afternoon the speaker was explaining the delusory relationship which exists between husband and wife. He said, "Who is husband? Who is wife? Nothing is permanent. All these things are just temporary and transient. In truth nothing exists." Then he added, "God alone is true. He is the only real truth." The housewife went back home and sat in her shrine room.

That evening the husband came back from his office half an hour early, thinking that his wife may not be well and perhaps he could help her in some way. He knocked on the house door and asked her to kindly open it. From the shrine room she answered, "There is no mother, there is no father, there is no house, there is nothing, not even a husband." He was quite alarmed by this behavior, but somehow he got her to open the door. When he came into the house he went straight to the telephone and called the psychiatrist. The psychiatrist came and examined her in detail. He gave his diagnosis. He said that after all this listening to these discourses she had developed some peculiar attitudes; but if she could be kept at home she would soon get over them. All arrangements were made to keep her from going to the lectures. Everyone was informed. The driver as well as every servant of the house was told not to let her go there.

After these restrictions had been put on her by doctor's orders, she did not go to the lecture for two days and she started behaving in a normal way again. So the detachment she had developed was only temporary and superficial. It did not last. Now the husband was happy. The normal daily routine resumed. After a week this lady went again to the place where the lectures were being given. On that particular day the speaker was expounding the teachings of the *Gita*. He explained that whenever one uses words one should tell the truth and one should not tell it in a compromising way. She heard this and returned home. Her husband told her that there was a marriage reception that day, and asked her to join him. She got ready and went there with her husband.

The marriage ceremony started. There was a tradition in those parts which calls for the auspicious necklace that is worn by the bride to be taken to every elder, who then touches it and blesses it. The father of the bride came to this lady, recognized her and asked her, "How is your mother? Is everything all right?" These questions were a matter of courtesy, exchanging a few words with her while he held out the sacred necklace, asking her to touch it and bless it. She answered, "My mother is doing fine. She is quite all right, but you know, a week ago my mother-in-law died quite suddenly and her body was taken to the cremation ground the following day."

The neighbor who was sitting next to her told her, "Why did you have to say such an inauspicious thing while touching and blessing this necklace, which is meant to impart a long and happy life to the new bride and her future family?" The housewife replied,

"Should I tell a lie just for the sake of this necklace? No, I will never tell a lie. It is a fact that my mother-in-law died last week and that the body was cremated the next day." One intelligent young lady sitting nearby told her, "Mother, certainly you should speak the truth, but you should also be aware of the circumstances and think through what is appropriate before you say anything."

Tell the Truth But Use Discretion In Your Words

Whenever you hear a spiritual teaching on a particular day, you will go about implementing it with a great deal of fervor and conviction; but only on that very day. But this is not the correct way to pursue your spiritual studies. You should use your intellect to understand the context in which you find yourself before you use words in a given situation. Whenever you do a particular thing or say something, you should know that truth is the royal means for reaching your ultimate goal. The tongue should not be tainted by untruth. The body should not be tainted by violence. The mind should not be stained by bad thoughts and bad feelings. It is only when you sanctify all these three, the tongue, the body and the mind and bring them into harmony, that you will be able to get the sacred vision of the Lord.

Students should be extremely careful in telling the truth. They should certainly tell the truth, but be careful not to go on talking and hurting others unnecessarily. Have control over your tongue. Whenever there is a misunderstanding with someone, if you tell him all his defects, with the justification that everything you are telling is true, then there are bound to be complications later. You should never hate others. When you have love in your heart, your words will naturally be very sweet. Even if anger develops, it will be of a fleeting nature.

There are four types of people. The anger of a person who is of a serene nature will be very short-lived; it recedes immediately. The *Gita* has declared such a one as a great soul. The second type will have this anger for a number of minutes, but it will soon fade away. The third category of person will have this anger continuously, all day long. The one in the lowest category will have this anger throughout his life.

The Four Types of Anger

The divine teacher has told this in another way also, "The anger of a good person is like writing on water; it is not at all permanent. The anger of the second category of person is like writing on sand, it will be washed away, one moment or another. The third type of person's anger is something like writing on stone. Over a long period of time it too will be eroded away. But the anger of the fourth type of person is like writing on a steel plate, it will never go away unless you melt it and cast it anew. Only when you put it into the fire will it get destroyed. Only through intense transformation is there any possibility of changing it."

Things which are highly relevant in day-to-day life can be found in the *Gita*. It is very difficult for you to take all the teachings that are in the *Gita* and practice all of them. But you should, at least, take those teachings which are directly applicable to your present life and put them into practice. That way you reap immediate benefits and will rapidly progress towards your ultimate spiritual goal.

REMEMBER GOD – FORGET THE WORLD

Of all the precious things in the world, time is the most precious. Think carefully how you are spending your precious time. Your primary duty as a human being is to offer your body, your work and your time to the Lord, who is the very embodiment of time.

Embodiments of Love,

Health which is spoiled and lost can sometimes be recovered with the help of medicines. But time which has gone by is lost for good; there is no way for it ever to come back and be used again. You have to make every effort to use this precious time in a sacred manner. Time is infinite; it goes on forever. But the time which is allotted to you is only a microscopically small fraction of that. Many of you are wasting your lives by thinking that the phenomenal world is real. As a result, you are using all your limited time for enjoying the pleasures of the world. If you reflect even for a moment on what you have achieved and how you have spent your priceless time, you will be very sorry to find that you have used it in such a wasteful manner.

Find Out Who You Truly Are

You cry when you are born, because you have come into this world without knowing who you are and why you are here. Your cry is an anguished plea to find out, "Who am I?" If you waste your entire life on only your physical existence, when will you ever be able to understand who you truly are? There is a deeper significance contained in your life than merely caring for the body. You have to start your life with "Who am I?", and you have to end your life with "I am that! I am God!" You have to recognize that you yourself are the divinity, and end your life in the supreme peace which is your true reality. Unfortunately, most of you concentrate your attention only on the worldly enjoyments you can obtain, aspiring for immediate pleasures, and do not think at all about the future consequences that will follow from your actions.

When a frog sees some flies or worms in front of it, it becomes so happy and enthusiastic that it would like to immediately jump on them, swallow them whole and enjoy them. But behind the frog there is a snake lying in wait, ready to catch the frog and eat it up. The snake is very happy to have found its meal in the form of this frog which for the moment is preoccupied with its own enjoyment. The snake does not know that a hawk is hovering overhead, ready to snatch the snake up in its claws. The hawk is so joyous at the idea of grabbing and consuming this unsuspecting snake that it does not pay any attention to the hunter lurking in the bush, ready to shoot it.

In the same way, you are also thinking only of fulfilling your desires and anticipating the comforts that you see before you, not thinking at all of what is stalking behind you, waiting to pounce on you. You are wasting your time without realizing the harm that may befall you in the future. You cannot know at what time, in what place and in what circumstances danger may present itself and come your way. Therefore, you have to sanctify the time at your disposal now, and use it properly, recognizing its sacredness and preciousness.

Youth Is the Most Precious Period of Life

You may be prepared to offer millions of dollars to buy whatever comes your way, but no amount of money can be paid to ever get back the time that has already been spent. Youth is the most precious, the most sacred period of human life. It offers you a golden opportunity to properly utilize your time and sanctify your life. In human life, the time of youth, like the waters that flow in the river, cannot be turned back again. Today's youth should recognize this fact. Utilize your time in a proper way and you will gain fulfillment in life. Always be aware of the many aspects of the wheel of time. Realize how extremely important time is. Think ahead as to what is likely to happen in the future and keep the goal of your life constantly in view.

In the chapter on devotion in the *Gita*, it is said that time is the most important element in your life and you must use your time wisely. Your time should be used to reach God. The divine teacher taught in the *Gita*, that even if you have not reached a highly developed detachment from worldly objects, if you use your time in constant awareness of the Lord, performing all your works and duties as worship and offering everything you do to the Lord, then you will have a blessed life.

Krishna told Arjuna, "Do your duty, Arjuna! If you have to fight, then fight. But fight, thinking of me. That way you will incur no sin. If you have offered everything to me, and have me steadily in your heart, you will not suffer any of the consequences of your actions. You are not being asked to go to the forest and do penance or to give up all your relations. You need not give up your family, your house and all your properties. Whatever you see, whatever you say, whatever you hear, whatever you think, whatever you do, do it as my work, and offer it to me. Offer your mind and your intelligence fully to me. That is the proper way to sanctify your time. If you conduct your life in this way, you have my assurance, you will be saved!"

Develop Self-Confidence and a Firm Resolve

Unfortunately today, one does not find this capacity for renunciation, this firmness of purpose, this deep level of faith and commitment, this willingness to completely offer up mind and intellect to God. Most people today do not have a vision that is steeped in faith. But you should develop such a strong faith. You cannot hope to know what kind of life you will be living in the future, or under what circumstances and in what place you will find yourself. No one knows these things but the Lord. If you offer everything to him, he will protect you in all situations. Such a deep level of renunciation requires strong self-confidence and a clearness of vision. Whatever work you do, you must have a great determination and a firm resolve. Without this you cannot achieve even the smallest thing.

A small bird laid its eggs on the shore of the ocean. It wanted to have a comfortable life. A number of times the waves came and washed the eggs away into the ocean. The bird became discouraged and also a little desperate, for every time it laid its eggs the ocean washed them away. In time it became very angry with the ocean. Now, you might think, 'what can such a small bird do to the huge ocean?' But it entertained no such doubts; it did not think of itself as just a little bird unable to do anything against the vast ocean. No, on the contrary, this small bird took a firm resolve and decided it was going to empty all the waters of the mighty ocean. That was its vow to which it stuck with great determination. Night and day it stood at the edge of the ocean, dipped its head into the sea, took a little water into its beak, flew to the other side of a nearby hill, released the water from its beak, and thus, drop by drop, resolved to empty out the whole ocean. It believed that ultimately it would manage, in this way, to conquer the ocean itself.

When it realized that it would not get very far on its own, it sought the help of Garuda, the eagle, which is Lord Vishnu's vehicle and which is endowed with divine powers. With the help of Garuda it was able to earn the grace of Lord Vishnu. Now the ocean became very frightened and humbly apologized to the little bird. The ocean assured the little bird that its eggs would never again be destroyed by its waves and that it would be most welcome to nest on its shores, without disturbance. How small was this little bird and how vast was the ocean! You also think of yourself as so small, but you should never get desperate and lose hope. You should not get dispirited thinking that you are so insignificant whereas God is infinite and all-powerful.

You might wonder, 'Why would God bother to pay any attention to me? What could I possibly offer him which he would be happy to accept, when the entire cosmos is already his? If even angels and divine beings cannot see him, how can I ever hope to behold his form?' But such self-demeaning and belittling thoughts will not get you very far. As long as you think this way, you will not be able to gain the grace of the Lord and be fit to serve him. Give no room for such displays of weakness. You have to establish the Lord in your heart and say to him, "Beloved Lord! I know you are residing in all the universe, but you are also here in my heart. With all my power I will keep you here, firmly established within me. You are, it is true, the biggest of the big. But you are also the smallest of the small. In that small form, You are ever residing in my heart." If you have such a firm faith in yourself, and a firm resolve to establish the Lord unalterably in your heart, then you will surely attain him and thereby, gain all the strength of the Lord.

Birth is Sorrowful, Life is Sorrowful and Death is Sorrowful

Gautama Buddha, with a firm resolve and a lot of penance, was able to achieve the state of enlightenment. One day, after coming to know that Buddha was begging for alms, his father sent this message to Buddha, "O my child, your grandfather was a king, your father is a king and you are also a king. I have heard that you, a king, coming from such a noble lineage, have been begging for your food. There is no dearth of property or wealth in this kingdom. There is no shortage of any luxury. You can have anything you wish. I am suffering untold pain knowing that you, who can enjoy all the luxuries and comforts of a king's palace, have taken to begging, and that you are lying down on the hard ground living an uncomfortable beggar's life. Please come back to the palace. I will welcome you and make all the proper arrangements for your return. The kingdom itself will be yours."

Buddha who heard all these things with total detachment replied to the person who brought the message, "Please tell the king, 'Yes, my grandfather was a king. My father is a king, and I too was a king. But now I have renounced this world. And I believe that my real parents are renunciates and that my true ancestors are also renunciates. If you want me to come back, you must first answer these questions: Do you have the power to save me from death? Can you keep diseases away from me and guarantee to keep me in sound health? Do you have the capacity to prevent old age and senility from descending on me? Do you have the power to free me from all these evils? If you can give me the correct answers to these questions, then I will immediately come back to the palace.'"

Buddha saw that birth was sorrowful, that life was sorrowful and that the end was also sorrowful. He replied to his father in the correct way. After having seen all the sorrows of life and after having watched so many people suffering, he could not continue to wallow in ignorance and illusion; that would have been sheer folly. Buddha's life can serve as an important lesson to you. In the limited time given to you, you have to realize your true nature. That is the real objective of human life. Your body is composed of the five elements, and some day it is going to perish. The indweller of your body is the only permanent entity. When you inquire into truth, you will realize that there is nothing like old age and there is nothing like death for the indwelling self. If you could understand that this indweller, who is your own reality, is the divinity itself, in all its fullness, then you will know the truth and enjoy infinite peace.

The Field and the Knower of the Field

Another way that the divine teacher spoke of the body and its indweller, was in terms of the field and the knower of the field. By the knower is meant the one who is conscious and filled with the highest knowledge, whereas the field is without such consciousness and knowledge. What is this field which is devoid of the highest knowledge? It is the body with its gross and subtle aspects; it is the dwelling place of the Lord. Know that the Lord, who has all knowledge and wisdom, resides in this field of the body. It is his residence here on earth.

In your day-to-day life, you refer to your body as *my body*. In other words, you acknowledge that you are not the body, but that this body is yours; it belongs to you. Similarly, the indweller considers that he is not the field, but that the field belongs to him. When you say, "this is mine", then you are declaring that you and the object are different. When you state, "this is my handkerchief", you are asserting your separateness from the handkerchief; it is something different from you. When you say, "this is my body", it means that you are distinct from your body. In the same way, when the Lord declares that the field is his, then he is free to give it up any time he wishes.

The body is given to you in order that you may realize who you truly are, in order that you may recognize its indweller. Without a body you would not be able to know him; you would not be able to perform any activity and follow any spiritual path. All your work, both worldly and spiritual, can only be performed with the help of the body. The body consists of 20 principles; these are the five organs of perception, the five organs of activity, the five vital airs and the five sheaths. When you add to these the lower mind, the power of discrimination, the seat of feelings and remembrance in the heart, and the ego, together with the indwelling self, then the total comes to 25 principles which comprise an individual. This knowledge of the body and the indwelling spirit relates to the path of wisdom.

The Whole World is Illusion

Foolish ones who are born in illusion and grow up in illusion, never recognize illusion for what it is. The whole world is illusion, all attachments are illusion, family life is illusion, death is illusion, all that you see and think is illusion. This life itself is illusion. Where are all those kings and emperors who were so proud of their accomplishments? They have all been ground under the wheel of time. Days, months, years and eras have all merged into one another. Time is one continuous flow, and in this flow everything and everyone, every object and every person, is being washed away. A thing which is itself being washed away in the flow of time cannot become the support for another thing which is also being washed away.

Who can save whom? The only permanent entity who is not being washed away by time and who can take care of all, is the Lord. He alone can protect everyone. He is the stable bank for this unending river of time. Hold on to him. That is the secret of life. That is the mark of a true human being. Believe in the Lord and do not believe in the world, that is the right way to live your life and enjoy it. Always remember these three principles: In the first place, **Do not forget the Lord**; in the second place, **Do not believe in the world**;

and in the third place, **Never be afraid of death.** These are the three guiding principles for all of humanity.

In the *Gita* you will find 64 qualities given as the attributes of a true devotee. It is impossible for any one individual to have all these attributes. If you can practice one or two of these it is enough. Have firm faith in the Lord. Once you have developed a deep faith you do not need anything more. In a match box there may be 50 match sticks. If you want fire, you can strike one stick. That will be enough. You need not strike all the 50 match sticks. In the same way, out of the 64 attributes, if only one single attribute is practiced to perfection, that will be enough. The most important attribute is selfless love. Swami has often said, "Love is God and God is love. Live in love." If you live in love and become immersed in the divinity, the Lord will take care of everything in your life. Krishna said to Arjuna, "When you have complete faith in me, when you are filled with devotion and leave everything to me, you will be very dear to me," .

The Four Types of Devotees

True devotion does not merely refer to the performance of various religious rituals like singing devotional songs, repeating incantations, engaging in silent or communal prayers or sitting for meditation. Devotion refers to this deep unshakable faith in the Lord. There are four types of devotees: the seekers of boons to relieve their suffering, the seekers of blessings for a full and happy life, the inquirers into the deeper meaning of life, and the knowers of the highest spiritual wisdom.

The first type is one who prays to the Lord when he is in difficulty or undergoing trials and tribulations. It is only at such times that he thinks of the Lord and worships him. The second type is one who entreats the Lord for the blessings of wealth, position and power. He prays to the Lord for progeny and long life and yearns to gain houses, property, cattle, gold, jewels and such things to serve his fellow man. Most people hanker after worldly boons, not realizing that true wealth is wisdom, that real property is a noble character, that the most valuable jewel is to be immersed in God's love. They are anxious to acquire worldly objects, but do not understand the subtle meaning and deeper significance of all these outer symbols of worldly wealth.

The third type of devotee is ever engaged in inquiry into truth. He constantly seeks to know, 'Where is God? Who is God? How can I reach God? What is my relationship to God? Who am I?' When you enter this stage, you become engaged in all these inquiries in order to gain spiritual knowledge. In the first place, you must try to find out, 'Who am I? Where did this world come from? What is my goal?' You puzzle over these three important queries and try to gain some understanding. You approach great people, listen to their teachings, serve them, and study the sacred scriptures. Through this process, indirect knowledge gets turned into direct knowledge, as the teachings you have heard and studied become your direct inner experience. Finally, when you have fully absorbed the teachings within yourself, you leave this stage behind and become the fourth type of devotee, the highest knower of truth, the one of abiding wisdom. This wisdom is true spiritual knowledge, the transcendental knowledge. It refers to the experience of unity, the experience of the One without a second.

Dwelling only on external things will cause you endless sorrow. If you base your experiences on worldly knowledge alone, you will have to suffer the reactions that result from this knowledge. For example, suppose you hit a table very hard and feel a sense of pride in doing this. You can boast that you have given it a good smack and that you surely must have hurt it with your blow. But, immediately afterwards, to your dismay, you discover that the object has hit you back with the same intensity and you end up being equally hurt by it. In knowledge of the world there will always be this response. Whatever you do will react back on you; whatever you say will resound back to you; whatever you think will reflect back to you. Everything in the world involves reaction, reflection and resound.

But in the spiritual domain there is no reaction, no reflection and no resound. Within this domain, there is only transcendental knowledge; that is the true knowledge. There you will find nothing separate, no objects which can react, nothing that can reflect or resound, because in the spiritual domain, there will be no other. There, all is one. Whenever there is a second entity there will be a wish to either possess it or to escape it; in other words, there will arise a feeling of desire or a feeling of fear. But when you are immersed in real knowledge, you will experience nothing else and no one else; there will be no second. Then neither desire nor fear can arise. That state can best be described as wisdom, the highest knowledge. In that exalted state, you do not see anything separate from self and you will not hear anything separate from self. You will only be immersed in supreme bliss. This is the eternal joy of the divine.

The Story of The Wealthy Man And His Four Wives

There is a little story which illustrates the four types of devotion that have been discussed here. Once, a wealthy man who had four wives had to go abroad for some important work. He spent a few months in a foreign country. Before he returned home, he wrote a letter to each of his wives. In the letter he mentioned that he would be coming home in a few weeks, and if there was anything they wanted from that particular country, they could send a list and he would be glad to bring back the various things to them.

His first wife was an unhappy lady; she was suffering from many ailments. She sent the husband a list of medicines, explaining that her health was not good and that she would like to have a number of foreign medicines which would help her feel better. His second wife had a great many desires. She wrote, 'Dear husband, please bring me some fine jewels, some silk saris and all the latest fashionable articles that are available there.' He received her letter and arranged to procure those items for her.

The third wife had a strong spiritual inclination. She wrote to the husband asking for any good books that were available in that country, books which dealt with the lives of great saints, depicting their life experiences. She was always looking for good spiritual books that would inspire her in her own spiritual aspirations, and so she asked her husband to see if he could find such books and bring them back for her. His fourth and favorite wife wrote, 'Dearest one, I do not need anything for myself. I will be very happy when I know that you have come back home, safe and sound.'

When he returned home he brought with him whatever they had asked for. The first wife got the latest medicines and tonics from abroad. The second wife got beautiful jewels and exquisitely textured silk saris. To the third wife the husband brought the finest copies of the scriptures and other holy books. And then he went to stay with the fourth wife, who had written, 'Please come home safely; I want nothing else.' She only wanted him. The other three wives became jealous of the favorite one since the husband had gone to stay with her. They sent messages asking, "After such a long time without seeing us you have not even once come to our houses to visit us. What is the reason for this?" The husband replied, "I have given each of you exactly what you asked for. One of you asked for medicines; I brought them. One of you asked for the latest jewels; I brought them. One of you asked for sacred books; I brought them. One of you wanted only me, so now she has me!"

God Answers Everyone's Requests

This husband is the Lord himself and the four wives are the four types of devotees. The Lord will give you exactly what you ask for. If you ask only for him then he will come and reside in your heart. God is the wish-fulfilling tree, the tree that bears every conceivable kind of fruit. He will answer everyone's request. He is omniscient. He is everywhere. He knows what you want and he will give it to you. In fact, this whole world is really a wish-fulfilling tree. The Lord uses the world to satisfy your desires and take care of all your wants. There are very few people who understand this. Here is another small story to illustrate this.

There was a traveler who had been walking for a long time in the hot sun. Finally he found a nice big tree and stopped there to take rest. He was very tired after his long walk in the heat and now the shade of the tree was giving him great comfort. While sitting under the tree he got thirsty and said to himself, 'How nice it would be if I could have a glass of cold water.' Seemingly, out of nowhere, a tumbler of fresh water appeared. He was sitting beneath a wish-fulfilling tree and did not know it. After drinking the water, a second thought came to his mind, 'How nice it would be if I could have a soft pillow and a comfortable bed; then I would really be able to rest nicely.' Immediately, a bed and a pillow came, given by the Lord himself. Now the traveler was very comfortable.

After getting the bed and the pillow, he thought, 'How very nice and comfortable this bed and pillow are! Now if only I could have my wife here, then how perfect everything would be.' His wife immediately came. As soon as she appeared, he became very frightened because he was not sure, 'Is she really my wife or is she some demon impersonating my wife?' The very moment this thought flashed though his mind she turned into a demon. Now, fear really overwhelmed him and in terror he wondered, 'O my! Will this demon swallow me up?' Immediately the demon pounced on him and swallowed him whole.

The moral of this story is that when you are under a wish-fulfilling tree you must be very careful what you think. Whatever thoughts you have will surely come true. The entire world may be likened to a wish-fulfilling tree. If you have good thoughts, you get good results, if you have bad thoughts, bad results will follow. Therefore, you should never harbor bad feelings or bad thoughts. That is why Swami has so often said, 'Be good, do good, see good. That is the way to God.'

You Are Not Mortal, You Are Immortal

The entire world is the creation of God and is penetrated by his will. Everywhere there is God. Do not have bad thoughts about anyone. Have complete control over your senses and think only good thoughts. Whether you are old or young, you should permit only good thoughts to come into your mind and always aspire to lead a good life. This is the real meaning of a human being. The word for human in Sanskrit is *nara*, which stands for that which cannot be destroyed, that which will always come back to the Lord. *Nara* is the one who will not be ruined, who is immortal. The ancient scriptures have declared, 'You are not a mortal being; you are the child of immortality.' A human being has also been called *manava*. This refers the one who is without ignorance. But today you are all behaving in a foolish way. By your thoughts, words and actions you are not giving the proper value to the word human.

It has been said that death is sweeter than the blindness of ignorance. You have to make ignorance flee away from you and never come back. If you want to drive away darkness, you must bring in the light. Where there is light there can be no darkness. If you want to free yourself from ignorance you must acquire wisdom. When you have wisdom, ignorance can have no foothold on you and will be swept away. To gain wisdom you must earn God's grace. A great poet sang, "O Lord! If I have your grace, what is there to fear? What can destiny ever do to me?"

Your life should not be ruled by lust, anger, greed, infatuation, pride or jealousy. These are your enemies. They must be conquered and subdued. They are the darkness, the product of ignorance. Your life must be ruled by light and by wisdom. Your life must be based entirely on the grace of God. From this moment on, aspire for God's grace and gain wisdom. To earn God's grace, think of God, everywhere, at all times and in all circumstances. In this age of darkness there is no greater spiritual practice than this. Engage yourself in the constant repetition of the sacred name of the Lord and keep him permanently established in your heart of hearts. Thereby, you will bless your life and set a sterling example for the rest of the world.

Part Two

PATH
of
WISDOM

Fifteenth Chapter

GIVE UP SELF-DELUSION –
KNOW YOUR REAL SELF

Krishna admonished Arjuna, "Give up this faint-heartedness! Pluck up your courage and fight! This weakness of heart that has overtaken you is not becoming of a great hero!"

Embodiments of Love,

What was responsible for Arjuna's despondency? It was ignorance. Because of ignorance he developed body-consciousness, and because of body-consciousness he became confused and weak-minded; he lost all his resolve and courage and was unable to accomplish anything.

Infatuation and Attachment Lead to Sorrow

Krishna told Arjuna, "As long as you are weak-minded, even the smallest task will not get done. You will be haunted by sorrow. Do you know what causes this sorrow? It is your attachment. You are infatuated with a sense of *my* people, *my* kinsmen, *my* friends. This possessive attitude stems from ignorance. Attachment and infatuation will always make you faint-hearted and plunge you into grief. These are the real enemies you must battle and conquer.

"As long as you are swayed by this possessive attitude, thinking only of *your* self, *your* family, *your* people, *your* things, you can be certain that sooner or later you will be cast into sorrow. You must shift your focus away from your little self and its concerns for *me* and *mine*. Align yourself with the will of the divine. Travel from selfishness to selflessness, from bondage to liberation."

More than ever, this teaching is applicable today. For example, think of the time when the school photographer came to take pictures of all the students in your class. When the photos came back from the lab, more than likely you were interested in finding your own photo; you were not as interested in the others' photos. Or consider when your father came home from a long trip, and brought with him presents for every child in the family. You were probably most eager to find out what he had brought for you. These are examples of a widespread selfishness which is prevalent everywhere. But, you should leave this kind of narrowness behind and become broad-minded and selfless. Then you will be a fit instrument in the hands of the divinity and contribute to the welfare of the whole world.

Infatuation Will Destroy Your Courage and Will

Before the great war referred to in the *Gita*, Arjuna had participated in a number of battles, but never before had he been overcome by despondency and attachment. Now, the same Arjuna was overwhelmed with grief when he realized that the opponents he had to fight were his own grandfather, his kinsmen and his teacher. This possessive feeling made him feel dejected. He became a victim of infatuation; the feeling of *my-ness* had crept in. As this attitude grew, its consequence, which is sorrow, also grew along with it. Previously, when Krishna went on his peace mission to the opposing side, Arjuna discouraged it. He urged immediate war. He tried to convince Krishna that the mission would fail, that talk would prove futile and only a victorious war could restore to them the kingdom which had been stolen from Arjuna and his brothers.

At that time, Arjuna told Krishna, "This struggle for right cannot be settled by peaceful means. Our enemies will never agree to the terms of your peace mission. Their hatred and greed is unappeasable. Why waste your time and efforts on them? Good and evil cannot coexist; they are incompatible; they will never join together. Your mission is bound to fail." Then, Arjuna was full of courage and determination because he was not seeing his grandfather, his teacher, his relatives and many of his friends facing him on the opposing side. Before this possessive vision emerged on the eve of the war, it seemed that Arjuna had a very broad vision. But now, standing in the middle of the battlefield, Arjuna's vision was beclouded. His eyes became dim. His heart was heavy and his mind confused. When he saw his close relatives and some of his friends arrayed on the other side ready to fight him, he felt dizzy. He said, "Krishna, I will not fight!"

Remember that Arjuna was about to fight a war to protect righteousness, a war for which he had been preparing for many years. He was already on the battlefield and the war was about to commence. Was that the time to look upon his opponents as relatives? When Krishna heard Arjuna's words he got very angry. He told Arjuna, "This is faint-heartedness. It doesn't become you! A fearless person like you, who has always walked proudly with his head held high like a true hero, now seems to be suffering from timidity. A person who suffers from such faint-heartedness cannot be my disciple. The war is about to start. The final preparations for war have been going on for the past three months, and now the battle plans have been set.

"If you had shown this kind of hesitation in the beginning I would surely not have taken on this task of driving your chariot. At this late stage you are hesitating, after you have convinced friends and relatives of the rightness of your cause and have persuaded them to join your side. Now with them all assembled here, you are laying down your weapons and giving up ignominiously. Is that the way for a hero to act? You are destroying the true spirit of your royal line, whose sworn duty is to protect honor and righteousness. If you continue in this way as a timid, faint-hearted weakling, the coming generation will laugh at your cowardice. You have taken the name of Arjuna but you are not living up to that name!"

Ignorance Is the Cause of All Sorrow

What is the meaning of *arjuna*? It means sacredness and purity. For such a noble person as Arjuna to lay down his arms and resolve not to fight a battle in which righteousness was at stake could only be due to ignorance. The Lord, being fully aware of the nature of this disease, resolved to eradicate it.

At the very beginning of the *Gita*, Krishna could have taught the principle of devotion and the commitment to duty and selfless action. But Krishna chose not to do so. In fact, he started speaking only after listening for a long time to Arjuna's weeping and lamentations. While Arjuna was carrying on, Krishna did not interfere at all. He patiently waited while Arjuna verbalized his confused state. Finally Krishna asked, "Arjuna, are you done? Have you vented all your feelings?" It was only at this point that Krishna started teaching.

Just as students become empty after writing their examinations, Arjuna also became empty after airing all his concerns. Then Krishna told him, "This awful defect of weak-mindedness has sprouted in you. I know how to deal with it. I will cure it! It is ignorance which is responsible for this infatuation. This ignorance is causing your weak-mindedness." Then Krishna started instructing Arjuna in the highest wisdom, the knowledge which distinguishes the true self from the false self, the eternal from the ephemeral, the sentient from the insentient.

When a person is overcome with anguish and is suffering from ignorance, what should be done to free him from his delusion? He is like a patient who is in great danger. The first thing the doctor must do is to see to it that the patient gets out of danger. After that the doctor can undertake longer-term treatments. Suppose the patient is in immediate danger of losing his life, then any treatments the patient is given will prove to be useless unless he is first brought out of the emergency. Once he is out of danger, then many therapeutic procedures can be undertaken. For example, if a person is drowning in a river, you must first bring him out of the water, lie him down on the bank, and give him artificial respiration. Then you can start your other treatments to bring up his circulation and get him over the shock. You certainly would not start those treatments while he is in the water, drowning.

The Cure for Ignorance

Krishna, therefore, gave Arjuna a strong injection of courage to save him from drowning in sorrow and dejection. His immediate first-aid treatment was to teach Arjuna how to discriminate between the true self and the personal self. He said, "Arjuna, as long as you are overcome with fear and anxiety, you will not be able to accomplish anything. Be courageous! Know that you are the *atma*, not this body; then you will be fearless. I can help you to achieve great things, but only if you base your actions on true knowledge and remain fearless." At this point Krishna was smiling, but Arjuna was weeping.

The one who is always smiling is the Lord. The one who is weeping is man. Krishna is the true self, Arjuna is the false self. One is the embodiment of wisdom and the other is filled with ignorance. Krishna said, "I would like to explain some things to you which are very important. Right now we are behaving in different ways. I am smiling while you are crying. But we could both be alike; either I could become like you or you could become like me. If I should become like you, then I would become weak-minded. But that is impossible! Weakness can never enter into me! On the other hand, if you were to become like me, then you would have to follow me and do as I say." At this Arjuna replied, "Swami, I will do exactly as you say. I will follow all your commands implicitly!" Having given Arjuna sufficient encouragement and strength of purpose, Krishna enabled Arjuna to recover his strong resolve. From that point on, Arjuna undertook to fight, following the directions given by the Lord.

Krishna started his wisdom teachings with some important truths relating to the body and mind. He said, "Arjuna, you think that these people are your relatives and friends. But, what is meant by a relative or a friend? Does it refer to the body or does it refer to the indweller? Bodies are just water bubbles; they come and go. These relatives and friends which you are so attached to now, have all existed before, in any number of births. But were they your relatives and friends then? No. You too have existed countless times before, and I as well. The body, the mind and the intellect are all just so much apparel. They are like the clothes you wear; you change them now and again. They are mere instruments. Why develop a close relationship with these things, getting infatuated with them and then having to suffer so much sorrow and grief?

"Do your duty! All the honor that is due to you as a prince will be bestowed on you. But on the battlefield there cannot be room for any feeling of weak-mindedness and feeble-heartedness. Fighting boldly to preserve righteousness and shrinking in weakness are completely incompatible with each other. To have this timidity on the battlefield is not becoming of a great hero. Your cause is just and you have come to fight. Therefore, fight!" With words such as these, Krishna cured Arjuna of his despondency and helped him to find his strength and courage. When Krishna finished his teaching on the battlefield, Arjuna regained his noble ideals and faced the upcoming fight with renewed valor.

The War Between Selfishness and Selflessness

This particular field on which the war was about to be fought had historically been a sacred place, where sacrifices and other sacred and auspicious acts had been performed. At the same time, it was also the place where the dynasty that sprouted the hundred wicked brothers had engaged in its nefarious activities. Therefore, this field was both sacred and corrupted by evil. This field is symbolic of the human body.

When a body is born it is pure and unblemished; it is not a victim of any of the six enemies of man: desire, anger, greed, infatuation, pride and jealousy. A new-born baby is naturally joyful. Whoever may look at it, whether that person is a thief or a king, the baby is happy. It smiles and laughs at anyone who comes towards it, whether that person has come to kiss it or beat it. Since a small child is pure, its body can be described as the field of righteousness. As the body grows, it goes on collecting bad qualities, such as jealousy, hatred, attachment, greed, selfishness. As these evil traits accumulate, the body becomes impure. Therefore, the body can be considered both pure and impure. Good and bad are both encased in your heart.

The impure qualities are associated with *my-ness*, the possessive tendency. The inner significance of this battle between the forces of good and evil, with the five Pandava brothers and Krishna on one side, and the 100 wicked Kaurava brothers on the other side, is the inner war taking place in each individual, an all-out war between good and bad, between righteousness and immorality, between selflessness and selfishness.

The Kaurava brothers represent those people who consider things which do not belong to them as their own. They represent the possessive nature. They consider the body as their very self. If you observe people of the Kaurava mentality, that is, those having this possessive attitude, you will find that they all identify themselves with the body and the senses. The great war between the Pandavas and the Kauravas lasted only eighteen days, but the war between the forces of good and evil goes on throughout your life. It has no end. This battle is fought in the field of your own body. In this way, Krishna explained some of the deeper significance of the war to Arjuna.

Foresight & Compassion – Qualities Found In a Pure Heart

You might wonder why the *Gita* was taught to Arjuna. Among the Pandavas, some of the other brothers, such as the oldest one, Dharmaraja, who was the very pillar of virtue, might be considered better qualified spiritually than Arjuna. Why was the sacred *Gita* not taught to Dharmaraja who was known for his outstanding moral strength? Or if you were to consider physical prowess, then Bhima, who was the most powerful among the brothers, would surely have qualified for the teachings. Krishna could have given the *Gita* to Bhima, but he did not. Why not? Why did he give it only to Arjuna? You have to understand the inner significance of this.

Dharmaraja was the embodiment of righteousness, but he did not have foresight. He did not think about the future consequences of his actions. Only after events had already occurred, did he think about their consequences and feel sorry for what he had done. He had hindsight but not foresight. If you take Bhima, he, of course, had great physical strength, but he did not have much intelligence. He was able to uproot a tree, but he was lacking in discrimination. Arjuna, on the other hand, had foresight. For example, Arjuna told Krishna, "I would rather be dead than fight against these people. It will mean so much suffering later on, even if we win the war."

In contrast to Arjuna's anguish about all the suffering that would be brought on by this war, Dharmaraja was quite ready to get on with the battle, although later he felt deeply depressed about all the killing when the war was over. Years earlier, Dharmaraja had been pulled in to a royal game of dice, in which he lost everything, including his wealth, his kingdom, and even his wife. Afterwards, he was filled with great anguish and remorse. Whenever a person without discrimination and foresight is called upon to make a decision while in the midst of difficult circumstances, he invariably regrets his actions later on. This was also the nature of King Dasaratha, who was the father of Rama, the divine incarnation 5000 years earlier. King Dasaratha lacked foresight and discrimination.

Early in his reign, Dasaratha had to fight a war to defend and preserve righteousness. In this war he took his young queen, Kaikeyi, with him. Kaikeyi had been a princess in a warrior kingdom and had been well-schooled in the art of warfare. It was Kaikeyi, in fact, who taught Rama archery and some of the methods of waging war. When Dasaratha was fighting during the war, one of the wheels of his chariot started coming off. Kaikeyi used her finger to keep the wheel from separating itself from the axle. In so doing, she saved Dasaratha's life, as well as her own.

After having achieved victory, King Dasaratha noticed that her hand was bleeding profusely. Seeing her plight, he was so overwhelmed with infatuation and so pleased with her courage and sacrifice that he told her, "Kaikeyi, you can ask for two boons. Ask for anything that you wish, and I shall do all in my power to grant them to you!" He granted the boons in gratitude for her heroic act in saving their lives. But his infatuation with her blinded him to her weak-mindedness. He did not specify what kind of boons she should ask for nor when they should take effect. He blindly granted the promise of boons without thinking of any of the possible consequences.

Kaikeyi waited until the time when Dasaratha decided to hand over the kingdom to Rama. At that point, Kaikeyi asked for Rama to be banished to the forest, and for her son, Bharatha, to be put on the throne instead. Then Dasaratha felt desperately sorry for having granted the boons without any pre-conditions. But it was too late to retract them, and the resulting grief brought on his death.

We know that Krishna had a great deal of affection for Arjuna, but is that the reason he taught the *Gita* to Arjuna and not to one of the other brothers? No. Krishna looked at all the consequences, all the implications, and found Arjuna alone qualified to receive the *Gita* from him. Arjuna foresaw what was going to happen after the war, and therefore declared that he did not want to fight, because the consequences would be very bad. He was not feeling sorry after the war was over, but before. That attitude of feeling sorry before taking action, instead of afterwards, can only be found in a pure heart. Arjuna certainly had such a pure and sacred heart and that is why Krishna was so fond of him.

The Transformation From Kinsman or Friend to Disciple

In those days people lived much longer than they do today. At the time of the great war, Krishna and Arjuna were already quite advanced in years, by today's standards. For over 70 years, Krishna and Arjuna had been inseparably together. Although they were together for so many years, at no time during all those years did Krishna teach the *Gita* to Arjuna. Why was this so? During all those years Arjuna treated Krishna as his brother-in-law and his close friend. Krishna did not teach the *Gita* to Arjuna as long as Arjuna was living with body-consciousness.

The moment Arjuna surrendered and accepted discipleship, then Krishna became his teacher and Arjuna became Krishna's student. Only after this act of surrender on the part of Arjuna did Krishna teach him the *Gita*. This means that if you really want to acquire spiritual knowledge from another, you have to relate to that person as disciple to spiritual teacher, before the transfer of knowledge can flow freely.

In the ancient scriptures there is a similar story of a great teacher. At that time there was no greater teacher than he. But he sent his own son to another teacher to attain spiritual knowledge. The father himself would not teach his son. He took this step because he knew that as long as the son considered him the father, the boy would not relate to him fully as the teacher, and therefore, the boy would not have been properly instructed in the highest wisdom. This was also the situation with Krishna and Arjuna. As long as the relationship of brother-in-law existed between them, Arjuna could not receive knowledge from Krishna. But once this feeling of brothers-in-law left his heart and the feeling of being in the presence of the supreme divinity entered Arjuna's heart, then Arjuna was able to learn from Krishna.

After Arjuna had surrendered completely and developed the feeling that Krishna was divine, he said to Krishna:

You are my mother,

You are my father,

You are my nearest kin,

You are my dearest friend,

You are my wisdom,

You are my treasure,

You are my everything,

You are my Lord, my loving Lord.

It was then that Krishna accepted him as a disciple. At that point Krishna said, "You do my work. Do everything for me and I shall take care of you." The most important thing that Krishna did was to free Arjuna from the feeling of body-consciousness. So long as body-consciousness persists, regardless of what path you follow, whether it is the path of selfless service or the path of devotion or the path of inner inquiry, you will not be able to practice the required disciplines that will lead you to the goal. Body-consciousness and the attachments resulting from it will constantly pollute your heart. Without emptying the heart of its dross, it is not possible to fill it up with sacred feelings. If a tumbler is full of water, how can you fill it with milk? You first have to empty the water. Krishna said, "Arjuna, you are full of body-consciousness. First you must completely rid yourself of this. Only then will I be able to fill your heart with sacred thoughts."

Be Courageous, Be Fearless, Be Discriminating

Krishna's teachings were aimed at freeing Arjuna of his infatuations, and the grief and sorrow which resulted from them. The two most important steps in this process are surrender and elimination of body-consciousness. Once Arjuna's body-consciousness was gone, Krishna was ready to reveal to Arjuna the highest spiritual teaching, that of self-knowledge. With that, Krishna awakened Arjuna out of his sleep of ignorance. He said, "There are a number of reasons for your sorrow but the most fundamental one is your ignorance. You have been unaware of your true nature and therefore you have become overwhelmed with grief. But now you have cried out for God. You have cried out for righteousness. You have cried out for me. When you cry for me, I will take care of you and give you everything you need."

You all cry for so many different things, but do you cry out for God? Do you shed tears when there is a decline of righteousness? When you do, the Lord will establish himself in your heart, teach you his highest wisdom, and make you an instrument in his mission. For this, you must have courage and inner strength. Krishna told Arjuna, "You should never have any kind of weak-heartedness. It is only after you remove such weakness from your heart that the divine power will enter and reside in your heart. If you do not have courage, even sheep will frighten you, not to speak of evil-minded men. You must have the capacity to face all circumstances. If you run away in fear, even monkeys will attack you. But, if you have a stick and stand your ground, the monkeys will not come near you. Whatever the circumstance, face it squarely and do not show your back. Then will you be able to achieve what you set out to do."

The essence of this teaching is, "Be courageous! Be fearless!" Courage is the primary instrument for achieving any kind of success. You need to have more courage and more determination. But you should not have blind and foolish courage. Courage must be accompanied by discrimination; only then will success be assured.

Sixteenth Chapter

BANISH IGNORANCE
AND SORROW WILL LEAVE YOU FOREVER

To gain wisdom, you need to undertake the practice of inner inquiry. In this practice you dissociate yourself completely from your mind and your thoughts. It is identification with the mind and its impurities that causes bondage. In this connection, Krishna told Arjuna, "Timidity, grief, sorrow... all these weaknesses and fears that you are experiencing are associated with the mind. What is the reason for this sorry state you find yourself in? It is the impurities in your mind, Arjuna. You have identified yourself with this impure mind, and as a result you are suffering."

Embodiments of Love,

The first thing Krishna did when he started speaking was to diagnose Arjuna's malady. Arjuna was suffering from ignorance. He was ignorant of his own true nature and the true nature of everyone else. Because of this ignorance, Arjuna came under the spell of delusion and duality. He had fallen prey to the impurities in his mind. He felt the anxiety of separation. As a result he became despondent. He was overcome with grief and sorrow. The cure for this disease of ignorance is wisdom. Therefore, Krishna started his teachings by expounding on the path of wisdom .

Your True Nature Is Eternal Joy

Life may be thought of as a flow, where different energies, feelings or states of being come together and then separate again. These are moments of transition, when a particular ephemeral quality changes to its opposite, or when a particular time period changes to another. For example, the junction between night and day, between sleep and waking or between health and illness are times of transition. The coming together of happiness and sorrow is also such a time. At the very moment of transition, you are neither happy nor sad. At that time when you transition from one feeling to another, your mind is in equipoise and you are not bound by either emotion.

But you do not remain there for long. Soon you move into the opposite quality, you feel happiness or fall into sorrow, and you come under the sway of that feeling. Of course, you aspire only for happiness and not for sorrow, but to permanently achieve that you must transcend all these temporary feelings.

When you become aware of the transitions you realize that your unchanging truth is neither of the opposites which you cycle between in life. The path of wisdom reveals to you your essence which is eternal joy. Your true nature transcends all these temporary joys and sorrows. When you are identified with your eternal self, you are not be affected by the pairs of opposites. The path of wisdom teaches the way to eternal joy through the practice of detachment and discrimination. This practice must be based on unwavering love for the divinity, present everywhere.

The Body Is the Outer Garment That You, As Pure Spirit, Wear

In the *Gita*, you will find reference to the master of the sense organs, and to the one who has acquired control over his sense organs. Krishna was the master of the senses and Arjuna had gained control over the senses. But at the beginning, Arjuna was steeped in body-consciousness and was not in control at all. Arjuna began worrying after he started thinking about the future consequences of the forthcoming battle with his relatives and friends. He was deeply concerned with what might happen following the destruction of these people. In other words, Arjuna was thinking only in terms of body-consciousness. The body can be thought of as a vessel or a container or apparel which the individual soul puts on. Just as it is natural to throw away a dirty or a worn-out article of clothing and wear a new one, in the same way, you also give up this body and put on a new one. Krishna showed that death was very much like getting rid of an old piece of cloth.

When ordinary people hear that the body can be thought of as a dress that you put on and take off, they get some doubts. After eighty or ninety years when old age has had its effect, one can easily accept that the body has become like a worn-out cloth. Then one would agree that these old clothes should be left behind. But if a person dies during youth or manhood before old age has set in, it would amount to leaving new clothes behind. Suppose a body of twenty years is left behind, how can it be called an old worn-out cloth? That is obviously a new cloth. Krishna answered this doubt with an example.

Suppose you had gone on a pilgrimage one year and while there you had purchased a piece of cloth. You brought the cloth home and kept it in a closet. Then after five or ten years, while putting some clothes in storage, you came across this piece of cloth and remembered that you had bought it many years earlier. You took this cloth to a tailor and got a shirt made. One day while wearing this shirt, you bent over to sit down and the back of the shirt tore. You thought it was a new shirt, but how quickly it had become torn! Why did it last only for such a short time? It tore because the piece of cloth was old; the shirt was new but the cloth came from old stock. Wearing a body and spending only a little bit of time in it may appear on the surface as if you are discarding a new body. But actually it is of old stock. It has come to you from many past births.

Here is another example that will help you to understand this. There are two individuals, a young person and an old one. The young man who is 18 years old has been striking a stone repeatedly, giving it twenty powerful blows with a hammer, but it does not break. He sits down to rest. Then an elderly person comes along and with only two strokes of the hammer breaks the stone. What is the reason for this surprising result, where the stone did not break after 20 strokes given by the strong, young person, but was quickly broken by a feeble individual of 80 years of age who gave it only two strokes? The mistake in thinking is to count only the two strokes given by the old man, believing that the stone had given way after the impact of those two strokes. But in truth, it gave way after 22 strokes. After the 20 strokes given by the young man it was given an additional 2 strokes by the elderly person; then it broke.

This Body Is Only One of Many You Have Worn

Similarly, you may have done a number of spiritual practices and enjoyed a variety of spiritual experiences in a previous birth, after which you gave up your life. Now in this life, you resume your spiritual journey and even before you attain old age you may gain spiritual fulfillment. In thinking about this kind of thing you may be taking only the present life into account, considering only the efforts and consequences of the actions of this birth. But in the eyes of the Lord, all your past lives, all your past efforts and past consequences are considered. Krishna said, "Dear child, in the end, each body is destroyed by time. Know that you have existed in countless bodies and have gone through countless cycles of births and deaths for ages past, as far back as anyone can count."

The very meaning of the word for body in Sanskrit, is 'that which wears out'. It is born as a lump of flesh. During its growth it becomes a beautiful attractive body, but then ultimately it becomes old and loses its strength and attractiveness. The body is an inert, insentient thing. During a lifetime it undergoes a number of changes and then eventually gets worn-out. But now you may have a doubt. How can the body be called inert and insentient? It is talking, it is walking, it is living, it sees, it hears, it feels, it experiences pain, it is full of activities. This living body cannot be called inert. But, once you wind the mechanism of a watch, it also starts working and moving. From that moment on, the hands of the watch will be going around and the bell will be chiming every hour. But that is not sufficient reason to say that the watch is alive. Because of the power it got when you wound it, this watch functions properly. In the same way, because of the life energy given by God, your body talks and performs various functions. Without the divine principle animating it the body cannot function, just as the watch cannot function without being wound.

But now another question arises. A watch is working but it does not change its form and size, whereas a body will be growing. How can you account for this? If it is merely an inert thing how can it grow? Inert things do not grow. But if you sweep the floor and collect the dust and put it in a dustbin, even that heap will grow. When you go on feeding this body with all sorts of food, this body also grows. As the food heaps up inside, the body grows. A heap of dust may grow but you cannot say that it has life. Similarly, just because you find your body growing you cannot infer that it is alive. The body itself is just an inert thing. But it is full of consciousness, because its very basis is divinity. Always remember that basis. It is this divine consciousness that supports and activates the living principle in all beings.

Ignorance is Being Unaware of Your True Nature

When Krishna called Arjuna ignorant did it mean that Arjuna had no education? No, it did not mean that at all. Arjuna had mastered a great number of skills; he was well trained in the martial arts, in the art of administration and many other professional skills. But in the field of spirituality he had no knowledge. Here he exhibited real ignorance. People use their capacities and faculties to specialize in one particular field and develop a proficiency in it. Some people use their faculties for mastering music, others write poetry, others develop skills in painting and sculpture. Among scientists, one person will achieve excellence in the area of physics, another in the area of chemistry, another in mathematics, still another in biology. In that way they may have made extraordinary contributions, each in his own particular area. But they do not know much about other areas of knowledge.

The only one who has complete mastery and proficiency in all areas is God. That is why he has been described as omniscient. One who is omniscient is also omnipotent and all-pervading. Only God has these three qualities, omniscience, omnipotence and omnipresence. Knowing the past, present and future, and knowing that Arjuna was ready, Krishna undertook to teach Arjuna the great spiritual truths. He told Arjuna, "Recognize the ephemeral nature of the body and never forget its unchanging basis. With that divine basis as your focus, discharge your duties. To begin with you must get rid of all your attachments. You are overwhelmed by attachment to the body. This attachment is very dangerous. It will destroy all your powers of discrimination." There is a small story to illustrate this.

The Danger of Being Attached to The Body

Once upon a time Indra, the lord of the celestials, was cursed to be born as a pig on earth. Being born thus, he was spending all his time living a family life in dirty, muddy water. The sage Narada, while passing by and seeing this pig and its family, recognized Indra reduced to that lowly form. Narada, who loved Indra dearly, took great pity on him. Narada spoke to the pig, "Indra, look at what a state you have degenerated into. How did this happen? How could you, a great deity with unlimited power, the lord of all the heavenly regions, have come to this? But never mind, don't worry, I will get you out. I will use all my accumulated powers of penance to help you." He spoke to him very sympathetically, lamenting that one who should be enjoying all the luxuries of heaven had been put into such a miserable state. How very unfortunate Indra's life had become, Narada thought.

But, Indra, in the form of the pig, replied, "Narada, why are you coming in the way of my happiness? The joy that I am getting in this dirty water I will not be able to get anywhere else. The wonderful life that I am enjoying here with my wife and children in this mud hole I cannot even get in heaven. Why have you come here to meddle with my life and get in the way of my joy? Please go your way and leave me be." Indra, who was under the spell of the illusion of attachment, did not realize his pitiful condition. Narada had to summon Indra's own weapon, the celestial thunderbolt, to render that pig body asunder and free a much-relieved Indra from his prison of attachment and body-consciousness.

When you are under the spell of attachment you will be completely deluded. This delusion is due to the irresistible power of *maya*, which veils your truth and keeps it hidden from you. If you want to destroy this power of illusion, you must develop your knowledge of the true self. Therefore, Krishna took it upon himself to start out his teachings by instructing Arjuna in self-knowledge. It is only after you have the direct experience of your eternal self, that you can truly do your work and discharge your duties properly. Without this knowledge you will not understand even the mundane daily activities relating to the world.

Listening to spiritual teachings can help you only to a small extent. When you are listening to the *Gita* you feel so happy and so full of joy. It all seems so simple. But this elation you experience is just a temporary phenomenon. When you undertake to put the teachings into practice many real problems and difficulties arise. But you must persist in your efforts. The teachings will do you little good unless you put them into practice. Whatever you have heard and whatever you have read you must enter into and completely make your own. Then you will gain something truly worthwhile.

You Must Live the Teachings

A great sage, while on a pilgrimage, reached a village in the south of India. In the temple of this village a number of people had assembled. A learned teacher was expounding the teachings of the *Gita*. The teacher was reading the text, the disciples would repeat the verses and then the teacher would give the appropriate commentaries. One particular disciple was found sitting in a corner profusely shedding tears. All the other people were holding the *Gita* and were repeating the lines, listening to the teacher's words very attentively. Their facial expressions would constantly change as the text was being expounded. Sometimes they would be joyful, sometimes serious. But the disciple sitting in the corner was not having any experience like that. His facial expression did not change at all. He was only shedding tears.

The sage observed all this. He addressed the man and asked him, "Why are you crying? When the *Gita* is being expounded in such a joyous way, what is the reason for your sadness?" The man replied, "Master, I do not know who you are. I do not know Sanskrit. I cannot pronounce the verses. Since I do not know Sanskrit I do not want to repeat these verses in the wrong way because I may be committing a sin that way. Therefore, I was just picturing in my own heart Krishna giving this *Gita* to Arjuna there on the battlefield. Krishna was seated in the driver's seat, Arjuna was sitting behind him in the chariot. I was crying because I was imagining Krishna having to turn his head back for such a long time, trying to convince Arjuna of these great truths. Keeping his head turned like that must have given him a great deal of pain. If only Arjuna had been sitting in front and Krishna in the back, then it would not have caused so much trouble to the Lord. Thinking of that hurts me very much."

The sage recognized that here was a true devotee. The man was experiencing so much love for Krishna and had immersed himself so deeply in identifying with the Lord giving the *Gita* teachings to Arjuna, that he had become a part of Krishna, himself. The sage concluded that experiencing such feelings was far greater than merely listening to and repeating the *Gita* verses.

Even now, while the *Gita* is being expounded, some of you are writing everything down reverently in your notebooks while some of you are holding the *Gita* in your hands and following the verses, trying to learn them. But these are all just outer activities which will not evoke very deep feelings of devotion. If you want your heart to become completely saturated with the essence of the teachings, you must seek the inner experience. Do this by putting the verses into practice in your daily life. Even if you practice only one of them it will be more than enough. What is the use of taking down a hundred of them? If you fill your head with all the contents of the book, your head will be just another book. What counts is what you get imprinted on the book of your heart. Even if only one of these teachings is imprinted in your heart that will be all that is needed. Let your heart become saturated with love. That is enough. Instead of filling your head with scholarship and book knowledge it is far better to fill your heart with love.

Ignorance Must Be Completely Dispelled

Krishna said to Arjuna, "There is no meaning in your grieving and lamenting, basing all your feelings on these outer bodily attachments and relationships. Go inside; let your mind become introspective. Then you will be able to understand all the things that I am expounding. You are grieving for people for whom there is no need to grieve. You are making yourself miserable without reason. You should not suffer so. You are feeling all this sorrow because your heart is full of ignorance. Drive this ignorance completely out of your heart. It is only when there is not even the least vestige of ignorance left in your heart that you will be capable of understanding wisdom."

Ignorance is like fire. Suppose a fire is extinguished almost completely, except for just a few glowing embers. If a breeze comes up, sparks from these few coals may develop into a huge conflagration. Therefore, there should not even be a remnant of the fire left. Ignorance is also like sickness. Suppose your disease is almost cured but there is only a small vestige of it left. If, after coming home from the hospital, you give up the proper diet, it may quickly develop and spread again. There should be absolutely no remnant of disease left.

You can also compare ignorance to being in debt. Suppose you have discharged all your debts; there is only one small loan of a hundred dollars left. But if you let the interest accumulate, what will happen? The debt will start piling up again. Therefore, you should discharge your debts completely. In the same way, if there are any latent impressions of attachment and desire left in your heart, your sorrow is likely to flare up and grow. That is why Krishna admonished Arjuna, "If you retain even the smallest trace of attachment in your heart, whatever I teach you will become useless. You must completely destroy all your attachment which has been fed for so long by the ignorance that is beclouding your heart. To help you do this, I am teaching you the path of wisdom."

The wisdom teaching is an extremely important part of the *Gita*. Once you understand the difference between the true self, the divine *atma*, and the false self which is associated with worldly things, then all the other teachings will become very easy to understand. You have to spend a number of days in concentration, trying to understand from the very core of your heart the distinction between the real and the not-real, and then detach yourself from the not-real. That is the central teaching of the path of wisdom .

Each word of these teachings is a rare jewel. It is only when you completely understand the nature of the wisdom path that you will be able to understand the *Gita* in full and live a life free of grief and sorrow.

Seventeenth Chapter

MASTER YOUR SENSES AND THE WHOLE WORLD WILL BE YOURS

Whatever you seek, wherever you look... whether you look for it here on earth or in the heavens or in the nether world... all that you will ever find are the five elements, and only the five elements. In all the worlds there is nothing else. Whatever you have ever desired, whatever you have ever used, whatever you have ever lost, all these myriad of things are but varying expressions of the same five elements.

Embodiments of Love,

Everything in the universe, everything that has ever been created, everything that will ever be conceived of, is made up of the gross or subtle aspects of the five elements, namely, space, air, fire, water and earth. These countless variations of the five elements have been and are forever changing with time. They are all temporary, endlessly cycling from one name and form to another.

The Transitory Nature of All Things

The flower which has blossomed today will be dried up tomorrow and it will be decomposed a few days later. Food that has been cooked today will be spoiled tomorrow and becomes poisonous the following day. Once it has become spoiled you cannot get the fresh food back. The beautiful form of today will have turned ugly by tomorrow. Even atoms making up the matter in the moon may in time end up here on earth, and atoms making up matter here on earth may go to the moon. Every seven years all the atoms which constitute the human body undergo a total change. It would be foolish indeed for you to think that the body and the sense organs which are made up of the five elements are permanent, or that any object made up of these elements has any lasting value. Only the senses will be hankering after such external, transitory things.

The *Gita* has shown that this impermanent complex of five elements which we call the body, mind and senses, consists of 24 principles. It is made up of the five gross sense organs, the ears, the skin, the eyes, the tongue and the nose. These reach out to the sense objects through the subtle sense organs, comprising sound, touch, sight, taste and smell. These gross and subtle senses are inextricably related. Without the subtle the gross cannot not function. For example, you may have eyes but no sight, you may have ears but no hearing, you may have a tongue but no taste.

The 24 Impermanent Principles

In addition to the gross and subtle senses there are also the five life energies which vitalize all bodily functions. One of these is related to breathing, another to elimination, a third to circulation, the fourth to digestion and the fifth to the upward flow which energizes the higher centers. Besides the 15 principles enumerated above, there are the four faculties comprising the 'the inner instrument'. This inner instrument is made up of all the different aspects of what we know as 'mind'. It consists of the thinking faculty which analyzes and reacts; the intuitive faculty, also known as *buddhi*, which knows the deeper purpose of life and discriminates between the real and the unreal; the subjective individual expression or ego self which is associated with the personality; and the reservoir of feelings and memory wherein the effects of past actions are stored.

All of the foregoing are contained within the five sheaths. These sheaths can be thought of as various bodies interpenetrating one another in a successively more subtle way, each one finer than the previous one. The grossest sheath is the food sheath which comprises the physical body. It is made up of physical matter. Next, the first of the subtle, intangible sheaths, is the vital sheath . It relates to the life breath and physical energy. Then there is the mind sheath which relates to the lower mind. The fourth sheath is the intellectual sheath. It is associated with the higher mind wherein the *buddhi*, the intuitive, discriminating faculty, is contained. These last-mentioned three sheaths, the vital, the mind, and the intellectual, all make up the subtle body of man. Finally, there is the bliss sheath, the subtlest of all the bodies. It is known as the causal body. It is beyond all aspects of mind. It is the source of all mind stuff. Within it, only a thin veil of ignorance remains to hide the true self, which is pure bliss.

The Immortal Self Beyond the Ephemeral Individual

Together these 24 principles comprise the individual being. The wisdom teachings deal with these various principles. Their purpose is to help you realize the one transcendent principle which is beyond all these. That is the *atma*. It is the immortal self, the one reality that underlies all these bodily principles, but which is in no way affected by them. It is true and unchanging, whereas these 24 are just manifestations of ignorance, constantly undergoing change. Together these 24 principles constitute the illusion which makes you appear as a separate being. If you go on spending your life depending only on these changing qualities, how will you ever be able to attain the eternal bliss which is your true nature, and which is not in any way influenced by these transitory things?

The joys that you experience through your sense organs, that seem so delightful in the moment, are likely to give you sorrow later on. Such joys come and go; they are not permanent. Krishna strongly emphasized that you should not believe in these sense organs and be led astray by them. However educated you may be, whatever office you may hold, whatever position you may have, unless you gain control over your senses you will not be able to gain peace of mind. Inner peace can be obtained only by controlling the sense organs. Perhaps you think that controlling the sense organs is too difficult for you to undertake, but in the *Gita*, Krishna taught a number of different ways which can help you succeed in mastering them.

The Noble and the Ignoble

Krishna said in the *Gita* that there are two types of people, the noble ones and the ignoble ones. The noble ones are those who follow the right path, the sacred path. They seek the company of great people and practice their teachings. As a result, they experience the great spiritual truths and enjoy the inner life of the spirit. Opposed to them are those who are full of unsacred thoughts and have impure hearts, who are under the spell of ignorance and live an unrighteous life. Their evil behavior can be said to be the direct opposite of the exemplary behavior of the noble ones, just as darkness is the opposite of light. Therefore, we can describe these two categories as that of gods and demons, or beings of light and beings of darkness. Krishna said, "Arjuna, I thought up to now that you were noble, that you were a true knight, but I see that you are entering the wrong path. You are getting steeped in darkness. You are following unsacredness. It would be wrong to call you noble. You are proving yourself to be otherwise."

Krishna gave Arjuna various such admonishments in order to encourage him to make a heroic effort to manifest the qualities of true nobility. He told him, "The primary cause of your present grief is your attachment, and the basis for your attachment is ignorance. It is out of ignorance that you allow your senses to govern your actions. If you want to free yourself from attachment and sorrow then you must control your senses. You have to clearly understand the nature of the senses. In the journey of life these sense organs are important; they are like the horses of your chariot which can take you to your goal. But only when you have full control over these horses will the chariot and the person riding in it be safe. If you leave them uncontrolled it is inevitable that the chariot and its occupant will come to grief. Therefore, if you want to reach the goal safely you must take charge of these horses. In other words, you must assert absolute control over your sense organs."

The Nature of the Sense Organs

When Krishna spoke of the sense organs he mentioned that they have the capacity to measure. For example, the tongue determines the taste of foods, deciding whether a thing is sweet or bitter. It does this by measuring the relative sweetness and bitterness of the food. Similarly, the ears determine whether some music is melodious or not and the eyes discern the beauty of objects seen. In this way, all the senses measure different qualities. Krishna also spoke of certain limitations of the sense organs, as ordained by God to insure their right use. For example, you can use the nose for smelling and for breathing. If you use the nose correctly, you are obeying the commands of the Lord and will surely benefit thereby. If, instead of using the nose for breathing and smelling good things, you use the nose to inhale noxious drugs, then you are not using it in the way specified by God.

As for the tongue, you have the Lord's gentle reminder, "Child, use this tongue to talk sweetly and not to hurt others' hearts. Use words which give them joy." The other function of the tongue must also be attended to. Use your tongue to take in fresh, wholesome food which is full of vitamins and proteins. On the other hand, if you use your tongue and sense of taste for smoking cigarettes or drinking alcohol you will be misusing the tongue. Then you will be disobeying the commands of the Lord and you will come to harm. In this way, you should use all of the sense organs for the specific tasks which have been assigned to them by God. Then you will be fulfilling the purpose for which each instrument has been given. This kind of regulated behavior will help you to achieve your life's goal.

As a result of the functioning of the senses, you may experience joy or grief. This joy or grief that you feel does not come from the senses themselves. It is only after the senses have come into contact with the sense objects that you will experience these feelings. For instance, suppose you are on a protracted visit to a friend in a neighboring town, and while you are away something happened in your home. No matter what happened, whether good or bad, you would experience neither happiness nor grief, joy nor sorrow, as long as your ears had not heard the news. But once you get a phone call and came to know what happened at home, if the news is good you would feel joy and if the news is bad you would feel sorrow. It is only after the senses became associated with the sense objects that the joy or grief would have come to you.

Those Bound by the Senses Are Destroyed by the Senses

There are a vast number of sense objects in the world, but you should see to it that your senses do not come into contact with too many of these. They are all impermanent things. By becoming captivated with small things your whole life becomes small and impure. You can see this in a number of living beings which are victims of one or two senses. For example, when a deer hears some melodious music, it becomes fascinated by it and can easily be captured. Therefore, a deer is bound by sound. A huge elephant can be controlled through the sense of touch and therefore becomes bound by touch. In this way a number of animals can be bound and controlled through different sense organs. Take for example a moth. When it sees light it gets strongly attracted to it; it becomes bound by the light and may be destroyed by it. In a similar way, a fish will swallow the bait and gets caught because it is bound by taste. And a bee will enter a flower and be bound by the power of smell; there it can get trapped for the night when the flower closes its petals.

Each one of these beings is bound by one of the sense organs; but man is bound by all five of them and, therefore, he is even more vulnerable than all these animals. Here is a small story:

Once upon a time a great sage undertook a tour of the country. He considered each one of the five elements as his teacher. Once he happened to go to the shore of the ocean; he was enjoying the waves and the various aspects of the ocean. As he was watching, along came a wave and brought some debris to the shore. He noticed that the moment any dross fell into the ocean the waves came and pushed it back out. The sage thought to himself, 'Why should the ocean which is so deep and vast find it necessary to throw out this little bit of filth? Could it not allow even such a small impurity to remain with it?' Then he went into meditation. In that meditation he understood that if the ocean were to allow any impurities to stay in its waters, these impurities would accumulate day by day and, in time, cover the whole ocean and pollute it. He decided that the ocean must have resolved not to allow any debris or impurity to come into it from the very beginning; in that way it had been able to remain clean and pure.

In the same way, right from the start, you should see to it that impure thoughts and ideas do not enter your mind, even in a small way. Not even the minutest impurity should be allowed to enter your heart. Before such an impurity can establish a foothold, you must immediately throw it out. If you give room to it, thinking that after all it is only a very insignificant thing and it cannot really harm you, then it will start growing in the heart. Therefore, if you understand the functioning of the senses and learn to limit them to the right use for which they were intended, then you will be able to benefit from them and not be disturbed by them. If instead, you allow the senses to rule you and bind you, neither joy nor peace of mind will be yours. Here is another small story to illustrate this.

The King Who Was Ruled by His Five Wives

Once there was a great king who had five wives. But his wives never listened to him. He might have been a king to everyone else, but he was not lord over his own wives. And so he was suffering very much. He had a crown on his head, but inside his head there were only worries. 'I have become a slave of these wives and I am suffering very much,' he thought. 'Is there anyone in the world who is not afraid of his wife? If there is such a one, how does he control her? How does he manage not to be dominated by her?' To inquire into this directly by asking individual citizens would not have been considered proper, so he decided to hold a public meeting and invite all his male subjects to attend. There were two stadium-sized tents put up at the meeting-ground. One was erected on one side of the field, the other was put up on the other side.

The king announced that the first tent was meant for people who had controlled their wives, and the second one was meant for people who were controlled by their wives. All the male citizens of that country started pouring into the capital; they all went straight into the second tent. The king went there and found that this huge tent, the one that was intended for those who were controlled by their wives, was filled to capacity. He got a little courage from this for he realized that he was not the only one controlled by his wives. But before beginning the meeting he saw one lone person waiting in the first tent which was meant for those who had control over their wives. That mammoth tent was totally empty except for this one man. The king was overjoyed to see him there. He went to him and told him how glad he was to see that at least one person in his kingdom had gained control over his wife.

The king questioned him, "Tell me, good man, what is your secret in controlling your wife?" The man, trembling with fear, replied, "No sir! No sir! That is not how it is. I cannot control her. It is I who am being completely controlled by her." The king said, "Then why did you come into this tent?!!" With his knees shaking and stammering his words, the man replied, "My wife ordered me to come into this tent. She forbid me to go into the other. That is why I am here. My wife ordered me not to go inside the tent where the slaves of their wives are staying. She made me go into this one." The king got very irritated with the man and commanded him, "You must leave here immediately! Under no condition can you remain in this tent! Go and join the others in the second tent!" The citizen turned white with fear; the blood rushed out of his face. He got down on his knees and implored the king with his hands folded in supplication, "My lord, please listen to me! You may punish me. You may do anything you wish to me. But I am terrified of disobeying my wife. Please! Don't make me go to the other tent!" The king then realized that there were no people anywhere in his kingdom who were not slaves of their wives.

The Mind With Its Five Wives, the Senses

This king is the mind, and he is never able to satisfy all his wives, namely, the senses. The eye demands, "Take me to a place where only the most beautiful sights are to be seen." The tongue demands that only the tastiest of foods be supplied to it. The ear commands that the most melodious sounds be played for it. The skin desires to feel only materials which are the most pleasing to touch. And the nose wants to smell the very best perfumes in the world. Who can satisfy all these desires of the senses? There is no coordination and cooperation among them. If you yield to the sense organs, they are going to give you a lot of trouble. Right from the beginning you must find a way to bring them under absolute control. Then you will have accomplished something truly worthwhile. The real hero in this world is the one who has managed to completely control his senses.

When the senses make their demands do not listen to them. Instead, turn your mind towards the higher intellect. Let it decide what is to be done. Then, the lower mind will follow and, in turn, give its commands to the senses. This way, the senses will have to obey. That is the proper way to curb the senses. A person who bases his life on his lower mind and senses will come to ruin and become worse than an animal. The wise one bases his life on his higher mind, which is his intellect, his power of discrimination and discernment and intuition. One who follows his higher mind becomes the most excellent of human beings. If you base your life on your higher mind, your *buddhi*, it will take you straight to the final goal. But if you base your life only on the lower mind and the senses, then every moment new changes will come about. It will become difficult to predict what will happen to you and where you will land. It is something like crossing a raging river or a storm-tossed ocean in a small boat. You do not know when your little boat will get flooded and when disaster will overtake you.

Being Ever Vigilant in Controlling the Senses

There was a great saint in ancient India. He was an extremely virtuous person; a truly wise man. He had complete control over his senses. One day it became known that his end would come soon. All his disciples assembled there and gathered around his bed. He was suffering from intense pain in the throat. He made heroic efforts to transcend the pain. He seemed to want to say something, but he could not speak. The disciples were very eager to find out what message their master was trying to give them during his last moments on earth. The disciples tried to help him in every way and implored him, "Swami you want to tell us something. We are eager to hear your message."

Summoning his last bit of energy, the sage found his voice and said, "My dear children, I have been followed all this time by *maya*, the power of illusion. Illusion told me, 'Everyone else has become my slave, no one has succeeded in becoming free of me, except you. You have been able to completely control your sense organs and, thereby, you have been able to conquer me.' Then I replied, '*Maya*, I may have conquered you up to now, but you know and I know that I have not fully conquered you yet. There is still a little life left, and a few breaths are still to come. Until my very last breath has been taken, I will not relax until I have conquered you totally.' My dear children, until now I have been able to control the senses and conquer *maya*, but I do not know whether I will continue to succeed until my last breath. During these last few moments, in order to free myself from *maya*, I have been thinking only of God and praying to him with all my heart." Then he fell silent, and thus he consummated his life.

As this story shows, you must be careful until the very last breath of your life not to yield to the sense organs. To realize the immortal self you must control the outgoing senses. Therefore, sense-control is an integral part of the path of wisdom, as taught by Krishna. Once you gain full control of the senses, you will easily be able to master the spiritual path.

In the beginning you may be subjected to a certain amount of difficulty. When you learn to drive, you first have to go to an open field and practice there. It is only after you have learned to control the car and have mastered the art of driving that you can take the car onto the main thoroughfares and the narrow streets of the city. If you try driving in city traffic before that, it will not only be difficult for you but also dangerous. Similarly, once you have mastered the senses and are unaffected by the allurements of the world, then you can face any situation without concern or problems.

Victory Over the Senses Through Self-Inquiry

To master the senses you should develop a broad view. Enter into the spirit of inquiry and find out who is the true self and who is the false self. After developing this discriminating power you can safely move in the world while continuing to keep your sight steadily on the goal.

The wavering senses can never give you permanent joy. Only when you gain the knowledge of the true self, the immortal self, will you experience true joy. All other knowledge and education will only help you to eke out a livelihood. Knowledge of the self alone is true education. With that you will be able to enjoy the unity of all existence. Once you identify yourselves with the divinity that is in everything then there can be no further clashes arising from any sense of difference. When you experience everything as God and see the whole world as God, then even the practice of discrimination falls away. Once everything is seen as one then there is no further need for discrimination.

As Baba has mentioned before, the senses can be very dangerous; they can be like horses running wild. If you do not use the reins to control them, they will run away with the chariot and go wherever they like. Rein the senses in with the help of your mind. Let your taste, your smell, your sight, your listening, your touch, all the various sense impressions come under your control. A number of times Swami has been telling you that you should not see or hear too many things. It is only when you see a thing or hear about it that you start thinking of it. Once you think of it you develop an attraction towards it. Then you want to possess it. Once you talk about a particular thing then you think of its form. Therefore, whatever may be the object, the first thing you should ask yourself is, 'Does it have any defects or flaws?' When you realize its flaws, that it will not last, that it is ephemeral, then you will not develop any attachment for it. If you want to reach God, you must be free of false vision, false speech and a false attachment to any sensory impressions.

Control of the Tongue, the First Step in Sense-Control

Spiritual practice begins with control of the tongue. The reason for this is that the tongue has two functions. The eyes have only the one function, that of seeing. Similarly, the ears have only the one function, that of hearing. And the nose has only the one function, that of smelling. But the tongue has two functions; it can speak and it can taste. Therefore you must make a special effort to control it. You have no right to criticize others. You have no right to think badly about others. It is far better for you to think of your own shortcomings. See the good in others and remove the unreal in yourself. If you have not even developed the power to inquire into your own true self, then how can you assume the power to look into others? First get fulfillment in your own life. It is only after you have saved yourself that you can become an instrument to save others. Therefore, you should not use harmful words or give condescending looks or think impure thoughts towards any other person. Spend your time only in good thoughts, in good listening and in good talk.

In order to exercise self control you have to do some spiritual exercises. Constant practice and detachment are essential for gaining control over your senses. If you understand that all things are impermanent, you will be able to gain control over your senses and develop detachment. Your true nature is nobility. You are not base and ignoble. Enter into good paths and develop your own innate sacredness. Only when you have the light of wisdom shining inextinguishably within you, will you be able to help others through your good thoughts, good sight and good counsel. Those who do so are veritably gods. Those who display the opposite traits are demons. Demons seek only darkness. But you must resolve to give up darkness and fill yourself with light. If you choose the path of light, then whatever has been your past, the Lord will accept you and shower his grace upon you.

The Pure Brother of the Impure Demon King

The brother of the lord of the demons surrendered to Rama and fell at Rama's feet. Seeing him, the generalissimo of Rama's army warned Rama, "He is the brother of Ravana. Like his evil brother he is a demon. He loves darkness. Just because he has had some quarrel with his brother and left him, you should not trust him and give him shelter. Even though he now proclaims himself to be an enemy of his brother, it is still dangerous to believe him." Rama smiled patiently and told his commander, "Brave warrior, I accept him not because he has opposed his brother, but because he has surrendered himself to me. I will give protection to whoever comes to me and says, 'I am yours'. I do not care who he is."

The commander then said to Rama, "You have given this demon your protection, and assured him that when this war is over and his brother, Ravana, is overthrown, you will make him the king of Lanka. But suppose this evil Ravana came to you now and surrendered himself at your feet. What kingdom would you give him?" Rama replied, "If Ravana had such fine ideas and were to surrender himself to me, I would ask my own brother Bharatha, who is ruling the kingdom in my behalf, to step down. And I would make Ravana the king of my capital city of Ayodhya. I have never asked anyone for anything; asking for favors is not my way. But if Ravana were to have such good thoughts, I would ask Bharatha to give up his throne."

Throughout the ages, divine incarnations have been espousing sacred thoughts and broad ideas such as this. In that way, they set an example for the whole world to follow. The point of this story is that whatever your past, whatever impure and unsacred environment you may have been brought up in, if your resolve is pure and you surrender yourself fully to God, he will take you in. Start by mastering your senses. This is the first step in leading a noble life and getting closer to your divine source. Sense-control is the basis for all sacred action and for enjoying a worry-free life.

Krishna said, "Arjuna, there is nothing that you will not be able to achieve once you have gained complete control of your senses. You will be master of the world. But, if you are a slave of the senses and get caught up in desire, you become a slave of the world. Therefore, master your senses. Make the senses your slaves. Only then will you be able to function as an instrument in my mission. Arise, Arjuna! Learn to control your senses! Do not get elated by joy or dejected by grief. The primary reason for this grief of yours is ignorance. You do not know the difference between truth and illusion, between reality and appearance, between the true self and the false self. Begin now to discriminate between them. Practice discrimination and your senses will come under control. Then all will be yours."

Eighteenth Chapter

YOU ARE THE INDWELLER –
YOU ARE NOT THE BODY OR MIND

*K*rishna said, *"Arjuna, I am your very self. Focus your
mind steadily on me, and with your mind fixed on me
do your duty."*

Embodiments of Love,

If you do your work, being aware of your own reality, you will accomplish great things. Actions performed with the awareness of
the *atma*, your true self, are free from bondage. To carry on your
work while at the same time, being fully aware of your identity
with the *atma*, requires perfect control over the senses. Sense-control is an essential precondition for being illumined. Once you enjoy
complete control over your sense organs you can be described as a
person imbued with the highest wisdom.

When you consider all the pairs of opposites, such as joy and sorrow, heat and cold, profit and loss, honor and dishonor, with an
equal mind, and are established in your true reality, then you have
gained the characteristics of a wise man. It is the nature of the wise
to treat everything equally. Once you recognize the nature of the
senses, it will be easy for you to follow the path that leads to true
wisdom. But if instead of identifying yourself with the *atma*, you
continue to identify yourself only with your body-mind complex,
then it will be impossible for you to obtain that exalted state.

You Are The *Atma*, You Are God

Krishna told Arjuna, "Always remember that you are the indweller, not the body. You are the one who wears the cloth; you are
not the cloth itself. You are the resident of the house; you are not
the house. You are the witness, the knower of the individual, you
are not the individual. But now, Arjuna, you are mistaking yourself
to be this limited individual. Enjoyment of impermanent things can
only give you impermanent happiness. Eventually, all these momentary pleasures and enjoyments will only turn into sorrow. Keep
your mind steady and discharge your duties, remembering the *atma*.

Do not think or worry about birth and death, or the joy and sorrow which accrue to you. Birth and death are relevant only to the body. They do not refer to you. You are not the body. You are the permanent entity which is free from birth and death. You have neither a beginning nor an end. You were never born and you will never die. Nor will you ever kill anyone. You are the *atma*. You are all-pervasive. Verily, you are God. Your very self is God and God is your self."

After realizing that it is in the nature of fire to produce heat, would anyone grieve over the fact that fire burns? Would anyone suffer from sorrow after learning that ice cools? The very nature of fire is to burn and the very nature of ice is to cool whatever it comes in contact with. In the same way, everything which is born will some day die. This is natural. Whatever is free to come must also be free to go. Therefore, you should not brood over things which are natural, like birth and death, joy and sorrow. Recognize the inherent defects and weaknesses of all things. One day or another, everything existing in the world will have to undergo change. The same five elements which are to be found everywhere in the world are also to be found in you and in everyone else.

Whatever things you desire, whatever things you are seeking, even if you pursue your search for them into the farthest corners of the world, you will discover that you are really just seeking the five elements. These five elements are all you will ever find in any of the things of the world. But since they are already part of you, what is the point of seeking them in the things outside? It is natural for you to seek and aspire for something which you do not have. It is unnatural for you to seek and aspire for something which you already have. There is only one entity which transcends the five elements. That is the divinity. That is what you should aspire for.

Keep the *Atma* in View and Nothing Can Harm You

Wisdom is seeing the one everywhere. That all-pervasive unity is the *atma*. Seek out this unity and keep it constantly in view. When all your actions are based on the *atma*, they become sacred and pure. When all your activities are performed for the sake of the *atma* or for the pleasure of God, then you become sanctified and filled with spiritual wisdom. A number of sages, right from ancient days, have made heroic efforts to attain this supreme state of being immersed in the highest wisdom.

Once upon a time, the King of Greece, Alexander, reached the banks of the great river on the north-western border of India. He intended to enter India, to conquer and plunder it. For this purpose he had come with a mighty army. In those days there were no royal roads; the few roads that existed were more like footpaths. The king crossed the banks of the river and entered the forest with his army. The scouts preceding the army found a *yogi* lying under a tree, with his legs spread out across the path, deep in sleep. This *yogi* had attained the stage of enlightenment; he was a truly wise man.

One soldier went up and awakened the *yogi* and commanded him to move out of the path. But the *yogi* was totally indifferent to the orders given by the soldier. He did not move. The Greek soldier started threatening the *yogi* and boasted that the great emperor of Greece, Alexander, was coming with his army and that this emperor had decided to invade India and plunder the entire nation.

While the soldier was shouting at this *yogi*, Alexander arrived on the scene. The Greek soldier was enraged to see that even after the emperor had come, this *yogi* remained completely unconcerned. The *yogi* was not paying the proper respect and courtesy due to the emperor. At this, the soldier threatened to cut off the *yogi's* head. The moment the *yogi* heard that the enraged Greek soldier wanted to cut off his head, he started laughing and stood up. On the *yogi's* face there was no trace of fear. He was amused, but at the same time he remained completely serene. The emperor saw the great effulgence on the *yogi's* face and spoke to him. "My soldier has just threatened to cut off your head and yet you seem very happy and unaffected. If you were an ordinary person you would immediately fall at his feet, beg for pardon and try to save your life. But you are only smiling. What is the meaning of your behavior?"

The *yogi* replied, "I am the eternal truth. I am pure awareness. I am infinite bliss. I am forever free. Your weapons cannot harm me. Fire cannot burn me. Water cannot wet me. Wind cannot blow me away. I was never born and I will never die. I am the immortal *atma*, the one true self. I am indestructible. Thinking that I am just this body, your soldier is threatening to destroy me by cutting the head off this body. Isn't that ludicrous? Hearing this provoked me to laughter."

When the emperor heard these words he was astounded. He thought to himself, 'It is natural for people to get frightened when someone threatens to kill them and they are about to face death, but rarely will anyone laugh and be so happy when they are about to die. In India there are people who have attained such a high spiritual state that they are not even afraid of death. How can I conquer a nation such as this? No, I won't succeed here with my weapons.' Having concluded that India could not be subdued by him, he turned his army around and penetrated no further into India.

Sense-Control Is Easy When You Understand the Senses

From times immemorial, great beings such as this *yogi* have existed in India, and, in the way in which they conducted their lives, taught other nations the highest truths about spirituality. They showed the spiritual heights that could be achieved through control of the senses. People who do not know the method of controlling the sense organs get lost and stray onto the wrong path. But, actually, controlling the senses is quite easy. When you do not understand the fickle nature of the senses, all attempts to control them are fraught with difficulty. But once you understand their limitations controlling them becomes easy, because you realize that all the pleasures and enjoyments you gain through them are filled with sorrow.

The first step in controlling the senses is to investigate the defects and problems associated with the various objects of the world. For the sake of temporary joys and pleasures you are subjecting yourself to many difficulties and problems that will hound you long after the little fleeting joys are forgotten. A person who has a disease may take some food items which are not prescribed in the diet and feel temporarily happy. Having ignored the diet and taken food which is prohibited, he may experience some temporary joy; but in a short period of time he will experience the unhappy consequences of his acts. It may even lead to a dangerous situation. In the same way, man, yielding to temporary joys, will suffer a great many problems in the long run.

How many powerful kings have there been who have created huge mansions and palaces, enjoyed luxurious comforts, eaten a variety of luxurious foods, traveled in luxurious cars and indulged themselves in countless vanities, all the while thinking that they were enjoying all the great pleasures available on the earth? What has happened to them in the end? Ask yourself, 'Is a king who indulges himself like that really enjoying the luxuries or are the luxuries enjoying him?' You will have to conclude that it is the luxuries which are enjoying him. It is he who is being enjoyed by the sense objects. They are literally eating him up. Soon he becomes weak, he becomes diseased and gets old.

If the king were really enjoying the sense objects, then he should have attained unbounded health and strength from them. But, as he is the one who is being enjoyed by the sense objects, he loses all his health, and his life span gets reduced. Not recognizing this truth he temporarily experiences some happiness. He fixes his vision on these transient sense objects without realizing the dire consequences which ultimately must come his way because of his indiscriminate desire to enjoy the senses.

Realize the Transitoriness of All Sense Objects

A certain man went to a palmist who told people's future by reading the lines on their hand. The man showed the palmist his hand. The palmist told the man that there was a line on his hand which signified that he would become very wealthy. The moment the man heard this he was overjoyed. After looking at his hand some more, the palmist told him that the line also showed that he would get a lot of honors. The man felt even more happy.

Then, after examining the hand still further, the palmist said, "You are going to occupy a very high position." The man felt so happy, it was as if he had just been told that he would become prime minister that very day. After a while, the palmist told him that he was going to have many children. Joy was now heaped on joy. Then after telling him all these things, the palmist said, "But your life span is going to be very short!" The moment the man heard this, all his joy left him; he got totally dejected and shrank down in despair.

Whatever may be your property and wealth, whatever position you may occupy, whatever honors you may get and however many children you may have, if you only have a finite life span, then what will be the use of all these things in the long run? If you are not going to be alive then how can any of these things be of lasting value to you? How many kings and how many emperors have lived? In what circumstances have they left this world?

In the history of India, there once was an emperor who ruled over all the hundreds of kingdoms comprising this huge land. He was most powerful, but did he not have to leave this world? In ancient times, there was an even mightier emperor who ruled over the entire world; could he take even a handful of earth with him? King Rama built a magnificent bridge spanning the ocean from India to Lanka; where is that great bridge now? So many kings have come and gone. Not even one person can carry a handful of dust with him. If you think and reflect over the past history of mankind, you will be able to understand how impermanent this world really is. Therefore, two important defects to be noted about the worldly pleasures: They are impermanent and they are harbingers of misery.

All that you see in the external world is but a reflection of what is inside you. There is only one thing which is real and true and all-pervasive. That reality, that truth, is always within you. It is eternally true, it is eternally auspicious and eternally beautiful. Make every effort to realize that permanent truth. Live in that auspiciousness. Be one with that divinity. It is the very embodiment of all beauty.

Focus on the Divinity, Your True Self, and Do Your Duty

After explaining the qualities of a wise man to Arjuna, Krishna directed him to enter the battlefield and fight. Krishna told him, "Keep all your attention on me. Concentrate on me alone. Obey all my commands and do your duty. This body has been given to you for the purpose of discharging your duty. It is because of your actions in the past that you have gotten this birth. Now, you must use your actions to sanctify this life."

The only light in this world which does not get extinguished is the light of the atma, the light of the immortal self. As long as there is electricity, the electric bulbs will burn. The moment the power goes off, the bulbs do not shine. Only as long as there are batteries in the flashlight, the flashlight will function. In the same way, when the senses are not receiving any power, they will cease to function. Even the sun and the moon, which do not need either oil, batteries or electricity, will lose their effulgence in the end.

When the sun and the moon are likely to lose their light, what about you? When this is true of these mighty mountains, then what about this small pebble that is you, deluded as you are, with body-consciousness? Krishna told Arjuna, "Because of the grief arising from your attachment to relatives and friends, you are getting drowned in ignorance. You are being washed away by the tears from your own eyes. Arise! Awake! Do not stop until the goal is reached!" Thus Krishna rescued Arjuna and put him on the right path.

Intellect Surpasses All Your Senses

The sun and moon shine in the world but they cannot illuminate God. The light shining inside the house can illuminate the objects inside but it cannot illuminate God. How do you know that the sun and the moon shine and that fire burns? On what basis can you declare that these things are bright and luminous? It is because of your eyes that you can recognize their brightness. If you did not have eyes the radiant light of the sun and moon would not be seen by you. But as for these eyes, what is it that helps them to see? Even when you are sleeping or when your eyes are closed there is an unmistakable radiance shining in your awareness. It is your highest intellect, your intuitive faculty, your *buddhi*. Therefore, you can conclude that even more effulgent than your eyes is your intellect. There is a small story to illustrate this.

There were two friends, a blind man and a lame man. They would go begging together from village to village. The blind one had good legs and the lame one had good eyes. The lame man sat on the shoulders of the blind man. So, with the help of each other they were able to go from village to village. Once, on their way, they came across a beautiful field of melons. The lame man said to the blind man, "Brother, there are some very fine-looking melons in this field. Let us go into the field and eat some; afterwards we can take a little rest and proceed on our way."

The blind person said to the lame person, "Brother, be careful. There may be some watchman keeping an eye on the field." The lame man said, "No, there is no one there." The blind man went on, "Please tell me if there is a fence or a gate around this garden." The lame one said, "There is neither a gate nor a fence. We can go and have our dinner." The blind person immediately said, "Brother, these melons must be very bitter and inedible, otherwise why is there no watchman, no fence and no gate to protect them?"

A person may not have eyes to see, but if he uses his intellect he is greater than the one who sees with his eyes. Therefore, it is really the intellect which lends a shining quality to the eyes. But from where does the intellect get its power? The intellect is shining because of the *atma*. Therefore, because of the *atma* the intellect is illuminated, and because of the intellect the eyes shine and can see, and because the eyes see, the effulgence of the sun and the moon can be perceived, and because of the sun and the moon the whole world shines. We see that the ultimate source that illuminates everything is the *atma*. Therefore, it is the *atma* which you should worship.

A Wise Man Never Forgets the *Atma*

It is only when you keep the *atma* constantly in view, in everything you do, that you will be able to reach the stage of true wisdom. A wise man is sometimes thought of as having something to do with worldly people. This confusion comes about because it has been said that, 'When everyone is awake, the wise man is asleep, and when he is awake all the other people are sleeping.' According to such a definition, you would conclude that those who work night-shifts, such as the night watchman and the station master, who are awake at night when others are sleeping and asleep during the day when others are awake, are all wise men. But, obviously, this is not the correct meaning of the word.

All those people who base their lives on this impermanent world, will be fully awake to this world and its objects. The wise man on the other hand, will be asleep and indifferent to worldly objects. Ordinary people will not be alive to the beauty of the *atma*; they will be sleeping through that. But when it comes to this world and its sense objects they will be fully alert and awake. Therefore, a wise man is one who is asleep to the principle of the world and who is fully awake to the principle of the *atma*. A wise man is not one who has renounced the world and gone to the forest. Krishna said, "Do your work in the world. Live in the midst of the things which are necessary for your daily life. But keep your attention and concentration constantly on the *atma*. That way you will gain abiding wisdom. "

Here, a doubt may arise. Why does such a wise person need to work at all? He will have no interest in work nor have any ambitions regarding work. And yet for the good of mankind he will take up work. If a wise man had the attitude that he did not need to work, then he would not be able to inspire others to work. The sage has to set an example for ordinary people so that they will be able to follow him. "Therefore, Arjuna," said Krishna, "Become an ideal human being. You are very close to Krishna. You are his relative and you are very dear to him. Keep the inner significance of all these teachings in your heart. I want to raise you as an example to the world. I will use you as my instrument. You will be my instrument in doing many great things in the world."

Whatever Krishna has said is for the welfare of the entire world and for setting an ideal example for mankind. All *avatars* undertake activities which are absolutely sacred, but ordinary people will not be able to recognize these activities as divine activities. In this context, Krishna told Arjuna, "Arjuna, I have not accepted the job of being the driver of your chariot because I like this task and want it so much. It is not for the sake of my love of horses either that I'm doing this. Don't you think that I have chariots and horses of my own? Do I need to drive your chariot and your horses? This body-consciousness that you have saturates your whole being. It is in your blood. I am enacting the entire play and I have taken on this task of driving your chariot in order to see to it that you become permanently cured of this disease of body-consciousness."

God Does Not Wish to be Praised by Anyone

Arjuna frequently addressed Krishna using an affectionate phrase that referred to Krishna as his closest and dearest relative, the light of his heart. Krishna once told Arjuna when they were sitting on the banks of a sacred river, "Arjuna, I do not like to be revered by you as your dearest relative, without reason."

In the world many people will freely praise God, using terms of great respect or familiarity, but God will not accept such adulation. Praises will be very common for people to utter in order to gain favor. It is as if they were going to some government officer to get into his good graces. But, praise which has no real basis, is like perfumed water. It can be smelled but it cannot be taken as nourishment. You will hear all manner of flattery but it will not touch your heart. God accepts only true feelings that come sincerely from the depths of your heart.

Krishna said to Arjuna, "I don't want to ask you to give up calling me your closest relative, and yet you are saying it out of praise rather than because it is really true. Therefore, I want to become your relative so that you can say it sincerely, knowing in your heart that it is true." Shortly afterwards, Krishna offered his sister in marriage to Arjuna and became Arjuna's brother-in-law.

Krishna's brother Balarama did not approve of this marriage, and would not even come to the wedding. Instead, he went off to a forest. From that time on, Balarama did not feel much love for Krishna. But, for the sake of harmonizing thought, word and deed, Krishna was willing to risk his relation to his own closest kin, his older brother, who as a divine being had taken birth for the express purpose of assisting Krishna in his mission.

This trait that we see here in Krishna, of putting principles before considerations of kinship, is truly extraordinary. His actions were always commensurate with his words. Unity of thought, word and deed is the very nature of divinity. It is also the true nature of man. Whatever you think must be in harmony with what you say, and whatever you say, that you must do. This harmony of thought, word and deed is the deeper meaning of Swami's often repeated statement, 'The proper study of mankind is man.'

Krishna told Arjuna, "I want to make an example of you to the whole world, that is why I am teaching you here on the battlefield the qualities of an enlightened being. First, I will turn you into a wise man and then, through your example, I will teach others. To begin with, you must understand this most important principle, which is that you are not the body; you are the indweller. When you understand that, you will no longer be bothered by body-consciousness.

The body is temporary. God is eternal and permanent. You are not the cloth but the one who wears the cloth. The body is the temple of God, but the indweller is God himself. This world is impermanent and full of sorrow. There is no use taking refuge in it. All the people you know will change. God is the only fixed entity. He is the one lamp which does not get extinguished. Take shelter in him. He is the supreme light. He is the light of the soul. He is the undiminishable light of pure consciousness. He is the one light, without a second."

Through such inspiring words, Krishna transformed Arjuna's heart which had been filled with impurities. By explaining all these noble principles to him, Krishna made Arjuna's heart bright and pure. Krishna turned Arjuna into a true wise man, one who manifested all the divine qualities.

Nineteenth Chapter

SENSE CONTROL –
THE KEY TO THE HIGHEST WISDOM

Once you have gained true detachment, then even the attainment of the highest heavenly worlds will seem trivial and insignificant to you. Arjuna asserted, "Krishna, even if I were given rulership over the three worlds and I were made master over all of creation, it would mean nothing to me. I have no interest in any of these things."

Embodiments of Love,

Arjuna had achieved great strength of renunciation at the time when he surrendered himself and was ready to receive the *Gita* teachings. At that point, he had detached himself from the world, and attached himself firmly to the transcendent principle manifested before him in the form of Lord Krishna. Such detachment from the world and its objects, and attachment to the divine principle, which is your true essence, must become your goal also. This is the destiny of every human being. In the course of your spiritual evolution, you will, as will every other individual in time, develop renunciation and dispassion towards the objects of the senses, and at the same time, develop an intense aspiration to realize the *atma* within.

Sense-Control, the Foundation for Self-Knowledge

If you were to construct a house, even a simple and ordinary one, wouldn't you take great care to lay a proper foundation? If that is true for a little house, then how much more care must you take in laying down a solid foundation for the great treasure house of self-knowledge. It is to provide such a foundation that Krishna, in his teachings to Arjuna in the *Gita*, emphasized the need to control the senses by developing a strong detachment from the objects of the world. This is an essential requirement for building up a solid foundation. If the foundation is not strong, the mansion of self-knowledge will not last long. It will soon collapse.

Renunciation does not spring up suddenly to become the foundation of self-knowledge. Such strong detachment does not just happen on the spur of the moment. This quality must be steadily developed and practiced, together with devotion and sense-control. If you want to light a lamp, you will need oil, a container to hold it, and a wick. In the same way, in order to light the lamp of wisdom, there is a need for detachment, devotion and control of the senses. Detachment can be thought of as the container and devotion the oil. Sense-control may be compared to the wick. If you bring these three elements together, the Lord himself will come and light the lamp of self-knowledge inside you. Before lighting this lamp in the heart of Arjuna, Krishna told him that he first had to establish complete control over his senses.

Such strict control over the senses is not something which can be achieved by most people. Even if they were to make an effort in this direction and achieve some measure of sense-control, ordinary people would not continue with these efforts because they would be convinced that by giving up sense enjoyments their very life would come to an end. They consider sense enjoyments as the only true source of happiness. This is what they experience day after day. But, the unbounded joy of self-knowledge is something they have not experienced even once. When you have a bird in your hand, would you let go of it and try to catch the two birds which may or may not be hiding in the bush? Reasoning in this way, they consider it madness to give up the sensory enjoyments which they enjoy every day in order to gain the bliss of the *atma* through self-knowledge, an experience which they have never known.

Sense Enjoyment Is An Illusory Joy

It is for these reasons that you will find many people criticizing the doctrine of detachment and control of the senses which is taught in the *Gita*. They say it is not really useful and applicable for ordinary people in their daily lives. But this criticism arises because they are ignorant of the real process that is taking place. All the momentary pleasures which they enjoy are just reflections of the true joy that always exists in the heart. By thinking again and again of a particular person or object, the mind departs from its own resting place and goes out to that person or object and takes on its form. Then it deludes itself into thinking that it is enjoying that object. But this can never be real joy. It is only a limited kind of joy which is imagined in the mind, a reflection of the true inner joy which is the source of all joys. To make this clearer consider an example.

A small baby may be sucking its thumb and drinking its saliva. It gets delight from this because it thinks that it is getting milk out of its thumb. But, the fact is that the saliva, which the baby thinks is milk, is coming from its own mouth, not from its thumb. It deludes itself into thinking that the source of its joy originated from outside its mouth. Consider another example.

A dog has found a hard bone. Once he has this bone it becomes very dear to him and he does not want to share it with any other dog. So, he takes it to some solitary place. There, he looks at it, admires it and starts gnawing on it. Since it is an old bone it is very hard. With all his enthusiasm and strength he goes on biting until he dislodges a tooth from his gums. Some blood spills out and oozes onto the bone. The dog is convinced that the blood has come out of that bone, and he immensely enjoys the taste of it. But the blood has not come out of the bone; it has come out of his own mouth. The dog does not realize the truth. Just as in the case of the baby, he has become deluded by following the imaginations of his own mind.

All Joy Comes Only From the Self

In a similar way, the ignorant think that they are getting joy out of the sense-objects. But, this limited joy that they experience does not come from outside of themselves. Ever present within their own hearts is true joy. It is this unchanging inner joy that gets superimposed on an object, making that object appear as if it is the source of joy. In this way, they believe they are deriving joy from the things of the world, but their joy is merely a small reflection of the unlimited joy that is hidden within them. Once they delude themselves into thinking that the joys and pleasures which they have in the outer world are true experiences, and the joy which they might get from the inner world is only an illusion, they lose all interest in practicing detachment. Then they give up pursuing the transcendental joy and continue to pursue only the worldly enjoyments which they believe can be obtained from sense-objects.

If an object truly gave joy then everyone would experience that joy to the same extent. If the joy were really inherent in the object itself, then the joy derived from that object should be the same for all people. Yet we know that this is not the case. If a particular object gives joy and pleasure to some people, the same object may be repulsive to other people, giving displeasure to them. For instance, some people may greatly enjoy cucumbers, whereas others may not like them at all. If joy were an integral part of cucumbers then there would be the one experience for all. Cucumbers would not give a feeling of joy to some and a feeling of dislike to others. Why is there this difference in reaction between different people? Why are there things which you may like that are disliked by others? It must mean that the joy you experienced was not directly associated with the object but that this joy came from within you. The feeling that you experienced was but a reflection of your own inexhaustible inner source of joy.

Sense Objects Can Only Give Temporary Joy

These likes and dislikes that you now feel, are just temporary phenomena. They are not permanent. Consider for a moment that at some time you felt very hungry. Now suppose that you were served some food which you found very tasty. What made this food so delicious? If you examine this question carefully you would conclude that it was your hunger that made everything taste so good. As long as you were hungry you found the meal that had been served to you to be most delectable. But after your hunger was satisfied, even if the most sumptuous delicacies were placed in front of you, they would not have appealed to you. When you are hungry, ordinary food will taste quite good, giving you great joy. But once your hunger is satisfied, even the most delicious food is not at all tasty to you. The only way that you can understand this change is that all these likes and dislikes emanate directly from you, the individual. They do not come from the objects as such. All your feelings of joy and sorrow emanate from the inner being, not from the external objects.

Ordinary people think that the joy or pain which they get from being with people whom they like or dislike comes from those people; but it is not so. It is one's own likes and dislikes which are responsible for one's joys and sorrows. It may be observed that when people have a strong liking for others, holding them very dear, then whatever be the attitude or the actions of that person, they will still like them all the same. What is the reason for this unshakable fidelity, this affectionate regard one may have for another person, despite a number of unsavory things which that person may be saying or doing? The reason is that when you like someone, the things which that person says and does will appear sweet to you. When you consider a person as very dear to you, then you feel that you love that person very much. This quality which you call 'love' is really a feeling of attachment in you that you are directing towards the other individual. In such an attachment both the love and the joy which appear to be present, originate only from you. Whether or not the other person has similar feelings, the feelings which you actually experience come from within you, only. They are not a part of the other person, at all. A similar thing was told by a great sage to his wife, in the ancient scriptures.

The sage said to his wife, "Dear one, you do not love me for my sake but for your own sake. Everything you love and hold dear, you love only for the sake of the *atma*, your highest self. The *atma* is the dearest of all, and it is for its sake that someone is dear to you. These feelings you have for others are all just manifestations of that great love you feel for your own true self."

Body-Consciousness Taints the Pure Love of the Self

In the whole world each person, whoever he may be, will love another only for his own sake, not for the sake of the other. If he loves an object, he loves it for the self alone, and not for the sake of that object. That self is the *atma*, the true self. But, when the pure love of the *atma* becomes tainted with body-consciousness, and the senses hold sway, attachment and selfishness arise. This inevitably leads to sorrow.

The body is impermanent. Death is certain for all. Even if someone were to live for a hundred years, he would still have to face death one day. Everyone knows that. But, isn't it strange that the would-be dying are crying and feeling sorry for those who have already died? Everyone is sure to meet death and so everyone may be thought of as among the dying. Yet, even though they themselves are dying, people feel sorrow and grief when thinking of someone who has died. It is as if death were a totally unusual and unexpected thing, rather than the natural conclusion that must come to all. This sorrow that comes on, particularly when someone near and dear has died, can only be there because of attachment. After knowing full well that death is certain, if you still worry about somebody, it must be due to the attachment which you have developed for that body. It is this attachment which is responsible for all your grief. Therefore, when someone has died the primary cause for sorrow is attachment, not love.

Basically, every human being, at all times, is a seeker of joy. He thirsts for joy and does not ever want sorrow. Man always aspires for profit, never for loss. That is his very nature. Profit, joy and bliss are inherent in his makeup; they are at the very core of his being. Every man, right from the beginning, would like to have only gain, not pain. For a business man, the first thing he thinks of is his profit. Here in India, when measuring out some staple such as rice, if the number of kg's goes above six, then the shopkeeper will not say '7', but '6 + 1'. This is because the word for seven also means 'weeping'. The shopkeeper will use another word to avoid uttering this unhappy word. In this way, man never wants to face unhappiness and loss. He wants only profit and gain, and the happiness they bring.

Self-Knowledge Gives the Greatest Joy

Of all the possible profits and gains, the supreme profit of all, which gives the greatest joy, is self-knowledge, the knowledge of the *atma*. That is the joy you must seek and make your own.

Consider a beautiful rose; the moment you look at a rose joy emanates from your heart. Similarly, when you see a handsome person or any beautiful thing in this world, you instantly feel joy. Many people undertake trips to go sight-seeing. Why do they go? In order to derive joy from it. Therefore, you can see beauty in nature and you can see beauty in people, and you can derive great joy from all the beauty that you see. But how long does this kind of joy and beauty last? The rose that you picked today starts to dry out tomorrow; then its beauty gets lost. The moment the beauty fades away, the joy that you previously derived from it also subsides. It is the same with the different stages of life: childhood, youth, adulthood and old age.

Childhood may be said to reflect divinity. During early childhood the individual does not suffer much from hatred, jealousy, anger and so forth. Jesus said that since children do not have any really bad qualities, they could be considered divine. During that period of life, there are no bad thoughts or bad traits, either in the mind or in the body. Little children are beautiful because they do not have impure feelings arising out of impure thoughts. As they grow up they gradually develop tainted qualities. The moment such negative qualities grow, the beauty of the small child fades away. Therefore, it is the coming in of impure thoughts which lead to impure words and impure deeds, which then results in the child losing its beauty.

Beauty and Joy

We see that the beauty possessed by a person is transient. It gradually fades away and, therefore, it cannot give permanent joy. Even a new-born donkey is very beautiful, but gradually as it grows up it develops a big stomach, gets a splotchy coat, and becomes ugly to look at. As long as there are no negative qualities everything looks beautiful. But, whoever be the person or whatever be the sense-object, you will find that its beauty is limited and, therefore, the joy derivable from it is also limited. Joy and beauty always go together. What is the one principle which has permanent joy and permanent beauty within itself? It is the *atma*! It never changes; it has no modification. In fact, it has no form at all. Beauty and joy are its form.

Although joy naturally emanates from the core of your heart, you think that you are deriving joy from the sense-objects and the sensory organs. But this is not so. All joy comes from within you and you have deluded yourself into thinking that it comes from something outside. The scriptures speak of the ethereal joy that emanates from the heavenly world of the creator. The joy which can be experienced through the contact of the senses with the sense objects is extremely small when compared to that creative joy. The sensory joy may be described as a drop in the ocean of bliss that is the creator's joy. But even this vast ocean of joy experienced by the creator of the universe, is itself as small as an atom when compared with the boundless joy that radiates from within your spiritual heart. That is the primary source of all joy. It is the joy of joys. The heart can be compared to a most splendorous and effulgent light which shines everywhere. Try to understand this brilliant spiritual light, which is ever luminous and all-pervading, and is your inner truth.

The Light of *Atma* Illuminates Everything

During the day, the sun illuminates the various objects of the world; at night, the moon plays a similar though lesser role. Therefore, you can declare that it is the sun and the moon that are responsible for the luminous nature of the world and its objects. But during the dream state you also see various things; where are the sun and the moon in that state? The sun that you see in the daytime during your waking state is not there in the dream state; nor is the moon there, nor is any other source of light visible there to illuminate the various objects. Yet you can see an entire world, namely, the world of the dream. What is it that illuminates that world? In the deep-sleep state there is absolute darkness. There is neither knowledge nor wisdom in that state. But how do you know that it is dark? What is it that enables you to apprehend this darkness?

The deep-sleep state has been described as the unconscious state; the dream state has been described as the sub-conscious state; the waking state has been described as the conscious state. There is a fourth state which transcends all these other states; it may be described as the super-conscious state. In the super-conscious state you are able to see everything, everywhere, and enjoy bliss supreme. What is the light that illuminates this bliss state and permits you to experience this unmitigated joy? That light is the effulgence that emanates from the *atma*. It is this light which illuminates all the other states as well and enables you to see them.

In the *Vedas*, the sages have spoken of this super-conscious state. They declared, "We are able to see a state which transcends the others, including the darkness of the dreamless state. Beyond the dreamless state is the supreme light of the *atma* which illuminates the waking, the dream and the deep-sleep states." To understand this a little better, consider an example from the waking state. When you close your eyes for a minute, what exactly are you seeing? You will say that there is nothing there, only absolute darkness. But then the question arises, 'How is it that I am able to perceive this darkness? Since I seem to see it and am able to describe it, there must be a light of consciousness which illuminates this state and enables me to see even this darkness.' That light is the light of the *atma* It is only through this transcendental light that all the other lights can shine.

We celebrate a festival of light in which we light a candle, and from that one candle go on lighting all the other candles and lamps. This first light is the basis for lighting the others. It is because we have this first light that we are able to light so many others. For living beings, this first light is the divine light of the one *atma*. With it, all the individual lamps, representing the countless individual beings, are lit in turn. It is because of this divine light that the eyes are able to see. It shines from inside and illuminates all beings. But it is not only the source of all living beings, it is also the source of all objects and all the external bodies of light, such as the sun and the moon.

You may wonder, since you cannot see this divine light, how can you be sure that it illuminates all these other objects and lights. Here the example of a battery will be instructive. You cannot see the electrical power which is in the cells, but if you switch on the current flow you can see the light in the bulb. If there had been no electric power in the cell, you would not have been able to get any light from the bulb. The body may be thought of as an electric lamp driven by this battery cell which is the mind; your eyes are the bulb and your intelligence is the switch which controls it. In this battery cell of the mind, a very special type of energy derived from the *atma* is stored. In ordinary electric batteries the power gets exhausted very quickly, but the *atmic* current flows continuously through the mind. The *Vedas* have declared that the mind is the receptacle for storing the *atmic* energy. It is this inexhaustible source that provides the temporary flow of pleasure when some pleasing object is perceived.

The Joy of the Self Is the Only True Joy

All the joys and pleasures which you enjoy in this world are only temporary, and are just the reflections of the immeasurable joy which is inside of you. Out of ignorance you believe that your joy comes from sense-objects and that this momentary joy is true. But only what is permanent is true. These temporary joys which are associated with the things of the world are not the true joy. Only the eternal bliss that is the *atma*, is true; these others come and go. All the things that you see in the waking state disappear in the dream state. All the joys and sorrows which you experience during the dream state you leave behind when you come back into the waking state. People and objects that you see in the waking state will appear as changing reflections in the dream state, and then they get completely absorbed and disappear in the deep-sleep state. In this way, your joy changes as these states change.

All the worldly joys which you think to be so permanent will give you a great deal of trouble in the end and lead you to grief. "Therefore," Krishna told Arjuna, "pay attention only to your inner truth, the basis, from which springs all manifestations. Then outer appearances and sense-impressions will not bother you." The basis does not change, whereas the manifestations which depend on that basis continuously change. If the basis were changing along with the manifestations, it would be impossible for you to even live. Consider this small example.

At various times you may have used different types of vehicles, such as cars, trains or buses, to travel from one place to another. The car might be moving fairly fast, so might the bus, and even if you are just walking you might be going quite fast. In each case, this movement will be in relation to the road which remains steady and unchanging. Suppose along with the moving car or the moving bus, the road itself is also moving rapidly, as in violent earthquake. Then what would happen? You would certainly be moving, but you could end up in any direction. You are not likely to reach your goal despite great efforts and hardships along the way. In order to reach your goal the road must be steady.

It is because the *atmic* source, the indweller of every heart, is permanent and steady that people are able to enjoy the things of the world, which are impermanent and changing. But, Krishna warned Arjuna, "Do not be satisfied with these furtive pleasures, which you mistakenly believe come from the world. The world is fleeting. It is fickle and full of sorrow. It is the ever-changing outer manifestation. It is not the permanent basis. It cannot lead you to your truth. How can you count on the world for your support when it is undergoing so many changes and modifications? Would it be possible for you to derive permanent bliss from it? Let go of the world and turn towards the transcendental principle. Turn towards the *atma*. It is forever steady and unchanging. There you will find the unending joy that you have been seeking futilely outside in the world."

Do Not Drive With Your Foot on the Brake

Now, some of you may be thinking that if young children are taught sense control they would turn into inert, helpless human beings? But nobody is telling them that they should not make use of their senses. It is only that they should learn to control them properly. There are brakes in a car, and whenever there is danger you use the brakes to stop the car. When Swami is asking you to control the senses and to control the mind, some of you might be wondering if you would be able to live at all and carry on your routine functions. Swami is not asking you to drive with your foot on the brake, but to use the brakes when necessary to control the car, whenever there is some danger. It is when there is some danger, such as impure thoughts, impure feelings, impure sights, impure hearing and so on, that you have to exercise control. If you do not have any brakes at all you will surely come to grief. A bullock which cannot be brought under control, a horse without reins, a car without brakes, a person without sense control, are all extremely dangerous and heading for disaster.

"Therefore, Arjuna," Krishna said, "control your senses and your mind, and recognize the defects that are inherent in all the objects of the world. When you turn from the changing manifestations and establish yourself in the unchanging basis, then you will be able to live happily anywhere, because you will be established in the source of all happiness, the *atma*, which is eternal bliss."

The wisdom teachings do not admonish you to give up your family or give up your worldly duties. Be in the world. Use your senses. But do so in a proper and ethical way, appropriate to each time and circumstance, never forgetting your true purpose. The *Gita* teaches the importance of discipline, of observing limits in all your activities. The brakes are used in a car for the welfare and protection of the passengers, so that they can safely reach their goal. In the same way, the senses must be brought under control and used for the welfare and protection of the individual, so that it can complete its journey safely. That is why Krishna was so insistent that Arjuna develop sense-control.

Detachment, Devotion and Sense-Control

This sense-control is something like the wick in the lamp of your heart. Merely having the wick of sense-control is not enough. You must also have oil, which is the fuel for the lamp; that is your devotion. And there must be a container which holds this oil, and that is your detachment. If you have the container, the oil and the wick, you will be able to light the lamp easily. Still, someone has to come and light it. That someone is God. Once you have detachment, devotion and sense-control, then the divinity will come and light the lamp in your heart. In the case of Arjuna, it was Krishna who performed this sacred act of lighting the lamp and revealing the splendor of the *atma* in Arjuna's heart.

Suppose you have some flowers, a needle and some thread, will these automatically turn into a garland? No. There has to be someone to string the garland together. You may have gold and precious stones, but without a goldsmith to create it, you will not be able to obtain a beautiful jewel made out of these articles. You may have a high intelligence, you may have books containing the highest knowledge and you may have keen eyes to see them, but without someone to teach you to read, they will all be meaningless and useless to you.

The *atma* is always present; it never changes, it never comes and goes. The spiritual teachings will also be ever-present; they will be there waiting for you when you are ready to receive them. And, inwardly, you may have an intense yearning for illumination. All these may be there for you, but unless the true *guru*, the spiritual teacher, comes and transmits the immortal knowledge to you, you cannot become enlightened. If you are ready to realize the underlying reality of all the objects of the world and to discover the divine principle within you, then you need the true teacher, the highest source of knowledge to come and instruct you. To gain the sacred knowledge of the self, that teacher is the universal teacher. It is God himself who comes to guide you to your goal. He may take on different forms. In the case of Arjuna, the divine teacher was Krishna, the *avatar* of that age, and he started by teaching Arjuna sense-control.

You must take some time to reflect on the deeper significance of all these teachings on sense-control, which were given by Krishna to Arjuna, not in an *ashram* setting but on the battlefield, at the eve of a great battle fought to preserve righteousness and to counter the forces of injustice and untruth that had become rampant.

WORLDLY KNOWLEDGE IS USELESS
WITHOUT SELF-KNOWLEDGE

*K*rishna *taught in the Gita that once you acquire true spiritual knowledge your troubles, difficulties and sorrows all disappear.*

Embodiments of Love,

As long as you identify yourself with your body, you will be exposed to countless problems and sorrows. The primary reason for having obtained your body in the first place, is to enable you to undergo the consequences of your past actions. This is your *karma*, the results of activities you have engaged in which have not yet fructified. Why did you accumulate this *karma* in the first place? Why did you engage in activities which bear consequences long into the future? The reason for *karma* is the desire or attachment you have for some things and the dislike or repulsion you have for other things. And what is the reason for this attraction and repulsion? It is because your mind is steeped in duality. You believe that this world is real and is filled with objects and things which are separate from you. But, where did this false view, this duality, come from? The reason for duality is your state of ignorance, the beclouding of your consciousness by a dark veil that covers the knowledge of your true reality.

The Light of Wisdom Dispels the Darkness of Ignorance

You have forgotten the fundamental unity of all beings. You have become unmindful of the divine basis of all things. You have lost sight of the *atma*, your real self. It is because of this ignorance that you experience so much grief and sorrow. If you want to be free of this darkness of ignorance, you have to obtain the light of wisdom. The only thing that can remove darkness is light. Similarly, the only thing that can remove ignorance is wisdom or spiritual knowledge. Ignorance has covered the knowledge of divinity and you are not able to perceive the truth. Just as the embers of a fire are covered by ashes, your light of truth has been covered by the ashes of ignorance and, therefore, you have not been aware of your own reality.

You may have the power of sight in your eyes but if there is a cataract covering the surface of your eyes, you will not be able to see. It is only after an operation is performed that you will be able to get your sight back. Similarly, it is only after a spiritual operation is performed and the cloud of ignorance is removed, that the sun of wisdom will shine freely. It is just like the sun's rays beaming into a room the moment you pull back the heavy drapes covering the window. The principle of divinity exists in everyone, so it is impossible for any person to be completely devoid of wisdom. There is no doubt whatsoever that, in time, the clouds of ignorance will be dispelled for all of humanity and the full light of wisdom will shine forth. All will realize their divine state.

When human life is infinitely expanded it becomes the one divine principle. Man plus infinity is divinity. When the human mind is expanded to infinity it becomes the divine mind, it becomes the creative principle which brought forth this universe. The *atma*, the self in man, and the divinity that dwells within him, are one and the same. Add infinity onto yourself and you become the divinity itself. You will have merged into the *atma*. Unfortunately, having become embodied, you have forgotten your divinity, your unlimited infinity. You are aware only of your limited individuality. If you want to attain your infinite reality, you must make an inquiry into the divinity which is inherent within you.

Atma Remains Unchanged, the Individual Changes

Consider a person who has built a house for himself. From the moment he completed the house he has been considering it as 'his' house. When he dies, the house goes to his heir, who then starts calling it 'his' house. Suppose, as time goes on, this new house owner becomes poor and has to sell the house to discharge his debts. Another person buys the house and begins calling the same house 'his' house. Now, who does this house really belong to? Does it belong to the one who constructed it, to the one who inherited it or to the one who bought it? There is no change in the house. In other words, the object remains as before. There is a change only in the persons who claim to own it. The house just continues to be there, but the claimed ownership undergoes repeated change.

In a similar way, there is the unchanging entity, the *atma*, which, like the house, remains unaffected by the countless owners who come and go. Each one claims personal ownership of this inner house which they call *I*. Each one believes the *I* to be their own personal self, but, in truth, it is the one, unchanging *atma*. And so this *my-ness* goes on constantly changing, but the *atma* which is being claimed as one's personal property, expressed every time one says *I*, remains unaffected by all these assertions.

Is there any medicine to cure this disease of *I-ness* or *my-ness*? Both the revealed and the written scriptures have declared that it is the mind which is responsible for this possessive nature. It has been said that along with the five senses of perception, the mind may be considered to be a sixth sense. But it is not just another sense equal to the other senses. In fact, it is the master of all the senses.

The Two States of the Mind, Pure and Impure

If there were no mind, neither the motor organs nor the sensory organs would be able to function at all. For all these various senses, the mind is in the position of the controller. It acts as the bridge to the inner life of the person. You may be in a lecture hall and your eyes and ears may be taking in all that is happening, but, if your mind is not there, if it were to wander off to your home town to think over some events going on there, you would not register anything which was taking place in the hall. Afterwards, you might question your neighbor, "What did the lecturer say? My mind was not here." What is the reason for your not hearing, although your ears are there? What is the reason for your not seeing although your eyes are there? The reason is the mind.

If your mind is absent, even if your eyes are here, you will not be aware of who your neighbor is; even if your ears are here you will not be aware of what is being said. The inner significance of this is that the mind is the master of the senses. All the senses should properly be subservient to the mind. When the mind is in a position of stillness, the senses will not be able to function at all.

The mind has two states. One is the impure mind, which is the thinking faculty, and the second is the pure mind, which is the seat of deepest feelings, experienced as the spiritual heart. When the mind allows itself to be subservient to the senses, it is impure. But, when the mind exercises control over the senses and follows the dictates of its highest inner knowing, it is pure. In other words, when the lower mind follows the *buddhi*, the higher mind, which knows the dictates of the heart, it is pure. Impure and pure are just aspects of the same mind. In its natural state, the mind is pure. Through the thinking process and its association with the senses, the mind becomes impure. Consider a small example.

The nature of a handkerchief is pure whiteness. The white color is natural to it. When you use the handkerchief it acquires dirt, and then you describe it as being dirty. After the washerman cleans it, you again think of it as a clean cloth. The dirty cloth and the clean cloth are one and the same. The same cloth, having acquired some dirt, has become a dirty cloth. Once the cloth has been washed and the dirt has been removed, it has become pure and you call it a clean cloth. You say that the washerman has made the cloth white. But really, he has not made it white; whiteness is its natural state. He has only removed the dirt. Similarly, when the mind absorbs impurities from the senses it can be described as an impure mind. But when the sense impressions have been removed and the mind is no longer turned towards the senses, it becomes pure again.

It is in this context that you can understand the meaning of these two states of the mind, pure and impure. When the mind is intimately associated with the senses it is impure. Then it is nothing but a bundle of thoughts; it can be conceived of as the process of thinking itself. In this process of thinking, revolving around duality and its polarities of attraction and repulsion, the mind gets dirty. It absorbs the impure impressions of the sense-organs and becomes impure. At this point it does not have any specific form; it is merely the thing which thinks.

Give the Mind Some Peace – Turn It Towards God

When the lower mind is free of the dirt and impurities of the senses and is turned towards the higher mind, it again becomes pure. Higher mind is always aware of the inherent divinity. When you turn your mind to the divinity, you will be able to free it from all the troubles and sorrows associated with impure thoughts which arise from the impressions of the sense-organs. Therefore, you have to make every effort to turn your mind away from the senses and towards God. This can be described as meditation or *yoga*, union with God. This is the process whereby you cleanse a mind which has become impure, and again make it pure.

The mind needs a certain amount of peace. Just as the body needs rest, the mind needs peace. How can the mind get peace? It is only when you control the thinking process and slow the flow of thoughts that the mind gains some peace. The mind will always try to go out through the sense-organs toward various sense-objects. This then, gives rise to the thinking process. If you control this tendency of the mind to go outwards, and instead turn it inwards towards God, impure thoughts will diminish. Then you will be using the mind properly, and giving it some rest as well. This has been described as the *yoga* of constant inward-directed practice. Let us look at this further.

How To Cross The Turbulent River of Worldly Life

When you are traveling on a wide, powerful river, what is the most important knowledge you should possess? You should know how to swim. That comes first; that takes precedence over all other knowledge. If you go on a great river but do not know how to swim, however educated you may be, you run the risk of getting drowned. There is a story for this.

A highly educated scholar had to cross a wide river to attend an important meeting. The wind and the river current were going in opposite directions, so the journey was quite slow that day. Now, *pundits* have the habit of constantly talking, whether it is to themselves, going on repeating verses from the scriptures, or whether it is to anyone within easy earshot. On this particular day the boatman was quietly concentrating on steering the boat in the river. This *pundit*, who was the only passenger traveling in the boat, had no one else to speak to, so he started a conversation with the boatman.

"Do you know how to read and write?" the *pundit* asked. The boatman answered, "No, I don't know reading and writing."

"You seem to be quite a strange person," the *pundit* said, "In these days in every village the government has established schools, and you should know at least a little bit of reading and writing."

Just to while away the time, this *pundit* continued speaking to the boatman. Next he asked him, "Do you play any musical instruments?" The boatman answered, "Swami, I've had no chance to learn an instrument." "Well, do you know any of the latest popular songs?" asked the scholar. "No, I don't even know that," replied the boatman.

"What a strange person you are. In every street there is a movie house, and there are loud-speakers all around it playing the latest hits. And the radio broadcasts are filled with all the current pop recordings. Shouldn't you at least take a little of your income to buy a cheap transistor radio and listen to music?"

The boatman confessed, "I do not even know what a transistor is."

The *pundit* replied, "If in this modern age you don't even know about a transistor, you have wasted much of your life; at least a quarter of your life has been dumped into the water."

He asked the boatman another question, "Do you have a newspaper with you?" The boatman replied, "I don't have any education at all; what is the use of my having a newspaper, Swami?" The *pundit* went on, "Without having an education and without being able to read a newspaper, you've wasted even more of your life. At least half of your life has been dumped into the water."

After a few minutes the *pundit* asked again, "Do you have a watch? Can you tell me what time it is?" "Swami, the truth is I don't even know how to tell time. Then what is the use of my having a watch?" the boatman answered. The *pundit* rejoined, "Look at how much of your life has been wasted. If you don't have a radio to enjoy music, and you can't read a newspaper to find out what is going on, and you don't even know what time it is, then three-fourths of your life has been dumped into the water."

Meanwhile a strong wind came up and it quickly turned into a powerful gale. The boat started swinging from side to side and the river was soon in full flood. The boatman could no longer maintain control of the boat. He asked the *pundit*, "Swami, do you know how to swim?" The *pundit* replied, "No, I never learned how to swim."

As he was about to go overboard, the boatman said to the *pundit*, "O Swami, what a pity! What a waste! You don't know how to swim? Now your whole life will be dumped into the water."

When you are traveling across a turbulent river, you should know how to swim. Without knowing how to swim, all your other knowledge of philosophy, physics, chemistry, botany, commerce, mathematics, political science, etc., will be of no use to you. In the journey of life, you are traveling on a rushing, unpredictable river, and you should know how to stay afloat and cross that river. To swim safely across the river of life, you must have the knowledge of the *atma*, and you must develop a strong power of discrimination, to know that which is useful and that which is useless for crossing this river. If you have not developed a capacity along these lines there will be no way for you to find fulfillment in life. You will drown in the river of worldly life.

External Freedom and Inner Freedom

As long as you base your life on wealth, property and worldly things, you will never be able to derive any real joy. There are two things which every person has to attain; one is external freedom, the other is inner freedom. External freedom speaks of independence, being free of external bonds and limitations. Inner freedom speaks of liberation from the bondage of the senses, having them under your full control. Every individual should realize both of these freedoms.

In the external world, as long as you are under the control of people who are unsympathetic towards you, such as some foreign king or ruler, you will not be able to get real joy. In the inner world, as long as you are a slave of the senses, then you will also not be able to enjoy real freedom. Even for the outer freedom, sense-control is important. But for becoming master of the inner world, the single most important faculty that you must develop is the control of the senses and thereby gain control over the mind. Once you have control of the mind you will be able to turn it away from the world and towards God. Then you will get real joy, both externally and internally, for then you will see the divinity everywhere.

Control of the mind and control of the senses is the victory that must be won by all human beings. Up to now you have been craving for different types of joys and pleasures; you go on uttering prayers for attaining happiness but you are not making any real effort to discover where that happiness is to be found. Krishna told Arjuna, "You are deluding yourself, believing that you can get happiness and peace in daily life. But, you won't be able to get real joy there. Sense-objects cannot give you the joy that you are seeking. It is only when you control your senses that you will be able to get peace and joy."

Whether you are a believer or a non-believer, you will have to gain control over your senses. Be the master of your senses. Do not allow them to get excited and run after sense-objects. When the senses get excited and you follow them, you will become weak and forget the Lord. Keep your senses under control and keep your mind firmly fixed on the Lord. Follow his teaching and directions. Without his grace your strength will leave you, and you will not be able to undertake any useful work.

You Need the Lord's Grace to Achieve Anything Worthwhile

As long as Arjuna had the blessings and the company of Krishna, he was a mighty hero and he was able to accomplish many heroic deeds. Once Krishna left his mortal body, Arjuna, through body-consciousness and attachment, was overcome with sorrow and self-pity. He felt that Krishna had left him, and as a result, he lost all his valor. Arjuna, the great hero, now became weak and unable to accomplish even the smallest tasks. When Arjuna was bringing the surviving women and children from Krishna's household to shelter, robbers attacked him in the forest. Arjuna tried his best to fight against them and to free the women and children from the grip of these murderous robbers; but he could not do it.

During the many battles of the *Mahabharata* war, Arjuna was able to fight and defeat so many great heroes. He was unconquerable, no matter the odds against him. But, the same Arjuna was not able to even vanquish the robbers in the forest and rescue the women and children who were under his protection. What was the reason for this? Until that time, with Krishna at his side, Arjuna had felt great strength. Not recognizing where that strength came from, he believed it was his own valor and his own strength that had provided the victories he was able to gain. But this delusion stemmed from ignorance. Arjuna's strength had not been his. That strength had been given to him by the divinity.

Even though a person may be endowed with divine strength, he deludes himself into thinking that the strength he has is all due to his own human capabilities. So it was with Arjuna. But, once he lost the strength of divinity, he was not able to accomplish even the smallest thing. Man has been able to undertake many types of activities because the divinity is inherent in him and has been providing all his inner strength, sustenance and power. Without this divine power, man would not be able to accomplish anything. Without the stamp of divinity not even his smallest undertakings would reach fruition. That stamp is all-important. Consider the following example.

Let us say that you have made a beautiful envelope out of heavy art paper. You have written Swami's address on it in colorful decorative script, and you have enclosed a beautiful letter, carefully written with calligraphy and adorned with striking colors. The borders of this envelope are also artfully embellished with many exquisite designs. You have inserted the letter inside the envelope, you have sealed it and posted it. Yet, despite all your great efforts and skill, the letter never reached Swami. Why is that? The reason is that you did not put a stamp on the envelope. All your decorations and all your beautiful handwriting could not help in getting that letter to Swami.

Even a letter which has been dropped in the postbox at the college hostel will not reach the temple here, less than a mile away, without a stamp. But with a stamp on it, a letter could even have traveled thousands of miles and reached its destination. The postal department will not look at all the decorations, the ornate letters, the striking colors and designs. They will not pay any attention to all your beautiful art work. They will only look at the address and check to see if the envelope has the correct stamp. So, what was most needed was for you to procure a stamp and properly place it on the envelope.

God's Grace is Earned Through Purity of the Heart

As in the example just given, God will not pay attention to all your elaborate efforts unless you have addressed your efforts correctly and have procured the stamp of divinity and affixed it onto your work. How do you obtain that stamp? Through purity of the heart. By bringing all your efforts in alignment with noble values. God does not care for all your scholarship, your accomplishments, your wealth and position. Worldly-minded people will have their eyes on that, but not God. God only looks in your heart. What is the use of earning many degrees and achieving great scholarship in a particular subject if your heart has not become purified by all your education? It is the values that you practice every day in the area of truth and honesty which will carry you through life and be your greatest asset. That is why we emphasize values so strongly in the system of education we have here at the *ashram*.

Would a hungry man have his hunger satisfied if you just showed him some different types of delicious food? Would a poor man be freed from poverty if he merely heard stories of great wealth? Would a sick man be cured if you just described to him the various medicines that could make him well? No. And in the same way, if you merely listened to the great teachings of the *Gita* you would not be able to derive much benefit from them. You have attended many discourses and you have heard many great truths expounded. Now you must put into practice at least one or two of these truths. Then you will be able to experience real joy.

For your efforts to succeed and be truly worthwhile you need the stamp of divinity. Purity of heart will earn for you that stamp. This means practicing the noble values that the *Gita* has been teaching. But even before these values can be put into practice you will have to control your mind and turn it one-pointedly in that direction. This can happen only if you master your senses. Therefore, the crucial lesson in all these teachings is the control of the senses. Krishna told Arjuna, "Arjuna, if you want to accomplish anything truly worthwhile in this world you must gain control over your own sense-organs." The same thing was said by Prahlada to his father, the demon-king, "Father, you have been able to conquer so many worlds but you have not achieved the real victory. You have not been able to conquer yourself!"

There are Many Beings but Only One Underlying Divinity

If a person has not conquered his own mind and senses, how will he ever be able to taste the sweet nectar of divinity? To achieve control of the mind and senses, it is important for you to know the deeper reason for all your efforts. The ultimate goal of your life is to realize the one divinity that underlies everyone and everything. You must become established in the one *atmic* principle that exists in every heart.

The sun is one for everyone. There is not a separate sun for different beings and for different species in different parts of the world. There may be thousands of different vessels all filled with water, standing on the ground. Some will be earthen pots, some will be brass vessels and some will be silver or copper ones. Above them in the sky is the one sun, reflecting itself in all of these vessels. From the many reflections it would appear that there are many suns, but even though the vessels are all different and the reflections are many, the sun which is being reflected is only one. The values of the vessels will also be different; the silver vessel is very costly compared to the earthen one, nevertheless, the sun which is being reflected is one and the same.

Similarly, right from the highest scholar to the most ignorant dullard, right from the wealthiest man to the poorest beggar, from the greatest emperor to the humblest citizen, the bodies and the apparel in which they are clad will be different, but the one who is the resident of all these bodies, the *atma* which is reflected in all these bodies, is one and the same. The clothes that you wear and the jewelry with which you adorn yourself may be very expensive. A poor person would not be able to have such costly things. But, these are just like the differences in the value of the vessels. The divinity inside all these bodies is only one.

Once you become aware of this truth and recognize the unity in all beings, you will be able to exercise sense-control quite easily. Instead of seeking to control others you will seek control over yourself. Instead of correcting others you will take charge of your own mind and senses. Defects and faults abide in everyone. Then who is to exercise power and authority over whom? If a person has committed some mistake it may be your job to show him the right way, but your main focus should be to correct yourself. Discharge your duty, do your assigned work but always remember the one divinity resident in everyone.

Only Wisdom Can Conquer Ignorance

Ignorance is very deep. It covers your inner truth. It is impossible for you to remove this thick layer of ignorance by encountering it head-on. In the early morning at 7 o'clock, although you may be only 5 feet tall, your shadow will be 50 feet long. How can you reduce the length of this 50-foot shadow? Is it possible to fight with it? If you admonish it, will it listen to you? If you criticize it, will it be reduced? Whatever you do, its length will not come down. But as the sun goes on steadily rising, the length of the shadow diminishes automatically. Once the sun occupies the position over-head, the shadow, by itself, will have come down to your feet, obliterated itself and disappeared from view.

You may be 5 feet tall but your ignorance is 50 feet long! Therefore, you have to develop inner inquiry so that your wisdom will grow. As long as the sun of wisdom goes on rising, ignorance will go on diminishing. In this way, your ignorance can be totally destroyed. This is one method.

There is still another method for dealing with this shadow that is 50 feet long. You realize that you cannot conquer it by turning to-wards it and trying to run over it. You realize that by facing it, your shadow will not get any shorter or disappear from view. But, if in-stead of turning your face towards your shadow, you turn your face towards the sun, then your shadow will automatically be behind you, and however big it is, you will not be aware of it anymore. It will continuously remain out of sight. Therefore, instead of think-ing of this ignorance, always think of the sun of wisdom. That way you keep the ignorance behind you and the sun in front of you, and you will not be affected by this shadow anymore. This means al-ways turning your vision towards God.

Both methods should be employed. Always turn your vision to-wards God and use your intellectual and intuitive faculties to in-crease your wisdom. These are two major *yogas* or spiritual paths, the path of devotion and the path of wisdom. If you do not turn to-wards God and increase your wisdom, but continue to turn towards the world, then as with the shadow and the setting sun, your igno-rance will go on increasing and you will get lost. "Therefore," Krishna warned Arjuna, "use your *buddhi*, your highest intelli-gence, to increase your wisdom. That way your ignorance will get destroyed. The moment your ignorance is destroyed, duality will vanish. When duality goes, your attraction or repulsion to sense ob-jects will also disappear. And, once these attachments or revulsion to objects disappear, your body-consciousness will also disappear. If there is no body-consciousness then there is no sorrow."

Develop Wisdom Through Inner Inquiry

We have seen that if you want to overcome body-consciousness, you must first overcome your attraction or repulsion to sense objects. Once this goes, duality will be destroyed. And, when duality disappears, ignorance will vanish. This will all happen when you develop wisdom. Therefore, the *Gita* has declared that it is through wisdom that you will be able to destroy ignorance and reach your ultimate reality.

What is this wisdom that you should develop? Can it be gained by acquiring secular knowledge in the world? No. It does not deal with external phenomena at all. It deals only with internal experience. It is only when you have developed self-confidence, confidence in the indwelling *atma*, that you will be able to develop a strong confidence in the Lord. If you do not believe in your self, you cannot truly believe in God. When you have faith in yourself, then you can have faith in God. To develop such a firm belief in yourself, to realize the indwelling divinity which is the same in everyone, you need to constantly engage in the practice of self-inquiry.

From the moment you get up in the morning until you go to bed at night you go on saying *I, I, I,* and *myself* and *mine*. But even when you say *I,* do you know who this *I* really is? You say 'this is *my* body', 'this is *my* intelligence', 'this is *my* inner feeling', 'these are *my* senses', but do you ever ask yourself, 'Who am I?' If you never inquire into your own truth what good is all the education you have acquired? If you will not make the effort to inquire into your truth, then who else will come and remove the writing that is on your forehead? Who will remove the *karma* that is imprinted there? Instead of engaging yourself in self-examination, you just allow impure thoughts to enter your head, and so all your thinking becomes dull and null.

You should realize that when you say, 'this is *my* handkerchief', the one who is the *you*, is different from the object which, in this case, is the handkerchief. You say, 'this is *my* body'. You do not say, 'I am this body'. When you say, 'this is *my* body' you are declaring that you and the body are different and separate from each other. If you then inquire who is this *you* who is saying this, then you will be led to the indweller. You must inquire who this indweller is, in other words, who is owning all these things. Only when there is an owner can there be any meaning in saying 'this is *my* property, this is *my* land'. Only the master who owns the property has the right to say 'this property is *mine*'. For the body-mind this master is the indweller. This master will not undergo any change. He will never leave you. Therefore, by means of inner inquiry, you should try to discover and recognize this unchanging indwelling divinity which is your true reality.

Every spiritual aspirant should take up inner inquiry. In all your spiritual practices that you engage in, you should spend three-fourths of your time on self-inquiry. Then you will get the full results. Only by using your time properly, by sanctifying your body and by sanctifying all your actions, will you be able to reach the goal. The most important reason for all these sorrows you are prone to, is the weakness you develop because your senses are not under your control. Use the strength you have to keep your senses under control. Put your mind on the right path and develop a firm resolve. You will gain great strength thereby.

The *Gita* declared that you should control the senses, not that you should destroy them. The Gita does not say that you should renounce action, but that you should renounce the fruit of your action. Therefore, you have to do your work. Although there is no need for the Lord to perform any particular work, you will find that he is working all the time. If he is working constantly, should you not be working also?

Perform your work and use all your senses correctly. Use them within the proper limits for the purposes for which they were intended. Do not ever use them in the wrong way. This is the message of the *Gita*.

Twenty-First Chapter

TO KNOW THE DIVINITY
IS TO BECOME THE DIVINITY

Krishna said, "If you are a slave of your desires you will be a slave of the entire world. But when you make desires your slave the whole world will be yours."

Embodiments of Love,

Have faith in the indwelling divinity, the *atma*, which is the basis of every happiness and joy that you will ever experience in the world. People are suffering immensely because of their erroneous belief that the joys of the senses and the delights of worldly objects are real and will last; but these are only temporary and cannot last. People have not inquired to find out what is the basis for the joys associated with the sense objects and all the luxuries of the world.

The *Atmic* Light Gets Hidden by the Impure Senses

In the *Gita*, the human body has been compared with a container having ten holes, within which is an inextinguishable light. If you were to cover this container with a thick cloth, then you would not be able to see any light shining through it. If, however, you gradually lift this thick cloth covering the container, then you would be able to see the light shining from each of the holes. At that point, it looks as though there are ten lights. But when you take the container away and leave the light, you realize that there was always only the one light. That one light shining within the container, which is the body, is the self-effulgent *atma*.

The splendorous light of the *atma* has been covered by the body and its sense organs. There are five gross and five subtle sense organs associated with the human body, which can be thought of as the ten holes in the container through which the light of the *atma* shines. This container of the body, in turn, has been covered by the thick cloth of *my-ness* and attachment, which obscures the pure light of the *atma*. First of all, you must remove this cloth of self-ishness and *my-ness*. This *my-ness* stems from ignorance. It is a form of delusion which makes you feel separate and keeps you bound up in duality. It arises from the cosmic illusion, or *maya*. *Maya* can be thought of as the outer vesture or garment of God. God has been described as having illusion as his outer form. This illusion veils and hides him from view. Once you take away this cloth of illusion, then the inner light becomes revealed, shining radiantly through the sense organs.

The light which you see through your eyes is but a reflection of the one self-effulgent divine light that is inside you. Every sensation you feel through your skin or hear through your ears is but a reaction to that same inner light. And every sound which you make through your mouth is but the resound of that one divine inner light. All that you have been able to do and experience through the senses is only a reflection, a reaction or a resound of that one splendorous radiance which is your immortal self, the *atma*. But as long as you still identify yourself with this container of the body, you will not be able to see the one *atmic* light. Only when you identify yourself completely with the *atma* will you be able to experience this one *atmic* light instead of a multiplicity of many different lights.

See Unity In All Diversity

Up to this time, you have been seeing diversity and separation in what is actually unity. But now you have to correct this wrong vision. The ancient wisdom teachings have emphasized that you will not be whole until you can see only unity in the illusion of diversity, that appears to be around you. When can you see and directly experience this unity? Only when you destroy your sense of identity with the body. Then you will be able to experience all as one. It is *maya* which causes this delusory experience of seeing diversity when there is only unity. But it is the universal experience of the great sages and mystics that there is only the one unity to be found within all the multiplicity of the world.

This unity is the basis of everything everywhere. It is the *atma*. It has to be experienced in every object and in every being. This is the sum and substance of the *Gita*, which itself is the essence of all the ancient wisdom teachings. The *Gita* has described the experience of unity as *yoga*, the process of becoming united with and immersed in the one divinity. You must make an inquiry, taking instances from your own daily life, to see how you can experience this oneness within all the diversity, and, thereby discover the divinity which is inherent in everything.

Take the example of some food preparations. For instance, you can consider some different types of sweets, such as cookies, cakes, candies, desserts, or other sweets which you might enjoy. The forms and names of all these items are different but the inner substance which gives them all their characteristic sweet taste is the same. That underlying sweetness comes from sugar. It is because sugar is present in these items that there is sweetness in all of them. Flour by itself has no sweetness; its taste is insipid. But, when flour is associated with sugar, then you enjoy it as a sweet. It does not matter what flour you use, whether it comes from rice or wheat or other grains. When it is associated with sugar, it becomes sweet. Similarly, the objects of the world are tasteless and insipid, but because the sugar of divinity has been mixed in with them, you can enjoy so many things in the world, considering them desirable and sweet.

You Are A Human Being, Not an Animal

Do not waste your life running after worldly enjoyments. Realize the truth that you did not get this human birth for the sake of enjoying food or sleep or wasting your time on meaningless activities or entertainment. When you look around you can see any number of animals, birds and worms which live only for the sake of food. Why have a human life if you use it only to enjoy the pleasures that animals, birds and worms enjoy? What is the use of acquiring a higher education, and then spending your time reveling in lowly pleasures that even without benefit of higher education, the animals, birds and worms also indulge in? What is the special ideal which has been held out for humanity? What is the inner significance of the statement that it is extremely difficult to obtain a human life?

Human life has not been given so that you can act like an animal. Human life has not been given so that you can act like a demon either. Man has taken human birth in order to realize his divine essence. Human life has been given to you so that you can reach the highest plane of God-consciousness. The same thing was taught by Jesus when he said, "Man does not live by bread alone."

You have to attain an achievement which is of extraordinary significance. You have been given life so that you may realize the divinity which is inherent within you. Your primary duty as a human being is to give up the things which are impermanent and attain those things which are permanent. But today you are not aspiring for such extraordinary qualities. Instead, you are living a wasted life, filled with attachments. This was also Krishna's admonishment to Arjuna. He said, "Arjuna! This body consciousness and attachment to the body is binding you. You are wasting your life. Give up your attachment to the body now!"

You have to inquire why you develop attachment to the body. Consider this small example. Everyone knows that it is not right to utter a lie. Many people, at some time, take an oath resolving that they will not lie from that moment onwards. But, the very next time they get into a conversation, they tell a lie. Or take a businessman who knows that he should not deceive. He makes a resolution that he will limit himself to earning only a fair and modest profit. But the very next day, he resorts to unfair means. Or a person decides he should not gossip or hurt others with his talk, yet within minutes he has totally forgotten his vow and begins to criticize someone.

Man seems not to have a steady mind at all, and without a firm and steady mind he is unable to control his actions. On a holy day he may feel that he should be thinking of nothing but the Lord and abstaining from taking any food. But after some time he excuses himself and says, "Let me at least have a few biscuits with tea." When man is constantly deviating in this way from his own firm resolutions, there must be some very powerful entity which is working inside him, constantly defeating him. If there weren't such a powerful instinct or urge working within him, he surely would not have changed his resolve and he would have been able to use his will to hold to his announced discipline.

Desire Makes You Break Your Resolutions

So, there is some power, some force that is hidden within man, that he is not able to control or understand. If he thinks deeply and tries to discover just what exactly this power is, he will find that it is related to the three worldly qualities which are inherent in the human condition. These three attributes which comprise worldly life characterize the mind and its thinking process. They are the slothful or dull, the active or passionate, and the serene or calm tendencies. These three attributes, in various combinations, will dominate a person's life. They will be fostered or diminished by the quality of the food taken in and by one's tendency towards indulging in or depriving oneself of sleep.

Of these three attributes, the first two qualities mentioned, that of slothfulness and furious activity, are likely to encourage you to take the wrong path. Slothfulness gives rise to dislike, repulsion and anger. An excessively active nature gives rise to attraction, desire, or attachment to worldly things. Desire is the most powerful urge making man give up all his resolutions. It acts as the leader or captain of all the bad qualities.

You can plan certain programs to defeat your external enemies, but all your plans and strategies will be of no use until you have conquered your inner enemies. Once you have yielded to your inner enemies, how can you hope to conquer your external enemies? When these inner enemies have subverted your will power and defeated all your good intentions, how will you be able to challenge and conquer your external enemies? This captain of the bad qualities, desire, has made a hole and entered the house. The others like hatred, anger, greed and jealousy then follow him into the house. The moment these enemies have entered into you, you lose all your discrimination and wisdom. The moment you lose your wisdom you also give up your resolution. Therefore, the most important reason for not fulfilling your own firm resolve is the welling up of desire. Let us try to understand this further.

When palaces are constructed as residences for great emperors and kings, there is usually a fortified wall surrounding the palace, protecting it from intrusion from outside. There will be a number of guarded gates within this wall. Similarly, a temple is usually situated within a compound having a protecting wall around it in which there will be a number of gates or doors. The body can be thought of as the compound wall enclosing God, who resides inside in the temple of the heart as the *atma*. An external fortress or a temple will be constructed with the help of bricks, cement, sand and mortar, but this temple of the body is constructed out of flesh and blood. In this body of flesh there will be a number of gates in the form of the sense organs. It is through these gates of the senses that desire and the other bad qualities break in, and invade the inner sanctuary.

The Body Is Given to You to Realize the Indweller

The body gains its luster from the indweller, who is God. As long as the indweller resides in the body, it will be full of fragrance and full of life. The moment this indweller leaves the body, the body becomes foul and offensive. Without the indweller the body is a reprehensible thing. Far from being fragrant with perfume, it just emits a bad smell, moment to moment. The process of transforming a body with such repugnant qualities into an instrument for serving mankind and realizing the divinity can provide great joy and inner satisfaction. But man thinks of his body only as a means for giving him physical pleasure, and so he uses his body primarily in self-defeating ways. Krishna admonished Arjuna that this was not the mark of a real human being. He told Arjuna, "The body has been given in order to understand the indweller. Arjuna, use your body only for that sacred purpose. Animals and birds have not been given this discriminating power."

You have the capacity to experience great things through your unique ability to inquire and engage in self-examination. You have to use all your powers to understand the principles which constitute human nature. First, you must understand the power of worldly desire which makes you give up all your resolutions. Of course, there must be some desire. Without desire you cannot live for even a moment. But you must use all your desires for good. Your desires should be to help others. That constitutes living as a true human being. If you do not have the welfare of the whole society as your goal you cannot be called a human being.

Since you are born in society, since you live in society and get so many benefits from society you have to serve society. In serving society, you will be serving the Lord. Be it a small job or a big job, whatever you do must be done for the sake of the Lord. Whatever work you do must be converted into divine work. It must be transformed into worship. You must question every action you undertake and ask yourself, "Will it lead me towards the goal?" When you see the Lord everywhere in everyone, then you will be doing everything with God-consciousness.

All the lights or energies in the body originate from the one divine light coming from God. They are all the reflections of the inner light of the *atma*, which is the effulgence of the supreme Lord. Similarly, all the lights shining in individual beings come from that one light of the divinity, the one *atmic* light pervading everywhere. You should always have this in your consciousness. You are able to see the external body with its features, but since you cannot directly see the *atma*, you have not developed the right understanding of the infinite splendor of the Lord, who abides as the indweller in all beings. Consider a small example for this.

Everything Comes From the One Indwelling Divinity

There may be a great downpour. Huge torrents of water will be flowing from the trees, water will be coming from the roof and the rain-gutters, it will be coming from the overhangs, it will be spilling over from the roof of the adjoining house, and running off from there onto your house, it will be flooding the ground all around causing rushing rivulets and streams. The water will be everywhere and will seem to be coming from so many different sources, but every drop of all this water can only have originated from the sky above.

Similarly, all this speech, all this strength, all this beauty, all these skills, in whomsoever they appear, are all coming from only the one source, the one divinity pervading everywhere. You have to recognize the unity which underlies all these different traits. Once you have a firm grasp of this unity, all diversity will disappear. And once the diversity disappears, the desires will also disappear. Then, when desire goes and the attraction to worldly objects goes with it, there will be no more room for repulsion and dislike leading to anger. Therefore, when you gain divine wisdom you conquer desire and anger.

It is through spiritual practice, particularly through inner inquiry, that you will be able to realize the unity and enjoy the divinity which is always within you. This yearning to gain the light of divine wisdom, to see the one in the many, is expressed in the great prayer:

> From the unreal lead me to the real,
> From darkness lead me to the light,
> From death lead me to immortality.
> Om, Peace, Peace, Peace.

> Asatoma satgamaya,
> Tamasoma jyothir gamaya,
> Mrityorma amritam gamaya,
> Om shanti, shanti, shantihi.

Whatever work you do, if you do it for the sake of the Lord and offer it to the Lord, then the work takes on a sacred value. Anything that becomes associated with the Lord, thereby becomes sacred and highly potent. Consider, for example, an ordinary rat, which is a despicable thing. If you see a rat inside your house, you take a stick and try to kill it, or set a trap to destroy it. When you see it you feel revulsion. But, traditionally in India, the rat has been associated with a particular form of the divinity, Lord Ganesha, who is the embodiment of divine wisdom. The rat is Ganesha's vehicle which carries Ganesha around. Now, if you are a devotee of Ganesha and you see images of the rat associated with Ganesha, you revere it as the sacred instrument of the Lord. What is the reason for this? The high value that the rat carrying Ganesha has been able to obtain is due to its association with this representation of the divinity.

Similarly, when you come across a snake you may feel some fear and go to get a stick to drive it away. Or you may get a snake charmer to catch hold of it. But when the same snake adorns the neck of Lord Shiva, you worship it and offer it your prayerful salutations. What is the reason for this? The reason is that it has offered itself to the Lord and serves him alone. Therefore, it has also become divine like the Lord. Even if it is a poisonous snake, once it has offered itself to God, it acquires fame and nobility.

Association With the Divinity Makes You Divine

Once upon a time, Lord Vishnu sent a message to Lord Shiva. He sent the message through Garuda, the eagle which is Vishnu's vehicle. Garuda came to Shiva, flapping its wings. When the snake, which was adorning Shiva, caught a little feel of the wind which was being produced by the flapping of Garuda's wings, it started hissing. Although an eagle is the deadly enemy of snakes and a snake would normally slink away when an eagle comes near, now, this snake began hissing at Garuda. It had the courage to do this because of the great strength it got by virtue of the position it occupied around the neck of the Lord. When this snake fearlessly continued hissing, Garuda said, "O snake, you are there around the neck of Lord Shiva; therefore I must excuse you. But just come aside a little, come away from there for a moment." The instant the snake leaves its position, it becomes a meal for the eagle. As long as it remains in its position it gains great strength because of its nearness to divinity.

Truly, the only *I-ness* that is acceptable is when you link your *I* with the Lord, and when you say, 'I am one with the Lord.' If instead you give up your nearness and dearness to the Lord and ego takes hold of you, then you become very mean and weak and vulnerable. Even if it is just a small thing, a valueless thing, once it takes shelter in the Lord its value will be greatly increased. An ordinary stone may be lying in the street, but when a sculptor comes and shapes it into a sacred form, it is revered and worshipped in the temple. You can reflect on the extraordinary value you will gain once you associate yourself with the divinity and become one with it.

There is no possibility whatsoever of any kind of smallness finding a place in divinity. In the Rama story we have the occasion when Sita, Rama's wife, had been kidnapped by the demon king, Ravana, and kept captive in his palace. At that time, Ravana was suffering great mental anguish. Even though ten months had elapsed since she had been abducted, Sita would not yield to him.

She would not even utter a word to Ravana. Whatever threats he made against her, she remained totally indifferent to him. This fact was noted by Ravana's wife, who went to her husband and tried to correct him. She said, "Ravana, you have infinite powers. You have done a great deal of penance. You are an extraordinary devotee of Lord Shiva. You have acquired extraordinary powers to disguise yourself. You went disguised as a mendicant to abduct Sita. You have the power to go in any disguise whatsoever and appear in any form. Since you can take on whatever form you want, why haven't you gone to her in the form of Rama? Then Sita would have immediately accepted you? Why haven't you done this?" Ravana told his wife, "If I were to disguise myself as Rama and take on his sacred form, I would not have been able to retain such lustful desires!"

When you become one with divinity, all your little mean thoughts and ideas will vanish. They can no longer come and disturb your tranquillity. "Therefore," Krishna told Arjuna, "When you are fighting the battle, fight; but while fighting think of me. That is the proper way of discharging your duty. In that way you will be upholding the high ideals of protecting righteousness and you will be setting a good example for others. You will also gain a great deal of renown. If you offer everything to the divinity, you will be successful in every endeavor. To do this you must gain control of the senses. Slowly but surely you must exercise control over your sense organs until they come under your complete control. Then you will be able to realize your full potential as a human being. Then, also, you will have developed equal-mindedness, and you will be called a truly wise man.

"Now you are still living with so many attachments; when you are so bound up, how can you develop equanimity? You are keeping inner peace far away from you. All these relationships and associations that you are cultivating are constantly changing. They are impermanent and cannot possibly help you in the end. Recognize the truth which is permanent. Attach yourself to the divinity. It is ever with you. It will never leave you."

Twenty-Second Chapter

THE THREE WORLDS –
THE GROSS, THE SUBTLE AND THE CAUSAL

*A*ll *the myriad objects you see in the world are just combinations of the five elements. Everything, without exception, is made up of the five elements and only the five elements. There is no sixth element to be found anywhere.*

Embodiments of Love,

There are three types of spaces which can also be considered as universes or worlds. They are the gross physical universe, the subtle universe of the mind, and the subtlest and most pervasive of all three, referred to as the causal universe. Beyond these and serving as the basis for all three of them is the transcendental, the divine principle, the *atma*, the supreme self.

The Five Elements, Gross and Subtle

A devotee who is anxious to know the divine principle and merge with it should have an understanding of these three universes. The first of these, the gross physical universe, is made up of the five great elements, that is, ether, air, fire, water and earth. Ether, which is also called space, is the first of the five elements; it is all-pervasive and very subtle. It does not have any specific attributes except sound. After that comes air. Air can be felt but it cannot be seen. It has only two attributes, sound and touch. Next is fire. Fire can be seen. It is denser than air. It has three attributes, namely, sound, touch and form. Following fire there is water. Water is still more dense, and like fire it can be seen by the naked eye. It can also be tasted. Water has 4 attributes, namely, sound, touch, form and taste. Earth, the last and densest of all the elements, has five attributes, namely, sound, touch, form, taste and smell. You can see that the last three elements, fire, water and earth, have form. The first two, ether and air have other qualities but no form.

All things found in the physical world, are impermanent and subject to continuous change. In time, all objects undergo complete modification from one name and form to another, and then to still another, and so on. In the physical universe, everything is in constant motion. Let us inquire deeper into the nature of physical objects made up of these five elements. Consider the various atoms which exist in a given place and a given time. They will comprise the various objects which appear there at that moment. As the atoms move and change their position, the forms they make up also change. The atoms in all the objects undergo such rapid change in position, that it is hard to say when a particular change has taken place in an object. There is an ongoing process of change. All the objects made up of these changing atoms will be changing their forms continuously with time.

The atoms which make up the human body, like the atoms in any other form, change every moment, causing the body to undergo modification. All these different changes are very much like waves, such as the waves you find in the ocean. For the waves in the ocean there is no beginning or end. The drops of water in one wave get merged into the next wave. The waves in which those drops have been merged again get merged into other waves, and so on. This process of forms changing and merging goes on continuously. This is the very nature of the physical universe.

Life Is a Series of Waves

Humanity can also be described as a series of waves; and other living beings such as animals and birds can be thought of as other waves. Plants can also be thought of as waves, as can the insects and crawling things. The demonic forces can be described as still other waves, and the divine forces are yet other waves. In nature, it is impossible to say what aspect of any wave will merge with any other wave. Therefore, just as drops of one wave in the ocean will mingle with and get merged into another wave, so also you may find that a wave containing human characteristics may merge into another wave containing characteristics of other living things. It is one continuous process of change and modification. In this way, life itself can be described as a series of waves.

In the same way that the body undergoes change, the mind also undergoes change. Human nature is associated with the thinking process, which is the result of a continuous string of thoughts. These thought processes are all impermanent. They constantly undergo change. We see that everything comprising human life is undergoing change. Unless you are able to recognize the six principal types of changes which occur in life, namely, birth, growth, maturity, decline, degeneration and death, you will be deluded into thinking that life is permanent. The root cause of such lack of understanding is ignorance, which gives rise to the ego and egoistic feelings of self-delusion.

The physical universe contains billions of suns, each with its own world. There are countless planets, big and small and innumerable beings. In this entire vast universe, the earth is smaller than even a tiny drop. On this earth, India is just a little country. In this little country there is a small state. In this small state is a very little district. In this little district there is just a minor village. In this village there is an insignificant little house. And in this little house there sits a very small body. Isn't it ludicrous to think that such a small body could ever feel egoistic and blown-up with self-importance, considering its minute size in this huge universe? When you think of this world and your own place in it, you can see that physically you are the merest speck in that vast totality. Can such a tiny speck ever hope to understand the totality? Can a mere little ant ever hope to measure the whole ocean? And yet, this ocean is itself constantly undergoing change… and so does the whole earth… and so does everything else in the physical universe.

The world in which you are living is completely temporary and transient. How can an insignificant, temporary thing living in a transitory world try to understand the infinite, limitless, permanent entity? To understand the permanent entity you must occupy a permanent place within that permanent entity. Body, personality and individuality are all temporary. They can be compared to a mirage. Man is trying to quench his thirst from a mirage. A mirage appears to be made up of water, but there is no real water there. No cloth can be wetted from a mirage; no bucket can be filled there. You can never slake your thirst there. In the same way, your body and your individual nature can never satisfy your thirst for the true joy that you are seeking.

But for the Divine Principle, The World Is Totally Inert

The whole vast physical world is something like an atom in the mental world, just as your body is like a infinitesimal atom in the universe. But this incredibly huge mental world is itself only the size of a mere atom in the causal world. The physical world, being made up of the five gross elements, can be apprehended by the five senses of perception. But since everything in the physical world is made up of the five elements and only the five elements, this world is totally inert and insentient. Yet, the divine principle is inherent in it. This divine principle is also to be found in the mental world. Since the mental world is made up of the same five elements (in their subtle aspects), this world is also inert and insentient. But just as the divine principle, as indweller, is inherent in the inert body, activating it, and is inherent in the inert mind, vitalizing it, so also it is inherent in these inert physical and mental worlds, energizing and vitalizing them.

This divine principle which brings energy and vitality to the physical and mental worlds, shines forth most splendidly from the causal world, the subtlest of these vast universes. To understand this process consider the reflections in a mirror. The image or reflection has no independent existence of its own. It can shine and be seen only when the object which is being reflected is luminous, and it can move only when this same object being reflected, moves. All the apparent luster of the things making up the world arises from the causal world, and is then reflected by the mental and physical worlds, which act as mirrors. Just as the effulgence of the sun gets reflected by the moon, the effulgence present in the causal state gets reflected in the subtle mental state and the gross physical state.

Now suppose you wanted to decorate the reflection which you see of yourself in a mirror. Could you do it so that it would remain there permanently? When you see your face in the mirror, could you paint a dot on the forehead of your image in the mirror and keep it there? No, it would be a futile effort. If you were to paint a dot on the mirror where the center of your forehead is on your image, then as soon as you move, the image would also move, and the dot which was formerly in the center of your forehead would now be over your ear. Whenever you moved to one side, the image would also move to one side and the dot would no longer be in the center of the image. Then, is there any way that you can put a dot on your forehead of your image in the mirror so that it will remain there, no matter what happens? Yes. You must put the dot on you, the object which is being reflected. Then you can move in any direction, or even turn the mirror to one side or the other, and the dot would not move on your image. Here is a small story which will illustrate this principle.

The Artist Who Tried To Capture the Image of the Lord

There was once a world-famous artist. He had an extraordinary talent for figure and portrait painting. He came to Krishna, in his capital city of Dvaraka, and wanted to paint Krishna's portrait. With a beaming smile Krishna said, "Well, if you want to paint my image you can certainly do so. Tell me what I should do." The artist requested, "Swami, if you would kindly just sit still for an hour in the same place, I will draw an outline, and then later on I will fill in the details." Krishna sat down on for the artist and remained without moving. The artist made some preliminary sketches. After a while, he prostrated at Krishna's feet and said, "Swami, I am done now." Smiling, Krishna asked, "When are you going to show the picture?" The artist answered, "Swami, by tomorrow at this time I should have completed it."

Throughout the night, he worked untiringly on this difficult task of accurately painting a likeness of the Lord on canvas. When the picture was done the next morning, the artist was extremely pleased with his work. He covered the painting with a beautiful cloth and brought it to Krishna. But when the cloth was removed, it was seen that in the intervening 24 hours the form of Krishna had undergone a remarkable change. The artist put the portrait directly alongside Krishna. He looked at the picture and then looked at Krishna. He realized that there was very little resemblance between the two. Krishna also looked at the painting and pointed out, "My dear fellow, there seem to be a number of defects." The artist said, "Please forgive me, Swami. Please give me another chance. Let me try again and I will do better." It went on like this for ten days.

Each day the artist did his work over again, but it was impossible to get a proper picture. Now the artist began to feel ashamed. He decided it would be best if he just disappeared from there, and so he hurriedly left the city. On the way, sage Narada happened to meet the artist departing from the city. Narada asked the artist, "You seem quite disturbed. Tell me what is making you so unhappy." The artist explained to him all that had happened. Narada told the artist, "Well, Krishna is a master actor and a master director. He is enacting this whole drama. Using your methods you will never be able to get a true likeness of him. But if you really want to succeed then listen to my words and follow them implicitly.

The artist agreed to do exactly as Narada instructed. He returned to Dvaraka, and the very next day went to Krishna, carrying with him a picture covered with a fine cloth. He told Krishna, "Swami, I have finally been able to bring you your exact picture. Please have a look. This will always give the correct likeness of you. Whatever changes come into your expression and form, the image that is seen here will show all these changes faithfully." Then he got ready to remove the covering cloth and said, "Please accept this as my best picture of you." When the cloth came away, it revealed a clean mirror.

If you want to paint a portrait of the Lord who is permanent with temporary materials like brushes, paint, etc., you will not be able to succeed. In the physical universe everything is temporary. All forms are constantly undergoing change. Such transient forms cannot give a proper vision of the permanent Lord. If you want to have a clean and unchanging vision of the Lord, you will be able to obtain it only in the clean mirror, which is your own purified heart.

To Reach the Permanent, Go Beyond the Impermanent

Trying to know the Lord through the changing forms found in the gross physical universe, is a type of delusion. The permanent unchanging entity cannot be known through impermanent, changing forms. Whatever knowledge you get this way will be impermanent. Whatever joy you may derive from trying to know him in this way will only be temporary. The basic nature of these five elements is that they are constantly undergoing change. To reach the state of the permanent, you have to go beyond these five elements and their changing forms.

Suppose you go on a pilgrimage to a temple to have a vision of the Lord. Coming there, you may have had to undergo a great many difficulties. Then, when you finally arrive there and have a chance to go into the temple, you stand before the likeness of the Lord with your heart filled with yearning. You look at the sacred image, but immediately you find yourself closing your eyes as you experience the intense feelings of being in the divine presence. Spontaneously, you close your eyes and turn your vision inwards. Having gone to so much trouble to get there to have a look at the holy image, why, once you are there, do you close your eyes and look within yourself? What is the inner significance of this? You turn your sight inward because you realize that in order for you to get a permanent and true vision of the Lord, you have to look inside your heart. You know intuitively that the pictures taken in through your eyes will remain fleeting impressions, superimposed on impermanent thoughts. After having registered these visual images in the thoughts, they must be fixed so that they can become unchanging impressions in the heart.

Although you cannot get a direct experience of the divinity in the physical universe, the indirect vision of the divinity that you can get there will give you some sacred experiences. Just because the physical world is transient and changing you should not renounce these feelings of connectedness with the divinity, even though they may be short-lived. These feelings will give you some temporary joy. First, you will have to secure this temporary joy and then slowly and gradually make the journey towards permanent joy. This journey will take you through the three worlds, the physical, the mental and the causal, going from the grossest to the most subtle. It is only in the causal that you will find the image of real truth. The causal arises from the transcendental state, which interpenetrates these three worlds, and is beyond them. That transcendental source which illuminates the causal is the unchanging light of the *atma*.

You Are Not Just One But Three

You can get some understanding of all this by contemplating the statement that Swami has often made, 'You are not one person but three... the one you think you are, the one that others think you are and the one you really are.' The one you think you are, the body, is ephemeral and untrue. Whatever life you are living today, whatever experiences you are having today, they are all transient. Both the body and its activities, are temporary and associated with the physical world. Now, when others think of you, they do so not only in terms of your physical makeup but also in terms of your personality and character traits. Theirs is a more mentalized image of you. Therefore, the one that others think you are, relates to the mind and the mental world, which is also changing and untrue. But, the one you really are, is the *atma*, the unchanging truth, shining in the causal state.

A piece of ice in your hand will start melting until it becomes water again. Why is this so? Because melting is the very nature of ice. Similarly, changeability or transitoriness is the very nature of everything that appears in the physical world. Even while you are trying to understand the gross physical universe, you have to think of the finer, subtler inner worlds. The physical world is at the gross level. You experience it during the waking-state. The same thing in a subtle form is associated with the mental world, which you experience in the dream-state. In the waking-state, you are able to see objects because of the light emanating from the sun and the moon. But the sun and the moon of your waking state are not present in the dream-state. It is only the light which emanates from the mental world which helps you to see the objects of that world.

The moment you push aside the gross, the subtle light becomes evident inside. During the day you are not able to see the stars. But just because you cannot see them does not mean that they are not there. Stars continue to shine even in the daytime, and yet because the sun's effulgence is so great, you cannot see them. As the light of the sun becomes dim at dusk, you begin to see the shining stars.

Behind the Gross the Subtle, Behind the Subtle the Causal

Behind the outer, grosser experience lies the subtler, finer experience, from which the outer has sprung. And within the subtle can be found the template for the gross. Even in the childhood of a great spiritual teacher, you can see the mark of one whose mission it is to bring light to mankind. And when you apprehend this underlying subtle quality of that being, you clearly see how it has shaped every aspect of that life through all its outer manifestations and through every major period of life.

There is another state that transcends both the gross and the subtle. That is the causal. The causal state does not have any movement; it does not undergo any change. Within it is to be found the self-effulgent light of the *atma*. It is because of this all-pervasive light of the *atma* shining in and through the causal state that you are able to experience the mental and the physical worlds. If there were no subtle mental world there could be no gross physical world for you. But, if there were no causal, there would be neither subtle mental nor gross physical worlds for you. To realize your divine state, your journey has to take you from the physical through the mental to the causal. Your truth is rooted in the causal. You must use the physical to reach the mental and the mental to reach the causal.

Ultimately, it is the light of the *atma*, the indweller, which activates and vitalizes all of these states of experience. The *atma* is the source and the substratum of all three worlds. In the ocean you will find waves and swells and foam on the surface, large-scale currents below the surface and the stillness of the deep ocean regions, far below. The waves and foam, the currents, and the deep ocean waters are not different. Water is the common element which interpenetrates all of them. But, it appears as if the waves, the currents and the deep ocean are different.

In the phenomenal world also, you have to discover the common element that underlies all experience and unifies the physical, the mental and the causal worlds. You can associate these three universes with the three states of consciousness. You can think of the waking state as the physical, the dream-state as the mental, and the deep-sleep state as the causal. Beyond these three states, interpenetrating them and common to all of them, is a fourth state. That is the superconscious state, the transcendental state. The unconscious state of deep-sleep is associated with the causal. It has a very profound quality of peace. But by itself, the deep-sleep state will not provide you with a permanent experience of real bliss. The bliss is there but you are not conscious of it. It is only after you come back to the waking-state from deep sleep that you remember the serene feeling of total rest you were enjoying. However, in the super-conscious state, you will be able to enjoy eternal peace and bliss, and be fully conscious of it always.

Samadhi Is Equal-Mindedness

The experience of that bliss has been referred to as the state of *samadhi*. What is the meaning of *samadhi*? *Samadhi* is ordinarily mistaken to be an emotional state in which a person acts abnormally, as if in a state of high excitement or trance. You may think that *samadhi* is something different from the waking, dream or deep-sleep states. But, truly, *samadhi* is something common to all three states. The meaning of *samadhi* is inherent in the word itself. Its root syllables *sama* or equal, and *dhi* or mind, together mean equal-mindedness. To be equal-minded in cold or in heat, in profit or in loss, in praise or in censure... that is *samadhi*. Therefore, a person who is immersed in *samadhi*, whose mind is in equanimity, will always be in a state of bliss, whether he is in the waking state immersed in his every-day life, or whether he is in the dream-state or in the deep-sleep state. Everyone yearns for such a beatific state. To attain it, a great deal of spiritual practice is necessary. You also have to earn the grace of the Lord by living a life replete with the virtuous qualities that are pleasing to him.

After describing the noble characteristics of a truly wise man, Krishna told Arjuna, "Arjuna, there is no value whatsoever in your basing your actions only on considerations involving the body. Follow my commands! Discharge your duties while all the time thinking of me. Then you will be able to experience and enjoy the divinity that is everywhere. This divinity is the unity which underlies all the diversity in the world. Base your actions on that. Constantly concentrate on that divinity. I am that divinity and you are very dear to me. When you concentrate on me, then I will be fully concentrated on you." For a wise man, whatever be the state he is in, his thoughts and feelings will not undergo any change. He will have developed an unwavering attitude, being focused at all times on the divine principle within.

Who will be surprised to hear that fire is accompanied by heat? Burning is the natural state of fire, just as cold is the natural state of ice. So also, everyone who is born will die. This should be considered as totally natural. Anyone who recognizes this truth will not be subjected to sorrow. In all places and in all circumstances, develop an equal-mindedness. Whatever happens, always keep your mind firmly fixed on the divinity, which is your true self. In order to develop this ability to think of the *atma*, your divine nature, in all places and at all times, you will have to gain a deep understanding of the characteristics of the three worlds, the physical, the mental and the causal.

In the evening you take your food and shortly afterwards you go to bed. Soon after that you are asleep and get a number of dreams. Many things happen to you in your dreams but after getting up nothing remains of the dream state. In the waking state you engage in many different activities and have numerous experiences, but then later on, when you go back to sleep again all these activities of the waking state are superseded by the events in the dream state. We see that so many changes come about in just 24 hours.

You Alone Are True

There are a number of striking differences in your experiences of the dream-state and those of the waking-state. Considering this, what should you believe and what should you not believe? You may ask, 'Which is true, which is not true? Am I the one who experiences all these various happenings in the waking state, or am I the one who experiences all those other happenings in the dream-state?' The wisdom teachings give the answer, 'You are neither this nor that. You are not the one experiencing the waking-state, nor are you the one experiencing the dream-state, nor are you the one asleep in the deep-sleep state. You transcend all these. You are the transcendental reality itself.'

That which you think exists really does not exist. That which you do not believe exists really exists. When you acquire wisdom you realize that there is only the One which really exists and is eternally true. That is the *atma*, the transcendental principle. But this principle of *atma* is not easily accessible to ordinary people. All that you read, listen to and experience are merely attributes of the physical state. Starting with this you have to reach out and try to achieve your goal. From the form you have to progress to the formless, from the changeable you have to progress to the changeless, from the attributeful you have to progress to the attributeless. Beyond all these, transcending all attributes and going even beyond the attributeless and formless, is the unchanging and unwavering superconscious state. This is the goal of all spiritual aspirants. One who has become immersed in this state is described as a wise sage. You may wonder if Arjuna achieved this state. Yes, Krishna himself conferred this state on Arjuna. Krishna transformed Arjuna into an instrument of the divine and thereby turned him into a truly wise being.

If a wise man does not engage in activities he will not be able to set a good example to the common people. In schools you will find a director of physical education and a drill master. The drill master takes his orders from the director. During the calisthenics drill, the director will keep quiet, but the drill master will call out, '1..2..3..!' and perform all the drill movements. He has to set the example. Only then can the others be expected to follow him. Similarly, the wise man, while taking his orders from the inner director, sets an example so ordinary people will be able to follow.

When Krishna gave Arjuna the *Gita* he transformed him into an ideal man. Krishna told him, "I will turn you into my instrument to do my work, so that you will be an example to all of humanity." What is the deeper meaning of Krishna doing all this for Arjuna? *Arjuna* means the one with a pure heart. Arjuna was always living in Krishna. A number of times Krishna referred to Arjuna as 'the one who lives in the effulgence of God'. All the deeper aspects of the relationship of Krishna and Arjuna can be gleaned from the names that Krishna gave to Arjuna. Arjuna's only duty was to implicitly follow Krishna's commands.

The Qualities of the Truly Wise

Arjuna said, "Swami, I will obey your commands, whatever they may be. Whatever you ask of me I will do. I will not undertake anything on my own, anything that is outside of your directions." This is the true attitude of a sage. He will not have the feeling of *I* and *mine*. He will not have any egoism or attachments. His every action will destroy any traces of ego or possessiveness. He will accept and follow only the commands of the Lord, who is no different than his own inner director. Because these noble qualities are so important for spiritual unfoldment, the characteristics of a wise man are explained at great length in the second chapter of the *Gita*.

But, just describing the qualities of a wise sage would not have been of much use, so Krishna began by explaining the qualities of the three states and the different aspects of the three worlds. Arjuna had the intellectual capacity to grasp the true significance of this. After being given the vision of the cosmic form of the Lord, he immediately understood its deeper meaning. He realized that it meant the union between the physical, the mental and the causal. After having had the vision of the cosmic form, whenever Arjuna closed his eyes thereafter, he would continuously see Krishna as an indelible impression on his heart. He realized that what he had seen with his eyes wide open was in the physical plane. Then, after closing his eyes, whatever still registered in his mind and was being seen by him internally, was in the mental plane. The indelible impression of this vision that remained in his heart was in the causal plane. It is something like print on paper. Once a picture is printed, it is impossible to separate it again from the paper. In this way, the cosmic form of Krishna became a permanent impression in Arjuna's heart.

Arjuna was the ideal man. Yet, in order to serve as an example for all of humanity, he undertook all kinds of common activities just like an ordinary person. Inside, within himself, he always kept his mind firmly fixed on Lord Krishna, who was the formful expression of his own true self, the *atma*. Arjuna knew that this physical body was for the sole purpose of obeying the commands of the inner director, manifested for him in the divine form of Krishna. In the *Gita*, Krishna held out this quality of inner surrender as the ideal mark of a truly wise man.

Twenty-Third Chapter

LIMIT DESIRES, BE EVER CONTENT
AND YOU WILL BE DEAR TO GOD

Whatever is born passes through six stages of life, namely, birth, growth, maturity, decline, degeneration and death. But, what is never born, never dies. For it these stages do not apply.

Embodiments of Love,

The second chapter of the *Gita* relates to the path of wisdom. The principle that underlies the wisdom teachings is that whatever is born must die, but what was never born, can never die. What is never born and will never die? The *atma*. *Atma* has neither birth nor death. It never undergoes any kind of modifications. *Atma* is permanent. It is immutable. It is everlasting. It is attributeless. It is your own true nature. The body is born and the body experiences the various phases of life and dies, but the indweller of the body remains unaffected by all these bodily changes. This indweller is the *atma*. It is free of illusion, devoid of *maya*. Once you understand this divine principle you will recognize it as the only thing of true value, the only thing worth knowing. Everything else is ephemeral and impermanent. You must make every effort to acquire the knowledge of *atma* and thereby gain lasting joy.

Be Satisfied, Do Not Chase After Desires

Do not encourage the multiplication of desires. Be satisfied with whatever you have been given. In the chapter on devotion, Krishna enumerated the 26 noble qualities which endear a devotee to the Lord. Of these, contentment stands out as one of the most important characteristics of a devotee. It means not running after worldly enjoyments. You have enjoyed so many luxuries and so many sensual things in your life but you have not gained peace and fulfillment from them. Give up chasing after them and you will gain contentment.

The heart of a person who does not have contentment is like a bamboo basket riddled with holes. If you try to draw water out of a well using such a basket, by the time it comes up, all the water will have leaked out. There will not even be a drop of water left to quench your thirst. Similarly, when you are suffering from pangs of desire and greed, all your contentment leaks away before you even have a chance to fulfill your desires. When contentment leaves your heart, discontent remains behind to take its place.

Desire breeds more desire. A person who does not have anything at all may feel very happy and contented when he gets 100 rupees. But once he gets the 100 rupees, he thinks how nice it would be if he could get 1000 rupees. If by chance he gets the 1000 rupees, he desires to have a million rupees. Then he would aspire to become a major property owner. From a property owner he would want to become a legislator and then a minister and then the prime minister. Finally, he would want to use all his status and wealth to attain the God-state. But you can never reach divinity with the help of power and wealth. As the person's desires cross all limits, he becomes discontented and his wealth gains him no inner peace at all. You must learn how to gain contentment from whatever you have, being satisfied with whatever wealth you have been given. Your responsibility is to take care of the possessions you have received through the grace of God, and be happy.

You Must Win God's Love

You all praise God, but it is far more important that God praises you. You declare your love for God, but you have to find out if God has declared his love for you. You believe that God is yours, but has God told you that you are his? Suppose you send a registered letter to someone. You will gain full satisfaction only after you receive an acknowledgment from the addressee that the letter has been received and read. Declaring your love for God and declaring that God is great can be compared to sending a registered letter. But that alone will not satisfy you. You experience the deepest contentment only when you get the positive acknowledgment from God that you have his love and that he considers you great also. It is only when he says, "You are my very own. You are most dear to Me!" that you attain total fulfillment.

Arjuna got such an assurance from the Lord after he said to Lord Krishna, "Swami, you are my all, I am yours! I surrender everything to you!" Previously, Arjuna had a number of desires, but when he surrendered fully to the Lord he renounced all his wants and desires. Then he earned the declaration from the Lord, "Dear one, you are mine!" To gain this result you have to engage yourself in spiritual practice. The hope and fruit of all spiritual practice is to get this declaration from the Lord that you are his. This becomes your greatest treasure, the consummation of your life.

Even if you are highly educated, even if you occupy a very high position in life, even if you are very wealthy, whatever be your station in life, when you go abroad you must have a passport to travel in a foreign land. A person may say, "I'm highly educated. I'm very wealthy. I have vast land holdings. I would like to have a passport." But just by saying that he will not get the passport. All these things may be personal attainments and accomplishments, but if you want to go to another country there is a particular procedure that you must follow. This procedure cannot be different for educated people and for uneducated people, for wealthy ones and for poor ones.

Even in such a small thing as going somewhere by bus or train or plane, no one will care to know your position and accomplishments. As long as you have a ticket with you, no one will ask you if you are a wealthy person or an educated one and what position you are holding. They will be satisfied to know that you have a ticket, and they will take you to your destination. If you do not have the ticket you will be left behind, no matter what your credentials are.

In the same way, if you want to gain entry into the kingdom of liberation, you need to have the grace of God. That is required for entry. The grace of God is your passport. But even a passport is not enough. If you merely have a passport, then there may still be some objections and problems. You should also have a visa; that gives you the right to enter your place of destination. In addition to the grace of God you must also have the merit of your spiritual efforts and yearnings.

The giver may be ready to give the gift, but the receiver must also be ready to receive it. God is prepared to give, but you must have the capacity to receive. Through your surrender and spiritual efforts you become ready to receive God's grace. Therefore, to enter into the kingdom of liberation you must have God's love and you must also have the merit of your own spiritual efforts. When these two come together you will be able to gain liberation.

Contentment Is the Real Wealth

The *Gita* taught that if you want to enter the kingdom of liberation there are 26 noble qualities that you should acquire. But, truly, it is enough if you have gained just one virtuous quality. That will be sufficient to qualify you for entry. Of all of the virtuous qualities given in the *Gita* chapter on devotion one of the most important is contentment. Only the one who has contentment can be considered great. Swami asks quite often, "Who is the greatest human being in this world?" The answer is, "The one who is always satisfied." Therefore, develop this contentment in yourself.

Do not get lost in the world aspiring for impermanent joys, impermanent wealth, impermanent position and luxuries. There is no objection to your enjoying the happiness which comes your way. But never forget that the world is made up only of the five elements. It has no eternal value. Your body also consists only of the five elements. As long as you consider this world real, you will tend to have attachments to the body and to a given place. It is best if you do not waste your time caught up with these attachments. Instead, always remember the goal. Here is a small example.

There was a wealthy man who had traveled the world over. He resolved to build a palatial mansion without equal anywhere. It was to be a house of such extraordinary grandeur that it would be beyond the imagination of anyone. He resolved to construct this unique structure even if it cost him tens of millions of rupees. A number of engineers and architects were called from various countries for this purpose. Ultimately he completed his beautiful mansion, and he now had a house which satisfied people from all points of view and different cultural backgrounds. Tens of thousands of people came to look at it. This wealthy man made all the arrangements for a grand inauguration of his unique place. Before the inauguration, he called a number of experts and asked them, "Do you find any defects, any faults in this building anywhere, even in the smallest detail?" They could find none. It seemed to be perfect.

He invited all kinds of people to the function, including many wealthy citizens and high officials. He also invited great sages to gain their blessings. Among the invited guests there were a number of truly wise men. All elaborate arrangements were made for their stay. After they were assembled, he prayed to them, "I humbly ask you to let me know if there are any defects, any shortcomings in this structure?" The engineers who had constructed the building echoed his sentiments and also asked the assembled crowd, "Who can come forward and just point out a single flaw in this beautiful building? We feel that it is absolutely flawless and magnificent. It is totally unique and modern, perfect in every detail."

At this point, a *yogi* who was standing in the corner, stepped out and addressed the wealthy man who was hosting the affair. The *yogi* said, "Esteemed sir, I see two major flaws in this building." All the people assembled there were greatly surprised. The engineers and architects were shocked. Everyone was most curious to know what these defects were. The wealthy man, whose house it was, folded his hands in supplication and said to the great sage, "Swami, please tell me what those defects are that you have spotted. Everyone is anxiously awaiting your answer."

The *yogi* said, "O rich man, these are faults for which you are not to blame, nor your engineers or architects or workmen. These defects are not within your reach or anyone else's to correct. One defect is that with the passage of time this building, and everything that is now standing here, will fall down and be reduced to rubble. This is a defect that cannot be changed. The second failing is that the person who built this structure will also perish and be forgotten. This too cannot be changed. Even though these conclusions may be delayed for a short period of time, they will both come to pass. Not realizing this truth you think that you have accomplished something flawless and great, that your achievement will be permanent. But it is not so. These defects that I have mentioned will always prevail in the end."

Such is the state of affairs for people who forget death and think that they, or their works or reputation, will be permanent. Only when you keep your focus on the *atma* will you be filled with contentment and feel unending joy and bliss. When you have such everlasting peace and contentment, you will be established in a mansion that can never perish, for then you are abiding in the *atma*, your unchanging permanent self. It alone has lasting value. There is nothing that can be compared with that dwelling place. Unlike the mansions you find in the world, it is perfect and permanent, free from all defects. Therefore, you have to recognize the truth that in this mundane world everything is impermanent. Keep your sight and concentration on the permanent *atma*. Constantly engage yourself in spiritual practice in order to achieve this inner vision and remain ever contented, undisturbed by worldly affairs.

Atma Is Never Born, *Atma* Never Dies

To dispel Arjuna's confusion about his outer role and his true identity, Krishna said, "Arjuna, you are disturbed because you think you are going to kill some people. You have lost sight of the truth that underlies all beings. Know that you are the immortal self and your kinsmen, though they have been engaged in evil deeds, are in essence the very same immortal self. Then who is going to die and who will be engaged in killing? You who are the *atma* do not kill and your kinsmen who are the same *atma* will not be slain by you. Death relates to the physical body, not to the true self. *Atma* cannot be killed. *Atma* is never born. *Atma* never dies. It is only when you understand and practice this truth that you will be following the wisdom teachings and performing your duty, unaffected by outcomes. Recognize the immortality of *atma* and fight to uphold righteousness. Then you will act in harmony with divine will and even in the thick of battle you will be immersed in inner peace. When you recognize the principle of the *atma*, realizing its permanent nature, you will know that there can be no defect or flaw of any kind in it. Then no disturbance can come into your mind and no doubts will ever becloud you."

All this must be understood in its deeper meaning. These statements that one does not kill and that one is not going to be killed, are quickly accepted at face value by most people who read the *Gita*. But they make no attempt to understand the deeper significance of these declarations, which are based on the principle of the immortal and unchanging nature of the *atma*. If you look about to see how people are practicing this teaching you will see that they are not practicing it at all, although they will freely repeat all the verses and even give lectures on them to others. Here is a small example of this.

There was a certain hunter, a very bad man who had killed a great number of animals. His killing soon spread to include human beings. He began murdering all the people who passed through the forest and came his way, in order to strip them of whatever possessions they were carrying. When he was caught and convicted, the judge decided to sentence him to death by hanging as punishment for all the horrible crimes he had committed. It was announced that the judgment would be read in court the next day. When he was led into court for sentencing, this criminal brought with him a copy of the *Gita*, which he kept in his pocket. The judge declared that by 7 o'clock the following morning, he would be hanged. But now, quite boldly, the criminal spoke up, declaring, "Sir, why are you inflicting such a drastic punishment on me?" The judge replied, "This sentence is being given because you have murdered so many innocent people."

At this point the convict took out the *Gita* from his pocket. He showed it to the judge and said, "According to this holy scripture, Sir, I am neither the killer of those people nor have they been killed!" And he brazenly added, "How can you deny these statements made by God himself?" Well, the judge was equal in cleverness to this man. Without a moment's hesitation, the judge said, "Yes, it is certainly true that you have not killed, nor have those people been killed. Similarly, as pertains to my judgment, I am not killing you nor will you be killed. Nevertheless, the hanging will take place at 7 o'clock tomorrow morning."

Reduce Your Desires and Remember the *Atma*

You cannot use the *Gita* to change the circumstances to suit your convenience. You have to practice the truths that are contained in the great statements made in the *Gita* after realizing their inner significance. The *Gita* has not just been taught to Arjuna. This sacred teaching has been given to all people born on earth. The *Gita* has been given to the entire world with Arjuna as the medium. Arjuna stands as the representative of all mankind. These teachings which have been given to the representative of humanity are applicable to humanity as a whole.

To follow these teachings you have to gradually reduce your desires and wants, and gain an understanding of the principle of the *atma*. That will bring you to a permanent state of contentment. Examine your life to see if you are practicing these teachings in your day-to-day activities. Just by memorizing the 700 verses of the *Gita* you will not be able to experience the great truths that are hidden there. These deeper truths will reveal themselves in the circumstances of your daily life. It is there in everyday situations that you will be able to experience these truths directly. You have to clearly understand the qualities that have to be practiced while discharging your duties. You have to recognize how each of these 26 qualities will help you reach your goal; and then you have to apply them in your daily life.

Therefore, keep your desires and your greed under control and be ever content. This will earn for you the love of God. Your profession of love for God is not enough. That you love God is not of much use unless you get His love directed towards you. You have to learn how to earn His love and grace. There is no point in shouting and saying that God is yours. You have to aspire to hear from God the declaration that you are His. That is the most important thing you must achieve in this life.

From this moment on, develop the sacred qualities which will evoke this priceless declaration of love from the Lord, and thereby sanctify your life.

PATIENCE AND FORBEARANCE –
THE HEART OF SPIRITUAL PRACTICE

Of all the noble characteristics that a devotee must possess, none is more vital than forbearance. When you have forbearance you shine with a peaceful forgiving quality that remains undisturbed under all circumstances. When you have forbearance, then no matter how others treat you, whether they are caring and friendly or whether they are hostile or indifferent towards you, you will feel only love towards them.

Embodiments of Love,

Forbearance is the heart of all spiritual practice. It is the one quality which all spiritual aspirants must achieve in their lifetime. For the truly wise, for the great sages and great souls, forbearance is their very splendor, their penance, their sacrifice, their righteousness. It is their wisdom, their immeasurable love. Forbearance is the essence of their nonviolence, their compassion, their depth of happiness. Forbearance is the very mark of all great beings. Truly, forbearance is everything. Without forbearance it is not possible to realize the truth of the *atma*, to manifest the everlasting and ever-luminous divine presence, that shines undiminishably within you.

Realize the *Atma* Through Your Direct Experience

As long as you think that your body is real and your divinity is not real, you will not understand the principle of *atma*. And as long as you identify yourself with your body and not with your essential truth, your real self, you will not be able to gain the direct experience of your indwelling divinity. The *atma* has been spoken of in many ways, but you can comprehend it only through your direct experience.

Someone may describe the exquisite sweetness of mango nectar to you in elaborate detail and with great enthusiasm; but unless you have tasted the nectar and experienced it directly, you will not be able to appreciate its unique sweetness. When the nectar is on your tongue and you delight in its taste, then you understand what is meant by its sweetness. Similarly, unless you seek the direct experience of the Lord, unless you engage in spiritual practices and develop the noble qualities that are dear to the Lord, you will never be able to savor the divine sweetness arising from the *atma*.

What is the way to immortality? It is the removal of immorality. Swami has often spoken of this. Only when you remove the immorality within you, will you be able to gain immortality. When you remove the weaknesses, such as jealousy, hatred, anger, pride and all the other evils which have obscured your truth, then you will be able to enjoy the strength of the unchanging presence of divinity inside you. It is when you embody at least one or two of the 26 virtues which have been mentioned in the *Gita*, when you understand their deeper meaning, practice them and make them part of your daily life, then it will become possible for you to realize the immortal nature of the *atma*. Of the many virtuous qualities that a devotee can develop, forbearance is at the heart of all of them.

You Gain Forbearance Through Difficult Circumstances

Forbearance cannot be learned by studying books. It cannot even be acquired by the teachings of a *guru*. It is not something which can be purchased in the bazaar. It is only by faithfully sticking to your spiritual practice, when you are under trying circumstances, that you will be able to acquire forbearance. It is when you are under test, in situations which are full of problems and difficulties, that the cultivation of forbearance takes place. Under those trying circumstances, weaknesses which are hidden within you will show their ugly heads. They will manifest in you as anger, fear, arrogance, hatred and many other evils that cover your essential truth. It is at such times that you must recognize these weaknesses and rise above them. Whatever action you must undertake that is appropriate to the situation, your inner state must be unaffected and rooted in unwavering peace and love. This is the practice of forbearance.

If you have not developed forbearance then you will suffer a lot of unhappiness and lack of peace in your life. Without forbearance you may take to harmful and evil ways. Therefore, it is essential that you recognize the importance of forbearance. All the education, strength and renown that you may have acquired will be of no use to you if you do not have forbearance. There have been a number of accomplished people who have acquired great powers by means of penance, but they were unable to enjoy the fruits of their penance because they lacked forbearance. Dearth of forbearance has made great scholars lose their prestige. Lack of forbearance is the most frequent reason for the loss of kingdoms by ruling kings. Forbearance is the shining jewel that decorates a human being. If this important quality is lost, you will suffer innumerable problems and sorrows. Therefore, develop forbearance. It is essential for your spiritual progress. Without this quality you will come to ruin.

Cultivate forbearance by the arduous practice of putting yourself to the test in very difficult circumstances. Forbearance is your vital protection. When you are equipped with forbearance you will not be troubled by grief or difficulties, by problems or unexpected situations. There is nothing extraordinary about returning good for good, but doing good in return for bad is an extraordinary quality. What is meant by doing good at all times, no matter whether it is right or wrong action that is directed towards you? When you are established in your essential truth, when you are in touch with your reality, you cannot but give the proper response under all circumstances, and it will come from the infinite reservoir of goodness and love, which is your unchanging nature. The practice of such a virtue requires a great deal of skill and courage, and a deep commitment to the essential truth of the one divinity, present in all hearts.

However much other people may criticize you, however much they may undermine and condemn you, you should never lose forbearance; you should remain unperturbed and continue to enjoy inner peace. When others admonish you, what will you lose – you, who in your essence are immortal? How can they possibly harm you? When you have forbearance and you are established in your divine nature, how can anyone diminish you? How can anyone affect your essential truth, which is unwavering, no matter the circumstances? But if, because of weakness, you lose forbearance and forget your truth, then you are subject to endless suffering, and you lose everything.

The Tree, the River and the Cow

There are three important aspects of nature which are very useful to man. These are the tree, the river and the cow. Without trees, rivers and cows, humanity would not be able to function very well. Whatever violence is done to a tree, however much trouble is given to it by cutting its branches and taking some of its wood, the tree continues to give protection from rain and sun to any person who takes shelter under it, and it will try to continue to give that person joy. Trees have been doing good for people by giving fruit, flowers and fuel, even though in return, people may have been doing harm to them.

In the case of rivers, however much the rivers are polluted by people, in whatever way people may use and abuse them without showing any gratitude towards them, they will still continue to serve humanity by bringing the fresh waters from the clear mountain sides. And even as the rivers serve all, their concentration is on reaching the ocean which is their home and goal. The waters of rivers give life to humanity. Whether you put their pristine waters to good use or bad, the rivers do not mind. They will continue to serve as they return home to their ultimate source.

Then there are the cows who deny milk to their own calves in order to provide milk for humanity. They freely give such a fine and nourishing food to mankind. Whatever troubles you might give a cow, it will always give you sweet milk, not bitter milk. So cows also have been doing only good for humanity, whereas humanity may be giving all kinds of troubles to cows. Men may beat or encage them, they may starve them or abuse them, but cows retain their peaceful inner disposition and continue to serve, under all circumstances. These three, the tree, the river and the cow are good examples of this sterling quality of forbearance.

There are Times When You Should Withhold Forbearance

But, sometimes, the outward signs of forbearance must be tempered, to provide the appropriate response to a particular situation. Although at all times, you should have forbearance deeply ingrained in your heart, you should not go on displaying it under all circumstances that come up in the world. When practicing forbearance you must carefully examine the conditions that apply and employ discrimination. It is well known in Indian history that a vicious invader threatened the northern kingdom, and gave a lot of trouble to its good king. This merciless assailant invaded the country 17 times. Whenever he came, he caused widespread destruction in the country and took away a great deal of wealth. He put the entire populace through innumerable difficulties and losses. In spite of this, when the kingdom's ruler caught his enemy, he excused him and allowed him to return to his own country.

Because of his generous heart, the good king, lacking in proper discrimination, forgave his ruthless foe. Whenever the king vanquished his foe and the defeated villain asked for pardon and protection, the good king excused him and sent him back home, without inflicting any punishment. But the heartless invader did not show any gratitude at all. He was an absolutely unrepentant, wicked fellow and he continued with his hatred towards the king and his greed to conquer the kingdom. The moment the invader was freed and back in his own country, he invaded again and again. Finally, through deceit, he succeeded in catching hold of the good king. Mercilessly he put out the king's eyes. To people who are ungrateful like that, who are vengeful like snakes, you should not display forbearance. You need to use discrimination and respond appropriately.

When To Use Forbearance and When It Is Inappropriate

In the great epic, the *Mahabharata*, which chronicles the war of righteousness between the Pandava brothers and their wicked cousins, there is an incident depicted in which Arjuna dragged the murderer of all her children, before Draupadi, the wife of the five Pandava brothers. The Pandavas had just won the war when the horrendous deed was committed. Even though Draupadi was overcome with sorrow, she pointed out to Arjuna the circumstances under which a wicked person should be excused. Draupadi told Arjuna that it was not proper to execute a person who was overwhelmed with fear, or a person who was humble and penitent and pleading for mercy, or a person who had lost his sanity and become deranged, or a person who had acted out of inconsolable grief, or women and children, in general, even if they deserve such punishment. For such, it is proper to show forbearance and treat them mercifully.

But, for people who are repeatedly ungrateful and malicious, who are unrepentant and untrustworthy, it is not appropriate to display forbearance. You need to deal with them firmly, according to the circumstances. But remember that all such actions relate only to your outer worldly life. In your heart, you must never lose your peaceful inner state of forbearance. For your spiritual life, forbearance is an essential quality necessary to reach the divine state, and you must practice it assiduously.

In the case of Jesus you can also see his highly-developed quality of forbearance. There were 12 disciples living and traveling about with him. Jesus extended all love and compassion, all protection and shelter to them. But one of them, Judas, was tempted by money and became a traitor to his master. Despite Judas' infidelity, Jesus remained unperturbed and continued to extend Judas his love. There is no need for you to pray to God to see that such people are punished. As was the case with Judas, their own acts will bring them to ruin. Whatever wicked actions a person commits, the fruits of those actions will have to be borne by him alone. No one can escape the fruits of his own actions. You may not be able to predict when and under what circumstances he will suffer the consequences, but the suffering is certain to come some time.

In both great Indian epics, the *Ramayana* and the *Mahabharata*, there are a number of instances depicted which show how people suffered in the end, when they did not practice forbearance. Consider the great suffering the five Pandava brothers underwent, having to go to the forest and live on roots and leaves, because of the hasty action of the eldest brother, Dharmaraja, in accepting a challenge to play a game of dice. Dharmaraja, as the king, felt it his righteous duty to respond to the challenge, and although he knew the game was rigged against him, he was in such a hurry to defend his honor, that he ignored the instructions given by Krishna and the advice given by his brothers. With a determination to be true to his principles, he hastened into the gambling game and had to suffer the consequences. As a result, he and his brothers lost their kingdom and were banished to the forest for fourteen years, undergoing untold deprivations and difficulties. It is only because of Dharmaraja's haste and lack of forbearance that all these consequences occurred.

You even find that a great soul like Rama, at times, did not have sufficient patience. At the end of the *Ramayana*, there is the incident in which Rama, after hearing the criticism and comments of one worthless washerman, immediately decided to banish Sita from the kingdom. Afterwards he suffered great pangs of separation. But, Rama was the avatar of his age, the embodiment of all the divine principles. In the case of the divinity, there will always be some deeper meaning and significance to the avatar's actions. Still, when you try to understand Rama's actions in a worldly sense, you can see that because of losing patience, Rama banished Sita and then had to suffer afterwards. Of course, when people who do only good and live only for the welfare of others, experience various troubles they will suffer their problems graciously. In this way they act as an example and teach the value of patience and forbearance when undergoing hardships in the world.

Undue Haste and Delay Are Two Extremes to Be Avoided

The qualities of patience and forbearance must be used with great discrimination, depending on the circumstances and conditions. There are circumstances when you are justified in acting quickly. You must always think ahead and be aware of the consequences of what you do. Under certain conditions, exercising unrestrained forbearance may lead to great troubles later on. Under most circumstances, haste creates problems. But if you are unduly slow, it may also lead to problems. It is said that undue delay can turn nectar into poison.

Slowness and haste are two extremes. On the one hand if you are too hasty your actions may be fatal, but if you delay too long they may also be poisonous. So, you must use your discriminating power and exercise patience to the degree appropriate to the circumstances. If first-aid must be given immediately, or if you are attending to a person who is very sick and is likely to lose his life in a few minutes if medicine is not given, then you must act quickly. In such situations there must be no delay. Delay would be poisonous and you must act fast and do the proper thing.

There are also circumstances when you are faced with people who are wicked and who are pursuing harmful ways. Then it may be necessary for you to warn them and correct them or otherwise deal with the situation. In such a case, appearing to lose patience may be your best recourse. Frequently, all that is necessary is just to change the sound of your voice a little. It doesn't mean that you have lost your inner quality of forbearance. Even if you elevate your voice and appear to be angry, you can still maintain the sacredness of your heart and not lose your peace, inside.

To Adhere to Truth Is the Same As Practicing Forbearance

By following the path of truth, you will be naturally practicing forbearance. In all circumstances, always stick to the path of truth. But sometimes you may have to change the tone of your voice and the volume of your speech in a way that will deal appropriately with a difficult situation. There is a well-known story in the *Mahabharata*. Ashvattama, the son of the teacher of both the Pandavas and their wicked cousins, and one of the three remaining warriors on the opposite side, had taken a solemn and powerful oath on the last night of the war, that he would use all his strength and accumulated power of penance to destroy the Pandava brothers before the sun rose the following morning.

Krishna, of course, knew of Ashvattama's murderous resolve and also knew of Ashvattama's considerable wealth of spiritual prowess to carry it out. Therefore, Krishna, out of his deep love for the Pandavas, took steps to protect them. It was getting close to midnight and Ashvattama had been unable to find the Pandavas. Krishna knew that Ashvattama would go to the all-knowing sage Durvasa and ask him where the Pandavas were. Now, a great sage like Durvasa would never tell a lie. He was well known for his anger, but his anger was used only to protect righteousness and to quench the fires of wickedness and evil. Even in his anger he would stick to the truth, but often times he would change the volume and sound of his voice, as he was declaring that truth.

You May Have to Raise Your Voice a Little to Tell the Truth

On this particular evening, Krishna went to see Durvasa. Durvasa was supremely happy to receive Krishna. Durvasa told Krishna how greatly blessed he felt to be honored by the Lord's visit. He asked Krishna, "Swami, please tell me what is the purpose of your visit?" Krishna replied, "Durvasa, I need your help."

In his heart of hearts Durvasa was overjoyed that Krishna, who was the protector and master of all the worlds, had approached him for help. But even for this there is a limit. Durvasa, who was extremely intelligent and who knew all things, said to Krishna, "Swami, I am prepared to give you any help you ask for, but I'm not prepared to tell a lie." Krishna told Durvasa, "I am the indweller in the heart of all beings. I am born again and again to protect *dharma*, to safeguard righteousness. How could I ever ask you to utter a lie? *Dharma* means right conduct; its very basis is truth. Certainly, I would never ask you to tell a lie." Durvasa replied, "In that case, I am ready to do whatever you say. What is your plan, Swami? I will implement it."

Krishna asked that a deep pit be dug which could hold five people. Krishna then told the Pandavas to get into that pit. Wooden planks were put over the pit to cover it completely. A rug was put over those planks and then Durvasa's chair was put on top of the rug. Krishna asked Durvasa to sit on the chair. He told Durvasa, "Ashvattama will come and ask you where the Pandavas are. You must tell the truth. But in telling the truth, you might just change the sound of your voice a little." As was predicted by Krishna, Ashvattama came. Offering his salutations to the sage, he asked Durvasa, "Swami, you know all things in all the three worlds. Please tell me where I can find the Pandavas?" Durvasa did as he was instructed by Krishna. He told the truth. He said to Ashvattama, "Pandavas is it? **Pandavas, is it? Yes, they are here! They are certainly here! THEY ARE RIGHT HERE UNDER MY FEET!**"

When Durvasa, pretending to be very angry, told Ashvattama that the Pandavas were directly under him, Ashvattama got very frightened. Durvasa's anger was well known and much feared. Ashvattama thought that instead of killing the Pandavas, he himself might be killed by Durvasa's yogic power, right then and there. Suddenly overwhelmed with fear, he ran away. Durvasa had uttered the truth. In keeping with his own integrity and stature as a great sage, he followed the commands of the Lord to give protection to good people by sticking to truth. But, he did change the impact a little, by raising the tone of his voice.

Negative Qualities Must Be Uprooted and Destroyed

You must have patience and forbearance, but at the same time, you should know under what circumstances and in what manner to use them. As we have shown, there are situations in which you must temper your outward expression of forbearance. You need to use your discrimination to know how and when to express the quality of forbearance, which should be ever firmly established in your heart.

Forbearance and patience are indicators of your inward state. They are instruments which you use to counter the negative qualities that are within you, the unwholesome character traits which come in the way of realizing your divine truth. Consider the ability to exercise forbearance in difficult circumstances as a test. It is in these times that the negative qualities buried within you will rear their heads and will tend to manifest themselves in wrongful or harmful actions. Welcome such difficult situations as challenges and opportunities to expose and destroy these negative qualities. You do this through your forbearance, patience and restraint, when otherwise your impulse would have been to use words or actions to harm. It is only after you achieve patience and forbearance and establish them firmly within you, that you will develop the inner peace and equanimity that is needed in order to understand the true principles of spirituality and divinity.

There are many negative qualities which must be completely shunned by devotees. In particular, you should not have any attachment, any hatred or any jealousy within you. If you have attachment, hatred and jealousy, even in the smallest measure, you will not be able to progress spiritually. Attachment, hatred and jealousy, and their hand-maiden anger, are the great enemies of devotees. They are the opposites of patience and forbearance. We will take up these negative qualities next and learn how to completely uproot them.

Twenty-Fifth Chapter

JEALOUSY AND HATRED -
TWIN PESTS THAT DESTROY YOUR PEACE

*The divinity is one. It is eternal, unchanging and everlasting.
It is the indweller of all bodies. As the indweller of the
body of living beings it is called the atma, the immortal
self. As the indweller of the world it is called God. It is the
one divinity present in different forms. Just as the physical
being can be thought of as the body of the atma, so also the
world can be thought of as the body of God.*

Embodiments of Love,

The body is impermanent, it comes and goes; but the indweller of
the body remains the same. Another name for the indweller is
atma, the immortal self, the universal spirit, which underlies everything that can be named or spoken of. It is the one permanent unchanging entity which pervades all space and all matter, and
which is the basis of all living beings. It may be called God, the
atma, or the indweller. *Atma* and God and indweller are exactly
the same. They are the one divinity.

Discover the Indweller Through Your Own Inner Practice

The sacred scriptures provide guidelines for seeking out and recognizing the indweller; but scriptural teachings in themselves will
not be sufficient to know it. You cannot attain the divinity by
merely studying the scriptures. Using the declarations in the scriptures as your basis, you have to make a determined effort to develop
inner vision. Scriptures can only show the path. They are like
guideposts; they give the directions. To reach the goal you have to
walk the path yourself. Following the directions given you have to
undertake this sacred journey and unwaveringly adhere to it until
the goal is reached. For this the *Gita* has laid out the path.

In the *Gita*, the directions for the journey commence with the
eleventh verse in the second chapter. That is the beginning of
Krishna's teaching. It starts with the injunction not to grieve *for
those who should not be grieved for*. Who is it that should not be

grieved for? What is the way to prevent grief? The *Gita* teacher declared that there is no point in grieving over things which are impermanent and transient. Bodies and personalities are impermanent and transient. All the things of the world are impermanent and transient. Krishna said, "Arjuna, all your grief is for nothing."

The Five Characteristics That Make Up Everything

Each of the myriad of things that can be found in this manifested universe is made up of five basic characteristics:
1. Each one *is*. It exists. It has *beingness*.
2. Each one shines with an inner light. It has luster. It is innately alive with energy.
3. Each has a deeper purpose. It has a reason for its existence. It is dear and a source of joy.
4. Each has a specific name, a category or designation.
5. Each has a given form, either tangible or subtle. It has a distinguishing feature.

These, then, are the five characteristics that are found in everything that can be spoken of. Whether tangible or intangible, once something has been conceived of, we can say that it exists, it shines, it has a purpose, it has a name, and it has a form.

The first three of these five characteristics make up the eternal truth which never changes. This is the permanent reality. It is the *atma*, it is God, it is the indweller, it is the divinity. It is referred to in Sanskrit as *sat-chit-ananda*, meaning existence, consciousness, bliss. For *sat-chit-ananda* there is no birth and there is no death. *Sat-chit-ananda* may be described as the mark or signature of the divinity. The remaining two characteristics speak of the body of the divinity. Name and form are only transient and illusory. They are really just imagination. So, of the five basic characteristics that make up everything, three make up the underlying divinity which never changes, and the other two are the changing names and forms which make up the world.

Realize that all the created things which you see in the world are artificial. They all have come at some time and will go some time in the future; in other words, they are subject to birth and death. They can be compared to relatives. Relatives come for a while to stay with you and then go back. They will not stay in the house permanently. Just like relatives, happiness and grief come and go. Similarly, everything having name and form is impermanent. To understand spirituality, you must realize that all created things are transient and temporary. Any day these things will disappear; they are constantly undergoing change. Grieving over such things which are impermanent is foolish indeed.

If you want to understand the three underlying qualities which are permanent, you have to develop certain noble qualities and virtues. As has been declared by Krishna in the chapter on devotion, the aspirant who has attained the 26 noble qualities is very dear to the Lord. But there is no need to have all 26 qualities. In a match-box you will find a large number of matches. If you want a fire, you do not have to strike all the matches; only one needs to be struck to provide all the fire you want. If you fully develop one or two of these virtues within you, then the others will also develop of their own accord. But they must become an indelible and integral part of you before you can hope to understand the principle of the *atma*. In striving to acquire these virtues, you will encounter certain negative qualities within you. They are your internal enemies. They will try to keep you from manifesting these virtuous qualities.

Jealousy and Hatred

In the previous chapter, the virtues of forbearance and patience were discussed. Now we will take up their opposite evils, jealousy and hatred. Jealousy and hatred are twin thieves. The one cannot live without the company of the other. There is an inextricable relationship between them; they will always take shelter within each other. Hatred may be compared to an underground pest and jealousy may be compared to an above-ground pest. Together they can destroy a tree. Consider a tree which is very green, which is flowering and producing fruit, which is very attractive to look at. When pests enter this tree the tree will become dry within days. One of the pests will go to the branches and leaves above while the other strikes at the roots below. While the one spoils the beauty of the tree the other will try to destroy the very life of the tree. They will always accompany each other.

So it is also with jealousy and hatred. Wherever there is jealousy there will also be hatred, and whenever hatred is visible you will find jealousy lurking invisibly behind. Hatred takes on a particular form. It manifests itself in various ways. For jealousy there is no form; it remains hidden under the surface. It has been said that there is no person in the world who does not suffer from some jealousy; there will be at least a small tendency towards jealousy in every person. To make sure that this jealousy and hatred do not enter your system you have to develop selfless love. Where there is selfless love there is no place for jealousy and hatred to enter and take hold. When jealousy and hatred are kept out, you can have the experience of divine bliss.

Beauty is a form of bliss. Wherever there is beauty you will also find joy. A thing of beauty is a joy forever. What is beauty? Is it the world which imparts beauty to a thing or is it already inherent in the object? We have seen how all things undergo change. Consider all these things which undergo change, how long can they remain beautiful? Only that which is permanent can be beautiful. The one permanent entity is God, and so God alone is beautiful. There is nothing in the world which is more beautiful than God. The most important duty of a devotee is to drink the nectar of bliss which emanates from that beauty. To imbibe and fill yourself with this divinity, which is so full of beauty, there is the need for acquiring certain virtues. In order to develop these virtues you will have to destroy the weaknesses and shortcomings that fester within you.

Being Jealous of the Divinity

Jealousy can even come into your relationship with the divinity. It is a form of arrogance, wherein you think of yourself more than you think of the Lord, and become jealous of the undue attention you feel is being given to the Lord. There is an example of this in the *Mahabharata*, the great epic detailing the war between the forces of righteousness and evil, in which Arjuna fought on the side of good, and Lord Krishna was his charioteer. During that great war, Arjuna was seated in the chariot behind Krishna, who was driving the chariot. On the eve of the war, Arjuna had heard all the teachings explained and expounded by Krishna, which make up the *Gita*, but he was not yet fully ready to practice them. He felt that Krishna was a very great person, a divine teacher, but he was not able to understand the full divinity of the Lord.

The great war was going on and some of the most fearsome weapons were being employed on the battlefield. On one particular day, Arjuna was battling with the grandfather, Bhishma, who was the generalissimo of the other side, and was considered one of the greatest warrior of that age. During that fight, a number of very powerful and terrible missiles shot by Bhishma entered Arjuna's chariot, but caused no harm to Arjuna. Arjuna fought brilliantly all day, skillfully wielding his bow while directing the chariot, using his feet to push against Krishna's shoulders, who would then steer the horses, to turn the chariot to the right or left.

The battle raged unabated with neither side gaining an upper hand until finally towards the end of the day, Bhishma swooned in his chariot and withdrew from the scene. At that point, Arjuna, exhausted but triumphant, blew his conch to proclaim victory in the fight that had been raging that day. Arjuna certainly had faith in the divinity, but at that moment he also felt a little arrogant. In that moment of glory, he felt that he was responsible for the victory and that, after all, Krishna had not fought, but had only driven the chariot.

It was after sunset when they turned the chariot towards home. As soon as the chariot reached the Pandava camp, Krishna halted it some distance from the tent, turned to Arjuna and said, "Arjuna, please get down and go into the tent." Arjuna who was a little puffed up with egoism thought to himself, 'I fought and won the battle today. Krishna was only the charioteer directed by me. Properly speaking, he should get down first and open the door for me. That would be the correct protocol.' And so Arjuna said to Krishna, "I think you should get down first." But Krishna insisted, "No Arjuna, you get down first." As this interchange continued, Arjuna developed some dark thoughts and began to feel some resentment towards Krishna.

Arjuna said to himself, 'Here I have been thinking that Krishna was so great, and it is surely because I had complimented him and expressed my admiration for him that he is now acting like this, considering himself more important. Well, it is my own fault. But yet, the war is continuing, it has to be fought and I need Krishna, so it would be best if I didn't develop any strained feelings between us. Getting into an argument with him now would certainly not be in anyone's best interest.' So, very reluctantly, Arjuna got down from the chariot. After he got down he stood near the chariot. Krishna continued pressing Arjuna, "Don't stand here. Go into the tent." Left with no alternative, Arjuna entered the tent. Krishna jumped down immediately, leaping a long way from the chariot. The moment Krishna came out, the entire chariot exploded into flames and was destroyed to ashes.

The Divinity Never Has Selfish Motives

Arjuna and Dharmaraja, his eldest brother, who were both watching from a distance, were astounded. Arjuna asked Krishna, "What just happened here? What is responsible for this spectacle?" Krishna answered, "Arjuna, no one understands my actions. For the divinity there is never any selfishness or egoism. The protection of my devotees is my only concern. The benefit and encouragement of my devotees is my only wish. I kept all those fearsome weapons which were employed by Bhishma and had entered the chariot, harmlessly under my foot. As long as I had my foot on them, they were not able to exercise their powers over you. If I had alighted from the chariot first, these weapons would have destroyed you along with the chariot. You would have been reduced to ashes. Being unaware of this, you asked me to get down first."

The moment Arjuna heard these words of Krishna, he realized his own arrogant and ignorant behavior. He was exhibiting all the signs of jealousy. Finding fault with the divinity and thinking that he was greater than Krishna can be seen as a form of jealousy.

There are a number of important signs of jealousy. Jealousy makes its appearance when you meet a person who has earned greater fame than you. Or it will develop when a person has more wealth than you. Jealousy will also show its head when you come into the presence of a person who is more beautiful and handsome. For students, jealousy will soon appear if there is another student who scores higher marks than you. It is the weakness of ordinary human beings to develop jealousy whenever they come in contact with people who excel them in terms of wealth, position, beauty, intelligence, and other such qualities.

Jealousy will not live harmlessly inside you. The moment jealousy enters all the virtues which you have cultivated over a long time, all the great qualities which you have developed, are destroyed. It ruins the human nature; it strengthens the animal nature; it promotes the demonic nature. It has no scruples. It does not look forward or backward. It is such an insidious quality that you must see to it that jealousy will never possess you. Enjoy the prosperity of others. Enjoy the progress of others. Enjoy the welfare of others. Enjoy the beauty of others. This is true virtue. This is one of the most important teachings of the *Gita*. Desiring the good of others is a laudable quality which everyone should possess.

Conquer Jealousy and You Can Conquer Anything

There is an ancient story of a devout woman who had a reputation of being completely equanimous and free of jealousy. Even her name meant 'without jealousy'. When the three aspects of divinity, Brahma, Vishnu and Shiva, which are the creative, the preservative and the destructive principles of divinity, came to test her, her extreme purity of heart was able to win them over and turn them into little babies. She became like a mother to them. In her presence, they remained happily nestled in her arms.

The three aspects of divinity also represent the three qualities in nature, the active, the passive, and the cyclical, which govern all phenomenal life in the world. These three qualities make up our experiences in the world, and the three aspects of divinity are the substratum of these qualities. Therefore, the deeper meaning of this story is that when you are free of jealousy, everything in the world will be like a babe in your arms. You will be its mother, it will look up to you and follow you. Truly, once you are free of jealousy you will be able to conquer anything.

But it cannot be emphasized too strongly that when you have jealousy, it will destroy all your good qualities. You may think that it will destroy others but in fact it will destroy you, not the others. It will make you sick. You will not be able to sleep well. You will not be able to eat well. Even if you are totally healthy, once jealousy takes hold of you it will cause all kinds of physical ailments to sprout up in you. It is like an inner consumption. Just as tuberculosis creeps in and consumes, so also jealousy weakens you without your realizing it. It can get into you in any number of ways and will ultimately destroy you.

Jealousy is a vicious disease which must not be permitted to gain a foothold. You must feel that God will always bless you with his grace. Even if you are in a lesser position than you think you deserve, you should enjoy the happiness of others. You should be glad to hear of their accomplishments and not feel sad just because they have things which you do not have. Jealousy is all-pervasive in this immoral age. It is prevalent in all types of people, be they worldly or spiritually inclined. It is mostly because of jealousy that people lose their peace of mind and waste their lives. Along with jealousy, backbiting and hatred soon make their ugly appearance. If you are the target of these evil qualities in others, your best protection is the great virtue of forbearance. Here is a small story.

Forbearance Will Overcome Hatred

Buddha was walking along the country-side begging for alms. He was approaching a village. Many people in that village had a great affection for Buddha. But just before he reached the outskirts of the village, some young rowdies loitering along the road began to jeer at him. A little surprised at this reception, Buddha stopped and sat down on a rock. He said to them, "Well, gentlemen, what pleasure do you derive from criticizing me?" Without giving any reason, they increased their denunciation of Buddha. Buddha said, "Continue as long as you want." They berated and reviled him to a point where they got tired of their own invective. Buddha's forbearance was so well developed that their hatred could not touch him. At first they were having a good time, but finally, having exhausted themselves without getting the reaction they wanted, they decided to go away.

As they were walking away, Buddha called out to them, "Children, I want to tell you something. In the village just beyond here, there are many people who love me very much. If they were to hear that you have been denouncing me in this vile way, they would cut you to pieces. In order to save you from that danger, I have stayed here on this rock and allowed you to criticize me. In that way I have given you a gift. Without spending a single cent, without making any effort, I have been able to give you so much enjoyment by allowing you to berate me. Rather than feel unhappy with your criticism, I am glad because I have been able to give you some pleasure and spare you from serious harm."

Then Buddha explained yet another important point to them in a way that made an indelible impression on their hearts. "Suppose a poor monk comes to your house and asks for alms. You bring some food out to him. But suppose the type of food you are offering is ritually impure and not acceptable by the monk. What will happen then? Since he has not accepted your offer, you will have to take it back and it will remain with you. Similarly, you are offering me all this criticism. These are the alms you are trying to give me. But I have not accepted your offerings. Well then, you will have to keep them; they remain with you. So you see, all your criticisms are really just being redirected to yourselves. You are not criticizing me at all!"

One can send a letter by registered post to a friend. If the friend does not accept this registered letter, what will the Postal Department do with the letter? It will redirect it back to the person who sent it. If you are criticizing someone but this person does not accept your criticism, then inevitably the criticism comes back to you. Do not think that by voicing the jealousy and hatred you may be feeling, that you will be troubling those to whom these odious sentiments are directed. In truth, you will only be troubling yourself. Jealousy and hatred will create great difficulties for the one who is infected with them. Jealousy and hatred spring from egoism. Here is a small example.

Behind Jealousy and Hatred Is Egoism

There was a devout religious man who took great joy in cultivating a garden full of beautiful flowers and fruits. Even though he was steeped in spiritual knowledge, he had developed a strong touch of egoism within him. The moment egoism developed, jealousy also entered. When egoism and jealousy make their appearance, hatred automatically joins them. God took a personal interest in this errant devotee. God saw that this person, although he had all the proper religious outer trappings, had nevertheless, filled his heart with poison. God decided to correct him by teaching him a lesson. The Lord manifested himself in the form of an old mendicant and took a stroll by that garden.

The old mendicant went to a recently planted tree and greatly extolled the beauty of that tree. Noticing the garden owner nearby he asked him, "Who is the gardener responsible for cultivating such a fine tree?" The proud owner puffed himself up and said, "Sir, it is I who have brought up this entire garden. I grew this tree and I raised all the other trees that you see here, as well. By my own efforts I developed all these pleasing paths and made this beautiful garden. I alone look after everything here. There is no hired gardener. I am the one who draws the water. I spread the manure. I pull the weeds and I remove the pests. I clean the paths. I am developing these beautiful flowers and fruits, doing all these things for the sake of giving joy to others." In this way he went on repeating *I... I... I.*

Appearing to appreciate the beauty of the garden, the old mendicant continued to dwell there for awhile, while the owner busied himself nearby, grooming his garden. After some time the mendicant left. A little bit later a cow entered the garden. She was so weak that she was about to fall and destroy the plants that were there under her body. The owner of the garden saw that this cow was about to spoil his beautiful garden. So he took a small stick and threw it at the cow to chase her out. But the moment the stick touched the cow, the cow fell down and died. Now, in his religion, cows are considered very sacred, and should never be molested or harmed. Having thrown the stick from which the cow dropped dead, he would now have to suffer the great sin of killing a cow. He was aghast at this terrible turn of events.

It was not very long afterwards that the same old mendicant came back into the garden. Walking along the path where the cow had strayed, he saw the dead cow and was shocked. He sought out the owner and urged him to quickly come to the spot. The mendicant asked, "Who killed this cow? Who committed this outrage?" When the owner did not answer immediately, the old mendicant asked more directly, "Tell me, do you know who killed this cow?" The owner replied, "Surely it was the will of God. Without the will of the Lord, would she have died just like that? Unless she was meant to die, would she fall down and expire just because a little stick touched her?"

The moment the old mendicant heard this he told the man, "Previously you told me how it was you alone who was responsible for raising this whole garden, how you alone planted and nurtured all these plants and put in all the paths. You were taking credit for all the good things that have happened here. But for anything that is wrong and inauspicious you put the blame on God. You are an arrogant, self-serving fool, so puffed up with your own importance that you won't even acknowledge the Creator's hand in bringing forth all the beauty that is here. You are taking credit for that which belongs to God. You are even jealous of God. If not for the will of God, there would be nothing in your garden."

At this point, the old mendicant revealed his true identity. He said, "I am the Lord himself. I have come to destroy your egoism." The erring devotee fell at the Lord's feet in contrition. The devotee realized how ego had stolen into him, had gained a foothold, and then had completely taken him over. Now, he understood the deeper meaning of the spiritual teachings that he had been mouthing for so long. He realized that everything is imbued with the divinity, and therefore, he should see the divinity everywhere and live his life with the knowledge that down to the minutest detail, everything is under the control of the divinity.

Destroy Egoism, Jealousy & Hatred with Love & Forbearance

You must take care that you do not develop egoism and its henchmen, hatred and jealousy. Once they take root within you they will be very difficult to eradicate. When you have become infested with these bad qualities you may not be so fortunate as this devotee and get the attention of the Lord so directly, to help you eradicate them. You will not be able to exterminate jealousy merely by reading scriptures or engaging in spiritual rituals. But by making a determined effort to transform your thoughts and develop selfless love, you can destroy this pest. Offer up all your negative thoughts at the feet of the Lord and fill yourself with unwavering love and forbearance.

So long as you have jealousy you can never shine. All the great virtues in you will disappear. The *Gita* has taught that the primary spiritual practice is to develop ideal virtues and apply them in your daily life. In this way, you create favorable circumstances for yourself. When you lead a virtuous life, you will be able to experience the principle of the *atma*. But if you do not develop the great qualities and apply them to your daily life, you will never be able to realize the divinity.

The light of the *atma* is everywhere. It is not limited to any one person or form. It shines as an effulgence, filling the entire universe. It may take any form and any name. It is the very basis of every name and form. Take for example the light that is emanating from a bulb, or the breeze you get from a fan, or the heat you get from an electric cooking stove, or the work you get from an electric motor. The effects are all different. The work done by the motor is different from the breeze obtained from the fan. The light obtained from the bulb is different from the food cooked on the stove. The effects are different, the machines are different, but going through all of them is the one electric current. The same is true for the principle of the *atma*. In different bodies it manifests differently, but underneath there is the same unity.

The luminosity of the electric light is proportional to the current that flows in the bulbs. The light that shines forth from the bulbs can be compared to the *atmic* effulgence which shines in individuals. Light has no shape or form, but bulbs come in various shapes and strengths. An incandescent bulb has a particular form; a fluorescent light has a different form. The dining-room bulb may be very bright; the bulb in the bedroom may be quite dim. Because of ignorance you may think that if the one type of electric current powers both the bedroom bulb and the dining-room bulb, why should there be a difference in the light? The difference comes about because of the bulbs.

Similarly, there is a difference in the expression of love in various hearts. If your love is wholesome, full and complete, you will be able to manifest the fullness of the *atmic* effulgence and shine brightly. If you have a narrow selfish love, it will be something like a dim bedroom bulb. It is not a question of current; the potential for providing any amount of current is available and ready. You must change the bulb in order to get a greater light. If you are filled with jealousy, then the power of the light will be very small. If you have the effulgence of selfless love, then the power will be something like a 1000 watt bulb. Therefore, develop your love. It is possible to recognize the divinity only with the help of love.

Only Through Love Can You Experience God

In order to see the moon, there is no need for you to shine a flashlight on it. By the light of the moon itself you can see the moon. If you want to see and perceive God who is always love itself, then only through love will you be able to see him. It is impossible to see him if you are filled with hatred. Hatred is the very opposite of love. Hatred is something like blindness.

However powerful a light you shine on a blind man, he will not be able to see the light. As long as you have bad qualities, the divinity which is very near will not be perceived. When you are free of jealousy, when you are free of egoism and hatred, you will be able to directly experience the effulgence of the divinity. A person who has opened his eye of wisdom will shine with the God-presence. A person who has closed his eyes with ignorance will not be aware of God. By closing your eyes you will have to search all over for a towel which may be directly above you on a shelf, very close by. If you open your eyes you will be able to place your hand right on it. The wise person whose eyes are open to the divinity and who is not beclouded by ignorance, directly perceives God and reaches him.

You become wise when you become fragrant with virtues. But if you are saturated with bad qualities, with doubts and all sorts of jealousy and hatred, you will not be able to understand anything at all. That is why it has been said, 'Death is sweeter than the blindness of ignorance.' You must free yourself from ignorance. Jealousy is an evil which develops that ignorance. Therefore, students who have very tender hearts, who have a bright future ahead of them and much progress to make, should never give room to jealousy.

If any person in your class gets an outstanding grade you should not succumb to jealousy. You can also work to attain an outstanding grade. If you have not achieved that and you also feel jealous, then you will be making two mistakes. In the first place, you have not studied adequately, otherwise you would have done better; and in the second place, you have darkened your heart with jealousy. Then crying over it is your third mistake. You should not develop these bad qualities which are sure to cause you so much trouble; they can even destroy a whole family which was previously happy and enjoying all the goodness of life.

Jealousy and Hatred Destroy Those Who Possess Them

While explaining these principles to Arjuna, Krishna told Arjuna, "For your evil cousins, the one hundred brothers who have been plotting to destroy the Pandavas' joy and happiness, it is their evil qualities which encouraged them to do all their wicked deeds. People who are jealous attract bad people for company. These cousins have with them their evil uncle, who encouraged them in their enmity towards the Pandavas. He is filled with jealousy. These are all blind people. Just as their father is physically blind, all hundred brothers are mentally blind. They join together and fall in line with one another. But you can be sure, Arjuna, that the bad qualities in these people will destroy them." As Krishna predicted, not even one of these hundred brothers survived the war to perform the funeral rites for their parents. This is the great tragedy of falling into hatred and jealousy.

If you want to really understand the *Gita*, then you have to start by developing all the good qualities and virtues that have been discussed. Once these good qualities are part of you, you will be able to experience the divinity directly.

Anything you desire can be gotten from a wish-fulfilling tree. The *Gita* is such a wish-fulfilling tree. It will grant you whatever you are ready to receive. It will give you the level of understanding which reflects your own particular desires. In this age, people are interpreting the *Gita* incorrectly, because they are filled with so many wrong desires. And so, the *Gita* has been of little use to them. But, you must develop your virtue and fill yourself with love. Then the lofty message of the *Gita* will shine within you and inspire you to reach the divinity. To reach the divinity is your birthright. It is your unchanging reality, your undying truth.

Twenty-Sixth Chapter

TRUTH AND GOOD CHARACTER –
THE VERY BREATH OF LIFE

*K*rishna said, *"Wherever there is exemplary behavior, wherever there is righteousness and sacredness, wherever duty and truth are adhered to, there will be victory. When you conduct yourself in an honorable way, when you live by the principles of right conduct, those very principles will protect you. Arjuna! Always live a sacred and honorable life. Then you will be leading a life that is truly worthwhile."*

Embodiments of Love,

There are seven facets to living a sacred life, which are like the seven colors contained in the rays of the sun. They make up the standards of virtuous behavior and moral excellence which are the very fabric of spiritual life. The first facet is truth. The second facet is good character. The third is right conduct. The fourth is sense-control. The fifth is conscious living with emphasis on restraining one's desires. The sixth is renunciation or detachment, and the seventh is nonviolence. All of these principles of right living have been laid down for the protection of the individual and for the well-being of society. Collectively they are referred to as *dharma* or righteousness.

Truth and *Dharma*

Truth is the very basis of righteousness. Just as burning is the nature of fire, coolness is the nature of ice, fragrance is the nature of a blossom and sweetness is the nature of sugar, so also, truthfulness is the nature of a human being. Truth and good character are your very life breath. When you recognize the innate truth which is your essential nature, then you understand your own reality.

To achieve success in the field of spirituality, good character is essential. Good character can be spoken as having three aspects. The first aspect is best conveyed by the words sacredness, holiness and goodness. The second aspect is best described by the words tolerance, compassion and forbearance. And the third aspect is given by the words resolve, determination and commitment.

Whatever education you have, however wealthy you may be, whatever position you may occupy, whether you are a great scholar or a statesman, if you do not have these three aspects of character, you are as good as dead. Whatever else you may have earned, without these three aspects of character, all your attainments and achievements will be worthless. People pay attention to external human beauty, but God recognizes only the inner beauty. Truly speaking, for human beings it is their sterling character which makes up their real beauty. A person devoid of good character is nothing but a stone. You have to follow these seven facets of *dharma* and let each one of them shine within you, for each one of them is completely natural to you.

The foundation step is truth. Truth does not simply mean abstaining from lying. You have to take truth as your very essence, as the foundation of your life. You should be prepared to renounce everything for the sake of truth. The world conducts itself in the fear of truth and is always subservient to truth. When there is no truth, man develops fear and becomes too frightened even to live. On the other hand, truth confers fearlessness on man. It is truth which protects the entire world and makes it function. Truth drives away all fear. It is such an important quality that only when it is being faultlessly observed will you be able to attain divinity. Character is the breath of truth. Important for character is virtue and good behavior. Humanity will not shine without good behavior. Virtues, good qualities, good behavior, all these lend splendor to humanity.

Truth Needs to Be Established from the Earliest Age

In order to serve humanity and realize your innate divinity, you have to take truth, character and good behavior as your basis. Right from childhood make the necessary efforts to establish yourself in these noble virtues. Early in life, children are likely to make a number of small mistakes, either knowingly or unknowingly. Fearing that these errors will become known to the elders and that there might be some punishment or criticism, children will try to hide their mistakes.

In this way, from an early age, there is a tendency for the child to develop the habit of straying from truth, to avoid blame. Eventually, this habit will destroy the very foundation of life.

Untruth will destroy one's humanness. Therefore, children should be strongly encouraged to always tell the truth no matter what, without fearing the consequences, be these consequences joyful and profitable to the child, or should they result in chastisement and punishment. Just as a foundation is very important for a mansion, just as roots are the very basis of a tree, so, truth is the very basis of life as a human being.

If you are wavering in truth, there will be no safety and no protection for your life. An example of strict adherence to truth can be seen in the life of a great king in ancient times. Because of his uncompromising stance on truth, he was forced by circumstances to give up his wife, his son and his kingdom. He considered truth as his penance. Even in the most difficult situations that assailed him, he was not prepared to tell an untruth or deviate from *dharma.* Eventually, he lost his kingdom. Banished and alone, he took up work in a cremation ground. When his son died, his wife brought the body to the cremation ground. Although he knew that it was his wife, and the body was that of his son, still he felt bound to discharge his duty as the person in charge of the cremation ground. Under the most trying tests, this king never gave up either telling the truth or following *dharma.* He considered truth and *dharma* like two eyes or like two wheels of a chariot or like two wings of a bird, each indispensable to the other.

Even a Little Fib Can Lead to Unhappiness Later

Right from the very beginning, it is incumbent upon elders to teach youngsters the importance of telling the truth. Here is a small example to show how making up stories to playfully befuddle a younger sibling, can produce unhappy consequences for a child. Once upon a time, a father wanted to give a special gift to his son on the son's birthday. Because of the love he felt for his son, this father gave the boy a gold coin, asking him to go to his mother and get a ring made out of the coin. The next day the son had his examinations; he kept the gold coin on the table where he was studying.

Now this boy had a younger sister who was very curious and mischievous. She entered the room and saw the gold coin. She took it in her hand and asked, "Brother, what is this?" He told her, "It is a gold coin." She asked, "Where did you get this?" Jokingly, he said, "Well, it grew on a tree." "How could this gold coin come from a tree?" his little sister asked. He then made up a story and proceeded to tell her a number of fibs. He said, "If you treat this as a seed and sow it by putting it in the ground, then pour water on it and tend it and protect it, a tree will soon come forth. Then from this tree you will be able to get many more gold coins."

She started asking some more questions, but he said, "Listen, I don't have time to talk to you now. I have to study. Ask me later." Seeing that he was busy, she took the opportunity to pocket the gold coin and left. From there she went into the yard and dug a small pit. She put the gold coin into the hole and covered it with soil. She poured water on the mound. All the while, she was thinking of what her brother had told her, how a tree would grow out of the gold coin, if it was planted.

A maid-servant, who was watching this little girl from a window, saw her put the gold coin in the hole. When this little girl went inside the house, the maid dug up the hole and took the coin. After some time, the mother came and asked the son to get ready to go to school. He wanted to give the coin to his mother so that she would have a ring made out of it for him, as his father had suggested. But the boy could not find the gold coin anywhere. He went to his younger sister and asked her whether she had seen it. She said, "Brother, I thought if we could grow a tree out of it, we could get lots of coins like that; so I've planted the coin in a hole I made in the garden." They went to the place and dug around, but the coin was not to be found.

Now the boy was very distressed. On his birthday, when he should have been very cheerful, he was crying. He told all this to his mother. His mother asked him, "But, tell me, son, why did your little sister take the gold coin and bury it in the garden?" The boy did not know, so the little girl was sent for and asked why she had done what she did. She said, "Brother explained to me how this would turn into a gold-coin tree; so I did as he said." His mother told the boy, "Because you made up this story and knowingly told an untruth to your little sister, the consequence is that instead of being happy and enjoying your birthday, you are weeping. And not merely that, you have also lost the gold coin that your father gave you."

If children are permitted to tell lies and harbor untruths at their tender age, this habit will grow and grow with the years. On the other hand, if you teach them from the earliest years to take truth as the basis of their lives, they will grow in character and be able to achieve many great things.

When One Bad Quality Goes the Rest Cannot Long Remain

There once was a great teacher who helped many people develop in spirituality. Whenever anyone came to him to be initiated by him, he used to inquire into their behavior and their character to determine the type of qualities they had. Appropriate to their qualities and stage of evolution, he would then give them a sacred incantation, a *mantra*. A thief, after recognizing this teacher as a great man, went to him and asked him for a *mantra*. The *guru* said to him, "Well, child, what are your qualities? What are your defects?" The thief said, "My bad qualities are going from house to house in the middle of the night, breaking in and stealing things. Since I spend the night in stealing articles, during the day I drink myself to sleep. Drinking is my second bad habit. If the police were to catch me, then to save my skin I would make up lies and tell them a lot of false information to put them off. That is my third bad quality."

The spiritual teacher asked him, "Well child, you say that you steal, you drink and you tell falsehoods. Can you give up one of these three bad qualities?" The thief thought for a while to himself, 'If I don't steal, how can I take care of my family, my children and my wife? No, I cannot give this up. Only when the body is healthy and strong will I be able to escape when I'm caught. So I have to get lots of sleep, and drink helps me get to sleep in the daytime. But it is unlikely that the police will catch me very often. So, I shall give up telling lies.' Then the great man asked him, "Do you promise that you will always tell the truth from tomorrow onward?" The thief replied, "Most certainly. Even from today I will only tell the truth." This is what the thief firmly resolved to do. And indeed, from that day onward he made it a habit to tell the truth wherever he went.

One hot summer night the thief was out prowling in a nearby town looking for a good place to break into. The mayor of this town, a very wealthy man, was taking rest on the terrace of his house. In those days, there were no air conditioners or even fans. Because of the heat and the still, sultry night air, he was not able to sleep. The thief managed to climb up to this terrace. As soon as the thief scrambled onto the terrace, the rich man spotted him, realizing that he was a thief. The rich man accosted him, saying, "Hey there, who are you?" Because the thief told only the truth, he replied, "I am a thief." In order to find out what this man's plans were, the rich man said, "Is it so? Well, I'm also a thief."

They decided to work together and planned to steal certain valuable things that were kept in that house. The rich man told the thief, "There will be quite a few valuables locked up in the safe inside the house of this rich man, but it will be very difficult for us to get into the safe unless we get hold of the keys. Let me break into the house and see if I can manage to steal the keys." The rich man continued, "I have been waiting for someone who can keep a watch for me. Now that I have been able to get a friend like you, I will go inside."

He left the thief and pretending that he was breaking into the house, he went inside; busying himself here and there, he delayed coming back for some minutes. Then he took the keys and stealthily came out. Now he told the thief, "I have the keys, but I looked everywhere for the safe. I couldn't find it. Let me keep watch and you go inside. See if you can locate the safe and get the valuables that will be kept in it by the rich man." As it turned out, this rich man had three big diamonds inside the safe. This thief went inside and soon found the safe. He opened it and took out the three valuable diamonds.

Immediately a problem arose in his mind. How to distribute the three diamonds between the two of them? As this thief followed the path of truth, a certain amount of righteousness had also automatically entered into him. He brought all three diamonds out but he told the rich man, "Brother, one diamond you can keep. The other diamond I will keep. The third diamond cannot be broken into pieces. I will put it back in the safe for the owner of this house. Let him keep it for himself." Deciding on this, the thief went back into the house to put one of the three diamonds back in the safe. Then he returned to the terrace.

After settling this transaction, the thief was about to leave when the rich man said to him, "Well, brother, perhaps we can have this kind of partnership now and again in the future. Please give me your address where I can contact you." As he was bound to tell the truth, the thief gave his correct address. The next morning, this rich man who was also the highest public official in that area, took the address and sent orders that a police complaint be lodged regarding the loss of some diamonds out of his safe. He told the police to go to the village mentioned in the address and arrest the thief who was living there.

In that particular village the thief was well-known. The police went there and had no trouble finding him. They caught hold of him and brought him to the mayor. The thief did not recognize the robed official in front of him as his partner of the night before. The mayor then questioned the thief, "Well, how did you enter the house? How did you get hold of this diamond?"

The thief narrated meticulously all the details of his adventure. He told how he had climbed onto the roof, had gotten into partnership with another person, entered the house, opened the safe, took out three diamonds, gave one to his partner, kept one for himself and again went into the house, again opened up the safe and put back one diamond. The mayor called in his head official and said, "Go and find out if there is a diamond remaining in the safe." The officer took the keys to the safe. To himself he thought, 'Can there be any thief who will put one diamond back?' Thinking this way, he opened the safe, saw the diamond that had been returned there by the thief, pocketed it, and went back to the mayor, reporting that there was no diamond in the safe. But then, the mayor searched the pockets of the officer and recovered the diamond. Immediately, he dismissed the officer from his service.

The mayor now addressed the thief. He said, "I know that in everything you have related, you have told the truth to me. Therefore, from today onward, I appoint you as my head administrative officer. Only a person who is truthful should be a public official. Unfortunately, you have become a thief; but your nature is not like that." This person now gave up thieving and became a high official; he continued to practice telling the truth and automatically, in the natural course of events, he gave up drinking as well as his thieving and became an honest and upright human being.

In the beginning, by adhering to truth, you may be put to a lot of trouble. In spite of the trouble you encounter, if you pursue the path of only telling the truth, eventually this truthful nature will fill you with joy and happiness and give you success in all your endeavors. Therefore, it was to promote the happiness and welfare of mankind that in the *Gita*, Krishna taught that one should always be truthful. He proclaimed that truth was life's royal road and that the path of truth was the only way to foster right conduct in society.

Dharma Is Changeless But Its Practice Changes In Each Age

Sometimes it has been said that righteousness has declined and that the *dharma* has diminished. But that is not correct. *Dharma* is based on truth. Truth is absolute; it can never undergo change or be diminished. However, in any particular age, the practice of *dharma* may undergo change. God incarnated as Krishna, not to re-establish *dharma*, but to re-establish the practice of *dharma*. *Dharma* never left, nor did it ever change; but it was out of use.

The seven facets of *dharma* have been present in all the past ages. However, each age has had practices most appropriate to that age. For instance, in ancient times when spiritual awareness was very high, the appropriate spiritual practice was meditation. In the age in which Rama incarnated, the most appropriate practice was penance and sacrifice. In the Krishna era, the practice was ritual and ceremonial worship. And in the past five thousand years of this present materialistic age, in which spiritual consciousness is at a low ebb around the world, the chanting of the holy name is the most appropriate practice. But, just as in the earlier ages there were also many believers who practiced the repetition of *mantra*, evoking the name of God, so also, in this age there are people who take to meditation, there are people who take to doing penance and there are people who take to ritual worship. But the principal practices depend upon the general character and mood of the times.

Different practices give different forms, so to speak, to *dharma*. But the inner flow of *dharma* is always the same. Truth will never change. Truth is always one, never two. In all the three times, past, present and future, in all the three worlds, earth, heaven and the nether world, in all the three states, waking, dream and deep sleep, and in all the three worldly qualities, passivity, activity and equilibrium, truth is always one. Since truth is one and the very basis of *dharma*, *dharma* cannot change. It never wavers or undergoes any modifications. But duty and practice will undergo intermittent change.

For example, take a person who is doing a job. How long will this job be his duty? Until he retires from that particular job. Until then, he goes to the office every day. Once he retires, his duty changes. After retirement, he might get involved in doing business. Then he says that pursuing his business is his duty. In doing business, he may be tempted to gain some extra profit by taking to under-handed methods; he may try to earn money through lying and cheating. Even though he may have now taken to lying and cheating in order to earn money, he will still consider the work he is doing as his occupation and his duty. When so many changes can come about in duty, how can it be described as *dharma*? These changing activities that occupy your time in the interest of providing for your living needs, cannot automatically be described as *dharma*. Duty becomes *dharma* when it shines with the virtues that make up the facets of *dharma*.

Not Harming Others Is Dharma

There is a simple meaning to the word *dharma*. All those actions which do not come in the way of others, which do not impinge on the freedom of others, can be described as *dharma*. Here is a small example for this.

You are holding a long stick and playing with it, moving it this way and that, and at the same time you are walking down a main street. This street is a busy public thoroughfare. You may feel, "I have every right to move wherever I want." Well, if this is your right, then the person who is coming in the opposite direction has every right to save himself from being hit by your stick. You are indulging in an activity which is likely to put other people walking on the street in danger. However, correct conduct expects you to act so that you do not interfere with the freedom of other people walking on the same road.

If you can conduct yourself in a way that is not detrimental to others or that does not impinge on their freedom, then you are behaving according to *dharma*. Later, we will take up Krishna's teachings in which he points out that merely refraining from doing harm is not enough. You should also be friendly and compassionate to all beings. But if, at the very least, everyone were to consider it their duty to conduct themselves without causing any harm to others, then there would be peace, prosperity and joy aplenty in the world. Acting in this way is your real duty, a duty which has to be performed for the sake of setting an example to others and for upholding the essential ideals of *dharma*.

Social Duty, Obligatory Duty and Family Duty

In your daily life in the family, there are three types of duties which may be considered to be three aspects of *dharma*. There is social duty, there is obligatory duty, and there is family duty. These duties express themselves in different ways. First consider an example of social duty. Assume that tomorrow is Sunday, which is a holiday for you. You may want to invite some people to come to your house for tea. Suddenly in the night, you develop a fever. While you are sick, you realize that if you were to invite your friends to visit the next day, you would not be able to receive them properly, and so, it would not make you or them happy. Therefore, in consideration of your obligations to your friends, which you would not be able to perform while sick, you decide to postpone the tea party. On the basis of the change in circumstances and your consideration for your friends, you change the tea party to the following Sunday. You are free to make the arrangements that fulfill both your wishes and your social obligations.

Next, consider an example of obligatory duty. Let us say you are a lecturer in the university. In connection with the upcoming examinations, the department head has directed that the whole teaching staff of the department assemble for a meeting. As this is an important department meeting, you will have to attend. Even if you are suffering from fever, you take some aspirin pills and go to the meeting. This is an obligatory duty and you have no right to cancel this. The scheduling of this meeting was not in your hands, and once it has been called, you are expected to attend.

Now, consider an example of family duty. You are in your own house. There is a small family quarrel between husband and wife. Inside the room, the husband and wife are having a tiff. She is very angry. Suddenly, the door bell rings and he goes out to answer it. He finds that a co-worker had dropped by for a casual visit. As soon as the husband sees the visitor, he greets him with a smile and a fond hello. He asks the visitor to be seated. With the visitor he is quite cordial. When he enters the bedroom and tells his wife of the visitor and finds that she is still very angry with him, he may resume his stern tone. But as soon as he goes into the other room to meet the colleague who has come by, he carries on with his friendly conversation. It is his duty to protect the good name of his family by conducting himself in such a way that an outsider would not know that he had quarreled with his wife.

If a person who is angry with his wife inside the bedroom comes out into the living room and irritatedly asks the visitor to leave the house, then the guest will be appalled. It is important to see to it that the secrets and confidences of the family are not thrown out into the street. This is an important duty of a family man. He must be ever vigilant to protect the honor of his family. If by his indiscretion the family honor is destroyed, then there will be no happiness for him or his family throughout their lives.

Sense-Control Is the Key to Doing Your Duty Properly

To protect the good name of your family you must remain alert and aware of others' needs; this requires sense-control. If you do not have sense-control, as was explained in a previous chapter, you become arrogant. One who is arrogant and devoid of sense-control is nothing but a demon. If you want to practice and protect *dharma*, you have to develop sense-control. For everything worthwhile in life, sense-control is very important. Krishna said to Arjuna,

"Arjuna, be a wise man, and have complete control over your senses. Do not obey the fickle cravings of your senses. The senses must be under your control. You should not become a slave of your senses. Make them your slave. Be their master. It is only when you have mastered the senses that you will have earned the right to be close to the one who is the originator of all the senses and has complete dominion over them."

In the second chapter of the *Gita* all the qualities of a wise man have been explained. Of all these qualities, sense-control is one of the most important. In this chapter we have been exploring some different aspects of *dharma*, which can be seen, like the rays of the sun, to have seven colors or facets. As has been pointed out at the beginning, this sunlight of *dharma* contains the rays of truth, character, righteous behavior, sense-control, penance, renunciation and nonviolence. You must make all of these your own.

Try to understand the meaning of these *Gita* teachings and practice them in your daily life. It is Swami's wish that when you have taken so much interest in studying these teachings that you should also evince the same degree of interest in practicing their meaning, and thereby acquire all the good qualities that are conveyed by them.

KINDNESS AND COMPASSION –
THE MARK OF A TRUE HUMAN BEING

Love all. Do not harbor enmity or hatred towards any being. The divinity in all its fullness resides in the heart of every being. This is the basic teaching of the Gita.

Embodiments of Love,

Whenever you hate someone, it is really God whom you are hating, for God is installed in every being. Whenever you criticize or admonish someone, it is the very Lord whom you worship that you are criticizing or reviling. That same Lord is the resident of all hearts. This awareness of the divine essence in every being is the basis of the teachings of universal brotherhood that have been given in the scriptures of India since ancient times.

The Unity of the Self, the One *Atma* Existing Everywhere

The *Gita* proclaims that the divinity is present everywhere and in everyone, as the all-pervading reality we call God. But the *Gita* declares an even higher stage than this. It teaches not only that God is everywhere, but that the inner truth behind the *I* that you refer to when speaking of yourself is your immortal self, your highest self, one and the same with God. And that highest self in you is also the highest self of everyone. It is the *atma*, one with the divinity. In essence, you and everyone and everything are God.

Therefore, in addition to teaching the unity of God, expressed through universal brotherhood, the *Gita* also teaches the unity of the *atma*, the one self existing everywhere. The *Gita* shows that the *atma*, which exists as the true self in you, exists as the same self in all other human beings, and in animals and birds and every other kind of being as well. Just as the *Gita* instructs you to regard happiness and misery as equal, so also it instructs you to recognize the one *atma* as existing equally in all beings, whether they are humans, animals or plants.

You must have the conviction that right from microscopic creatures and insects up to the creator, the same divinity exists uniformly everywhere. That is why a great poet, brimming with devotion, sang:

> *O Lord, You have been living in the ant as well as in the creator.*
> *You have come as Krishna and Rama. But truly, you live in*
> *every form. I see you everywhere, in every being I encounter.*

Harmonization of Thought, Word and Deed

Today, human nature is such that when you see some ants and roaches you don't mind killing them. At the same time, when you go into a temple and see an image of one of the forms of God, you pay homage to it. You act differently in the two situations, even when you know and profess that the one God is present everywhere. Saying one thing and doing the opposite is a common disease of humanity today. That is why, instead of attaining the status of a *mahatma*, a divine being, people have not risen very far above their lower natures. The *Gita* teaches truth in action, which is the harmonization of thought, word, and deed. This is the real mark of a human being. It is in this way that you manifest your divine nature in everyday life.

Develop your faith and see the same divinity existing in every living being. Spread your love, which is the very essence of your divine nature and the divine nature of all living beings. Look upon every person with compassion and love. Unless you adopt this approach in your dealings with others, all your spiritual exercises will just be a waste. Worshipping God while harming your fellow human beings can never take you to your goal. The *Gita* teaches that man himself is God, and that God is man. This unity of God and man has repeatedly been emphasized in the *Gita*. "Only the one who treats all alike is a true human being," Krishna proclaimed.

Whatever education you might have acquired, if you do not have human kindness then all your schooling and accomplishments amount to nothing. Kindness to all living beings is one of the most important virtues of a human being. You have to use your discrimination and discover how to develop this kindness and apply it in your daily life. Kindness to living beings refers to looking after people and other living things which are in distress and going to their rescue. You have to make the necessary effort to reduce their pain, their sorrow and their troubles. It is no use to repeat 'love, love, love' an endless number of times. You have to act with love and kindness in everything you do. Kindness must be an integral part of your life. You have to believe that kindness is the same as divinity. You have to believe that the heart which houses kindness is the temple of God.

Kindness Is the Hallmark of a True Human Being

There are a number of weaknesses that have invaded human beings. As a result, they lose their innate kindness and become cruel. They behave more like wild animals dwelling in the jungle. But clearly this is not the true nature of a human being. It is the very opposite of humanness. The very word human or humane is used to denote kindness. Of all the different flowers of devotion, God accepts the flower of human kindness with the greatest love. Offering ordinary flowers and worshipping God with the ordinary thoughts and intentions that accompany them, will not evoke the love of God. That will not please him, nor will he accept such offerings.

What offerings will God accept? What does he appreciate? He will accept the flowers of human kindness, the flowers of love, the flowers of compassion blooming in your heart. How should you express this feeling of kindness? It is not enough for you to just do some good. You must transform your heart. There must be a leap of faith. You must develop a deep-seated belief in God's omnipresence. You have to live the conviction that the same God exists in every heart. Then you will be able to recognize other's pain and sorrow as your own pain and sorrow. Here is a small story.

In a village there lived a couple who had a young daughter. It was just a small family of three. It was not a well-to-do family; in fact, it was a very poor family. But poor as they were, these parents decided to provide a proper education for their child. There was no school in the village in which they lived, so they had to send their child to a neighboring village. She had to traverse a forest every day to go to the village where the school was. City people might be afraid of walking through a forest, but villagers do not mind; it is part of their daily life. So this little girl spent her time going to the school in the neighboring village, learning her lessons there, and then coming back home in the evening.

A Child Suffused With the Nectar of Human Kindness

Along the way, in the forest, a small shelter had been erected to provide rest for wayfarers. One day, when passing by, this girl found an aged man in the shelter. He appeared to be undergoing some suffering. She realized that he would not be able to reach the next village where he could get medical help and protection.

Because of want of food, his body had become weak, and as she passed by she could see that his condition was not good. Daily she had been carrying some food for herself, and from the next day onward she gave this food to the sick man, who continued to lie in that small shelter in the forest. Every day, in the morning on her way to school, she would leave the food, and then in the evening she would collect the empty food container on her way back home. After ten days of ministering to him in this way, he regained some strength.

One day, as she was coming by on her way home, he took the hands of this little girl and asked her, "Dear child, you have been giving me food every day. Please, tell me where this food is coming from. Do your parents know that you are bringing me food every day? Or are you taking it from somewhere without their knowing it? Is this, perhaps, the food that has been provided for your daily lunch, and you are giving it to me instead? Tell me what you are doing. Please answer my question." She replied, "Honorable sir, I have been brought up to take things only with permission, and I can assure you that my parents know of my bringing food to you. Ours is a very poor family and we have very little money, but still we have been able to manage to provide food for ourselves and those in need. So, I have been bringing food from my family especially for you."

He asked her, "But if you have so little money how are you able to buy this food?" She replied, "Beyond here in the forest, there is a fruit-bearing tree. On my way, I collect fruits from that tree and sell them before going into the school. With the little money I collect, I buy the food. The next morning I prepare it and bring it you." The old man was overjoyed at her sacrifice and her intelligence and straightforwardness. He questioned her further, "How did you get such a noble mind?" She said, "Whatever good I am able to do is because of the upbringing and teachings given to me by my parents. As long as I can remember, my parents have been telling me that we must share with others and serve others. Ours is a very poor family, yet we always try to help others. We feel very blessed when we have the chance to do so. It gives us so much satisfaction." In this way, she told the sick man a little bit about her family and then went home.

Gradually the man recovered his health and was able to walk to the village where this girl and her family lived. What was the result of all the kind actions directed towards the sick man by this sweet little girl? The man told the family how he had been praying to God, "O Lord, give health and prosperity to the parents of this girl. When I was sick and helpless, I could not be of any use to the world. Now I am much better and can be helpful to others. I pray to you out of a heart filled with gratitude to bless this family." In this way, he shared with them his prayer that God bless good families such as these who generously help those in need. Then he left.

God Showers His Grace On Those Who Have Kindness

Whatever this girl did in the way of kindness, she never expected any reward for her actions. Without expecting any result or any fruits, she had faithfully been serving the sick man every day. Now God showered his benevolent grace on her. One evening, the Lord came to that house with a chest full of gold and asked, "Is this the home of the child who has given so much food and water to one in distress?" The Lord continued, "It was I who assumed the form of the sick man who languished in that shelter, until your little girl came and took care of me. Now I am leaving this gift so that the child can grow up and become highly educated. I lived in that shelter for ten days to test this girl. This child's heart is very sacred and pure. It is full of kindness. Her heart is my dwelling place, my own temple." He handed over the chest to the parents telling them to use the money to secure her happiness and prosperity.

But the parents were not overjoyed at the prospect of getting such a large amount of wealth. They fell at the feet of this divine person who had blessed them with his visit. They said to him, "Revered sir, we do not have any need for so much wealth. Wealth beyond one's own capacity is harmful, it can take away one's peace of mind. It can increase one's ego and make one forget God. We do not want so much wealth," But, having blessed them, the divine visitor disappeared, leaving the entire treasure there. This person who came was not merely a great man. The family members recognized him as the Lord himself. Without keeping the money just for their own family, they used it for the welfare of the whole community in which they lived. They asked everyone to conduct themselves in the belief that present in every being is the full manifestation of God. They showed by their own lives how God could be obtained, by expressing love and compassion and kindness to all beings who were in need.

You should not narrow your belief in God by thinking that he exists only in a certain place. You have to experience God everywhere. How will you be able to develop this feeling? God exists both inside and outside. If God existed only inside, inner purity would be sufficient. As God exists externally as well, external purity is also required. Therefore, since God is both inside and out, you need to have both inner and outer purity; only then will you be able to become fully aware of the omnipresence of God.

Inner and Outer Purity

What is the meaning of external purity? Of course, external purity means keeping the body pure and wearing clean clothes. But it means much more than that. The place where you live must be kept clean. The books which you read must also be clean and wholesome. Be it your body or your mind, you should not allow dirt and bad qualities to accumulate. The statement that you should take a daily bath means that every impurity in body and mind has to be cleansed. Where dirt accumulates, germs will gather and bring on disease. Therefore, do not allow impurities of any kind to remain on you.

Every day in the morning, you should brush your teeth and also clean your tongue. Let there be no impurity in the main entrance. Whenever there is some dirty water outside, mosquitoes, worms and undesirable bacteria will soon fester. In the same way, wherever there is some dirt in your body, all these germs and insects are likely to accumulate. Not merely that, in the surroundings of your house you have to keep everything clean. There is a saying, 'Look at the house and you will know its resident'; in other words, the cleanliness of the house is a reflection of the cleanliness of the in-dwellers of that house. This principle of cleanliness is meant for your own good. Whether it be the house or its surroundings, if everything is kept clean, you will be happy. You have to keep yourself and everything around you clean and orderly in order to enjoy good health. When you have good health you will remain happy.

You may have only two sets of clothes, but when you wear one, you should make sure that the other is clean. Then, afterwards, you can wear the second set, cleaning the first. Actually, there is no need even for having two sets of clothes; just the one may be worn every day as long as you keep it clean. Whatever you have must be kept clean; do not allow yourself to become dirty. But just cleaning the exterior and wearing clean clothes, while keeping the heart impure, is not of much use. You have to make every effort to achieve inner purity, as well. For this purpose you need to keep all your thoughts and feelings sacred. Let your thoughts be directed towards the service of others. Do not allow jealousy or hatred to enter into you. Always try to develop feelings which are full of joy.

There is no need to bother yourself unnecessarily about others' affairs. Just always think good of others. In this context the ancient teachings declare, 'Let the whole world be happy.' To promote universal joy and well-being is the basis of the spiritual teachings and the object of all spiritual practice. Therefore, the sacred name of God should be continuously contemplated upon, so that it purifies your heart. Only when you take proper care to maintain inner and outer purity will you be able to prevent the entry of impure thoughts and harmful qualities, such as jealousy and hatred.

Conquer Your Inner Enemies

Prahlada, the great devotee of the Lord, declared that only when you conquer the inner enemies can you be considered truly great. He told his father, the demon king, "You are only a king now, but if you can overcome the inner enemies that have invaded you, then you can become a great emperor." These inner enemies, including such evils as hatred, greed, pride and jealousy, make up the delusion that besets human beings. You should never allow these inner enemies to enter your heart. If you keep them out, you will be free of all difficulties and problems. To achieve that, you must treat joy and sorrow, profit and loss, heat and cold as all the same. When you develop such equanimity, these inner enemies will not touch you.

But it will be difficult to treat joy and sorrow, misery and happiness as equal unless you are firmly established in the belief that God is dwelling in every heart. When you recognize that, then all the pairs of opposites will have been conquered and they can no longer disturb your equanimity. Then you will be immersed in divine grace, and no matter how unfavorable may have been your fate, the hand of destiny can no longer touch you.

When you have the firm belief that the same divinity exists in every heart, then every obstacle is overcome. When you have full faith in the indwelling divinity, then anything and everything becomes yours. That faith is the key. It is the very root of spiritual life. Catch hold of that. That is your goal. If you need to fell a tree, it's not necessary to first cut away all the branches and leaves. Cut the trunk and the whole tree comes down. Once you gain hold of the divinity, everything comes under your control. To do this, you must develop the practice of expressing your compassion for all beings, until this concern for the welfare of others suffuses every action of your life. And also, you must develop both inner and outer purity, keeping both body and mind sparkling clean. Only then will you be able to recognize the divinity that is everpresent everywhere.

You need to realize that when in your devotion you pray to God and offer him your obeisance, it is the same God who is dwelling in every heart. So you must be very careful not to criticize others. You must develop the strong conviction that any criticism you direct towards another being will go straight to God, residing in that heart.

The Two Banks of the River of Life

Life may be compared to a river. If you allow this river of life to proceed unchecked and unbounded, you are likely to destroy many villages. You have to take whatever measures are needed to see to it that this river remains within its bounds and reaches the ocean. It is only the ocean which can bear this river and absorb it. How to make this river of life reach the ocean? In the *Gita* it has been said, you must have two banks constructed. When the river has two banks, it can safely go on and reach the ocean.

What are these two banks for the river of life? They have been described as two powerful *mantras*. On one side you have a *mantra* which says,

> *He who has doubts will perish.*

On the other side you have a *mantra* which says,

> *He who has faith will attain wisdom.*

So the two banks for the river of life have to do with renunciation of doubt and the blossoming forth of faith. When you have these two banks channeling your life, then you will reach the goal and merge in the ocean. This teaching given by Krishna is the very essence of devotion. It enables you to reach the ocean of infinite grace.

The Three Principles That Take You to Your Divine Goal

Krishna said, "Child, that ocean of divine grace is the goal of mankind. It is the ultimate goal of all life. Don't forget that goal. Don't believe in the world and don't be afraid of death, but ever remember the divinity which is the very reason for your having taken birth. These are the three principles I give you:

> *Never forget God.*
> *Never believe in the world.*
> *Never be afraid of death.*

Take these three and inscribe them in your heart. Always remember them, for they will sanctify your life and bring you to me."

Twenty-Eighth Chapter

FEARLESSNESS –
SEEING THE ONE SELF IN EVERYONE

*F*ear *arises when you see another as separate from God. But when you know that the one divinity is the basis of all you see, then fear leaves you forever. Once you become established in that awareness of the divinity being everywhere in everyone and in everything, then you are permanently freed from the specter of fear.*

Embodiments of Love,

You must be firmly grounded in the belief that every name and form that can be found anywhere in the universe is only a combination of the five elements, and that the foundation of these five elements is always God. Then fear cannot gain a foothold within you.

Divinity Is The Basis For Everything

Everything without exception is made up of the same five elements. There is nothing else to be found in this manifested creation; there is no sixth factor at all. Consider some of the objects you see in this room. Here is a table, here is a chair and here is a podium; over there is a window and a door. For all these different objects, the difference consists only of separate names and forms; the content, which is wood, is the same in all. Similarly, mountains are rocky, trees consist of wood, earth consists of mud, the body consists of flesh, the ocean is made up of water... these are all different names and forms. But, in composition they are all just combinations of the basic five elements.

These five elements are five aspects or reflections of the one divinity. It is their divine basis that illuminates them and gives them their existence. Except for these five reflections of divinity, there exists nothing else in the whole universe. In all these five, the divinity is the same. It is one. Beyond it there is no second at all. When you know this without a doubt, then you will have no fear.

Of all the great virtues, fearlessness occupies the place of primary importance. It is the ideal virtue. Unless you have fearlessness, you will never be able to live comfortably. Be it in the secular field, in the battle of life in the world, or be it in your struggles in the realm of the spirit, you must never leave room for fear to creep in. It should find no place in your life. When you are obsessed with fear, you will become extremely timid. You will not be able to accomplish even the smallest job. When you are filled with fear you cannot shine in the world. Therefore, the *Gita* taught that you must become totally fearless.

Fearlessness Is Beyond Body-Consciousness

Fearlessness is not just the absence of fear. Both fear and the absence of fear are associated with body-consciousness. Absence of fear can sometimes be foolish, such as when the body is threatened with harm. But fearlessness is beyond body-consciousness. It can be experienced only when you recognize the truth that the one divinity resides in full measure in every heart.

It is said that a person charged with fear dies every step of the way, while a fearless person dies only once. "Therefore," Krishna told Arjuna, "give up your fear and become completely fearless!" Only a fearless person can achieve victory in great undertakings. A person who is truly fearless will have detachment from all the objects of the world and be saturated with the love of God. On the other hand, one who is egoistic about his body and his worldly accomplishments will be charged with fear. Attachments to the worldly objects and egoism will never be entertained by a person who is free from fear.

In the epics, you will find the story of a demon king who was charged with fear, whereas his son was completely fearless. The king had placed his trust in the world. The son, Prahlada, had placed his trust in God. The boy's teachers went to the demon king and said, "Sire, your son is not afraid at all. However much trouble we give him he never complains or cries about anything. Rather than shedding even a single tear out of personal hurt, he constantly praises the Lord and sings endlessly of the Lord's glory and magnificence." Why was the boy free of fear? It was because he had the firm faith that there was nothing else in the world except God. This conviction endowed him with unshakable fearlessness.

In another ancient classic we find a *guru* commending his disciple on his fearlessness. The teacher said to his disciple, Janaka, who was a great emperor and yogi, "I am very pleased with you. You are now totally freed from fear and you need never again worry about anything. You have kept your heart entirely absorbed in the Lord. You are existing only as an instrument of God in the world, serving him in everything you do. You have no attachments at all to the objects of the world. You believe that everything in the world has the form of God and is imbued with divinity. Wherever you look you see only unity in the diversity that others see. This awareness has made you totally fearless."

Fear Of Death – The Most Powerful of All Fears

Of all the fears that haunt humanity, the fear of death is the strongest. No matter how courageous and valorous you may be, no matter how highly educated, no matter how much you may be blessed with unlimited wealth, no matter what great talents and skills you may possess, the fear of death will be lurking in the background, annulling all your accomplishments and destroying your self-confidence. Most people become subject to despair when they see people dying. The moment they hear of someone's death they consider it very inauspicious and try to close their ears to it. Even when they are over 100 they get frightened when they think of death. They always want to live just a little bit longer. But however much more anyone may aspire to live, death is certain.

The fear of death will not save you from death. Distracting the mind by dwelling on the transient joys of life will not save you. Your relations and friends cannot save you. Your great accomplishments cannot save you. All the objects in the world and all the people in it, are equally washed away by the flow of death. What profit is there for you to take shelter in those who are also being washed away? The person who is seeking protection and shelter, and the one from whom shelter is being sought, are both being washed away. Only when you catch hold of the divinity, which is the immovable bank of this river of death, can you nurture any hope of being saved. When you truly know that all there is, is the divinity, then there is nothing to fear. Then you are saved. You will have conquered the fear of death.

Fearlessness may be compared to a great mountain while fear is something like the small waft of air created by your breath. Can this little current created by your breath ever shake such a mighty mountain? Of course not. The little wind of fear can never shake the great mountain of fearlessness. When this steadfast and unwavering mountain of fearlessness becomes implanted in a mind that is clean and pure and free of delusions, and when it resides in a heart that is immersed in bliss, then you are veritably expressing your divine nature. Then the truth will be established in your heart of hearts, that there is only the one divine reality existing everywhere. Once you know this all-pervasive divinity to be your essence you laugh at death, for then death no longer has any power over you.

Why should anything ever frighten you? What can possibly make you afraid? Death is really just a kind of joke in this play of life. If the role calls for you to fall and die on the stage, will you, the actor, be affected? What is so earth-shaking about the death of a body that is born to die. The body, which is made up of the five elements, has to be destroyed some day. For the sake of such an impermanent thing why should you worry? "Arjuna, you are not the one who is going to kill, nor will those you fight be killed. The only thing that can be killed is the body. You are the immortal self. You are not the body." This is the truth that Krishna taught Arjuna and thereby made him fearless. Fearlessness is a quality that is as vital and as important as your lifebreath itself. It is the foremost of the virtues taught in the *Gita*.

Fearlessness Is the Very Nature of a Human Being

In truth, human beings are divine and fearlessness is their very nature. It is the deeper meaning of the word *human*. *Human* refers to your divine essence. Here is a story to illustrate how human beings are not living up to their divine nature, but in their actions have become worse than animals.

Once there was a fearsome forest, and living in this forest there were a large number of animals. In most forests where there are lions there will be no elephants, and if there are elephants roaming about then there will not be any lions. But in this forest, there were all types of animals: lions, elephants, jackals, dogs, monkeys, the whole animal kingdom was present there. One day, a clever fox thought to himself, 'Human beings boast that there is something special and unique about human nature. They say that it is extremely rare and difficult to attain life as a human being. But human beings are born the same way that we animals are born. All these beings are born from the womb of a mother. The question is: Why are we all lumped together and called animals, while human beings are singled out and called humans? In what way are we inferior to them?'

The fox weighed all the various arguments and counter-arguments to this question that was perplexing him, and he resolved to prove that there was no distinction between humans and animals. From that day onwards, he started airing this problem to all the denizens of that forest. He sought out other animals and said, "Why should we accept the present state of affairs? People are considering animal life as inferior to human life. We should take steps to reverse this erroneous belief." In this way, he began to encourage all the animals living there to think about this issue and get excited about it. He showed how these false beliefs had been taught and accepted by all the animals, even by the mighty elephant who was stronger than anyone and the dauntless lion, who was their king.

The Grand Meeting Of All The Animals

The fox resolved to have a very big meeting of all the animals to discuss these points and frame some resolutions on which they could universally agree. The name proposed for this meeting was 'the great gathering of the four-footed ones'. It was decided that on a particular day, at a particular time, all of them would come together in a big open area and assemble for this special meeting.

Initially, three agenda items were agreed upon. The first was that human beings, just like animals, are born from the womb of a mother; therefore there should be only one name, both for humans and animals. Either humans should be called animals or animals should be called humans; but there should not be two different names and two different titles. That was the first resolution they wanted to pass at the meeting. The second agenda item was that animals had been called unwise, while humans claim to be endowed with wisdom. But animals should not accept this. In what way do humans have superior wisdom to the animals? The fox was particularly insistent on this point. He asked, "What is this wisdom that man has, that we do not have? We have to firmly resolve that there is the same wisdom in both humans and animals."

The third agenda item that the fox proposed was, "Humans are considered to be talking animals whereas we are dumb; that is considered to be a very great disadvantage to us, which they claim makes a big difference. But even if we are dumb, what is it that we are lacking? By having learned the ability to talk and by possessing that skill, what is the extraordinary happiness that humans have attained? Let us propose that talking and dumbness be considered more or less the same."

"Then there is also a fourth point we should consider," the fox added. "Human beings think of us as being restless and excitable whereas they consider themselves to be calm and peaceful in nature. But none of us should agree to this. The peaceful nature that we have, even man does not possess. We deserve the reputation and recognition that we are far superior in serenity to human beings." They all agreed that these four points should be discussed in the meeting. But then they wondered whom they should ask to preside over their meeting.

The fox pointed out that there were a number of great sages who had been doing penance in the forest. "We should select a very highly accomplished sage to preside over our meeting," he suggested. They all agreed and resolved to send the fox to find a wise man whom they could trust to be true and just, and request him to chair their meeting. After a long search, the fox came to a cave in which he saw a sage engaged in penance. His instinct told him that he had found the right holy man to chair their gathering. He reverentially approached the sage and prayed to him, "*Swami*, in the kingdom of animals we have decided to have a very important meeting and we request you to preside over it." The sage, who recognized everything as the living divinity, said, "All right, I will be happy to come and preside over your meeting." So, in a vast open field they arranged to have their gathering.

In that forest, every animal from the smallest to the biggest came with all their children, and many brought their grandchildren also, to attend this important meeting. They were all in very high spirits and extremely happy to take part in such a grand meeting. And they all showed a great deal of respect for their president. A high platform was provided for the president. Just beside the chair for the president, a chair was provided for the lion. The sage presiding over the function was also in very good spirits and was not the least bit afraid of the lion who was sitting next to him. This sage recognized the existence of God in every living being; therefore, he was full of fearlessness. Once all of the animals were seated, there was a need for properly welcoming the august assembly. The secretary for this great meeting was the fox. The fox began his welcoming address.

"Revered president, your excellency the king, honored minister, dear brothers and sisters! This day is a day which will be written in golden letters in the annals of this great forest and all its denizens. This is an unforgettable day which will never be forgotten in the whole animal kingdom, for today we will achieve a grand success in this most important meeting for which we have all assembled here. In coming together here you have all made some notable sacrifices. You have given up a great number of activities and have made time available in your busy lives to participate in this meeting. So, in the very first place, let me express my deepest gratitude to all of you." Then the secretary went on and explained the items on the agenda. As soon as the agenda had been presented, the lion got up and addressed the vast gathering.

In What Way Are Human Beings Better Than Animals?

The lion told them, "You have all heard what my brother has said to you. I want you to know that the great qualities you have, like valor and courage, humans do not really have. I myself am a direct proof of this. If you consider the courage and valor, the magnificent prowess and strength which I have, where will you find any human being who is my equal? Though I am king of the animals, I never take any wrong or unjustifiable actions. Without reason I do not kill animals. Only when I am hungry will I take a little food. I do not kill any animals for sport; I never waste any food. Consider our courage, our code of ethics, our high level of morality. Can you find such great qualities in human beings? No! They don't have them at all. Therefore, why should we be afraid of them? Why should we be thought of as inferior to humans? Today, let us resolve to wipe out this blot on our reputation." When the lion finished his address there was an uproarious cheer and the applause resounded throughout the entire forest.

When things quieted down, the elephant, who was sitting just by the side of the lion got up and said, "Humans are not even half as big as my leg. In form I am certainly mighty and magnificent. In intelligence I have attained proverbial greatness. Kings, emperors, distinguished leaders, all have developed great regard for me. If ever a coronation was to be performed and I were not there, it would have to be postponed. When I am so great, how can you say that humans are superior to me? My intelligence is extraordinary. Therefore, even if you consider just these two, my intelligence and my physical size, you must conclude that humans can never be equal to me." Again the audience cheered their agreement.

The fox got up and said, "The lion, our illustrious king, has just talked to you, and the big elephant, our distinguished minister, has also spoken his mind. Now we would like to invite a representative of the smaller animals to come and address us." At this point a dog who had strayed into the forest, and who had many experiences with human beings, was asked to speak to the gathering. It offered its humble salutations to the president, to the king, to the minister, to the secretary and to all in that great throng who had assembled there. Then it said, "Although I am very small and weak, in faith there is no one that can be compared to me. I have unswerving faith and unlimited loyalty to the person who has brought me up, and who looks after me. I will always be grateful and faithful, even if I lose my life. Even if I am hurt and harmed by my master, I will not return the harm in kind. Everyone knows that human beings do not have this sense of loyalty which a dog has. In this quality of loyalty I can never be considered inferior to human beings.

"Among themselves, humans often give trouble to the ones who most lovingly take care of them and guide them, such as their own parents or their teachers. Humans will not hesitate to do bad in return for the good which is given to them. They will criticize and concoct schemes to deceive and hurt the very ones who have looked after them so carefully. Humans do not have any gratitude at all. They do not have any loyalty. Only so long as their purposes are being served will they pretend to be obedient. The moment their own selfish interests have been taken care of, they start troubling their own teachers. When humans are like this how can we be considered inferior to mankind?" There was complete agreement in the audience. A nodding of heads and sounds of "Hear! Hear!" affirmed every point the gentle dog had made. In this way, one by one, others got up and had their say. Appropriate to their status and experience, they gave speeches, extolling the many fine qualities practiced by the animals but which were being ignored by human beings. Finally, there was the speech of the president.

Through Effort Humans Can Transform Their Lower Nature

The sage addressed the gathering, "Dear animals. All that you have just spoken of is true. Whenever a spiritual teacher does something or says something to us, it is meant for our own good. It is intended to promote our inner development and also our friendship and good understanding with others. But as soon as this friendship flowers and understanding blossoms forth, human beings become suspicious and think that something bad is being done to them. To your face, they will offer salutations and use words of praise but behind your back they will criticize and revile you. Filling themselves with opposites like that and with low forms of cleverness, they waste their intelligence and their lives. All the defects that have been pointed out here are certainly true and present in humans. As for food, sleep, breathing and such things, there is absolutely no difference between humans and animals."

The sage continued, "I do want to point out, however, that there is one specialty in human beings that is unique, in which they cannot be compared with the animals. Animals may inherit a streak of cruelty. Once they have acquired that they cannot change it. A tiger, however hungry he may be, will not eat rice and curry. He only aspires to have mutton. He will not settle for just a little tea and biscuits. However much he may try to change his habits, he will not succeed. On the other hand, if sufficient efforts are made by humans, they can transform their cruel nature and any of their bad habits. The most important difference between humans and animals is that humans, with effort, can bring about a complete transformation in themselves, whereas animals will not be able to accomplish that. These special capacities and skills for transforming themselves are only available to human beings."

The fox got up and said, "Swami, we will concede that human beings have these special capacities for changing themselves, but if they do not make use of these capacities, do they deserve the high status that they now enjoy?" The president declared, "If anyone has the capacity to change himself but does not use it, then he is much worse than an animal." At this all the animals burst into an uproarious applause. The cheering went on and on until the president gaveled for order. The sage then repeated the principal point he had just made… that any human beings who had the capacity for doing good, but who did not use this quality to improve their own behavior and develop the good within themselves, were, without a doubt, worse than animals. Then the sage added, "What is the use of all the learning that human beings accumulate? Will it change their faith? As soon as bad thoughts enter their heads, their thinking becomes dull and they become like idiots. In learning and skills, humans have attained a high status. But all this learning is only for the sake of procuring some bread. They use their education only to fill their bellies and to eke out a livelihood."

At this point, the fox got up and added to what the president had just said, "In the process of eking out their livelihood, humans use all kinds of unethical means. In this respect, it is clear that we animals are much better than human beings." The fox got carried away by his own rhetoric. He continued for some time on the same theme. "We are always fair in gaining our livelihood. In all respects, when compared to humans, we are far better. Really, we are the BEST!" He got an exuberant, almost riotous ovation from the whole four-footed assembly. Everyone agreed whole-heartedly with this appraisal and urged the fox on to say more. But now the enthusiasm had exceeded its limits and the president pounded the gavel and called for order. The sage arose and made a few additional remarks. He explained the second major difference that make human beings unique. He said, "Man has been able to conquer *maya,* he has been able to master illusion. Once he has achieved that, he is able to experience the *atma,* his own true divine self. Then he can reach the state of *nirvana,* the exalted state of eternal bliss. This is a vital difference between humans and animals.

The Vital Difference Between Human Beings and Animals

"Human beings have the power and also the authority to conquer *maya* and totally free themselves from delusion. If man takes the trouble and makes the effort, he will be able to directly experience the *atma* and, thereby, know himself as the divinity that he truly is. With the help of spiritual exercises he can reach *nirvana* and be immersed in supreme bliss. In the interest of truth, I have to point out that you animals do not have these powers and potentialities with which human beings have been endowed." The sage added, "Dear children, in the English language, human beings have been collectively called mankind, using the generic term m-a-n. The same is given in Sanskrit as *manava.* The inner significance of m-a-n is that human beings can separate and remove this illusion, *maya;* they can get the vision of *atma,* and immerse themselves in wisdom and joy in the state that is called *nirvana.* This, then, is the meaning conveyed by these letters m-a-n, where 'm' stands for '*maya* removed', 'a' stands for '*atma* realized', and 'n' stands for '*nirvana* attained'. Attaining *nirvana* means that man becomes one with joy and bliss. So, a true human being is one who has removed the ignorance of *maya,* who has had a vision of the *atma* and who has become merged in the supreme state of bliss."

When the sage had finished, all the animals bowed their heads and there was a deep reflective silence as they mulled over the words the president had spoken. They had to agree that these were three possibilities, which they, in their present forms, could never hope to achieve. But then a question was raised by one bold buck, "Have all human beings been able to attain this?" The sage responded with a resounding "No!" He said, "Only very, very few people care at all about these extraordinary treasures which are their birthright. Most people fritter away their lives, never pursuing these invaluable opportunities of human life. Their pursuits reek with selfishness and they treat each other much worse than animals. Although humans have this great capacity for wisdom and bliss, they do not develop themselves in this direction and, so, they have not been able to derive any real joy from their lives."

Most Human Beings Behave Even Worse Than Animals

The animals came to a consensus and agreed that those people who do not make any effort at all in these directions are just like them and there is absolutely no reason for distinguishing them from animals. The sage agreed. Then, on a personal note, the president explained the reasons why he had come into the forest to live. He said, "Human beings do not care much about these noble qualities. Animals give trouble only to those who give them trouble; otherwise they will live in peace with one another. But humans hurt those who do not hurt them at all. Without any reason they begin to blame and cause trouble, harming people who are unblemished and who have given them no cause for provocation.

Humans also enter into all kinds of improper work which they have no right to be engaged in." He concluded, "It is for these reasons that many true spiritual seekers have become renunciates, have given up the company of men and gone into the forest to live. Humanity is becoming increasingly selfish. Whatever people say, whatever they do, whatever they think, is laced with selfish motives. Animals do not have such selfishness. Animals are not harming other animals and accumulating wealth. Therefore, in many ways humans behave worse than animals."

In this context Krishna said to Arjuna, "Be a true human being, not one who is worse than an animal. Rise above the animal nature to your true human nature. There are two qualities of animals that you should never have. You are neither a sheep, which is timid and fearful, nor are you a tiger, which is cruel to others. You are a man. You are worthy of higher things. Be fearless! Do not ever allow yourself to be subjected to fear. In truth you yourself are the divinity. Sorrow and fear can never have any power over you."

When You Have A Firm Faith In God You Will Be Fearless

There is infinite power inherent in the human heart. But despite such power, you do not have faith in yourself. What is the reason for this? The reason is that you feel separate. You believe that you are different from the divinity. But in truth, the divinity is always inside you as your very core. This same divinity pervades the entire universe. When you develop a firm faith in God, you will never have any fear whatsoever. You will recognize that the God you worship is the one who is present everywhere in everyone and in everything, and also in yourself. That belief will remove all vestige of fear from your heart.

But if you do not have that faith then you will be ridden with fear. Every moment, every step, you will be frightened. When you have an examination you will be afraid. While going in an airplane, you will be afraid. When a truck comes in the opposite direction on the road, you will be afraid. Right from the very moment when you get up from bed until you again go to bed you will be afraid. And even in bed you will be afraid that thieves might break into the house and steal your belongings. You will be expending your entire time in fear. But this is not the way a human being should live. You should become steeped in the conviction that the divinity is present everywhere and thereby attain utter fearlessness.

Your faith in the omnipresent divinity is the key to developing fearlessness. Only when you lose faith will you develop fear. Only when you forget your true self will fear arise. You have forgotten your own true nature. You have forgotten the *atma*. You are considering yourself to be this little five-and-a-half-foot body, but the truth is that you are infinite in form and your power is unlimited. When you make an effort to remove the delusions and get a vision of the *atma*, you become immersed in the bliss of *nirvana*. Then you can call yourself a real human being.

If you make no effort along the path of self-realization, but demean yourself into dark, selfish pursuits and degenerate behavior, you become more like a demon than a human being. Do not fall to such depths. Conduct your life so that you can truly call yourself a human being and live up to the high ideals that you inherited when you were given this sacred human birth.

Develop Good Qualities And Gain the Grace of the Lord

One of the names Krishna used to address Arjuna was *the one who delights in being engaged in work*. When most of you are given some work to do, you quickly get disgusted with it. When Sunday comes and you have a day off from work, you are happy. But if ever a day came when Arjuna had no work, he would be very unhappy. Arjuna always felt a great deal of joy and delight when he worked. The different names Krishna used for Arjuna in the *Gita*, are associated with various noble qualities and virtues. You will be able to understand the nature of the divinity, if every day you take up one virtue and try to incorporate it in your life.

Patience, forbearance, compassion and nonviolence are some of the qualities that have already been taken up in these chapters. Now you have also learned about fearlessness. There are a number of other important qualities. Only when you develop these qualities in your daily activities, will you be able to earn the grace of the Lord. Without developing these noble qualities you will not be able to gain a place in God's house, irrespective of the education, position, and wealth you have been able to earn. A person is not permitted to go to another country without a passport. Similarly, in order to earn the grace of God, your good qualities serve you as your passport. You must develop these qualities.

Along with your education you should also acquire good habits and a sterling character. Without these, all your education will be of no use. This education you are now pursuing is only useful for living in the physical world. It will not take you to God. In the world of today, scientists have been able to glean a number of secrets from nature. But have they been able to gain peace of mind? Have they been able to get joy and happiness from the machines they developed? Happiness and peace cannot come from these. You can get peace only from the divinity.

The worldly happiness and peace you get is but momentary and impermanent. It cannot take you to the state of permanent bliss. The wisdom chapter of the *Gita* emphasizes the practice of recognizing the one all-pervasive divinity that is always very near to you. This chapter is a very long one; there are 72 verses in it. But you will not be able to get rid of your sorrow by just learning these verses and merely chanting them every day. That will not be of much use to you. You will have to make a very strong effort to practice the inner meaning of these verses and apply them constantly in your day-to-day experiences. Only when you practice them in your daily life and make them your own, will you be able to earn the grace of God and be forever united with him.

Twenty-Ninth Chapter

TURN TOWARDS GOD AND
GOD WILL TURN TOWARDS YOU

When you develop your power of discrimination and become fully awake to the indwelling divinity, you will not suffer sorrow nor be subjected to fear. But as long as you have attachment to the body and attachment to objects, fear and suffering will be with you. Therefore, Krishna told Arjuna to develop his discrimination and rid himself of body consciousness. He told him that once he was free of body consciousness he would be able to develop integral vision.

Embodiments of Love,

Mankind today has three types of vision. The first is body-oriented vision, which is totally superficial. When you have this kind of vision you see only the external appearance of others, such as the clothes and the ornaments they wear, their facial features, their body characteristics, their peculiarities of speech, etc. This type of vision is oriented only towards the phenomenal world.

The second kind of vision is insightful vision. Instead of focusing on the external characteristics of others, you focus on their inner feelings, particularly as it is reflected in their behavior and expressions. You gauge the thoughts in another's mind and the feelings in their hearts by carefully watching what they say and do. When you have this kind of vision, you become concerned primarily with the deeper feelings and motivations of the other person.

Sacred Vision

The third kind of vision is integral vision. With this kind of vision, you do not concentrate on another's external features or even their inner feelings. When you have integral vision you see the divine consciousness that pervades everyone, the inner unity that prevails everywhere despite body differences and differences in expression and emotional makeup. You realize that feelings, thoughts and behavioral characteristics all undergo change and transformation. But, you are not interested in characteristics that change with time. With integral vision you are wholly oriented towards the unchanging, indwelling divinity. Such a deep inner vision is a sacred vision. When you have this you are in the hands of God. More than that, not only are you in the hands of God, but verily you become God himself.

The truly wise say that one who knows God becomes God. As you perceive so you become. Therefore, when you gain integral vision, you take on the sacred nature of the divinity itself. To become a person of the highest wisdom, you must develop integral vision. You must steadily abide in the inner unity that is at the core of all the outer diversity. It is for this reason that Krishna commanded Arjuna to steadily turn his vision towards his highest self, and to maintain that vision at all times, under all circumstances.

Chariot Festivals

In India, there has been a tradition from ancient days for temples in villages and towns to conduct chariot festivals. During these festivities the idol of the deity installed in that temple is taken in procession. First, a huge chariot is constructed for this purpose. Then the chariot is elaborately decorated and a beautiful seat is provided therein for the deity. On the auspicious day, the deity is transferred from the temple to the chariot with appropriate rituals and incantations. The chariot is then taken through the streets in a colorful procession pulled by devotees and preceded by groups of dancers, musicians and singers. Along the course of the procession, many people offer worship to the deity by lighting sacred lamps and waving them as the chariot comes by.

During these festivals thousands of people gather, coming from all the surrounding villages. Three kinds of people come. The first kind, which constitutes the bulk of the people present for the festival, concentrate all their attention on the chariot and its external appearance. Then there are others who concentrate mostly on the sacred feelings generated by the procession, such as the fervent piety of those who are pulling the chariot, the ecstatic joy of the dancers and singers, and the reverence of the priests and devotees who are offering worship. Thirdly, there are a few who recognize the real purpose for which this festival has been arranged. Only this small handful cares to have a vision of the indweller, the sacred person who is seated in the chariot.

Of course, the festival is being celebrated for the purpose of installing the image of God in the chariot. Without the representation of God, the festival would have no meaning. This sacred figure inside the chariot represents the indweller, who is God himself. But only the rare individual will turn his full attention towards that divinity. Most people will see only the physical appearance of the chariot, its decorations and other such things as the fine raiment put on the sacred image inside, the costumes worn by the dancers and musicians, and all the sound and color of the festivities. The largest number will concentrate only on these external things. But there will also be some people who concentrate their attention on the rituals of worship and the offerings being made, such as the breaking of coconuts, the waving of lamps and incense, and the devotion expressed through these rituals. The number of people with this kind of vision and interest will be much smaller than those who concentrate on the decorations, the dances and dramas and all the external paraphernalia associated with the festival.

But the divine person who has been installed in this chariot, who is driving this chariot and who is the resident of this chariot will be seen by only a very small number of intensely-devoted people who yearn to have the sacred vision of the divinity. In the huge throng turning out for the festival, such people may be counted on the fingers of one's hand. For them, all the outer trappings and all the sound and excitement of the procession will only get in the way of their having a real vision of God. All they long for is to see and be with their beautiful Lord, whose representation is seated in the chariot.

The Chariot of the Human Body

What is the deeper meaning of this chariot? How many such chariots are there? The chariot that is being spoken of here is the human body. So there is not just one chariot but millions upon millions of chariots. Every day, these chariots move from street to street and house to house, taking the indwelling resident in procession. You have been developing your vision in such a way that you see only the body and its external features or the expressions arising from various feelings and emotional states, but you have not learned to develop the internal vision, the vision which perceives the indwelling person in this chariot of the body, and understands who he really is. It is a very rare individual who attempts to look deeper, beyond the external and superficial aspect of the body, and beyond the emotional and mental traits of the individual, to try to discover the sacred divine principle which is there inside.

The bodies of human beings are not the only chariots. The bodies of animals like dogs or tigers or elephants are also chariots. In fact, the body of every being is a chariot. For example, Lord Shiva is depicted as riding on Nandi, the bull. The bullock is Shiva's chariot. Yet, when you see a bullock, you do not think of Lord Shiva; still he will be seated there. When you see a rat, you will not be thinking of Ganesha, the elephant god, who represents the aspects of protection and wisdom in the divinity. Lord Ganesha will be there, riding on that rat. The rat is his vehicle, so it is also a chariot in which God is installed. In a similar way, lions, crows, dogs, snakes, eagles and so many other animals and birds are used as vehicles for the many different aspects of God. In truth, every living being is a chariot taking God in procession.

These days you are developing the vision that sees only the chariot. You are focusing all your concentration on the external decorations. In this age, almost your entire time is spent on adorning the chariot and seeing to the comforts and pleasures of the body. As a result, you are paying attention only to the external differences and you are not spending any time trying to see the indweller.

"Therefore, Arjuna," said Krishna, "know that all these people about whom you are so concerned, are only chariots. They may be grandfathers, they may be brothers, they may be cousins, whoever they may be, they are only chariots. In truth, you are seeing only chariots in the form of these various relatives and teachers. You have been keeping your vision clouded by seeing only the body. But a sacred person like you should not care so much for externals. You must concentrate your mind on the indweller who is seated in every human body. Then only will your vision become sacred. Such sacred vision alone can provide the basis for your victory.

"Only a person who has sacred vision can achieve success in great undertakings. Arjuna, people are giving the same value to the shadow as they give to that which is casting the shadow; they are giving the same value to the reflection as they give to the one whose reflection they are seeing. But that is not correct. The unchanging, sacred principle which has given rise to all these shadows and reflections is the eternal self. It is the *atma*. Its value is unlimited and beyond all measure. On the other hand, the external beauties of these bodies and all the thoughts and feelings and behaviors that are being manifested in these bodies, are all just images. They are only shadows or reflections without any real substance or lasting value."

When Arjuna gave so much value to mere reflections, he was displaying his ignorance. His was not a worldly type of ignorance, but ignorance related to the spirit. Arjuna had not developed his inner vision. He was not yet able to discriminate between that which is real and that which is unreal. In order to save him from all the misunderstandings and confusion which would inevitably arise when there is a lack of inner vision, Krishna undertook to teach Arjuna the sacred knowledge of the eternal self. Krishna instructed Arjuna in the spiritual exercises which had to be practiced in order to attain this highest wisdom.

The Field of the Heart

Before a farmer can raise a crop in his field, he has to do a great deal of preparation. Before the seeds can be sown, the land must be cleared of brush, stones and weeds, and then it has to be softened by plowing and irrigation. The farmer must determine what particular types of seeds will grow best on that land, and what kind of nutrients would be required to fertilize the soil. When all these preparations are completed, he finally sows the seeds. Therefore, before a crop can be raised, the entire field has to be made ready for cultivation. Stones and weeds have to be dug out and thrown away. Only then can the appropriate seeds be sown to assure a good crop.

In a similar way, a spiritual aspirant must also carefully prepare the field of his heart. The same principles of cultivation apply to that field. First, one has to remove from the heart all undesirable thoughts and useless habits. They have to be dug up and cleaned out. After that, you have to irrigate the entire field of the heart with the waters of love. These waters of love make the heart soft and cultivatable. With the help of spiritual practices, you have to plow the field of your heart and spread the fertilizer of faith in order to make the soil rich and nutritious for the seeds to grow well there. Only when all this has been done will the entire field of the heart be ready for sowing. When the heart is covered with bad weeds of base thoughts, when it is barren, hard and dry and infertile, how can good seeds grow there and have any chance of maturing into a bountiful crop?

It is in this connection that Krishna said to Arjuna, "Arjuna, you must cultivate and transform the field of your heart. You must root out your external vision. Develop a pure and strong flow of love for God. Sow the seeds of God's name in your heart and you will raise a rich harvest of unity consciousness there, for that is what grows best in that field. That is its very nature. Then you will become a man of steady wisdom and attain your spiritual goal. In the garden of your heart you will be able to enjoy the sacred fruit of liberation. Once you have that, fear can never again trouble you.

True Fearlessness

When you have steady faith and an integral vision, and when you constantly think of the indwelling divinity, you will not become elated by joy nor shrink away from sorrow. It is only then that you will become completely fearless. Fearlessness does not mean the absence of fear. True fearlessness completely transcends fear. It is altogether different and much higher than the mere removal of fear. The latter is a momentary experience; it comes and it goes. For example, if you happen to see a rope lying on the ground after dusk, you might think, in the failing light, that it was a snake. Fearing that the snake might harm you, you would switch on your flashlight to get a better look at it and see if it is a poisonous snake. But as soon as the light shines on it you realize that it is not a snake at all but a piece of rope, and with this realization your fear disappears instantly. Here you were subjected to fear and then you became free of fear; both were just transitory experiences.

Fear is only a delusion created by the mind; lack of fear is also a delusion created by the mind. Mistaking one thing for another leads to fear; recognizing the mistake and rectifying it leads to the removal of that fear. But, true fearlessness is not associated with these two at all. Fearlessness is a permanent state where there is no question of ever experiencing any fear. When you are imbued with fearlessness you are continuously aware of your own reality. At that point, it would be impossible for you to become subject to fear. You should not consider this quality of fearlessness as just the absence of fear. When you are truly fearless you will not be aware of any second entity, at all. You can have fear only when there exists a second object who evokes the fear in you. But, fearlessness is always associated with unity consciousness. It refers to non-duality, where there can be no two but always just one. Only in the state of non-duality will you be truly fearless.

When you forget your true self you will suffer from fear. When you remember only the world and not God, you will suffer from fear. When you are filled with desires and attachments, you will suffer from fear. When you are deluded by objects, you will suffer from fear. On the other hand, when you are immersed in the transcendental reality, you will be totally free from fear; you will never be afraid of anything. Then you will be truly fearless.

Krishna said, "Arjuna, there is only one thing you will have to develop. You need not develop further your vision of the phenomenal world; nor do you need to further develop your mind. You need only to develop the vision of the one existing everywhere in everyone. If you know it, and if you remember it, then you will not be subject to this constant cycling between fear and its removal. So long as you have the deluded perspective that the world is real and made up of separate objects, your vision will be clouded and you will be subject to fear. But when you recognize the truth of the unity of the whole creation, you will be forever fearless. A person like you should become wise and never again experience fear."

The Story of Gajendra, the Elephant

You will have to control your tendency to look outwards towards the body and its deeds and towards the mind with its thoughts and feelings. Instead, develop the inward vision of the sacred self. This is the true vision, the integral vision. There is a fine example of this in the ancient spiritual classic called the *Bhagavatam*. It is the story of Gajendra, an elephant who was caught by a crocodile. This elephant, Gajendra, had a strong ego and he was convinced that with his great strength he would be able to fight and free himself from the crocodile. But here two facts must be known; elephants are very powerful on land, crocodiles are very powerful in the water. When an elephant enters the water he will not have so much strength, and when a crocodile comes out on land he will also be less mighty than in his natural habitat, the water. In this case, because the crocodile was in the water he was able to exercise all his great strength. But the elephant, Gajendra, was very arrogant; he was blown up with ego and felt that no crocodile could ever be equal to an elephant, who was the lord of the forest. He did not know that a crocodile in the water would be more than a match for any elephant away from land.

For a long time they fought relentlessly. Finally the elephant got tired and lost all his physical as well as mental strength. He had placed all his confidence in his physical and mental prowess, but having exhausted all that, he began praying to the Lord. As long as his vision had been directed to his body he did not look towards God. As long as he had confidence in his own bodily and mental strength, the thought of God did not arise and the Lord's grace did not descend. When the elephant lost his physical and mental power and turned towards God, immediately Lord Vishnu hurled his sacred discus, and freed Gajendra from the catastrophe that had overtaken him. Now, the discus spoken of here does not refer to a mere weapon used by the Lord; but it refers to his grace. You evoke God's grace by turning your vision towards God. Then God turns his vision towards you.

Turn Your Vision Towards God And See Your Self

When will you acquire God's vision that will forever keep you in his grace? Only when you renounce all your egocentric beliefs in your own strength of body and mind. You gain God's grace when you turn your vision towards God, put yourself wholly in his hands and, just as the elephant Gajendra did, surrender yourself completely to his will. When you turn your vision towards the teacher you love, the teacher will turn towards you. Even if the teacher's vision were to fall on you, if you had not at the same time turned your vision towards your teacher, you would not have been able to experience the teacher's beneficent gaze. Now, all your vision is concentrated on the body. The effulgence of the shining sun may be all around you but its light will not have entered the room where you are staying. What is the reason for this? You have put curtains and shutters on the windows and kept the warm rays of sunlight out. Only when you break open these dark curtains and shutters will the effulgence of the sun enter your inner apartment.

In the same way, you have covered your vision with shutters of doubt and ego and thick curtains of body-consciousness, and so the rays of grace are not able to penetrate through and enter your heart. You might say, "I have not been able to get the grace of God." But how will you be able to get it if you do not turn your gaze on him?

When you do not look to God, then surely you will not be able to see God. If I am standing directly in front of you and you are standing directly in front of me, and we are looking at each other, what is it that we will see? Who will you see in my eyes and who will I see in your eyes? We will see each other, in each other's eyes. When we stand face to face, I can see my vision in you and you can see your vision in me. But if you stand behind or turn away, how can I see my vision in you, or you see your vision in me? It would be impossible. In the same way, if you want your eyes to meet the eyes of God, you must come and be directly in front of him and concentrate your vision on him. When you do, he will turn his benevolent gaze upon you, and you will see a vision of your higher self.

When the sight of the elephant, Gajendra, was turned towards God, God's sight met with it, because God's sight then turned towards him. Once that happened, all problems were automatically solved.

The Elephant of Arrogance and the Crocodile of Attachment

Who is this elephant? This proud elephant is arrogance and pride. When a man is full of arrogance and pride, he develops desire. Desire may be compared to thirst. When this proud man develops thirst, he goes to the waters of the world to drink. Even before he enters these waters completely, attachment catches hold of him. Attachment and possessiveness are the powerful crocodile that robs you of all your strength and makes you cry so pitifully. Before entering the waters of the world, before having gained so many attachments, you will have only rarely cried. For example, before marriage, a young man will feel free and unencumbered. But after marriage there will be a continuous growth of attachments. Then one has to take care of wife, children, parents, in-laws and quite a few other relatives, and soon it feels like the whole world has laid hold of him and is pulling him down under the waters.

Once you develop egoism and pride then desires follow. Soon attachments come, and from attachments all these bonds develop. When bonds develop, you will be so distracted you will not be able to turn towards God and see him. Only when you look towards God will you be able to see him. Then he will look towards you, and you will be able to perceive your own true image. "Therefore," Krishna cautioned, "do not become a victim of this bondage, Arjuna. Keep your mind clear and pure. Always look towards the immortal self, the universal principle. It is the one divinity existing in all things. Cultivate such sacred vision in your mind. Do not allow the weeds and shrubs of ego and body-consciousness to develop in your heart. Instead, grow the tree of God's grace in your heart. Turn your sight towards God. Let this be your objective. Make that your goal."

TO BECOME FREE
SURRENDER YOUR MIND TO GOD

The entire world is made up of three qualities. These qualities constitute illusion. They can be spoken of as density or inertia, action or reaction, and balance or harmony.

Although their effects are very different, all three qualities befog your understanding. As long as these qualities reside in your heart you will remain in bondage.

Embodiments of Love,

Among the three qualities enumerated above, the first two, namely inertia and excessive activity, are responsible for all the sorrows, grief, troubles and problems that you experience. Whenever torpor, laziness, drowsiness or sleepiness manifest, or whenever unconscionable fear or rage or hatred take hold of you, then you are overwhelmed by the quality of inertia or density, which in Sanskrit is called *tamas*. Whenever strong desires, frenzied activities, impatience, passion, emotional and self-interested actions of all kinds predominate, then the second quality, which in Sanskrit is called *rajas*, holds sway over you. When these two qualities are in control, your real human nature is forgotten. They bring out the animal nature and the demonic nature in human beings. Therefore, to begin with, these two qualities of *tamas* and *rajas* will have to be expunged from you.

Root Out the Weeds of *Tamas* and *Rajas*

A farmer who wants to gain a good crop starts by removing the weeds from his field. As long as the weeds cover the field, depleting the soil of nutrients and energy, the crops will not have a chance. Therefore, the removal of this unwanted growth is an essential precondition for raising a good crop. In the same way, if you want to gain enlightenment, if you want to realize the bliss of the eternal self, if you want to abide in the unending joy of the *atma*, you will have to remove from the field of your heart the weeds of *tamas* and *rajas*. They have rooted there in the form of desire, anger, greed, delusion, pride and jealousy, the baneful inner enemies which must be conquered. These inner enemies are the children of *tamas* and *rajas*. They keep you locked up in delusion. As long as these weeds remain within you, you will not be able to reap the bliss of the *atma*.

The first chapter of the *Gita* is filled with Arjuna's anguish and wailing. The two qualities *tamas* and *rajas* had taken over his heart and were responsible for Arjuna's grief and sorrow. Krishna taught Arjuna, that in the first place, he had to root out *tamas* and *rajas* from his heart, so that he could fully express his human nature. But, to express his true divine nature, even the third of the three qualities that make up illusion, the one which in Sanskrit is called *satva* and which is characterized by a balanced peaceful manner, had to be transcended. It is also a limitation which covers your divine nature, although with a very fine veil. All three qualities keep you locked into the individual personality and prevent you from fully realizing your divine self. Krishna told Arjuna, "Offer all three qualities, *tamas, rajas* and *satva*, to me. Then you will be free of timidity and sorrow, and you will be able to achieve victory in the world."

Clean Your Heart Thoroughly To Welcome God There

If you are inviting a great spiritual being such as a sage or a revered teacher to your house, there are certain preparations which you will have to undertake in cleansing, adorning and decorating your house. You will have to clean inside and out and bring order to the surroundings before the guest arrives. Great people will not enter a house which is full of dirt and which lacks sacredness. In the same way, when you have invited the governor or a high official to your town, you clean the roads and decorate the paths and keep everything ready and fit to receive the distinguished personage. Even though this person holds only a temporary position, you will still take great care to clean your house and make many preparations to welcome the honored guest to your place.

When you make so much effort to receive a worldly official, then how much more effort and preparation should you make to invite the very creator and protector of the world to come to your house? Clearly, when you welcome God into your heart, you must cleanse your heart thoroughly. Only when you purify your heart will God be pleased to enter it. Krishna said, "Arjuna, up to now you have been taking me only as the charioteer of your chariot, but you must take me as the charioteer of your life! The seat on which I am seated in the chariot is clean and well decorated. Now, think of how clean and grand your heart must be to make a seat for me there, if I am to install myself as the charioteer of your life."

If you go to a park and decide to sit down on the ground, you put down a mat, or a newspaper or a large kerchief and sit on that. When you take so much care about the seat for this body, which, after all, is just temporary and full of impurities, how much more care should you take when you are inviting God into the inner sanctum of your heart?

As long as the two qualities *rajas* and *tamas* are in your heart, your heart will remain impure. These two qualities continuously pollute and dirty the heart. As long as it is dirty, the divinity will not enter your heart; you will not be able to perceive the divine presence there. Therefore, you must first remove the quality of density and inertia, the *tamas* quality, and having done that, you must remove the *rajas* quality. Then the *satva* quality will shine in you, and you will become a self-assured human being, in touch with your divine source. Start now by making every effort to remove every bit of dirt that has accumulated in your heart. There is a small example for this.

Devotion, Wisdom and Detachment Will Keep You Pure

When ladies go out, they frequently take along a little mirror, a comb and a handkerchief, to make sure that they will present a neat appearance. Why do they take these three particular items? During the journey, it is quite likely that their hair will get disturbed. To put their hair back in order they take the comb. To see if their hair is properly in place, they take the mirror. And to wipe their face they take the handkerchief. If they leave any one of these behind, they will not be able to achieve perfection in their appearance. So, a comb, a mirror and a handkerchief are necessary to help maintain facial cleanliness and a neat appearance.

In the same way, if you want to correct the disturbed beauty of your heart, you have to take certain aids for that too. Whether your hair is disturbed or not is shown to you by the mirror. Whether your heart is disturbed or not is shown to you by your devotion, which acts as the mirror. This mirror must be pure. When the mirror is clean, you will be able to see if your heart and mind are pure or if they have become covered by impurities. When you recognize that your heart is disturbed, you have to correct it. And for this purpose you need a comb, namely, the comb of wisdom. Wisdom clarifies the heart and returns it to a state of order and beauty. Then, just as you have a cloth to clean the dirt that has come on your face, you have to remove the dirt that has entered your mind with the cloth of detachment. With the help of detachment you can wipe off all the dirt that has accumulated in your mind.

Just as ladies take these three things, the mirror, the comb and the handkerchief, along with them whenever they go out on a journey in the world, so also, in your journey of life, you have to take devotion, wisdom and detachment to keep your heart and mind pure.

The Characteristics of *Rajas*

We have already considered the *tamas* quality which binds you to your lower nature. Now, let us examine the characteristics of the *rajas* quality, which also locks you into the lower realms of being and keeps you from expressing your true human potential. A person who is filled with *rajas* will always be hasty in everything; he will have no patience or forbearance. He cannot be steady for even a moment. And he will exhibit a great deal of anger. Not only this, he will also have unlimited desires. These are all characteristics of the *rajas* quality. This becomes clear when you go to watch animals in a zoo. Be it a cheetah, a tiger or a fox, they will not be quiet and steady for even a moment. The reason is that they are filled with an excess of *rajas*.

When *rajas* enters your heart it makes you unsteady in body and mind; you will be restless all the while. Not only does it make you unsteady, it also keeps you in delusion. When you are deluded, you have strong desires for the objects of the world. As these desires manifest in your heart, you take action to procure these different things for yourself. In that way, delusion leads to desire, and desire leads to action. These three, delusion, desire and action are the powerful qualities which are the characteristic features of *rajas*.

It is because of *rajas* that you constantly move about. For example, when you sit in a particular place, you find you will not be steady for very long; some part of the body or other will always be moving. This may be compared to the aspen tree. Even if there is no breeze or wind, the leaves in such a tree will always be moving. The same applies to a horse. The word for horse in Sanskrit refers to that which has no steadiness. Whenever you see a horse, whether it be the head, the tail or the legs, some part of it will always be moving. That is why in ancient times, a sacrifice called *the sacrifice of the horse*, was performed as a symbolic ritual to elicit the help of the gods, in the practice of steadying the mind.

Remove All Three Qualities And Gain Liberation

The exemplar for the *rajas* quality is Ravana, the king of the demons. The exemplar for the *tamas* quality is another well-known demon in ancient lore, who slept for decades at a time. There was still a third demon whose heart was good and who surrendered himself at the feet of Rama. He is the exemplar for the *satva* quality; he chose the side of good, but nevertheless, he was a demon. All three of these demons are brothers. If you allow the first two into you heart, they will lead you into endless harm and grief. If you let the third one dominate you, he will lead you into activities and ways of living that are good. But, nevertheless, he will also keep you immersed in delusion and forgetful of your true divine nature.

If you want to enter the kingdom of liberation, you must remove all three of these demons from your heart. All three belong to the same demonic family. That is why the *Vedanta* has been teaching that you must transcend the three qualities and offer them to Lord Shiva. He will watch over them with his three eyes and render them harmless with his three-forked trident.

What is the best way to remove these three qualities? If you are out in the wilds and a thorn were to enter your foot. You need not take a big sharp knife to remove it. You just take another thorn and remove the first with the second. Once that has been accomplished, you throw away both thorns, without making any distinction between them. In the same way you have to remove the *tamas* quality with the help of the *rajas* quality. Then you have to remove *rajas* with the help of *satva*. Finally, you give up *satva* also. Before you can enter into the kingdom of God-realization, you have to cast out all three of these qualities that keep you bound up in delusion. That is why Krishna directed Arjuna to transcend all three qualities. He warned Arjuna that he would have to make a maximum effort and take great care to permanently rid himself of these three qualities.

After having taught Arjuna to recognize these various qualities, Krishna showed him how to rise beyond them. In that way, Krishna transformed Arjuna into a truly wise man. The primary cause of these three qualities is the mind. It is impossible to transcend this human nature and realize your divine nature until your mind loses its wavering nature and becomes still. Therefore, the best way to transcend these qualities is to offer your mind to the Lord. After you have offered your mind to him completely, God will take care of you in all respects. Here is a small story to illustrate this.

King Janaka's Challenge to Gain Self-Knowledge

Once upon a time, King Janaka sent a message to the people in his realm, saying, "If there be amongst you a great scholar, a *pundit*, a *mahatma*, a *yogi*, a sage, whoever he may be, let him come and teach me the knowledge of the *atma.*" In his message he said that he expected to attain self-knowledge within a matter of a few moments of being properly instructed. Even while climbing onto his horse and before he was completely settled onto it, he should have gained self-realization. He said, "If the person offering to teach me self-knowledge cannot assure me this experience of instant illumination then he will be banished from my domain, even if he is the greatest scholar or the most learned person or the highest educated person in the land."

Well, all the *pundits* and sages were a little frightened by this requirement. They saw that this would be a severe test on their scholarship and learning, and so no one dared to come forth and offer himself to instruct the king and meet the conditions that had been posed.

It was at this point that the boy Astavakra entered the kingdom. While he was going on the road towards the capital city, he met a number of people coming from there, including quite a few scholars and *pundits.* All of them had long faces, looking worried and grief-stricken. Astavakra asked them what the cause was for their worry and grief. They explained to him all the things that had happened. But Astavakra could not understand why they should get frightened over the king's pronouncement, if they had truly mastered the teachings and realized their truth. He said, "I will gladly solve this problem for the king." So saying, he directly entered the court of Janaka.

Astavakra addressed the king, "My dear king, I am ready to teach you the knowledge of the *atma.* But this sacred knowledge cannot be taught so easily. This palace is full of *rajas* and *tamas.* We must leave here and enter an area that is pure *satva.*" So they left the palace on horseback and went along the road leading out of the city towards the forest. As was the custom, whenever the king went outside the palace walls, the army followed close behind. But, when they approached the forest, King Janaka directed the soldiers to remain outside, and not follow them into the forest.

Astavakra and Janaka went deep into the forest. Astavakra told King Janaka, "I am not going to teach you the knowledge of the *atma* unless you accept my conditions. I may be only a young boy, but since I am to teach you, I am in the position of the preceptor. You may be an all-powerful emperor, but since you are going to learn from me, you are in the position of the disciple. Are you prepared to accept this relationship? If you agree then you will have to offer the traditional gift to the teacher, the gift that is given by the disciple to the *guru*. Only after you give me your offering will I start my instruction to you."

King Janaka told Astavakra, "The attainment of God is the most important thing to me, so I am prepared to give you absolutely anything you want. You can have my crown and the kingdom itself." But Astavakra replied, "I don't want any material things from you. All I want is your mind. You must give me your mind." The king answered. "All right, I offer my mind to you. Up to now I thought this was my mind, but from now on it is yours alone."

Janaka Achieves Self-Realization

Astavakra told Janaka to dismount from his horse and leave it by the side, and then he told the king to sit down in the middle of the path. Astavakra walked further into the forest and sat quietly under a tree. Outside the forest, the soldiers waited for a long time. Neither the king nor Astavakra showed up, although it was long after the customary time when the king would have his repast. Both the officers and the soldiers who loved their king and were very faithful to him, became anxious to find out what had happened to him. So, one by one, they stole into the forest to look for King Janaka and the little boy who was with him, suspecting some foul play.

When they went along the path leading into the forest, they were relieved to find the king seated there, in the middle of the path. His horse was standing next to him. The king had his eyes closed and he sat motionless. The boy, Astavakra, was not to be seen. The officers addressed the king, but he did not answer. They feared that Astavakra might have exercised some magic spell over the king and had made him lose consciousness. They went to look for the prime minister.

The prime minister came and addressed Janaka, "O king! O king! O king!" But Janaka did not open his eyes. He did not move at all. The prime minister became very frightened. Not only the prime minister but all the other officials from the palace who had come, were now getting thoroughly concerned. The king had always kept to a rigorous schedule. He took his supper at the same time every day. Now that time had long since passed but the king still had not stirred. In this way, the day went on and evening came, but the king did not move from his position, sitting there immobile on the ground.

Left with no alternative, the prime minister sent the chariot back to the city to bring the queens, thinking that if the queens spoke to the king he would surely respond. The queens came and addressed the king, "*Maharajah! Maharajah!*" The king did not stir; there was absolutely no response from the king. Meanwhile the soldiers searched throughout the whole forest for Astavakra. At last, they found him under a tree. Astavakra was immersed in divine ecstasy.

The soldiers called out to him and exhorted him to answer their queries. Astavakra came out of his self-absorbed blissful state. They implored him to come to the place where the king was. Astavakra asked them, "Why are you all so worried? The king is safe and everything is all right." But they insisted that Astavakra come along with them and brought him before the king seated in the middle of the path. The king had his eyes closed. His body was completely still. The soldiers said, "Here, look for yourself! See what has happened to the king!" Until that time, whether the prime minister, or the other ministers, or the queens, or any of the court officials or soldiers or common people, had called out and addressed the king, he neither opened his mouth in answer nor opened his eyes in acknowledgment. But now, Astavakra came and spoke to the king. King Janaka immediately opened his eyes and replied, "Master!"

Astavakra questioned the king, "Well, the ministers have come and the soldiers have come, and also many others have come. Why did you not reply to their entreaties?" Janaka answered, "Thoughts, words and deeds are associated with the mind, and I offered my mind entirely to you. Therefore, before I can use this mind for anything, I need your permission. What authority do I have to speak to anyone or use this mind in any way? Without your permission and command, I am not going to do anything." Astavakra told Janaka to put one foot in the stirrup and get up on the horse. By the time he had climbed up and seated himself on the horse and put his other foot in the stirrup, he had attained the direct experience of the *atma*. Then Astavakra said to him, "You have attained the state of God-realization."

For Self-Knowledge Total Surrender of the Mind Is Required

Once a person has offered up his mind, and with it all his words, deeds and thoughts, then he will not have the authority or the power to perform any actions without the permission of the one to whom he has surrendered his will. As was the case with Astavakra and Janaka, so also with Krishna and Arjuna. Krishna told Arjuna, "Arjuna, offer everything to me. Surrender all your actions to me. I will take care of you and I will guide you towards liberation and deliverance." So also, you need to offer all your physical, mental, spiritual and worldly duties, all your various actions, thoughts and words, to the Lord, the inner director installed in your heart.

But, you may wonder, if every duty and desire is relinquished and offered to the Lord, then does that mean that even the desire for liberation has to be given up? After all, that is also a type of thought. No. The real meaning is that when you offer up your load of desires and duties and responsibilities to the Lord, and allow him to make all your decisions, then he will carry all your burdens. And then you can be one-pointed in the one worthwhile goal of life, that of self-realization.

All this education that you acquire, all this learning that you pursue, is associated with the three qualities of delusion. Only when you transcend these three qualities will you be able to gain self-realization. In celebrating a marriage, a benediction is given so that the couple might be blessed with a successful career, with material prosperity, and with a fine family. These are three of the four primary goals of human life. The first refers to duties and responsibilities and position, the second refers to the accumulation of wealth and the third refers to the desire for progeny and the continuation of the family line. All three of these goals have to do with the worldly life. But there is a fourth goal of human life. That final and most important goal is liberation. The fourth goal relates to the spiritual life. The first three of these goals of human life cannot be considered equal to the fourth, which is liberation. Offer up all your little acts involving these first three goals. Give them all to the Lord, and trade them in for the one priceless treasure which he will give you in return, namely, liberation. Consider the following example.

In Indian currency, the smallest denomination is a paisa. It is a small metal coin. One hundred paisa is equal to one rupee. Conversely, 100 rupees is equal to 10,000 paisa. If you should have to carry these 10,000 paisa around with you, it would become a very large unwieldy bundle. Also, it would be quite difficult to hide and protect such a big bag of coins. If you were to heap all of these 10,000 paisa into one small cloth, the cloth would soon get torn and before long the coins would fall out.

Krishna told Arjuna, "Arjuna, I will give you a hundred rupee note. You give that whole pile of change that you are carrying, consisting of 10,000 paisa, to me. This one 100 rupee note and these 10,000 paisa are equal in value, but what a great difference there is in the burden of carrying them around with you. It is the same with all these many little duties and worries and thoughts of various types that burden you. Offer all 10,000 to me; I will give you a single 100 rupee note and relieve you of your load."

All your various thoughts, all your wishes and wants… all these small desires may be compared to individual paisa. When you have so many small paisa, unless they are all put together, they will not be equal to a one rupee note. Krishna said, "Arjuna, all these small desires can never be equal to the grace that I can shower on you. So give them all to me." This is how King Janaka was able to attain liberation after he had offered up his entire mind, all his thinking and doing and speaking, to Astavakra.

Offer Up Your Mind To the Lord

The sum and substance of all this is that you should offer up your mind to the Lord. In everything you do and think and say, follow his directions, emanating from the purity of your heart. That is what is meant by becoming mindless. Do not allow your mind to follow desires. Offer all these desires up to the Lord and follow only his dictates. Until you have done that, pleasure and pain, happiness and sorrow and all the other pairs of opposites will be present within you. If you want to become free of these opposites and treat all things equally, you have to become mindless. That is why it has been said in the *Vedanta* that it is the mind which is responsible for liberation or bondage. As long as you retain the mind, *rajas* and *tamas* will not leave you. So long as you have *rajas* and *tamas*, you will have no steadiness. Why is the mind so unsteady, constantly hopping from place to place? It is because of desires. These desires all relate to the body.

Consider for a moment that you have poured a little water into a vessel; when the vessel moves, the water also moves. If the vessel is steady then the water remains steady. In steady water you will be able to see your own image. In moving water your image will be blurred and indistinct. It follows then that if you want to enter the still state of meditation and have a vision of your true self, you must keep your body steady. The body is like a vessel; the mind may be compared to the water inside. If the body moves, it is like the movement of the vessel. Then the mind inside will also move. Therefore, if you want to keep your mind steady, you must keep your body steady. Considering how much you move the body, think of how much more the mind will move.

If you throw a stone into a well, ripples will start. These ripples or waves, which arise from the stone hitting the water, will soon spread to the far end of the well. In the same way, once you put a thought into the well of your mind, it spreads to the entire body. And whatever be your thoughts, they will subsequently influence your actions. So, you must constantly keep good thoughts, positive thoughts, in your mind. When you are having good thoughts, there will also be good feelings in your heart. If negative thoughts enter your mind, then, in whatever you see, in whatever you hear, in whatever you say and wherever you go, these negative thoughts will lead to harmful actions and grievous results.

Steady Your Mind and Your Body

When you are sitting, the posture should be erect... not like that of an old person, all bent over. You should be steady and straight. You should not go to the other extreme either, of raising your head up; nor should you turn your head to one side or the other. For meditation, it is very important to have an erect sitting posture. If you were to imagine a line going vertically down through the top of your head, it should go straight to the base of your spine, the center of subtle energy at the bottom of your spine. That way the entire spine will be in proper alignment. The *kundalini* power will then be able to travel unimpeded from the lowest energy vortex to the highest at the crown of your head.

Therefore, keep the body steady and straight. If from youth it is bent, then by the time you become old you will be completely bent over. Be it your head, your neck or your torso, there should be no bend. This is extremely important for students, and equally so for devotees. Therefore, I will be telling you this quite often.

Why are you studying at all? What is the goal of your studies? Truly, you are studying in order to steady your mind and body. Except when you are playing, you should not be moving too much. Even when you are talking or when you are singing, you should be steady. In this way, right from childhood, if you can keep your body under control, it will be very useful to you as an instrument to achieve meditation. Krishna gave these instructions to Arjuna in the *Gita*, in order to turn Arjuna into an ideal representative of mankind, one who would serve as a model for all of humanity. Krishna told him, "Arjuna, I am taking you as my instrument so that by your example you may teach all of mankind."

Arjuna became an ideal person. Since his wavering mentality was due to the *rajas* and *tamas* qualities, Krishna told Arjuna to systematically rid himself of these two qualities, and offer them to the Lord. Eventually, he would even have to give up being controlled by the third quality, the *satva* quality. In the second chapter of the *Gita*, the chapter on the wisdom teachings, Krishna explained a number of ways in which the three qualities that have been discussed here, can be conquered. When you have completely expunged them from your mind, you will become transformed into a sage, a wise being, one who is steeped in the highest wisdom.

Part Three

PATH
of
ACTION

Thirty-First Chapter

DO YOUR DUTY – BUT WITHOUT CONCERN FOR THE RESULTS

*K*rishna said, "Arjuna, you have work to do. Do it! But give
up all interest in the fruit of your work." Krishna did not
say that there would be no fruit. The fruit will certainly be
there. Every action has its consequence or fruit. But the
fruit is not your concern; you should not aspire for it.
Therefore, the essence of Krishna's teaching is that you
must do your duty, but do it without keeping the outcome
in mind.

Embodiments of Love,

For every action there is an outcome, and subsequently, this outcome gives rise to another action. This ongoing cycle of action and
result, result and action, manifests itself in a way similar to the cycle of the seed and the tree. The seed and tree also follow one after
the other, with the seed giving rise to the tree and the tree giving
rise to the seed. Without a seed you cannot have a tree and without
a tree you cannot have a seed. The same thing is true for an action
and its result. These are natural cycles in the world. When this is
so, with one always following the other, why should you take a
special interest in the outcome? Your duty and responsibility is to
perform the right action; have no concern about the result. Krishna
told Arjuna, "In this battle, you should be indifferent to what happens to your own people or what befalls you. Do your duty without
letting your mind dwell on the outcome."

The Shield of Devotion and the Armor of Wisdom

In battle, warriors wear shield and armor. This gives them some
protection against the powerful weapons that are shot at them by
their enemies. In the spiritual battle which you must fight, you
must also wear a type of shield and armor. Here the shield is devotion and love for God, and the armor is wisdom. In an ordinary war
relating to the world, the fighting may last only a few days, or it
may drag on for a few months or even some years. But the spiritual
battle goes on continuously; it never ends. It has been fought by

mankind unceasingly, right from ancient days. Since time immemorial there has been the fight between good and bad, between virtue and sin, between attachment and detachment.

Humanity has been waging an endless war with its feelings of *I-ness* and *my-ness*, with its feelings of hatred and jealousy and other evil qualities that have taken shelter within it. Egoism and attachment, in particular, have extraordinary strength. They are really dreadful. Compared to them, you, the individual who is fighting them, are not so strong. You are really quite weak. In fact, you have become so dominated by these negative qualities that, like Arjuna, you have identified yourself with them. Now, to fight such powerful enemies and qualities, you have to follow the directions of the indwelling Lord and you have to wear a very strong shield and armor. The mighty shield and armor that you have to wear in this spiritual battle are devotion and wisdom. They will protect you from such formidable enemies.

When you have a parasol to shade you, you are not troubled by the hot sun. When you wear sandals or shoes, you are not concerned about stepping on a thorn. When you wear a shield and armor, you are not too much bothered by the weapons being hurled against you. "Therefore, Arjuna," Krishna said, "in this inner battle you must don your spiritual shield and armor." When Krishna lifted Arjuna out of his despondency at the beginning of the *Gita*, he gave Arjuna the armor of wisdom. That was the first teaching that Krishna offered.

Use Wisdom to Conquer Your Inner Enemies

Krishna said to Arjuna, "All these attachments that you now have, all these desires to possess things, are not tendencies that you acquired yesterday or the day before. They have been with you for numerous births and they are responsible for all the pain that you are experiencing. You have no way of knowing when you will finally be able to rid yourself of the pain they have caused. But you cannot do much about the past, so do not worry about it. Focus, instead, on the means for eliminating the pain that would come to you in the future, were these attachments and desires to continue ruling over you.

"In the battle that you are about to fight, you have provided yourself with worldly armor. That will help protect your body from external enemies; but how will you be able to protect yourself from the internal enemies which you are battling inside you? To protect yourself from them, you have to wear the armor of wisdom.

You are concerned about your external enemies, but you are not thinking about the inner enemies at all. If you succumb to your inner enemies you will never be able to conquer your external enemies. Therefore, first conquer these inner enemies."

It is natural to search for a doctor when you are sick and suffering, but it is of greater importance to see to it that you do not contract any illness in the first place. It is said that an ounce of prevention is worth a pound of cure. From earliest times, the inner enemies have been subduing mankind and filling human beings with sorrow. As long as you are filled with egoism and attachment, you will not be able to free yourself from grief and sorrow. You have been engaged in wrongful actions, and these have been responsible for all your pain. Does this mean that you should abstain from action? No. You have no choice but to act. You must act, and you are free to enjoy your actions as well. But from now on, you must perform all your actions properly, in a way which will not accrue harmful consequences and pain to you in the future. In keeping with this, it is very important that you understand the underlying principles of right action.

Every Worldly Experience Can Be Traced to *Karma*

Action is called *karma*. You are born in *karma*, you develop in *karma* and you die in *karma*. It is *karma,* or the actions you perform, which are responsible for all good or bad, sin or virtue, profit or loss, joy or sorrow. Truly, *karma* is responsible for your very birth itself. *Karma* is really the creator for mankind. It shapes your life. It follows then that you should not look upon action with carelessness. Your entire life is associated with action. Therefore, recognize the importance of right action and engage in that, unwaveringly.

Do not think that action is just a small thing. It may start as a small sapling but it will grow into a very big tree. Before a seed can become a tree, it has to break out of the soil in which it was sown. Then, once it has become a big tree, it will offer you its fruit. Whether this fruit brings you joy or sorrow depends on the seed that you have sown. To get the very finest fruit, the seed of action which you have performed must be of the highest quality and it must break out of the soil of egoism. Then this action can be transformed into *yoga*. *Yoga* is union with God.

Egoism Develops When You Forget the Indweller

What is the root cause of egoism? Why should you ever feel egoistic? Egoism arises because of the ignorance which is inherent in you. You have to think out for yourself what is the birthplace of this egoism, where did it come from and where will it end?

Consider these facts of the physical universe: Light travels at the rate of 670 million miles per hour. At this rate, light travels a trillion miles per year. We consider the sun to be very near; the distance between the earth and the sun is approximately 90 million miles. For us, the splendor of the light coming from the sun is exceptionally bright. But this is the light from only one sun. There are billions of suns and stars. The distance to the nearest of these is almost 4 light years, or something like 23 to 24 trillion miles.

The stars look as though they are very close to one another, but the distance between any two stars is tens of trillions of miles. They look as though milk has been spread all over the sky. The stars that you can see with a high-powered telescope number in the billions. And there are many, many more objects in the heavens which you cannot see. What is the size of the earth in the context of such a vast universe, where there are billions upon billions of stars, spread over distances of trillions upon trillions of miles? And what is the place of this little planet earth in relation to the huge sun, which, nevertheless, is only a minor star among the countless stars that speckle the heavens?

On this earth, what is the size of the country in which you are a citizen? What is the size of the state you are living in? Within it how small is this district that you are now in? And how much smaller is the little town that you call home? And then, how very much smaller still are you on this tiny plot of land that you occupy within it? If such is the scale of the universe and such is your size in it, why are you so puffed up with egoistic feelings? If you were to take true cognizance of the vastness of the world, you would not have any egoism. Only when you are oblivious of the greatness of the universe in relation to your minute size can you ever be filled with such a foolish notion.

Perhaps you are proud of your own body. But the body consists of only the five elements. One day or another it will perish. Only the indweller is permanent. It does not have birth or death, it does not grow or decay. It shines everywhere. In the whole world it is the one permanent entity shining as the effulgent one, in a sea of changing forms. It is behind every form, it is the splendor animating every feature in the vast universe. Even in utter darkness it is there, for it is that which reveals the darkness to you. This all-pervading splendor is the indweller, the eternal flame ever shining inside this inert body. Look to this indweller, turn towards it, and you will not be deluded by pride and egoism.

The Body Is An Inert Thing Made Of The Five Elements

Take shelter in the indwelling Lord. Do not keep looking towards the body and feeling proud. The body is subject to so many diseases; it undergoes many changes. It is barely able to journey on this ocean of worldly existence and survive. The body is only an inert thing; it is nothing more than seven buckets of water, the iron from four 2-inch nails, the phosphorous from 1,100 match sticks, the carbon contained in four pencils and two pieces of soap. When you put all these things together with a few other assorted substances, it becomes a body. So, the body just consists of this inert matter. But it is able to move and exhibit life because there is an indweller inside.

Consider the wall clock that is hanging there. It has three hands: a second hand, a minute hand and an hour hand. As soon as you wind the clock, all three hands start moving at their own prescribed rate. How long will they keep moving thus? They keep moving as long as there is power in the spring to energize them. The moment that power is exhausted, they stop wherever they are. Your body may be compared to a clock. The breath may be compared to the spring. Your actions may be compared to the second hand; your feelings may be compared to the minute hand; and your joy may be compared to the hour hand. It is the divine energy within which empowers and vitalizes all this.

In the context of this example of the clock, you can answer the question as to why you perform actions at all. You see that the second hand, which represents your actions, moves quite fast and soon covers one whole revolution of 60 seconds. At that point, the minute hand, which represents your feelings, will have advanced one sixtieth of a revolution. It is only when the second hand has made sixty full revolutions of sixty seconds each, and the minute hand has gone once around, that the hour hand, which represents an experience of divine joy and bliss, will move one division. The hour hand moves so slowly that you cannot even detect its movement, although you can see the movement of the minute and second hands.

There is an inner secret here. Once every hour all three hands meet. When the action which is associated with the body and nature, when the feeling which is associated with the inner man, and when the unending joy which is associated with the divinity all come together, then you have the meeting of nature, man and God.

From Sacred Action to Devotional Feelings to Bliss

Nature has been described as the field of action; it gives you the opportunity to sanctify your work and reach your goal. When you perform 60 good actions, one good feeling will emerge. Therefore, to get the one good feeling you have to perform so many good actions. And it is only when you have sixty such good feelings that there will be one small movement of the hour hand, which represents the ineffable experience of divine joy. Therefore, Krishna told Arjuna to perform good actions. When you do innumerable good actions, you are likely to get one or two deeply-satisfying and lasting good feelings. And it is only when you develop innumerable such good feelings that you will be able to reach the bliss that is the eternal state of the *atma*. Therefore, you must start by performing many good actions.

The body has been given to you for this specific purpose of performing actions. It is impossible to spend even a moment without being active. That is why the performance of sacred activities, which includes ceremonial and ritual worship, has been given so much importance in the *Vedas*, the holy scriptures of India. But sacred actions do not just refer to performing sacrifices, doing penance and giving charity, each of which gives rise to an anticipated result. There are many actions that you can undertake from which you would not expect any fruit, at all. Such actions, which are performed without any concern for the fruit, can be termed *karma yoga*.

When an action is performed without desire and without any feeling of egoism, then it is *karma yoga*. That is the highest form of action, the most sacred of all, and it's one you should follow in every move you make in life. Remove your egoism. Drive it away. Remove your desire for the fruit. When you perform action with this attitude, it becomes work in the spirit of true sacrifice, it becomes penance and it becomes *yoga*. All three of these, sacrifice, penance and *yoga* convey the same idea. Every action you perform should be sanctified in this way. Even inhaling and exhaling are actions; they are also *karma*. Without performing *karma*, man cannot live for even a moment in the world. But *karma* associated with ego will always be narrow and harmful.

Food Gives Rise to Thoughts, Feelings and Actions

Therefore, perform all actions with only the feeling of sacrifice in your heart, not with a self-serving feeling of egoism. The results will be good or bad, beneficial or harmful depending on the type of actions you perform. The actions themselves depend upon the feelings of selflessness or selfishness you have. The feelings, in turn, depend on the thoughts you harbor. And the thoughts depend on the food that you consume. Therefore, you have the sequence of food leading to thoughts, thoughts leading to feelings, feelings leading to actions, and actions leading to results. These results, in turn, lead to more feelings, ones of pain or joy, depending on the nature of the actions, feelings, thoughts and food. From this you see the great importance of always taking in very pure and wholesome food.

Assume that a sage performing a *vedic* ritual makes a small fire, as is prescribed by the scriptures. The smoke pouring forth will depend on the type of fire that was made. A cloud will form as a result of the smoke that has risen up. Water vapor condenses due to the cloud and there are droplets of rain. The crop below depends on the rain, and so the food that is consumed depends upon the crop. Finally, the physical body, being the same as food, depends on the food that is taken in. Therefore, even food can be traced back to the type of actions, in this case, to the fire that had been built and the sacrifice that had been performed.

Focus On The Action, Not On The Fruit

If your actions are good, then your birth will be good. Your actions are the original cause, your birth is the final result. In this context, Krishna said, "Keep all your attention on performing good deeds; do not pay any attention to the fruit." The fruit will follow by itself, but your focus should be on the action.

In the past, you have been associated with a number of good or bad actions and as a result, you are now enjoying or suffering their consequence in the form of joy or sorrow. How do you get rid of the sorrow that is the result of your past bad actions? It is only by engaging in good actions that you can remove this sorrow. That is the reason why action has been given primary importance in the *Vedas*. Bad actions must be replaced by good actions, which then lead to totally selfless actions, where there is no personal interest in the fruit. This, then, becomes *karma yoga* and brings you into union with divinity.

If you are careless with your actions, or if you waste your actions, your whole life becomes a waste. Life has been given to you so that you engage yourself in good *karma* and ideal activities. *Karma* does not mean just performing actions with the body. *Karma* is the very name of the body itself. Since the body has come as the result of actions performed previously, one of the meanings of *karma* is body.

Body is the consequence of actions; it is associated with time, circumstance and causation. But this applies only to the waking state. In the dream state, the body is inactive, so there cannot be any action at all; there will only be the illusion of action, or *maya*. In dreams, all the senses will be still. In the state of deep-sleep, which has been called the causal state, there will not even be any mind. Beyond this state is the ultimate source, that which is called the great cause, the original cause. It transcends the causal state. This original cause is the divinity. Here is a small example to illustrate these states.

Those of you who are students walk here from the hostel, which is about one kilometer away. At 4:15 in the afternoon, you leave the hostel and by 4:30 you reach the gates of the ashram. So, it takes you about 15 minutes to move your body from the hostel to this complex. Your purpose for coming here is to hear Baba's lecture. In every action you undertake, there will be these same four factors, a time, an activity, a cause or purpose and a result. The time, as you have seen, was 15 minutes. The activity was to walk from the hostel to the prayer hall. The reason was to listen to the lecture. The result is that you will be sanctifying your life thereby. In this way, the waking state can be used for one's spiritual advancement.

Time, Action, Purpose and Result Apply Only to the Body

Now consider further, that after this discourse is over you return to the hostel. After you have had your dinner, you relax on your bed and go off to sleep. You have a dream. In the dream you find yourself wandering on a boulevard in Paris. When did you leave the hostel to travel to Paris, and how long did it take you to get there? That question cannot be answered. There is no specific time involved here. How did you travel there? Was it by ship or by plane? That also cannot be answered. There is no specific activity involved in getting there. Why did you go to Paris? You do not know; there is no apparent reason for being there. What is it that you have enjoyed there? What is the result of your going? Even that you cannot answer. There is no specific result accruing from your action that can be discerned there. So, in the dream state, there is neither time, action, purpose, nor enjoyment of the results; none of these are there.

Now, assume that soon after you fell asleep, some one came and woke you up. You got up and realized that you had been asleep for only five minutes. During the course of those five minutes you had your dream and you went to Paris. How is that possible? It is not possible. It was only a mental experience. You have not performed this action, either with your body or with your senses. That mental experience is associated with your subtle form. But it is the gross body which has these four factors of time, action, causation and circumstance. You have seen that none of these occur in the subtle or mental experience associated with the dream state. Only because of the tricks of the mind have you been able to create a new world there.

The mind created so many people on that busy boulevard in Paris, so much traffic, so many objects. The mind has this exceptional power. It has an extraordinary capacity to create anything, or destroy anything, not only in dream, but also in the waking state. For all your actions, it is the thoughts in your mind which are responsible. When you offer such a powerful mind to the Lord, then not only the mind but all your actions, everything you do, will have been offered to him. When you use your mind to think of the Lord, all your actions become sacred.

Turn Desire Towards Wisdom To Gain The Divine Light

A great sage used to say, "If you sing hymns of praise to the Lord and offer a light to him, then the entire world will shine with the effulgence of that light." In your worship you take a flaming lamp, and offer the light to the Lord. Your mind, which is made up of many desires, can be likened to the oil, the wick can be likened to the sacred wisdom you have gathered. When you join these two together, using your wisdom to turn your desires to God, then you get the effulgence of divine light blazing forth from their union.

For this oil and wick there must be some holder. The body can be thought of as the container which holds this oil of desires and the wick of wisdom. The blissful joy that you feel is the effulgence of the light coming from this sacred lamp. If there is only a wick and you try to light it, it will not burn. Or, if you want to light the oil itself, you will not be able to do it. But when the wick is associated with the oil, then it will be able to burn, and you will have light.

Another way of seeing this oil and the wick, is to think of action or work, which is associated with the mind and its desires, as the oil. The *buddhi*, or the intuitive intellect, which is associated with wisdom, can be thought of as the wick. When you combine these two, namely, action and *buddhi*, in other words, when you make all your actions sacred, following the dictates of your highest inner motivator, then the light will shine forth. This light is the eternal light of the *atma*. When all your actions become sacred, you will come into awareness of your eternal truth, you will be basked in the light of the one immortal self.

Now, the flame in the lamp has a number of individual characteristics. When there is a breeze, the flame will flicker. When water comes on it, it will sputter, making some sound. If there are impurities in the oil, it will give forth smoke. It also gives off heat; if you touch it, it will burn you. And, depending on the type of oil and the flow of air there will be different colors to the light emerging from the flame. These various characteristics belong to the flame, but they are not associated with the radiance that emerges from the light of that flame.

There is only one characteristic to that radiance; that is, it envelops all it touches in the splendor of its effulgence. The flame has a number of different attributes, but the effulgence of the *atma* has only the one attribute of illuminating and removing darkness. That immortal inner light of the *atma* is given equally to all people. That is its one all-encompassing quality. But, for the flame of life, there will be many individual characteristics. Many changes and problems will come into it.

The Three Types Of Actions

There are three types of activities emerging from different aspects of this flame of life. There are the ordinary actions which lead to ordinary results, which in turn, lead to more actions in an endless cycle. This is like a flame that burns steadily one moment and sputters the next, or burns in various hues and at various temperatures.

Then there are the good actions, those which always bring good results. These good actions are like an unchanging flame which is ever steady. This second type of activity applies to performing your worldly duties in a righteous manner, being active in good causes, engaging in devotional practices, etc. These are all good actions but along with them, there will still be a clear interest in the results. The *Vedas* have declared that even the best and most beneficial actions performed with interest in the results can only take you as far as heaven. You should not be under the impression that heaven endows you with immortality; when the merits of the actions have been consumed, you have to come back down to earth. So, this second type of action, also perpetuates the cycle of birth and death.

Lastly, there are actions which are not related to the attributes of the flame. This third type of activity is associated with the pure radiance, the effulgence of the *atmic* light. For such actions, interest in the fruit is not relevant, at all. Such actions emerge out of your inner nature, your deepest truth, which is divine. You perform all your actions as an offering to the divinity, knowing that the one divinity is in everyone. Such sacred acts can be called *yoga*, for then you are engaged in *karma yoga*. This is purity in action where there is no attachment to the outcome.

Realize that when you are interested in the fruits, they soon become exhausted, and new actions have to be undertaken again and again, in an endless cycle. Take, for example, a member of the legislative assembly who runs for election. If he achieves victory in the election, he can go to the assembly for five years. As time passes, his term of office runs out and at the end of five years he has to return home. Similarly, all the merits which you earn through your activities may be compared to this kind of limited term which lasts for a number of years. At the end of the period you have to come back into birth again.

As long as your merits last you enjoy heaven, but as soon as they get exhausted you must again descend into birth. Therefore, while describing the doctrine of *karma* to Arjuna, Krishna said, "Instead of aspiring for the temporary result of an action, which keeps you bound to the cycle of birth and death, aspire to realize the supreme divinity which is your own true self. When you know that the one divinity is the immortal self of all and act from that knowledge, then your actions are aligned with the divine will and they will be sacred. Then you will never have to come back into birth again. But, if instead, your actions are motivated by the results, which, in turn, leads you into to life after life and you are perpetually coming and going, then how will you ever be able to reach your permanent goal?" There is a small story to illustrate this.

Aspire For the Supreme And Never Come Back

An inveterate thief was caught in the act of stealing and was put into prison. It was decreed in court that he be imprisoned for six months. The six month period soon passed and the day arrived when he was to be released. The jailer came and told the thief, "Well, by tomorrow evening your term will be completed and you will have served your punishment. You can make your preparations to go. Collect all the personal possessions that we are holding for you, and be ready to leave." The thief was not overly happy to hear this, but he was not unhappy either. He was just indifferent, for he knew what was to happen. "Let the articles remain here," he said.

The jailer asked him, "Why, don't you want to take these things with you?" The thief replied, "There is no point in taking them with me. In a day or two I will be back. Soon enough, you will see me again in this same jail. Since it will be just a few days, why should I bother with them?" So, this thief knew that he was going to indulge in stealing again, that he would be caught and punished again and, undoubtedly, he would land right back in this same prison.

In the same way, your actions may be compared to this coming and going of the thief. You perform actions in your life here on earth. In time, you are motivated to make all your actions good actions and they produce good results. Afterwards you go to heaven. When your term there has expired you come back again to earth. Krishna said, "This process of going up and coming down is not good." At this point, Krishna gave Arjuna the sacred teachings. He directed Arjuna to seek out the place of eternal truth and abide there. Once you are established in that permanent place, abiding in your immortal self, actions can no longer bind you. Then there will be no need to ever come back again, for you will be established in the permanent bliss of the *atma*. Compared with this exalted state, earthly and heavenly joys are like mere atoms in the infinite universe.

THE YOGA OF ACTION -
RELINQUISHING THE FRUIT

*K*rishna *told Arjuna repeatedly, "Arjuna! Do your duty.
Engage yourself in rightful action. But do not aspire for the
fruit of your action." Krishna's intent was to turn all of
Arjuna's actions into sacred actions, into karma yoga, and
thereby help him to reach his spiritual goal.*

Embodiments of Love,

In the world, all actions are performed for the sake of the rewards, or what can be called the fruits. If there were no fruits resulting from their actions, if they were not compensated or paid in
some form or other, the great majority of human beings would not
undertake any work at all. What is Krishna's objection to Arjuna
aspiring for the fruit of his labor? When almost everyone performs
actions for the sake of the reward, what is the deeper meaning in
Krishna directing Arjuna to perform all his actions without expecting any reward? Krishna's sole interest was to see to it that all of
Arjuna's actions be transformed into *yoga*, in other words, that
Arjuna's will be aligned with the divine will. This would happen
when Arjuna surrendered himself fully to the divinity, offered all
his actions to the divine and gave up all his attachments to the results. Then his *karma* became *karma yoga*.

Transform All Your Actions Into Sacred Actions And Be Free

As long as you act with body-consciousness, that is, as long as you
identify yourself as the doer of an action, then that action cannot be
karma yoga. Any action performed with the feeling of ego, the sense
that *I did it*, or with the sense of attachment, that it is *my* act, can
only bring sorrow to you in the end. Such actions will always result
in further bondage. However, when you transform your actions into
yoga, then you become free from bondage. How does action or *karma*
become *yoga*? All actions performed as offerings to the divinity,
without any sense of individual doership and without seeking any
personal results, will be transformed into *yoga*.

Numerous troubles arise when one acts with a feeling of egoism. Inwardly, you might feel, 'This action was performed by me, so I should derive the benefits from this action. I worked, so I deserve to get paid. I am certainly entitled to the rewards accruing from these actions that I have performed.' Such feelings serve only to further strengthen the sense of ego, the sense of *I* and *mine*. As this sense of *I* and *mine* goes on increasing, the *atma* goes further and further into obscurity, and the joy emerging from the *atma* goes on decreasing. To destroy egoism completely, Krishna asked Arjuna to transform all his actions into *yoga*.

What is the method of transforming your action into *yoga*? You must become impersonal; you must not identify yourself with the actions or the results that accrue from them, but, instead, concentrate fully on the action itself, remaining indifferent to the results. In other words, you act because it is your nature to do so, offering all your efforts to the indwelling divinity, and remaining totally unconcerned and disinterested in the fruit. With such a feeling of detachment, whatever task you become engaged in will become sacred.

There is the example of King Janaka, who showed by his life that if you perform actions without any desire for the fruit and without any personal interest in the act, then your accomplishments can indeed become very great. While ruling a kingdom, and bearing all the responsibilities associated with it, King Janaka performed all his acts with the attitude that he was only the witness. Because he acted without any attachment to the results, Janaka became a sacred king, a monarch who was also a *yogi*.

Turn Actions Into *Yoga*

Every action that is offered to the Lord and is performed without any personal interest becomes a holy sacrifice and can be considered as *yoga*. But when an action is performed with a personal interest in the action and its results, then it is nothing but *roga*, which in Sanskrit means disease. The root cause of all such disease is attachment. From attachment follows hatred and anger. These are the demons that will hide all your human qualities.

It is the same for everyone; once attachment and hatred begin to show themselves in you, they encourage all the demonic tendencies and you forget your true human nature. Therefore, Krishna commanded Arjuna, "Perform your actions free from all attachments. Be impersonal. When you perform actions without having any personal interest, the fruit of these actions will not touch you. That is how I rule over all the three worlds. Can you not rule over even one little body that way?

"Develop the firm faith that when you remain disinterested in the rewards you will be able to achieve many great tasks. But when you have attachment to the results of a task, you will be subject to disappointment. If you get the fruits you expected, you will be overjoyed. If you do not succeed, you will be worried. Try to control this sense of dejection and elation. Become truly wise. Do not allow yourself to be subjected to these wavering feelings of elation and dejection."

There is no human being who is not engaged in actions. Every person has a human body for the express purpose of performing actions. To sanctify the body, you have to perform only good actions. For every action there will be a fruit. You should realize that the joy which you get in performing an action is much greater than the joy you get from the fruit of the action.

For example, on an auspicious religious festival, a family may choose to be together throughout the night with other devotees, relatives and friends to sing devotional songs. As long as they are engaged in their practice and involved in their ceremonies they are unaware of any feeling of fatigue. Even if some of them were suffering from fever they would not mind; they would be completely absorbed in the function. During that period, when they are immersed in their practice, no one feels tired. But when you visit this family soon after the function is over, you find them all looking rather weary.

The Joy of Doing Is Greater Than the Joy of the Rewards

You get joy while performing an action, but you do not experience joy to the same extent after the action is completed. You are simply deluded by the feeling that there is some joy in the fruit of the action. But, truly speaking, there is no joy whatsoever in the fruit. The joy which you believe you get from the fruit is only a reflection; it is a shadow of the real joy. It is just a phantom joy. It is not the permanent joy that you are seeking. When the actions themselves are temporary and transient, how can the fruits derived from them be anything more than fleeting shadows?

Perhaps you feel that by performing acts of charity or by doing good, involving yourself in good causes, participating in auspicious events or by engaging in various acts of personal sacrifice, you will earn heavenly rewards. However, Krishna declared that heaven is only temporary. He said, "Arjuna, there is something which is far greater than heaven. Of course, you should always do good. I am not saying that you should stop performing good deeds, sacrifices, austerities, religious rituals and the like. It is not only your right but your duty to continue with such good actions; but, do everything you do with only the welfare of the whole world in mind. Do not act with any selfish motive. Perform every action selflessly, disinterestedly, concerned only with the peace, welfare and prosperity of all living beings, everywhere.

"Do not be concerned with reaching heaven. Set your sight on a much higher goal, beyond heaven. Heaven will last only as long as the merits of your actions last. Once these merits are exhausted, you will have to come back to earth. Therefore, give up your longing for heaven, which is temporary and impermanent. Cultivate nearness and dearness to the Lord. Become merged in him; that is what is truly important. The principle of divinity is greater than heaven. When you understand the secret of action and perform all your actions from the proper perspective, you will be able to acquire the divinity itself."

The Gita Brings the Highest Wisdom Into Daily Life

The *Gita* has not asked you to renounce all worldly activities and become a *sanyasin*, a wandering mendicant. Some people are under the impression that the *Gita* should not be taught to children, for the youngsters might get a notion to renounce the world and go to the forest. Many people suffer from such wrong impressions. But consider the great number of people who have been teaching the *Gita*. Are they all *sanyasins*? Have they renounced all the things of the world? Did Arjuna, who heard the *Gita* directly from Krishna, become a *sanyasin*?

The inner significance of the *Gita* has to be understood in the context of human nature as it is expressed in the world, in the everyday activities of people. The most important objective of the *Gita* is to bring down the priceless, ancient wisdom to the level of the mundane world and to raise worldly life to the level of the highest wisdom. The *Gita* brings down *Vedanta* into daily life and elevates daily life to the level of *Vedanta*; it not only introduces philosophy and spirituality into daily life, but it also introduces daily life into philosophy and spirituality. Hence, it reconciles spirituality and daily life.

Human existence does not just involve the daily, secular activities; it is not meant at all for just eking out a livelihood. The *Gita* teaches the sanctity of human life; it directs man to his ultimate goal. It teaches him how to make his livelihood in the world, in a way that enables him to transcend the human condition, and in a way that does not bind him to further human births. You will not be bound by your actions when they are performed selflessly, without any interest in the fruits. The *Gita* teaches you to develop nonattachment to all your activities, duties and possessions. What actually happens by having this attitude of detachment is that your actions become sacred. The *Gita* does not encourage you to renounce work; on the contrary, it encourages you to do your duty and perform all the activities appropriate to your status in life. But you must transform all these actions into sacred works by offering them to the Lord.

For example, consider the work of a cook. Cooks perform their duties properly and do their job well when they keep their mind on the cooking. If instead, they do everything keeping only the wages in view, then they will not have much interest in their work and the cooking will not be good. Cooking should be performed with a sense of love and absorption in the work and with the welfare of all in mind, without concern for the monetary rewards. Then it becomes a sacred and pure service that nourishes and sanctifies.

In the same way, when you perform your assigned duties, whatever they are, with full concentration on the work, offering it to the divinity, and without any personal interest in the fruit, then your actions become sacred and grand. With this feeling of disinterestedness in the fruits, your work becomes steady and you will also progress steadily forward towards your goal. But when you have a personal interest in the work that you are performing, there will be ups and downs, fickleness will develop and your desires will quickly grow.

Krishna held out King Janaka as an ideal person because he ruled his kingdom with this sense of detachment, and thereby attained perfection. There are some people who have only outward vision. There are others who have developed inward vision. Outward vision sees only the illusory world outside. Inward vision transforms the mind and fills the heart with sacred feelings. In order to gain inner vision, you have to develop this quality of absorption in the work and detachment from the results, offering everything you do to the divinity within. There is a story to illustrate the great spiritual power of this lofty practice.

Janaka and Suka

Once, in the age previous to Krishna and Arjuna's, the young sage Suka, had entered King Janaka's kingdom and was traveling in the neighborhood of the capital city. King Janaka heard that Suka was in the vicinity, but did not know where Suka chose to make his camp. The king sent out messengers in all directions, to get news of Suka's whereabouts. They located Suka living in a shelter in a forest, near the capital city. Janaka, along with his ministers, went to visit Suka. Janaka did not go there as a king or ruler. He went as a servant of the Lord. Janaka had long ago removed all traces of ego and now went as a humble spiritual seeker. Suka was giving a discourse to his disciples on a spiritual topic.

During this discourse, Janaka stood and listened with full concentration. Evening came. Before he left, Janaka went to Suka and asked, "Swami, may I come every day and experience your inspiring discourses?" Suka replied, "Janaka, spirituality and philosophy are not anyone's private property. Whoever has the interest, whoever enjoys listening to these teachings, whoever believes in reaching the goal, has a right to this knowledge. Certainly you may come. You are most welcome." Janaka went back to his palace and returned each day to attend the discourses.

Now, Suka wanted to demonstrate to the world that King Janaka had inward vision, whereas most people have only outward vision. With this in mind, he moved to a spot on the crest of a hill overlooking the capital city, and made his camp there. From this place, he continued his daily discourses on *Vedanta*. One particular day, King Janaka, because of some urgent responsibilities of administration, was delayed in coming there. Suka purposely held up starting his discourse until Janaka had arrived.

Suka took no cognizance of the large gathering of people that were already assembled there, waiting for the discourse to commence. To demonstrate his interest, Suka started asking questions of this person and that, trying to find out why King Janaka had not come. He also told some people to go and find out what had delayed the king. He himself stood on the roadside and watched for the royal party to arrive.

At this, some murmur began among the people there. The disciples, the elders and youngsters who had assembled there, began whispering among themselves. One said, "Look at Suka. He is considered to be such a great sage who has renounced everything; but it does not seem to be true. Here he is waiting for King Janaka. Just because Janaka is an important ruler, Suka is not paying any attention to us and does not seem to care about starting the discourse."

Another person said, "Look at this peculiar behavior of Suka. Why does he show so much partiality to kings? For a sage, should there be any difference in his feelings for a king and for others?" Now, Suka noted all this talk that was going on. In fact, it was with the intention of teaching them a good lesson that he had conducted himself this way. Half an hour passed. An hour passed. Two hours passed. Suka continued to wait for Janaka to come; he did not make any attempt to start his discourse.

The Venom Must Come Out Before Teachings Can Go In

Meanwhile, those people whose hearts were a little polluted, gave expression to their feelings of jealousy and anger. All those impure feelings which were inherent in them, but had been hidden inside, now started coming out. That is just what Suka wanted, for only after the venom that was in their hearts had come out could the teachings of the *Vedanta* enter there. If there is nothing inside one's head, then it can be filled with sacred teachings. But if one's head is already filled with all sorts of impure stuff, how can it take anything pure and sacred in?

Without emptying the head of all the useless dross, sacred teachings will never take hold there. So, Suka's wish was that all these baser feelings should manifest themselves and be expressed. He wanted his students to pour out all the dirt and filth which was inside their minds. He knew that as long as their hearts harbored attachments and bad feelings, his teachings would not take hold. So he had them undergo this process of purification.

Meanwhile, with a great deal of anxiety, Janaka rushed to attend the discourse. Suka noted the approach of Janaka. He could be seen coming from a long way off because Janaka did not usually come alone. Although Janaka was not interested in bringing ministers and servants, they would invariably accompany him to provide security and protection to the king. Soon all the people became aware that King Janaka was approaching. Entering the area where the discourse was given, Janaka prostrated himself before the *guru* and humbly asked his pardon for coming late. Then Janaka spread his grass mat and sat down.

Immediately Suka commenced his discourse. Now, in the hearts of the young disciples who had assembled there, hatred fructified. Their faces began changing because of their feelings towards Suka and King Janaka. 'Look at this Suka!', they thought to themselves.

'He only cares about pleasing the king. That is the extent of his *Vedanta.*'

The Fire That Brought Out the Attachments of the Disciples

Suka decided to teach a lesson to all the people assembled there who were harboring such negative feelings. After some time, he interrupted his discourse suddenly and said, "Janaka, look at your kingdom. It is on fire!" King Janaka, who had closed his eyes and was totally absorbed in listening to the sacred teachings, took no notice of these words. He had fixed his mind on the *Vedanta*, and so he kept his concentration only on the *Vedanta*.

The other people who had assembled there saw the flames and smoke rising above the city. Some of the disciples, thinking of their relatives and belongings, began running towards the capital city, in the plain below. All the attachments which had lain hidden deep in their hearts now came to the surface and fully exposed themselves.

A few moments later, Suka told King Janaka, "Janaka, this fire has now spread to your palace." Even then, Janaka did not take any notice of Suka's statement; Janaka did not move from his seat. He had the true feeling of complete detachment and indifference to all things worldly. His interest was only in the *atma*. Except for this absorption in the *atma* he had no other feelings.

Among those in attendance at the discourse were a number of celebrated spiritual teachers having worldwide reputations. Suka wanted to demonstrate to them that they might be very great scholars but they had not killed their attachments. When these scholars saw the flames, they were apprehensive; they turned to King Janaka and began praying, "O, King! O, King! Please do something about this terrible catastrophe happening below!" But Janaka had entered into a state of *samadhi*; he was enjoying the bliss of the *atma*.

Tears of joy were coursing down Janaka's cheek. He did not waver for even a moment from the holy thoughts on which he had fixed his concentration. Suka observed Janaka's state and was very pleased. After some time, those disciples who had run away towards the capital returned, reporting that, in fact, there had been no fire at all. Then Suka began to explain to the disciples the meaning of all that had gone on.

Suka said, "Well, children, I did not delay starting my discourse for two hours because Janaka is the king and, therefore, a very important man. I delayed because he is a deserving person, a true seeker; and I believe in waiting for such a one. Because he has purged himself of ego and pride, because he has true humility, dedication and detachment he has the authority to hold up the discourse. You listen, but you do not hear what is said or put it into practice; therefore, you have no such authority.

"Instead of teaching hundreds of people who have made no effort in applying these teachings to their daily lives, I can teach at least one person who truly has a right to being taught, because he has integrated these sacred precepts into his very life. What is the use of teaching people full of attachment and egoism? It is something like throwing a stone into water. For any number of years the stone may lie in the water, but it will not absorb even a drop of water.

"Even if I can get just one person like Janaka, it is sufficient for me to go on. Why have useless shining stones in great numbers? If there is at least one gem which is truly valuable, that is enough. Why have ten acres of barren land if you can have even a small plot that is fertile and abundant in its yield? If one king like Janaka can become sacred, then he can transform his entire kingdom and turn it into a sacred realm that will be an example to the whole world." Suka's intent was to make Janaka a sacred king and at the same time to teach a valuable lesson to the conceited disciples who had gathered around him.

Through Arjuna Krishna Taught The Whole World

Krishna had a similar intent when he taught the *Gita* to Arjuna. Arjuna was also a sacred person, and he had qualified himself for the teachings by his character and his high ideals. Arjuna had control of the senses; he had won a great deal of spiritual power from the penance he had performed. He had, to a large extent, suppressed his worldly attachments. He had a highly developed intellect and had become skilled in many arts. And he had surrendered himself to Krishna in true humility.

Krishna decided that Arjuna was ready for the highest wisdom and resolved to turn him into a truly wise being. With the intention that if Arjuna could be corrected, the whole world would benefit thereby, Krishna took great care to give these sacred teachings to Arjuna. Arjuna had both the capacity and the virtue to rise to great spiritual heights. That is the reason he had been given a number of titles. The Sanskrit word *arjuna* means one who is pure.

Another title Krishna gave Arjuna was the sacred-hearted one; another was the jewel-of-men. Arjuna was such a powerful person that he could, if he wanted to, undertake acts which would terrify the entire world. But Arjuna always acted purely in keeping with righteousness. He earned the right to use a powerful weapon which could not be wielded by any other living person of his day. Originally, this weapon belonged to Lord Shiva. This same fearsome weapon which was originally with Shiva and then with King Janaka in an earlier age, in Krishna and Arjuna's time, became the *Gandhiva*, Arjuna's formidable bow. By earning the grace of Shiva, Arjuna was able to obtain this magnificent weapon. In every respect Arjuna was an outstanding hero, and it was such a noble and righteous human being that Krishna chose to teach the *Gita*, so that the entire world would benefit thereby.

It is through your mouth that you offer food to the stomach. Then it is through the stomach that the food reaches the entire body. In the same way as food reaches all the limbs of the body when offered to the stomach, the *Gita* was given to a pure and selfless person such as Arjuna so that it might reach the entire world. One of Arjuna's names is *Parthiva* which means son of the earth. All of you are children of the earth. Since Arjuna may be considered an outstanding representative of all mankind, Krishna felt that the whole world would in time be transformed by converting him into a sacred person.

Ordinary Actions, Detached Actions and Sacred Actions

Compared to ordinary actions which are done by thinking of yourself as the doer, actions done without any sense of doership will be much greater. But, an action that is done with complete selflessness, performed impersonally with total indifference and without any attachment—is greater still. But when the action is entirely offered to the Lord, when it becomes a holy sacrifice, it is even more sacred than all of these. Thus, Krishna commanded Arjuna to offer all his acts to the Lord. When Arjuna reached this state of evolution, that is, when Arjuna acted completely selflessly and offered everything he did to the Lord, Krishna began to teach him the *Gita*.

In the primary stage, every human being has to perform actions and be actively employed in the tasks for which he is suited. One needs to perform action in order not to develop laziness. A lazy person is absolutely useless to the world. Swami does not approve or encourage anyone to be lazy. First, you must perform ordinary actions. Then you should enter into the stage where you perform all your actions without any self-interest. Gradually you transform these actions into *yoga*, you transform work into worship. This is one of the core teachings of the *Gita*.

The *Gita* Will Give You Whatever You Are Ready To Receive

It is to utterly destroy selfishness, egoism, arrogance, pride, possessiveness, attachment, hatred and other such poisonous qualities that the *Gita* has taught the truth in so many ways. In the process, it has helped many different kinds of people to develop a sacred nature. The *Gita* may be compared to a wish-fulfilling tree. Whatever you desire from the *Gita* it will give. The meaning given to different teachings in the *Gita* depends on your outlook and stage of spiritual preparation. No one can say that he knows the one correct meaning for a particular verse; no one has the authority to claim that theirs is the only meaning.

The *Gita* teachings apply to every level of spiritual seeker. Therefore, the *Gita* may be described as the heart of the *Vedanta*. It is its very essence. The *Gita* is a treasure chest of gold; the *Gita* is a flower-strewn path; the *Gita* is the support of all earnest seekers and aspirants; the *Gita* allows them to swim and survive in this sea of worldly life; the *Gita* helps them to traverse all obstacles and reach their goal. A person who does not care for the *Gita* misses the very purpose of life.

Whatever be your feelings, the meaning you will derive from the *Gita* will be commensurate to your level of spiritual development. For example, many of the devotees here will know the Sanskrit chant which is used as an incantation for evoking the blessing of the Lord. Its first line translates, 'to the white attired Lord'. Lord Vishnu is this all pervasive one. He is omnipresent. He is described as ash-colored. He is also described as having the color of the moon, being whitish, which is the same as saying that he has the color of ashes. He has also been described as having four hands and a most pleasing and sacred face, which does not exhibit any feeling of elation or dejection. This is the feeling of believers, and it is in this way that they pray to the Lord. But non-believers may use the very same words, although the image they describe with these words may be completely different.

The Sanskrit word that starts this incantation also refers to the one who carries white clothes. In whatever situation you see this one, you find it does not exhibit any feelings; it is ash-colored, and it has four limbs. One can take these attributes, put them all together and say that these words describe a donkey. A donkey will be carrying white clothes from the washerman, it has four limbs, an ash-colored body and a most patient face. It is not tied down to any place, you can find it roaming in the roads, in front of the house, everywhere. This is the meaning given to these very same words by non-believers. So, whether it is the exalted Lord or a lowly ass, depends on how you look at it, whether you are a devotee or a non-believer, and whether you are interested in or oblivious to such spiritual expressions.

In the same way, the *Gita* yields up different meanings to different types of people. Based upon the state of your feelings, each of you will get the meaning which is appropriate to the stage you have reached on the spiritual path. So, this *Gita* is a great wish-fulfilling tree. It is a celestial cow, giving freely of its milk. You can take from it whatever meaning you like, whatever teaching you are ready to absorb. There is plenty of water in the ocean, but the amount of water you can take away from it depends upon the capacity of the vessel that you have brought to fill up. The water will be the same; the difference will only be in the size of the vessel. Likewise, there may be differences in your feelings, but the *Gita* is only one.

The basic message of the *Gita* is the same for all; its sacred purpose is to transform humanity into divinity. You should not take such a holy book lightly. You should approach the *Gita* with a deep feeling of devotion and commitment. You should chant the verses with genuine feeling and understanding. And you should practice daily at least one or two of the precepts given here. Only then will you gain complete fulfillment in your life.

Thirty-Third Chapter

DEVELOPING THE INNER VISION

Whether you are actively working in the world or have withdrawn from it, the most important consideration is not the work that you do or not do, but how effectively you have been able to uproot and destroy the deep-seated tendencies which lie hidden in your heart.

Embodiments of Love,

The principal objective of all spiritual practices is the removal of the deep-seated negative thought forms, impure habits, tendencies, and predispositions, which in Sanskrit are called the *vasanas*, and which have encased themselves deeply within you. They manifest in your thoughts and actions as the twin evils of attachment and hatred, or attraction and repulsion. You must cleanse yourself of all trace of these evils which have harbored themselves inside you.

You Cannot Run From Your Inner Enemies

If you just run away to the forest or to a cave without performing the appropriate exercises to remove your inner enemies, then, whether you like it or not, all your latent tendencies will continue to produce thoughts and actions that bind you. These impurities will lie there as seeds in your heart and prompt a stream of thoughts that will be saturated with likes and dislikes, desires and delusions. As a result, you end up forgetting your true human nature.

The *Gita* has shown that if you can root out the entrenched tendencies that cling to your heart, then you are free to perform any action without concern for the results. From that point on, you will not be bound by any actions that you may become engaged in. In other words, you will be freed completely from the fruits of your actions. People who do not understand this truth and end up renouncing all outside activities become mired in sloth and laziness. But the *Gita* has repeatedly warned that there is no room at all for laziness in the world of the spirit.

What the *Gita* teaches is the *yoga* of impersonal action, in which you remain totally detached and free of any personal interest in the work that you do and in the results that accrue from it. It means working with full concentration to the limits of your capacity for excellence, but orienting all your actions to the service of God and remaining established in God-consciousness. You will not be able to reach this high stage of desirelessness in your actions and renunciation of the fruits of your labors, as long as your *vasanas* which have arisen from past actions are unfavorable for spiritual progress.

Transform All Self-serving Actions Into Selfless Actions

You must first remove the negative tendencies which have driven all your ordinary, self-serving actions that have kept you bound, and replace these negative tendencies with positive, noble qualities which are associated with beneficial and selfless actions. Then, when you are firmly established in the stage of selfless service, wherein you perform only good actions, you can go on to the higher stage where you renounce the fruits of all your actions. From there, you will naturally rise to the stage of totally selfless, impersonal *yoga*. At that stage, you make sure that all your actions are of the highest purity and then you offer them all up to the divinity, to do with as the divinity wishes.

What is the inner secret of performing work? It is the *Gita's* proclamation that only through positive, laudable activities can the negative tendencies be removed. The *Gita* advises you to be engaged only in good actions so that you will steadily purify your heart. But it goes further than that. It asserts that true purity of heart can be achieved only by dedicating all your actions to the Lord. Every action that you perform must be offered to God; only then can your heart be fully cleansed. Consider an example.

When food is eaten after having been cooked and prepared in different ways, it is just ordinary food, and you are subject to the good or bad effects of eating that food. However, if special care is taken in the preparation of this food to make sure that it is pure and worthy of being offered to the divinity, and then, before consuming it, it is offered with full heart to God, then it becomes consecrated food. From that point on, this will no longer be ordinary food. Consuming it will confer divine blessings, for it will be the sacred gift of the divinity.

By the same token, all the many activities performed by you during the day fall into the category of ordinary actions. But when you perform these same actions, even if they are just little acts, with the intention of making them an offering to God, devoting their results not to your own pleasure but for the pleasure of the Lord, then your actions become sacred actions. In other words, your *karma* becomes *karma yoga*. It is only through such *karma yoga* that you will be able to rid yourself of all evil tendencies and make your heart pure.

Purify Your Actions Before Offering Them To God

What should be the qualities of the actions you offer at the feet of the Lord? How sacred should they be? Before an object is offered to an ordinary individual, you see to it that it has some utility, that it has some value, that it is pure and that it will be cherished. In other words, that it will be received with joy. That being the case in offering something to another individual, then how much more care should you take in making an offering to the Lord! How very pure and extremely fulfilling it must be! One must not offer all types of objects and all types of actions to the Lord. Before you offer anything to the Lord, you must first make it pure, you must make it sacred and great. Then it will be a fit offering for the Lord.

For example, if you want to offer a rose to the Lord, you first select a beautiful, fragrant bloom. Then you remove the insects from the flower. Next you remove the thorns and any imperfect leaves from the stem; and in a number of other ways you make your offering as beautiful and as pure as possible. Only then do you offer it to the Lord. Every action you perform should be like this flower which you offer to the Lord. Just as a fine fragrance is inherent in the flower you offer, so also your actions must be saturated with the fragrance of love and sacredness. Just as the flower that you offer is beautiful and pure, so also your actions must be good and pure. Such is true *karma yoga*. The *Gita* prompts you to offer only such kinds of action to the Lord.

You must be able to distinguish between wise action and unwise action, and for that you must understand the difference between wisdom and ignorance. You must develop your wisdom until it expands and merges with the cosmic wisdom, the divine wisdom. Anyone who wants to directly experience the Lord must develop this wisdom, and along with it a number of important qualities.

The Characteristics Of An Enlightened Being

These qualities of a person endowed with spiritual wisdom are patience, determination, purity of body and mind, selfless love, an everpresent awareness and yearning for the indwelling divinity, and the six qualities which are known as the spiritual treasures— namely, control of the mind, control of the senses, renunciation of selfish desires, endurance and indifference to all kinds of opposites such as pain and pleasure, an unshakable faith in the sacred teachings and contentment derived from a steady, unwavering mind. Let us consider the first of these qualities: patience.

Patience or forbearance is one of the most important characteristics that every person should practice and possess. Many kings have been destroyed because they abandoned this quality of patience. Even great sages have lost all their spiritual merit because they neglected this quality. Countless scholars have come to ruin because they overlooked this invaluable characteristic. Patience can be thought of as the most important shield and armor for facing the battle of life. You quickly lose all your human qualities if you lose patience. As you have already seen, the quality of patience is an extremely important sign of a great person; without patience it would not be possible to become an enlightened being.

A resolute nature, in other words, the quality of determination and being endowed with a firm resolve, is the pre-condition for developing patience. Now, a resolute nature should not be associated with stubborn foolishness. In matters relating to the spirit, firmness and a resolute nature refer to a mind that is free from delusion and unsteadiness.

Whatever obstacle is encountered, whatever troubles and problems arise, with a resolute nature you will remain firmly committed to pursue the tasks which you have undertaken until you achieve your final goal. If you do not have this quality of determination, then patience will have no basis and cannot develop in strength. Patience and determination are twins; one cannot exist without the other. Without determination, patience cannot establish itself, and without patience, determination will degenerate into arrogance.

Next, let us consider purity. Just as you undertake various actions to purify your body, so also you must undertake various good actions to purify your mind. Through these acts, you can remove the attachments and desires that have polluted your mind with egoism. Only when these negative qualities are eliminated will you be able to achieve self-control. Just as a tortoise is free to loosen its limbs and come out of its shell, or to withdraw itself back into its shell, in the same way, you should be able to control your senses and use them when you need them. The *Gita* has affirmed that these are also very important qualities of a wise person.

By Their Actions People Will Reveal Their Inner Natures

It is in the field of action or *karma* that you most patently reveal your character and the type of human being you are. That is why so much importance has been given to performing all your actions without attachment to the fruits. Just as a mirror can show you the type of face you have, your actions will reveal the type of inner feelings you have. When you have some dealings with others, you can easily find out the type of people they are by examining their actions.

People may appear to be very fair, to be serene and mild, and have a very peaceful disposition; in other words, they appear to have a *satvic* nature. They may also appear to be individuals ready to undergo great personal sacrifice. You may believe that they are blessed with a sacred heart. But their actions may prove them to be otherwise. Their actions may be totally devoid of love and compassion and true caring and consciousness of others. Their actions may reveal an animal nature or even a demonic nature. Through their actions their hidden nature is revealed.

Other people, by the outer impressions they first make, may seem to be cruel. You may feel that they are curt and abrupt and lacking in civility or gracious manners. They may appear, in every way, to be very *rajasic* or even *tamasic*, the lower animal-like qualities previously-discussed. But, if in their actions people exhibit compassion and other great human qualities, then you must conclude that they are truly *satvic* in nature. So, if you want to ascertain whether a particular person is predominantly *satvik, rajasic,* or *tamasic* in nature, whether his inner being is serene and selfless, or desire-ridden and quick to react negatively, or slothful, vicious and mean, then you need only to observe his actions. People's actions will unmistakably reveal their inner nature.

The *Gita* has pointed out the type of actions that should be performed in daily life. The *Gita* has not commanded you to renounce everything, take up *sanyasa*, by which is meant that you detach yourself from all worldly possessions and interests, and go to the forest. Rather, the *Gita* has shown that an important duty and responsibility of every human being is to undertake useful activities in the world. Furthermore, the *Gita* proclaims that the secret of human life is to recognize and follow the path of *dharma*, which means engaging yourself in selfless and sacred actions that promote the welfare of your fellow human beings.

The *Gita* declares that human life lies in action; you would not even be able to sustain the body if you abstained from all actions.

Therefore, every ordinary human being, as well as every spiritual aspirant, should enter into the field of activities and work. But the actions which you perform must be sacred actions; they must conform to the principle of *dharma*.

You have to convert your activities into *karmas* which are useful to others. You have to perform actions which are ideal, and you have to practice such ideal actions without any selfish motive. They must originate not from the compulsive drive of desire, but from the peaceful quality in your heart, devoid of self-interest and attachment to the fruits. Only then can your actions be considered *satvic* in nature. Ordinary people will not be able to perform actions completely without desire. You will have to orient your actions and your desires towards the purpose of seeking and experiencing God. When that sacred orientation becomes the basis of all your activities, then your *karma* becomes yoga. That will lead you straight on the path to your goal of becoming one with the divinity.

The Spell Of Illusion And Its Two Powerful Forces

However, involved with all your actions, there will be the spell of *maya* or illusion which will frustrate your efforts to reach your divine goal. There are two powerful forces which make up *maya;* these are the veiling power and the projecting power. There is no particular form or shape to these two. First, consider the veiling or covering power. How does it cover? With what does it cover? How can you uncover this thing which it has covered? If it does not have form itself, by what means does it cover? How can it be removed? These are all questions that cannot be answered.

Maya is mysterious and inexplicable. Delusion and confusion are its very nature. Consider a rope lying on the road. In the darkness you are deluded into believing that this rope is a snake. What is it that has covered the rope? Try to understand what happened. You were suddenly filled with a feeling of fear because you imagined a snake lying on the road before you. So, it was in your mind that the rope got converted into a snake and you got frightened. Is the snake really there? No, there is no snake there. Then how can the rope be converted into a thing which does not exist and never has existed? This is the delusion.

Under what circumstances does this delusion exert its influence on you? It is during twilight or in the dark that you imagine you see the snake when there is only a rope there. It is through darkness that the delusion comes and envelops you. In truth, no snake has replaced the rope, but the delusion beclouds the minds of human beings and obscures their clear perception. This delusion is *maya*. When you shine your light on the area, you find no snake there; there is only a rope lying there. Thus, in the light, delusion disappears and the real object is seen.

That which exists will always exist; it will never cease to exist. It remains unchanged forever. There cannot be even the slightest variation in its existence. It is only the delusion affecting it which comes and goes. The form that this delusion takes in the mind is the second powerful force of *maya*, the projecting power, which superimposes imaginary creations and objects on the unchanging basis. In this case the projection was the snake. Another time it will be something else.

Moods, pains, pleasures, all come and go. They are something like relatives that come to visit you but do not stay permanently. In the same way, this *maya* comes and goes as a delusion for human beings. The delusion in your mind which covers the rope and hides it from view is the veiling power. The illusion which has been projected by your mind onto the rope is the projecting power. With the help of the light you see the rope as rope, and the snake vanishes. So these two aspects of *maya* have come in the darkness and have disappeared in the light.

The Power of *Maya* to Delude Can Be Permanently Dispelled

Do these two powers of illusion always come at the same time, or can they come at different times? The veiling power and projecting power may appear and disappear at the same time, but, as happens in deep sleep when there is only the veiling power, they may appear and disappear at different times, also. *Maya* is inexplicable. It has no beginning. But it can permanently come to an end. When the light of wisdom shines on it, *maya* will finally disappear. Then the one unchanging reality will stand revealed. By teaching this great wisdom to Arjuna, Krishna was able to free him from delusion and helped him shine with the inner light.

Then as now, you are developing only superficial understanding and outer vision. But it is the inner vision that is important; it alone is true and sacred. You lose sight of the one reality, of your own truth, because you pay attention only to the impermanent outer vision and completely forget the permanent inner vision. God's mission is to restore this sacred inner vision. This is what he does when he comes as *avatar*.

Krishna said, "Dear one, whatever actions you perform during the time you are on this earth, know that they are all impermanent. In time, you will discover that everything in this world is temporary. Your relationships, your attachments, your accomplishments, the sense of individuality you have developed, are all going to disappear. Everything gets washed away in the flow of time. If you try to catch hold of things and cling to things which are themselves being carried away by this flow of time, what chance is there for you to be saved? What chance is there for you to reach that perfection which is forever unaffected by this flow, and which not only is never subject to it, but is always its master?

"Arjuna, the things you are holding on to are all being washed away. Develop the firm conviction that in attaching yourself to temporary things you are wasting your life, that you are wasting the sacred opportunity that has been given to you to reach the permanent state that is your true reality. Surrender yourself to the divinity, hold on to that permanent entity always established in your heart, and you will surely gain the eternal joy, the bliss divine."

A Pure Heart Is Free Of Attachment and Illusion

In this way, Krishna urged Arjuna to free himself from the attachments and illusions that were confounding him. Krishna said, "Arjuna, you yourself must purify your heart and remove the veil of ignorance that is beclouding you. Take to the path of righteous action, work for the welfare of the world and dedicate every act to me, your very self, residing in your heart."

There is no royal road for human life leading to spiritual awakening other than through *karma yoga*, through the path of sacred action. You will be able to enter the path of devotion only after you have laid a firm foundation through good actions. And only after you have purified your feelings and developed your devotion will you be able to enter the path of wisdom and proceed on to the highest level of God-realization. It is in the arena of action that you lay the groundwork for reaching up to the loftiest regions of the spirit, or plunging yourself down to the lowest depths of sorrow. Your good or bad circumstances are inextricably linked with your actions.

As part of your activities, you may perform the various scripturally-prescribed sacrifices and ceremonial rituals. But, as previously mentioned, these can take you only up to heaven. Krishna informed Arjuna that there was a state which was far beyond and far more sacred than heaven. "Do not consider heaven as a permanent place,"

Krishna said. "When you have exhausted your merits you will have to leave heaven and return to earth. Heaven is only a temporary camp; you will not be able to reside there permanently. Perhaps you think that in heaven you will be able to enjoy so many bodily and mental pleasures. But, in truth, the pleasures you get there are only a little greater than those you get here on earth. There is a state which is far, far beyond; far more sacred. That state may be reached by identifying yourself with God, by associating yourself with the *atma*, by merging your small individual self with your highest eternal self. In order to attain this state you will have to become totally desireless and selfless; you will have to perform all your actions without expecting any fruits from them."

Actions Without Attachment To The Fruits

Whenever you perform an action, there will always be a consequence, a resultant fruit from that effort. However, there is no rule that says that you alone should enjoy the fruit of your actions. A grandfather might have planted a seed which subsequently developed into a fruit tree. And this grandfather might have died before the tree produced any fruit. But the fruit of the tree might have been enjoyed by his grandchildren, some time later. Here is a case where a person performing an action did not personally enjoy the fruit; but some others had the chance to enjoy them.

The grandfather might have knowingly planted the tree without ever expecting to enjoy the fruit; he undertook the task originally with the broadminded view that the tree in the courtyard would give fruit to the generations who came along later; fruit which would be greatly enjoyed by them. And so, the fruit of his broadminded action was reaped by succeeding members of his family.

With what motive did the grandfather plant this particular tree? He might have done it with the slightly selfish motive that it would give enjoyment to members of his family. But the selfishness that comes from doing everything only for your own enjoyment is much baser and meaner than this grandfather's slight tinge of selfishness. The inner urge which leads you to undertake actions which are primarily for the welfare of others is always greater and nobler than the narrow feelings that lead you to act completely selfishly, expecting to derive all the benefits of your actions only for yourself. In this sense, the grandfather's action must be considered far superior to that of an individual who acts only for himself.

But, clearly, there is an even greater action, one that goes beyond all selfish considerations; that is when you perform an action as an offering to God. That is the greatest of all actions and that is what you should strive for. You should endeavor to perform all your actions selflessly and disinterestedly, offering them to God, without expecting to reap any of the fruits. Such action is truly *yoga*.

From Ordinary Actions To *Buddhi Yoga* to *Karma Yoga*

Using your intellect to plan out an action, the fruits of which would benefit someone else, as was the case of the grandfather planting a tree that was enjoyed by future generations of his family, can be called *buddhi yoga*. In *buddhi yoga*, you inquire into the consequences of your actions, and thereby base your actions on the reasoning power of your intellect. Intellect goes far beyond the narrow selfish considerations of the lower mind and the senses. But even here there is still a tinge of selfishness.

When you are completely free of all selfishness, totally indifferent to the results, acting effectively and with full concentration, but without any attachment or desire, and offering all your actions to God, then you are practicing *karma yoga*; that is far superior to *buddhi yoga*. Such a high state is not easily accessible to ordinary people. But that does not mean that you should give up trying to attain it. With whole-hearted effort and with God's grace, seemingly impossible things can be achieved. If you persist in your efforts, then with practice you will be able to reach this high level of *karma yoga* in all your activities.

To succeed in this, the inner vision must be developed. In order to firmly establish that inner vision, you must keep a particular principle constantly in mind. It is this: no matter how hard you search, whether it be in this physical world or in the world of your dreams and imaginations, or any other world, all you will ever see, wherever you look, will be combinations and variations of the five elements, either in their gross or subtle forms. They are the only things you will ever be able to find anywhere. There can never be anything else; there is no such thing as a sixth element.

These five elements are all reflections of the unlimited effulgence of God. They are his aspects. Their basis is the one divine principle. Therefore, perform all your actions with full consciousness, regarding all objects in the world not as the different, multifarious names and forms that they appear to be, but as mere combinations of the five elements, energized and illuminated by the one divine principle. When you know that, when you see everything in the world to be the sacred manifestation of divinity, then all your actions will automatically become offerings to God.

By keeping such lofty ideas in view while performing your actions, you effectively turn your vision from the limited outer vision to the liberating inner vision, and thus become a sacred human being. Constantly reflecting, in this manner, on the divinity that is everywhere, is the best way to develop the inner vision that will establish you in *karma yoga*. But such inner vision is very rare among people; even the greatest *pundits* and scholars are steeped only in the outer vision. Here is a story that illustrates this.

Astravakra At The Assembly Of Scholars

Once upon a time, King Janaka called an assembly of great scholars. Noted academicians participated. Famous *pundits* and logicians came from all over the realm. Scholars of renown, who were extremely articulate in their arguments, streamed in. A number of highly gifted persons who were capable of impressing the whole world with their intellectual and verbal prowess came to the great hall of the palace where the assembly was being held. This assembly was composed of such giants that there was no room at all for ordinary people to enter.

The daily meetings were presided over by King Janaka himself. Of the highly select group in attendance, only the most outstanding and accomplished were given an opportunity to speak and present their views. Into this magnificent and august assembly, young Astavakra, a young boy with a hideously deformed body, sought to gain admission. But who would permit Astavakra to enter? He did not have any credentials or any recommendation whatsoever. He did not have the help of any great teacher or sponsor. The only help he had was his deep faith in God.

Whoever has an abiding faith in God will not be put to any insurmountable difficulties. Temporarily there may be some obstacles, but in the end he is sure to meet with success. For three days Astavakra waited at the gate of King Janaka's palace through which all the participants to the great assembly entered. There, while waiting, Astavakra observed all the world-famous scholars who were coming to attend the meeting. Although only recognized scholars were being allowed inside, Astavakra was not prepared to give up his resolution to join the assembly and participate in its deliberations. 'I, too, have a chance,' he said to himself and continued to wait patiently at the gate, day after day.

There was one observant and sympathetic old scholar who noticed Astavakra standing by that gate whenever he entered and exited through it, morning and evening. The kindly old scholar informed King Janaka of the boy's presence. He told King Janaka that there was someone standing outside waiting for days to enter the assembly, although he did not have any of the usual qualifications necessary for being permitted inside. He told the king that this was not an elderly scholar, nor even a middle-aged one, but a very young person who did not seem to have much experience and who did not wear any of the accepted marks of achievement in scholarship, nor was he personally recommended by any of the *pundits* present. In short, nothing was known of this person or his qualifications except that he had been continuously waiting to come inside.

King Janaka directed his attendants to find the boy who was waiting at the gate outside and to bring him into the assembly hall. Shortly after King Janaka had taken his seat and the meeting began in the solemn and sacred atmosphere befitting such an august assembly, Astavakra entered the hall. The moment they saw this young boy with such a crooked form come to take part in the assembly, most of the great scholars who had gathered there began to laugh. King Janaka, who was keenly observing Astavakra as he entered, did not laugh.

Astavakra carefully looked around the hall, and then quite inexplicably started laughing even louder than the scholars who were seated there. This loud burst of laughter from Astavakra was quite inadmissible and greatly surprised the scholars. It became a real problem for them. 'Why should this young scamp be laughing at us?' they thought. 'There certainly is reason enough for our laughter, considering how funny he looks, but there is nothing at all strange about us, so what conceivable reason does he have for all this laughter?' They were very disturbed and irritated by what they considered the boy's impertinence.

You find this to be a rather common experience in the world, that when ordinary people see someone who has a physical defect which gives him a crooked appearance or makes him appear strange or unusual, they are inclined to laugh. Such gross behavior can only be considered a sign of ignorance. It is totally different from the warm smile of an innocent child. A small child will smile at any person, regardless of their appearance. When the child smiles, every other person seeing this child will also smile along with it. Such a child's smile, which infects everyone who sees it, arises from the sacredness of innocence. But in that assembly hall, the laughter that Astavakra met with was very different from a child's innocent smile. That hall was packed full with very great and noted scholars, persons of exceptional accomplishments in learning; but there was no child-like innocence to be found there.

The assembled scholars were eagerly waiting to find out why this strange-looking young lad who had just come in was laughing so loudly. One of the scholars was bold enough to speak to Astavakra. He asked, "Young stranger, who are you? We do not know you. When we looked at you as you came in, your form made us laugh. In response to our laughter, you are laughing even more loudly. What is the reason for this? What is so ludicrous about all the renowned scholars seated here that you have not stopped laughing even for a moment?"

Without Inner Vision They Were Shoemakers Not Scholars

Astavakra replied, "I entered this gathering thinking it to be a sacred assembly convened by the famous Emperor Janaka to discuss the holy scriptures. If only I had known what kind of people were attending this assembly, I would not have bothered to come. I waited patiently for many days and then entered this hall thinking that the greatest living scholars would be assembled here. I looked forward to being in the company of such sacred souls. But, alas, I find nothing but common cobblers here, only shoemakers, who stitch sandals and work with leather."

When they heard this, all the scholars became furious, feeling deeply insulted by Astavakra for using such abusive words. But Astavakra continued in the same vein, "Cobblers is the proper word to describe you. Only cobblers, only people who work with hides would think about the worth of a particular skin; others will not be bothered about it. All of you are laughing at my skin and have obviously decided that it is not worth much. But not even one of you has made any effort to know my spiritual understanding. *Pundits* should have the capacity to look inward, but you only seem to care about the outer covering. If you have not developed your inner vision but are only concerned with the superficial outer vision, then you cannot be considered scholars at all. Then you are only cobblers, shoemakers, specialists in hides." Thus spoke Astavakra.

The scholars hung their heads in shame. King Janaka, who understood very well what Astavakra was saying, invited him to take a seat in that assembly and subsequently bestowed numerous honors upon him.

As was the case then, so is the case now throughout the world. However great people may be, they have developed only the external vision. They do not bother to cultivate the inner vision.

When you examine a person, you pay attention to his physical features, his wealth, his status, his education and degrees and so on. On the other hand, when God examines a person, he looks at the purity of his heart, he pays attention to the peace that is within him. You should also develop such inner vision and inner peace. Whatever be the circumstances, you should not be subject to quick excitement. You should allow time for the nobler feelings to well up from inside you and manifest themselves.

Let All The Poisons Emerge Without Interference

Suppose someone insults you what will you lose by their insult? You should not respond to such insults with any agitation or excitement. If you remain peaceful, all the anger of the other person may freely pour out. But if you try to obstruct others' strong feelings by preventing them from venting their anger, it could possibly lead to a dangerous situation. Consider, as an example, that someone has become sick, that he is feeling quite nauseous and is throwing up the contents in his stomach. What is the reason for his being sick and vomiting? It is because some impurities, some toxic substances have entered his stomach. Wherever there are impurities you will soon find germs or poisons, and along with them come sickness and diminution of health. For this reason, it is most important that no impurities enter your system.

The body is carefully arranged to immediately throw up and expel any toxins that attempt to enter it. When the body reacts naturally by vomiting out the poisons, it would be incorrect to give medicines to stop that vomiting. If medicine is given, the toxins will not be thrown up; instead they will remain in the stomach and soon poison the whole system. Therefore, one should allow all the impurities to come out and not obstruct them by giving medicine which suppresses the nausea. After all the impurities have been thrown up, then one can give some healing medicines.

Once the vomiting and nausea are over, a person will feel very weak. Then he will do whatever you ask; that is when he will obey you. So this is the best procedure to follow when someone is vomiting out poison. The same thing applies whenever someone is very angry and is vomiting out poison, in that form. Let them do it; do not obstruct them. Whatever they want to say, let them say it as long as they want to. Until such time as it all comes out, you should remain peaceful and patient. Why should you subject yourself to a lot of disturbance and excitement? Instead of becoming upset, your patient attitude will actually promote feelings of peace and happiness within you. This itself is the experience of heaven, namely.

to maintain your equanimity and compassion under all circumstances. Why should you deny yourself the joy of such heavenly feelings?

Patience is a most important quality. Of all the good qualities a person can have, patience and forbearance rank at the very top. Baba has said a number of times that forbearance is truth, forbearance is righteousness, forbearance is nonviolence, forbearance is happiness. Forbearance really is equal in value to everything that you can find in all the worlds. If a person has forbearance, then he will be able to acquire all the other important qualities such as mind control, sense control, renunciation, fortitude, faith and equipoise. All these make up the state of inner purity.

You use soap and water and powders and perfumes of various kinds to purify yourself externally. In the same way, you develop these six spiritual treasures and put them into daily practice in order to purify yourself internally. Inner purity is extremely important; it is even more important than outer purity. The Lord is ever present both inside and outside. The entire place where the Lord is to be found must be purified and sanctified, both inner and outer. Then the indwelling God will protect you wherever you go.

The Six Spiritual Treasures

Krishna taught Arjuna all the qualities which make one an ideal person, firmly established in wisdom. They have been previously mentioned but let us examine them once again. They are:

1. peace of mind,
2. sense control,
3. renunciation of desires,
4. fortitude under all circumstances; this means that whatever be the test, whatever be the circumstances, you maintain a steady, undeluded and unwavering mind,
5. a firm faith in the teachings of the scriptures, as well as in the words of the *guru* and the great saints who have trod the spiritual path before you, and
6. being contented under all circumstances and having complete equanimity of mind.

Only when you have equanimity of mind will you be able to develop firmness and fortitude. Only when you have fortitude will you be able to develop firm faith. Only when you have intense faith will you have some sacred feelings and renounce desires. Only when you have disgust for the objects of the world will you have sense control. Then when you have achieved sense control, you will gain peace of mind. Where there is peace of mind there is inner and outer purity. And where there is inner and outer purity, patience will be second-nature to you and you will dwell automatically in that peaceful state. Therefore, you must make an effort to develop these basic qualities which are so vital to progress on the spiritual path.

By reading or listening to these teachings on the *Gita*, or even committing various passages to memory, you will not be able to achieve much. Along with these activities of the mind, you have to put at least one or two of the injunctions given here into practice. Only then will the fragrance of the *Gita* enter your heart. It is Baba's wish that all these great teachings which you have been enjoying be put into practice by you, so that they can become your inner treasure and be an integral part of your expression in all your day-to-day activities.

REMOVE BODY-CONSCIOUSNESS – REALIZE GOD-CONSCIOUSNESS

The world is filled with God. Saturated as it is with the divinity, the world is also filled with karma or action. Karma is the power of creation, the power of life; it is a power directly derived from God. You come into human birth in order to reap the fruits of your previous actions. In that way, actions lead to rebirth and then to more actions, thereby, keeping you bound to the cycle of birth and death. To free yourself from this bondage, should you engage in actions or should you abstain from actions? The Gita makes the answer clear. The path to liberation is through karma, through action. But it enjoins you to turn all your actions into karma yoga, sacred action which will take you towards union with God.

Embodiments of Love,

When the power of life takes on manifestation, it becomes a body. Life, which wears these various bodies, has also been called *karma*. The Sanskrit word *karma* means work or action; but *karma* refers not only to the action itself but also to the cycle of action and reaction, of work and its resulting fruits. Your body is formed on the basis of the *karma* or actions that you performed in an earlier birth. You get this human body and this life in order to enjoy or suffer the consequences of actions that you were engaged in during another life.

The body is directly associated with *karma*; it has no meaning outside of *karma*. Body means *karma*, and *karma* means body. It is through the body that every conceivable kind of action is performed. The place and the time where these actions occur are within nature or the world. When actions become sacred and righteous, when they are selfless and of the highest purity, and when they have been offered to God, then they become *yoga*; they lead to union with God. So, you can see, that in action God, man and nature all come together.

You Perform Actions In Order To Sanctify Your Life

Everything in the world is the result of *karma*. That is why the ancient wisdom teachings have declared, 'Offer your prostrations to *karma*'. Whatever happens is the consequence of some previous action, in other words, the result of *karma*. And, be they good or bad, be they virtuous or evil, all *karmas*, all actions are derived from the powers of God. The expression may be different but in the deepest sense, everything comes from God. That is the reason why a *yogi*, without caring whether it is favorable or unfavorable, accepts everything that happens to him as the will of the Lord, and considers the performance of righteous action as his primary duty.

The purpose for which you should be performing all your actions is to sanctify your life. It is only through God's grace that you gain the privilege to engage in righteous actions. It is through the teachings of the Lord that you get this sacred opportunity and direction. It is for that reason that this holy scripture is called the *Gita*. *Gita* means song. It is the song of the Lord. All those who listen to this song will be able to overcome grief and sorrow. Whether it be on the battlefield or on some other field, wherever this sacred song is sung, grief and sorrow will be dispelled.

When actions are performed as offerings to God, they become *yoga*. This is revealed in the prayer given by a great saint who sang,

> O beloved Lord. You are the atma, my very self. My body is your house. All my daily duties are my offerings to you. My life's breath is your praise. Wherever I walk I am circumambulating you. Whatever word I utter is a mantra in adoration of you. Every karma I perform is done as worship unto you.

This saint had purified every action performed by his sense organs and offered these actions to the Lord; thereby; all his deeds became acts of worship. When you transform your actions into sacred actions, suitable as offerings to God, then your actions will bring you into alignment with God; they will become *yoga*. You need to recognize the greatness inherent in such *yoga* and strive to purify every act you perform and offer it to the Lord. On the eve of the great war, Krishna commanded Arjuna, "Arjuna you must fight this war. But while doing so, think continuously of me and make every action pure and offer it to me. That is what pleases me." Obeying the commands of the Lord, Arjuna fought on the battlefield to preserve righteousness, keeping Krishna steadily in his mind.

Make All Your Actions A Sacrifice Not A Battle

To reach your spiritual goals, you need to obtain God's love. In fact, for a devotee, pleasing the Lord is itself the goal. It becomes your most important duty. You must make sure that every act you perform will satisfy the Lord. Krishna taught, 'Obey my commands and perform your duty.' In obeying the commands of the Lord and fighting in the war, Arjuna's actions became a sacred *yagna*, a sacrificial ritual which exalts the divinity and immerses one in the divine flow of grace. In contrast, there is a story in one of the epics of Daksha who wanted to perform a *yagna*, a ritual sacrifice. However, he disobeyed and disrespected Lord Shiva, and he also violated the commands of the holy sages. With a sense of egoism and attachment, he commenced the sacrifice. His egoism converted that sacrifice into a war.

You see that because Arjuna obeyed the Lord's commands and fought in the war, his battle became a sacred sacrifice. But for Daksha, who performed his sacrifice in violation of the Lord's commands, his sacrifice became a battle. What is a war and what is a sacrifice? All actions that are pure and selfless, and performed as an offering to the Lord, become a sacrifice. But actions which are undertaken in violation of the Lord's command, which are contrary to the scriptures and which are performed with a sense of egoism and pomposity, undertaken only for the purpose of promoting one's desires or hatreds ... all such actions become a war, even though the nature of the action may be that of a sacrifice. When the anguish and hatred in a person takes form in words, and these words, in turn, lead to argument and counter argument, then a battle will soon ensue. The root of all this is attachment and desire, arising from identification with the body.

You Are The Atma, You Are Not This Body

Krishna said, "Arjuna, obey my commands. Give up body-consciousness. Give it up completely. Stop identifying yourself with your body. The body is full of mucus and filth. You are not this body; it is only temporary and transient. You are the witness, the indweller, the *atma* inside this body. This six-foot frame is not you. You are the cosmic personality; you are boundless. This body is subject to birth and death. You, however, are the *atma* which is birthless and deathless. You are not a limited individual, subject to the passage of time. You are that most effulgent form which has conquered and mastered time itself. Discriminate between the permanent and the impermanent! Inquire into wisdom and ignorance! Distinguish between truth and untruth!"

Krishna continued, "Arjuna, recognize your real nature! Censure and praise are associated with the body; they are not permanent. Profit and loss are also associated with the body. They are a result of activity, of *karma*, but they are not characteristics of your essence, the *atma*. Be indifferent to all these polarities. Treat joy and sorrow equally. Only when you develop this kind of equal-mindedness, will you be able to realize true fulfillment and become a truly wise being." In this way, Krishna taught Arjuna the highest wisdom, the discrimination between truth and untruth, the recognition of that which is permanent behind all that which is impermanent.

God In Human Form Is Not Limited To The Avatars

God is everywhere. He is all-knowing, he is all-pervasive, he is all-powerful. He is not limited to the body. His power is not limited to the *karma* performed through bodies. The divinity is not just a particular body called Rama, born in a particular age, or another body called Krishna, born in another age. Those incarnations served as exemplary models for mankind to follow. But, the principle of divinity is not limited to any given body. The divinity is omnipresent and omniscient.

Again and again this truth has been taught to mankind. Krishna spoke of this to Arjuna. He said, "Arjuna, in remote antiquity, in many ages gone by, I have taught this *Gita* to the sun god. Then others in a long lineage of sacred beings came to know of the *Gita* when the sun god passed it on to the many great sages of those times. But thereafter, slowly and gradually, this knowledge became hidden and was finally lost. But it is this same ancient, sacred knowledge that I am now teaching to you here today."

When Arjuna heard this, a number of doubts entered his mind. He began thinking, "The sun god is a very ancient entity. Krishna was born only recently in this present age. How could Krishna have taught the sun god who is so ancient?" As soon as Arjuna had these thoughts, Krishna, who knows all minds and all hearts, spoke up immediately. He said, "Well, Arjuna, I know your doubts." With a smile on his lips, he continued, "You see, Arjuna, I am not this particular body. I am the one who has no birth. I transcend all time and space. I am not limited by circumstance. I exist in all ages, in all times. Basing your conception of me on my body, you are thinking that I belong to this particular age. But all these ages and all these eons are within me. Do not try to limit me to this body and to a given time. Bodies change but I never change. I take on different bodies, at different times, in order to perform *karma* and to fulfill a particular mission." The moment Arjuna heard this, spiritual understanding dawned within him and he recognized the timeless, unchanging principle of divinity.

Expand Your View Of Yourself To Understand The Divinity

All people will not be able to understand the omniscience of God. Even spiritually-minded people will base their view only on the visible outward actions of the Lord, thinking of him as an individual entity associated with a given form. Since they identify themselves with their own bodies, so they also identify the Lord with a particular body. They speculate on the future of this particular divine incarnation and fail to recognize the omnipresence and omniscience of the divinity. But this is not right. Krishna commanded Arjuna, "Develop a broad mind and expand your vision. You can start with the concept of the individual personality; but do not get stuck there. Do not waste your entire life thinking only of individuals.

"From the individual, you must move on to the concept of the society, which transcends the individual. Individuality and personality are associated with a limited name and form, but let your mind soar beyond name and form. Reach and experience that divine principle which is your very essence. You are still viewing everything in the framework of duality, and so your life is manifesting only duality. You are caught up in name and form, in subject and object. Make the effort to travel from duality and illusion to complete oneness with the divinity, constantly keeping this highest wisdom of pure non-duality as your goal. Make an effort to see the same divine principle everywhere and in everything, until you realize the ultimate truth that only the *atma*, which is your very self, is real and that it alone exists."

Buddha taught the same great truth, although he may not have made reference to the *Vedas* or used *Vedantic* terms. Nevertheless, he experienced and demonstrated the essential spirit of the *Vedas*. First he said *buddham sharanam gacchami*, meaning, 'I take refuge in the *buddhi*, my power of discrimination.' This deals with the individual; it speaks of the limited personality. Gradually, he added *sangham sharanam gacchami*, meaning, 'I take refuge in the community, I take refuge in the extended family of spiritually-minded beings.' He recognized that feelings associated with individual and personal considerations are selfish and narrow, and cannot take you very far.

Go From The Individual To The Society To The Divinity

You should not consider this individual self as everything; it is only a drop in the ocean. Along these lines, Krishna also directed, "Arjuna, expand your heart and become broad-minded. Include the entire human society within your scope." Society does not have any particular form; it is made up of individuals. When a large number of individuals join together, they become a society. Baba often says, "Expansion is my life." When you expand individual life to infinity it becomes divinity; that is to say, let yourself as an individual multiply and broaden to see the divinity in all, and you will reach divinity. Therefore, Krishna told Arjuna, "Live in society, serve the society, and develop broad-mindedness. Recognize the divinity to be present everywhere, in everyone."

The expansion from the individual to the society does not mean merely shifting your loyalties to a particular group, kinfolk, region, community or country. This is the first step, but you must go beyond that. These will still limit you and not take you all the way to the divinity that is your own truth. Therefore, Buddha added one more step, *dharmam sharanam gacchami*, meaning, 'I take refuge in *dharma*, I take shelter in truth and righteousness.'

Dharma, as used here, has a very broad connotation; it refers to the one who supports the entire world. When you investigate the general meaning of the word *dharma*, you find that it relates to the basic nature of a thing, its essential truth. It refers to the immortal *atma*, the indwelling divinity. Therefore, the deeper meaning of *dharma* is found in the true nature of everything, which is divinity. To take refuge in *dharma* is to become one with all the attributes of divinity. It has been said that *maya* or illusion is the body of God, but it is more correct to say that *dharma* is the body of God. It is his very form. That is why Krishna announced, "For establishing *dharma* I have come again and again." *Dharma* reveals the broad nature of the divinity in all its glorious aspects.

Krishna directed Arjuna, "Move beyond this short-sighted feeling of individuality. Do not keep this body as the entire basis of your life. It is only a covering, an instrument. It is what you see through your mortal eyes. Broaden your vision. Develop your insight; acquire God-vision. When your vision is filled with God, then the entire creation becomes God for you. Make *dharma* your vision and your vision will become God-vision; then you will see the entire creation as God."

Krishna continued, elucidating the correct means for practicing *dharma*, "As an individual you are a prince, belonging to the warrior class. Fighting to protect righteousness and organizing for battle is your duty, your *dharma*. It would not be right for you to go out and incite a war, but in this case, your evil cousins have declared war against you. My direction to you is that you honor your duty, and while performing your duty, remember me and follow my commands. In that way, all your actions will become suffused with *dharma*."

The Nature Of Dharma

In instructing Arjuna, Krishna revealed the essential form of *dharma*. "Arjuna, it is the very nature of fire to burn; if it does not have the power to burn, then it is not fire. Similarly, ice has the nature of coolness. If it is not cold, you cannot call it ice. And sweetness is the very nature of sugar. If sweetness is not there, the substance may look like sugar, but it may be salt or it may be flour, but it is not sugar. In the very same way, death is natural for every human body. When the human body moves on to its natural conclusion, why should anyone worry about it?

"Just as burning is natural for fire, coolness is natural for ice and sweetness is natural for sugar, so also death is natural for every human body. Without concerning yourself about the bodies of your relatives, fight this war; but do so keeping the attributes of a truly wise being in mind. If you want to obtain peace, then you must destroy your ego and attachments. And you must also give up your delusions. But do not give up God! He is within you. He is the very source of your being. Attune yourself to him and obey all his commands, and you will recognize the true nature of humanity."

Dharma, the divine quality which is natural to and inherent in man, will itself destroy *maya*, the illusion of world, individuality and separateness. Previously it was mentioned that the letters in the word *man*, where by *man* is meant a true human being regardless of gender, the letter *m* stands for 'maya removed', the letter *a* stands for 'atma seen' and the letter *n* stands for 'nirvana attained'. In other words, remove the ego *I*, have the vision of the inner Lord and merge in the joy of your immortal divine self, the *atma*... this is what makes up *dharma*; this is the essential duty of man. Repeatedly, again and again, you should contemplate on this.

Peace Can Only Be Found Within Yourself

Peace is not an object which is available in the market place. It is not a thing which can be bought and won, along with a kingdom. It is not a gift which can be given to you by your relatives. Peace is inherent in your own nature; it is within you. Only when you search for it within yourself will you be able to find it. Therefore, get rid of your outward vision and develop inward vision. Outward vision is appropriate to an animal, not a human being. A true human being has inward vision. "Therefore," Krishna commanded Arjuna, "sanctify your life by developing this unique potential of the human beings to turn their minds inwards."

The story has been told of how early in the career of the sage Narada, he was continuously having one type of worry after another. Now, Narada had learned quite a few things. He was a master of all 64 types of learning and had practiced all 64 human skills; and yet he felt no inner peace. He began thinking to himself, 'What is the reason for all this worry, this lack of peace that I am feeling? I have mastered all types of learning, I understand all fields of human knowledge; still, I have not been able to remove my sorrow.' He went to a great sage and asked him to explain the reason for his worries and lack of peace.

The first thing the sage asked Narada was, "What are your qualifications?" Narada replied, "I have learned and mastered every type of education; there is no field of human knowledge which I have not learned." The sage then said, "Well, that is very good. Then you must have learned the knowledge of the self?" Narada replied, "No, except for self-knowledge I have had every kind of education." The sage told Narada, "You can get peace of mind only with the knowledge of the *atma*. Only when you have learned that supreme knowledge by which you will know everything else, can you be called educated. Otherwise, you remain ignorant, no matter how many fields you have mastered. What is the use of learning so many things without understanding the one thing which is truly essential?" Here is a small example.

For A Marriage There Must Be A Husband

In a small village there was to be a marriage. The lady of the home where the marriage was to be celebrated, told the neighboring lady, "Dear friend, we are planning to celebrate a marriage at our house in a grand way. We have invited a famous Bombay band. We have also invited a number of noted singers. Several highly gifted cooks will come to prepare food for the occasion. We are planning to put up a very big marriage tent. It will be a truly grand affair. Please come. You will greatly enjoy this marriage. It will be a unique celebration." After hearing all these things, the neighbor lady said, "O, how wonderful. I certainly will come." Then she inquired, "Please tell me, who is the bridegroom?" At this the lady replied, "Well, that has not yet been decided."

For a marriage, the bridegroom is a very important person. If the bridegroom has not been selected, who will be married in the marriage tent? What good is the fine band and cooks and singers and priests when there is no one to be married? First the bridegroom must be chosen, then all these other things take on value. In the same way, if there is no peace of mind, what is the use of having learned so many things? The wise sage told Narada, "Only by acquiring *atmic* knowledge can you obtain peace of mind."

Today's man is an easy prey for attachment and hatred. He is overwhelmed by the possessive nature and filled with ego. Just look at the state he is in and what he is doing! He considers himself to be the most important being in the world. He deludes himself with the feeling that there is no one greater than he. Because of this delusion he has lost his power of discrimination, and so he has not even been able to reflect on his own confused state. He considers that it is he who is doing everything. He thinks that he can hire the whole world and do with it as he pleases. But it is not he who is running the world. He does not have that power, neither for good nor for evil. The one who is the creator of this world, the one who is the protector of this world, the one who is the father of this world, the one who is the mother of this world, the one who is the Lord of this world... only he has the power and the authority to run it. For this entire moveable and immovable world, there is only one master. This is an all-important truth that every human being must recognize.

Use The Hardships You Encounter As Opportunities & Tests

Do not give in to temporary excitements and anger, and thereby lose your peace of mind. Sorrow, loss, pain, worries are all tests to help you rid yourself of your weaknesses. They reveal whether or not you have developed firm faith and patience to endure hardships, and be unaffected by them. There is no use in merely passing examinations conducted by educational institutions. You must pass the examinations presented to you by life itself. It has been said, 'After acquiring all types of education, it is only a fool who doesn't know his own mind.' Whatever learning he might have acquired, a mean person will not acquire any good qualities from it. Then what is the use of all his education? After acquiring a lot of useless knowledge, he has only achieved the faculty for engaging in arguments and counter-arguments.

Why study so many things which have no value at all? Instead, make every effort to learn about that which has no death; that is the education which has lasting value. What is the knowledge which enables you to know that which has no death? That knowledge is the knowledge of *atma*, and that education is the *atmic* education. The one who has no death has no birth either. Everything which is born, which has come into existence, undergoes modifications and will eventually die, and thereby lose its form. The entire world and everything in it has a particular form. As it has form, it will undergo change. You should try to reach the state where there is no change at all. To do so you must gain self-knowledge, you must realize the *atma*.

No Need To Carry Your Luggage On Your Head

There once was an old, ignorant villager, who left his native place to set off on a long journey. He had never traveled by train before; in fact, in all his life he had never even had a chance to see a train. Now he had come to the railway station and was waiting for the train to arrive. A train made up of many wagons drew into the station. The villager was completely awed by this train. 'It has so many carriages,' he thought to himself, 'and it goes so fast. Look at how easily it balances on those narrow rails that a human being can hardly even walk on.'

Hundreds of passengers were waiting to board the train. The amount of luggage which most of these passengers had brought was very large. The villager sat brooding, thinking to himself, 'How is this train going to be able to carry so many passengers and so much luggage? Why do these people have so much luggage anyway?' Along with the others, the villager entered the train. Putting their luggage on the racks overhead or leaving it on the floor, the passengers took their seats and began chatting and relaxing.

The villager thought to himself, 'How cruel all these people are! Why are they giving so much burden to this poor train by throwing their luggage down in the compartment and relaxing?' So, this old man sat down, keeping all his luggage on his head. It was enough that the train was carrying him; the least he could do was to carry his own luggage and not place any further burden on this heavily-loaded train! A co-passenger asked him, "Sir, why are you carrying your luggage on your head? Why not put it down and be comfortable?" The old man replied, "When the train is carrying so much luggage already, I do not want to add my own luggage also. So I have put it on my head and will carry it myself."

Whatever you do with your luggage, the train will still be carrying both you and your luggage. By keeping the luggage on your head you are not helping the train at all. So you might as well put it down and enjoy your journey. Now, this naive old man had kindness and compassion, but he did not have much intelligence and discrimination.

Krishna told Arjuna, "Though you are highly educated, though you have sense control, though you have accomplished great feats and have developed many skills, you are, nevertheless, experiencing many difficulties. This is because you have not been able to understand the divinity. As long as you do not understand the divinity, you cannot be free from sorrow. If you want to free yourself from sorrow and earn the grace of the Lord, you must obey my commands.

"First of all, remember that you are not the body. These sense organs have no connection with you; they are associated with the body. Use the body for doing work, but do not identify yourself with the body or the work. You have taken birth in this body as the result of your past actions, your *karma*, and you must use this body for performing *karma*. So, get up! Arise, Arjuna! Do your duty. Perform actions and offer them all to me. Let me have the consequences of your actions. Shun selfishness, uphold justice, be fixed in faith! That is the *dharma* from age to age. If you obey my commands, I will take care of you."

Identify Yourself With The Divinity Not With Your Body

Krishna continued, "I want to tell you one other thing, the blind father of these evil cousins of yours had 100 sons, yet in the end there was not even one of them left to perform his funeral rites. What is the reason for this? All these sons were the children of God, but the blind king considered them as his. Arjuna, you are also becoming a brother to him. You are deluding yourself with the idea that this body is yours when it really is not yours, at all. By thinking that you are the body, you are developing the same blind outlook. That is complete ignorance. Unless you drive away this ignorance, you will not be able to realize wisdom. You have to develop discrimination and self-inquiry in order for wisdom to enter into you.

"Within your body is the spiritual heart, and within that heart is God. Also in your body is the individual soul. These two, God and the individual, appearing to live separately inside the body, are playing together, acting out their parts in a grand drama. They come together and go apart again, as directed by the author who has written this play. He assigns all the separate roles of good and bad, virtue and sin. But, in truth, there is only the one divinity that plays all these parts.

"From the standpoint of the body, there is the individualized soul manifested as this particular person of body and mind, and there is God who is the indweller of the heart. As long as you have the delusion of the body, these two, God and the soul remain separate entities enjoying their play with each other. As soon as the delusion disappears, they merge into the one all-pervasive divine principle. When you remove the false delusion of body-consciousness, you bring about the union of the individual and God. Then you are established in divine consciousness and enjoy eternal bliss."

Teaching in this way, Krishna was able to impart to Arjuna the knowledge for becoming a wise being and the means for reaching the bliss of non-duality. He said, "Arjuna, always have the sense that everything which exists is one and the same entity. Do not allow the senses to pull you away from this feeling of unity and equanimity. Let your heart be free from sorrow and elation, attachment and hatred. Be unaffected by censure or praise. Treat all people equally."

Krishna told Arjuna, "When you firmly believe that everything in this creation is the manifestation of divinity, then you will become steeped in wisdom and freed from illusion. Then you will have realized the true purpose for which you have been born as a human being. Arjuna! Carry out my commands! See me everywhere! Know me to be your very self, the *atma*! Realize the *atma* and be forever free!"